VERDI IN
VICTORIAN LONDON

Verdi in Victorian London

Massimo Zicari

https://www.openbookpublishers.com

© 2016 Massimo Zicari

This work is licensed under a Creative Commons Attribution 4.0 International license (CC BY 4.0). This license allows you to share, copy, distribute and transmit the text; to adapt the text and to make commercial use of the text providing attribution is made to the author (but not in any way that suggests that he endorses you or your use of the work). Attribution should include the following information:

Massimo Zicari, *Verdi in Victorian London*. Cambridge, UK: Open Book Publishers, 2016. http://dx.doi.org/10.11647/OBP.0090

In order to access detailed and updated information on the license, please visit https://www.openbookpublishers.com/isbn/9781783742134#copyright

Further details about CC BY licenses are available at https://creativecommons.org/licenses/by/4.0/

All external links were active on 28/6/2016 unless otherwise stated and have been archived via the Internet Archive Wayback Machine at https://archive.org/web

Updated digital material and resources associated with this volume are available at https://www.openbookpublishers.com/isbn/9781783742134#resources

Every effort has been made to identify and contact copyright holders and any omission or error will be corrected if notification is made to the publisher. For information about the rights of the Wikimedia Commons images, please refer to the Wikimedia website (the relevant links are listed in the list of illustrations).

Published thanks to the generous support of: Cantone Ticino (Aiuto federale per la salvaguardia e promozione della lingua e cultura italiana); Fondazione Fabio Schaub (Canobbio - Ticino).

ISBN Paperback: 978-1-78374-213-4
ISBN Hardback: 978-1-78374-214-1
ISBN Digital (PDF): 978-1-78374-215-8
ISBN Digital ebook (epub): 978-1-78374-216-5
ISBN Digital ebook (mobi): 978-1-78374-217-2
DOI: 10.11647/OBP.0090

Cover image: Ricard Urgell, *Opera* (1922), https://commons.wikimedia.org/wiki/File:Ricard_Urgell_-_Opera_-_Google_Art_Project.jpg

All paper used by Open Book Publishers is SFI (Sustainable Forestry Initiative), PEFC (Programme for the Endorsement of Forest Certification Schemes) and Forest Stewardship Council(r)(FSC(r) certified.

Printed in the United Kingdom, United States, and Australia
by Lightning Source for Open Book Publishers (Cambridge, UK)

Contents

List of Illustrations   vii

Acknowledgments   ix

Introduction   1

1. Music Journalism in Early Victorian London   15
2. *Ernani* (1845)   31
3. *Nabucco* and *I Lombardi* (1846)   45
4. *I due Foscari* and *I masnadieri* (1847)   57
5. *Attila* (1848)   77
6. Uneventful Years: 1849–1852   95
7. *Rigoletto* (1853)   113
8. *Il trovatore* (1855)   127
9. A Moral Case: The Outburst of *La traviata* (1856)   139
10. *Luisa Miller* (1858)   171
11. *I vespri siciliani* (1859)   181
12. The Years 1860 and 1861: *Un ballo in maschera*   191
13. *Inno delle nazioni* (1862)   209
14. *Don Carlos* and *La forza del destino* (1867)   217

15. The Late 1860s and Wagner's *L'Olandese dannato* (1870)	233
16. Verdi's *Requiem* and Wagner's *Lohengrin* (1875)	247
17. *Aida* (1876)	257
18. Music Journalism in London: The Late 1870s and 1880s	267
19. *Otello* at the Royal Lyceum (1889)	285
20. *Falstaff* at Covent Garden (1894)	297
Conclusions	309
Appendix I: Verdi's Premieres in London	321
Appendix II: Verdi and Wagner in London	325
Appendix III: The Periodicals	327
Select Bibliography	329
Index	335

List of Illustrations

Frontispiece: Giuseppe Verdi, from a picture reproduced in Frederick Crowest, *Verdi: Man and Musician* (London: John Milton, 1897).   x

1. James William Davison from a picture reproduced in Joseph Bennett, *Forty Years of Music, 1865–1905* (London: Methuen & Co., 1908). Image from https://archive.org/details/fortyyearsmusic01benngoog   19

2. Mr. Ap Mutton, alias James William Davison. From a drawing by Charles Lyall published in Joseph Bennett, *Forty Years of Music, 1865–1905* (London: Methuen & Co., 1908). Image from https://archive.org/details/fortyyearsmusic01benngoog   21

3. Benjamin Lumley, in a portrait from the frontispiece of his *Reminiscences of the Opera* (London: Hurst & Blackett, 1864). Image from https://archive.org/details/cu31924022334563   34

4. Giuseppe Verdi in *The Illustrated London News*, 30 May 1846.   44

5. Scene from *I due Foscari* at the Royal Italian Opera. *The Illustrated London News*, 26 June 1847.   60

6. Jenny Lind (as Amalia) and Luigi Lablache (as Massimiliano) in scene VI from *I masnadieri* at Her Majesty's Theatre. *The Illustrated London News*, 31 July 1847.   71

7. Jenny Lind (as Amalia), Italo Gardoni (as Carlo, to the left) and Luigi Lablache (as Massimilano, to the right) in the last scene of *I masnadieri* at Her Majesty's Theatre. *The Illustrated London News*, 31 July 1847.   76

8. Scene from *Attila* at Her Majesty's Theatre, London. *The Illustrated London News*, 15 April 1848.   83

9. Scene from *La traviata* at Her Majesty's Theatre. Violetta faints after Alfredo flings her "portrait" at her feet. *The Illustrated London News*, 31 May 1856.   142

10	In reporting on Marietta Piccolomini's success, the *London Journal* portrayed her as a real beauty, a charming singer, an impressive actress, and the daughter of a noble family. *The London Journal*, 23 August 1856.	159
11	Marietta Piccolomini. *The Illustrated London News*, 31 May 1856.	161
12	Adelina Patti, the first Aida in London in 1876, as seen by the American satirical magazine *Puck* in 1881. Image from Wikimedia, https://commons.wikimedia.org/wiki/File:Adelina_Patti,_the_everlasting_prima-donna_LCCN2012647299.jpg	258
13	Giuseppe Verdi, illustration by Théobald Chartran, *Vanity Fair*, 15 February 1879. Image from Wikimedia, https://commons.wikimedia.org/wiki/File:Giuseppe_Verdi_1879_Vanity_Fair_illustration_by_Théobald_Chartran.jpg	266
14	Joseph Bennett, from the frontispiece of his *Forty Years of Music, 1865–1905* (London: Methuen & Co., 1908). Image from https://archive.org/details/fortyyearsmusic01benngoog	268
15	Portrait of Giuseppe Verdi by Giovanni Boldini (1886). Image from Wikimedia, https://commons.wikimedia.org/wiki/File%3AGiuseppe_Verdi_by_Giovanni_Boldini.jpg	284
16	"Otello in Milan" from Blanche Roosevelt, *Verdi: Milan and 'Othello'* (London: Ward and Downey, 1887), p. 192.	286
17	A painting by Achille Beltrame portraying Verdi at the piano in his study at Sant'Agata on his 86th birthday. *La Domenica del Corriere*, October 1899. Image from Wikimedia, https://commons.wikimedia.org/wiki/File:Verdi_at_the_piano_at_Sant'Agata.png	296

Acknowledgments

The publication of this book was made possible thanks to the support of the Fondazione Fabio Schaub. My special thanks go to Mrs. Pia Schaub, whose generosity was pivotal in funding this book.
I want to express my gratitude to Hubert Eiholzer, Head of Research and Vice Director of the Scuola Universitaria di Musica (Lugano, Switzerland) for granting me the intellectual freedom necessary to carry out the research which has kept me deeply absorbed for many years.

Although a lonely enterprise, this volume was brought to a close with the help of many people. I would like to thank Alessandra Tosi and the editorial team of Open Book Publishers for the unflagging enthusiasm with which they welcomed my proposal and guided me through the challenges that such an undertaking involved. My thanks go to Katherine Ellis, who was director of the Institute of Musical Research, School of Advanced Study, University of London in 2009, when I started investigating this topic as Visiting Fellow there. Other musicologists have provided me with invaluable help, even unwittingly, by giving me advice on sources, singers and many other related questions. Special thanks go to Marco Capra, Director of CIRPeM (Centro Internazionale di Ricerca sui Periodici Musicali), Emanuele Senici, Marco Beghelli and Dorottya Fabian.

This book originates from a doctoral dissertation completed at the Faculté des Lettres, l'Université de Fribourg (Switzerland) which I defended on 12 March 2015. I am grateful to my supervisor Luca Zoppelli, to the second referee Alessandro Roccatagliati and to the president of the jury, Dimiter Daphinoff, for their incisive comments.

This book is dedicated to my children, Camilla and Samuele.

Lugano, February 2016

Giuseppe Verdi, from a picture reproduced in Frederick Crowest, *Verdi: Man and Musician* (London: John Milton, 1897).

Introduction

Giuseppe Verdi's first success was *Nabucco*, given in Milan on 9 March 1842. Although this was Verdi's third opera,[1] the composer referred to it as the first milestone in what would become a life-long, successful career. "With *Nabucco*," he declared to Count Opprandino Arrivabene years later, "my career can be said to have begun."[2] However, when Verdi made his first appearance as the young Italian composer with the necessary talent to forge an international reputation, Italian opera was said to be in a state of decadence.

Gioacchino Rossini, already a classic, had long quit the composition of operas to devote himself to smaller works and chamber music. Gaetano Donizetti, whose first works bear witness to the Rossinian influence, would die in 1848, but his last operas—*Don Pasquale, Maria di Rohan, Dom Sébastien*—premiered in 1843. Vincenzo Bellini, who had pushed traditional Italian opera towards a more dramatic style, passed away in 1835. Contemporary critics often remarked on Bellini's innovative use of *canto declamato*, and some were preoccupied with the alarming turn taken by modern vocal composition. Under the influence of Bellini's works, proper vocalisation was all too often sacrificed on the altar of dramatic poignancy, they believed, a choice that revealed the younger generation's limited talent. Saverio Mercadante, who outlived

---

1   As we know, Verdi's first opera was *Oberto, Conte di San Bonifacio* (libretto by Temistocle Solera); it was firstly performed at the Teatro alla Scala in Milan on 17 November 1839 with moderate success. Instead, *Un giorno di regno*, a 'melodramma giocoso' set to a libretto by Felice Romani and performed at the same theatre on 5 September 1840, was a failure.

2   See Julian Budden, *The Master Musicians: Verdi* (London: Dent, 1985), p. 21.

most of his colleagues and died in 1870, never attained the popularity of either Donizetti or Bellini. Having abandoned the *bel canto* style for the highly declamatory singing style adopted by Bellini, Mercadante for many years was said to be the only Italian composer to stand comparison with Verdi. However, although his operas were produced internationally, they were rarely revived and soon forgotten. In a contribution appearing in the *Gazzetta Musicale di Milano* on 30 January 1842, the author elaborated on the sad state of Italian opera and listed Giovanni Pacini, Federico and Luigi Ricci, Pietro Coppola and Alberto Mazzucato as the only representatives of the younger generation who were worth mentioning in the same breath as Bellini, Donizetti and Mercadante.[3] Although their names mean little or nothing to modern operagoers, their works enjoyed a certain degree of popularity in the first half of the nineteenth century. In a letter published in the *Gazzetta Musicale di Milano* on 6 February 1842 (one month before the premiere of *Nabucco*), the Belgian music critic François-Joseph Fétis summarised the reasons for the diminished state of Italian opera: "An exaggerated preference for the declamatory style, the shouting of the actors (I dare not call them singers), and a noisy instrumentation have become a necessity for the Italians; they no longer understand dramatic music but in this form."[4]

Verdi made his appearance when Italy, the cradle of *bel canto*, was craving fresh blood. As early as 1836, Giuseppe Mazzini, the man whose political writings and ideas were to contribute enormously to the cause of Italian unification, expressed the hope that a young composer would soon appear who might regenerate Italian opera. He prophesied the rise of a genius who would give birth to a new operatic genre and dreamed that the false ideals of classicism would be abandoned for a more strongly realistic music drama. The new genre should bring together two features traditionally associated with either Italian or German music: melody and harmony. Mazzini pronounced the epoch of Rossini over and the traditional combination of separate set pieces and pointless recitatives surpassed. It was time to restore the recitative to its

---

3   C. Mellini, "Della musica drammatica Italiana nel secolo XIX," in *Gazzetta Musicale di Milano*, January 30, 1842, pp. 18–19.
4   "Seconda lettera del signor Fetis, intorno allo stato presente delle arti musicali in Italia," *Gazzetta Musicale di Milano*, February 6, 1842, p. 22.

original dramatic function and dignity, and get rid of the stereotyped manners that then prevailed. In a word, it was time to emancipate opera from the bulky figure of Rossini and his worthless imitators. Of course, had he had the authority, Mazzini would have forbidden singers to add any arbitrary embellishments and cadenzas to operatic arias, for they impinged on the true expression of their dramatic content.[5] Since Verdi's first opera, *Oberto, Conte di San Bonifacio*, would be premiered in 1839, Mazzini could not yet be aware in 1836 that a young composer of genius was already at work to give Italian opera a fresh start.

When Alberto Mazzucato, a composer of some reputation and also the first editor of the *Gazzetta Musicale di Milano*, reviewed the premiere of Verdi's *Nabucco* in Milan, he drew the readers' attention to the innovative features the new opera presented and to the courage the composer thus demonstrated. Verdi, Mazzucato claimed, had put himself at the head of a group of composers who, regardless of the bad taste then prevailing, were committed to interpreting the dramatic content of the libretto and breaking away from the long hackneyed operatic conventions consisting of the unavoidable *cabalette, finali, strette* and *rondo*.[6] However controversial this claim may sound to us today— soon after the introductory choir *Nabucco* opens with the "Recitativo e Cavatina di Zaccaria," which consists of a typical cavatina-cabaletta structure, while the "Finale I" ends with a *stretta*—the degree of novelty represented by Verdi could not escape the critic's attention. In a review appearing on 20 March 1842, Mazzucato returned to *Nabucco* and elaborated further. Verdi's melodies were spontaneous, smooth and free from superfluous flourishes; they reached their highest point when, on occasion, they were given to the choral masses and sung in unison. In general, Verdi's melodiousness reminded the critic of Bellini, Rossini and even Giovanni Paisiello, whose *Nina, o sia La pazza per amore* (1789) was also mentioned as a reference model. More tranquil than Bellini's, less artificial than Mercadante's, less brilliant than Donizetti's, Verdi's melodies, although belonging to the Rossinian school, came to establish a new mould of song.[7]

---

5   Giuseppe Mazzini, "Filosofia della musica," in *Scritti editi ed inediti*, 94 vols. (Imola: Cooperativa tipografico-editrice Paolo Galeati, 1906–43), 8: 119–65.

6   Alberto Mazzucato, "I.R. Teatro alla Scala. Nabucodonosor, Dramma Lirico di T. Solera, Musica del Maestro Verdi," *Gazzetta Musicale di Milano*, March 13, 1842, p. 43.

7   *Ibid.*, p. 45.

Of course, not everybody agreed with Mazzucato on the value of Verdi's operas. To others, the popular success Verdi enjoyed in the 1840s meant little or nothing since, as someone suggested, the public also lay in a state of decadence. All too often, operagoers yielded to the blandishments of false idols, ignorant as they were of the difference between the true art that never perishes and the musical platitude they were served in its stead. With *Nabucco* the question of plagiarism was also raised, and Rossini's *Mosè in Egitto* (1818) and *Le siège de Corinthe* (1826) were hinted at when it came to specifying the models Verdi might have taken inspiration from.[8] Abramo Basevi, who contributed music reviews to the *Gazzetta Musicale di Firenze* (1853–1855), *L'Armonia* (1856–1859) and *Boccherini* (1862–1882), insisted repeatedly on the line of continuity that connected Verdi's *Nabucco* to Rossini's operas. With regard to the *grandioso* character and the melodic treatment of Verdi's arias, he recognised the strong influence exerted by Rossini's style rather than Bellini's or Donizetti's.[9] Basevi can also be counted among those critics who objected to the treatment Verdi reserved for the voice: "Considering the human larynx as an instrument, for such it is, Bellini treated it like a wind instrument while Verdi, one may occasionally say, like a percussion."[10] Verdi was well aware of these reproaches and as early as 1844 admitted to the librettist Salvatore Cammarano that he was accused of cherishing noise and punishing song.[11] On the other hand, in 1846 Benedetto Bermani, a contributor to the *Gazzetta Musicale di Milano*, claimed that Verdi knew very well how to employ the voice and how to make use of the individual artists he had to work with.[12]

This last issue was long at the core of the critical discussion regarding Verdi's new dramatised style. Some contemporary commentators

---

8   See Benedetto Bermani, "Schizzi sulla vita e sulle opere del maestro Giuseppe Verdi," *Gazzetta Musicale di Milano*, V/8 (Supplement), February 22, 1846, pp. i–viii.
9   Abramo Basevi, *Studio sulle opere di Giuseppe Verdi* (Florence: Tipografia Tofani, 1859), pp. 1–18.
10 Basevi, *Studio*, p. 162. See also Marco Capra, "'Effekt, nicht als Effekt.' Aspekte der Rezeption der Opern Verdis in Italien des 19. Jahrhunderts," in Markus Engelhardt (ed.), *Giuseppe Verdi und seine Zeit* (Laaber: Laaber Verlag, 2001), pp. 117–42.
11 Verdi to Salvatore Cammarano, Milan, 23 February 1844. See Francesco Izzo, "I cantanti e la recezione di Verdi nell'Ottocento, trattati e corrispondenza," in Fabrizio Della Seta, Roberta Montemorra Marvin, and Marco Marica (eds.), *Verdi 2001, Atti del Convegno Internazionale* (Florence: Olschki, 2003), pp. 173–87.
12 Benedetto Bermani, "Schizzi sulla vita e sulle opere del maestro Giuseppe Verdi," *Gazzetta Musicale di Milano*, V/8 (Supplement), February 22, 1846, pp. i–viii.

sympathised with those unfortunate singers who had to bear with the composer and endure the repeated strains he put on their voice. Even in the 1860s Francesco Lamperti, who taught singing at the Milan Conservatory and counted Sophie Cruvelli and Emma Albani among his pupils, lamented that the art of singing lay in a terrible state of decadence owing to the new and overwhelming tendency to assume a more dramatic character at the expense of true melody. This change was deplorable, leaving even a strong and sonorous voice sounding monotonous and wanting in the character and dramatic accent required by the lyrics and the quality of the music.[13] Basevi coined the expression that best describes the manner in which many commentators conceptualised Verdi's dramatic orientation: "The effect, nothing but the effect." In his view, composers like Verdi aimed uniquely at the applause of the public, for no matter how short a moment.[14] Basevi did not intend to pay Verdi and his colleagues compliments, for these composers, by feeding countless "effects" to their public, could be compared to those courtesans who manage to attain their prince's benevolence by way of blandishment and adulation. For this reason, he could not recognise in Verdi the founder of a new school, prone as he was to the ephemeral appetites of the public. In contrast to Basevi, however, Filippo Filippi,[15] who also advocated a radical reform in Italian opera, understood Verdi's mannerisms, that is to say Verdi's adherence to a distinctive manner or style in relation to each different operatic libretto he set to music. He considered this approach a quality and not a fault. Verdi's striving for new effects depended on the careful attention he paid to the dramatic content of the chosen librettos. His style stemmed from a deep sense of music drama and not from a gratuitous propensity for pointless mannerisms.[16]

Three main issues appear to have characterised the critical discussion that accompanied the first appearance of Verdi's operas in Italy: the continuity with an operatic tradition considered at its lowest ebb; the

---

13 Francesco Lamperti, *Guida teorico-pratica-elementare per lo studio del canto* (Milan: Ricordi, 1864), p. ix.
14 Basevi, *Gazzetta musicale di Firenze*, II/1, June 15, 1854, p. 1. See Marco Capra, "Effekt, nicht als Effekt."
15 Filippo Filippi was editor of the *Gazzetta musicale di Milano* (1860–1862) and music critic of the Milanese daily newspaper *La perseveranza* (1859–1887).
16 Marco Capra, "Effekt, nicht als Effekt," pp. 117–42.

composer's arguable preference for strong dramatic effects; and the new singing style, to which he sacrificed proper vocalisation. Although not every critic agreed on Verdi's talent and some objected that Italian opera had taken a dangerous turn owing to his works, Verdi's popular success in Italy was undeniable and in a few years he came to symbolise his country's artistic excellence and cultural identity.

But while the figure of Verdi in nineteenth-century Italy has been investigated at length, and a number of scholarly contributions have recently appeared which explore the manner in which his operas were received and his figure was conceptualised, little attention has been paid to Victorian London and its music milieu.[17] What was the London critics' initial response? Why did some of them react so harshly? When did their initial antagonism change? Who were these journalists, and what credentials did they possess? What biases and prejudices influenced their critical response? Why did London opera managers continue to produce Verdi's operas, in spite of their alleged worthlessness?

This story begins in 1845, when *Ernani* was performed in London for the first time, and unfolds chronologically until the first performance of *Falstaff* at Covent Garden in 1894. Each chapter touches upon the circumstances that led to the London premiere of a new opera, describes the contextual conditions of their performance and expands upon the manner in which they were received by the press.

Not every opera composed by Verdi reached London in his lifetime. *Macbeth* (1847), Verdi's tenth opera and the first set to a Shakespeare play, was not given in London until 1960. Others were performed in London during Verdi's lifetime but only after years of waiting, a circumstance that caused critical misunderstandings of his compositional development. A case in point is represented by *Luisa Miller*, which was premiered in Naples on 8 December 1849 and first given in London in 1858. Basevi considered *Luisa Miller* the turning point between Verdi's first and

---

17 In Italy, an increasingly strong scholarly interest in the reception of Verdi's operas is suggested by the recent publication of Marco Capra (ed.), *Verdi in prima pagina* (Lucca: Libreria Musicale Italiana, 2014). Extensive monographs investigating the reception of Verdi's operas outside Italy have been published in recent years, e.g. Gundula Kreuzer's *Verdi and the Germans* (Cambridge: Cambridge University Press, 2010), Hervé Gartioux's *La reception de Verdi en France* (Weinsberg: Galland, 2001) and George W. Martin's *Verdi in America: Oberto through Rigoletto* (Rochester: University of Rochester Press, 2011).

second style; in the first style, the composer followed Rossini's example, resulting in the grandioso and the passionate prevailing over other dramatic features.¹⁸ In contrast, Verdi's second style was characterised by a more tranquil treatment of the voice and a more careful portrayal of the *dramatis personae*, a trait that Basevi associated with Donizetti.¹⁹ In *La traviata* (Venice, 1853) Basevi recognised a third style and argued that Verdi was then looking to the French comic opera.²⁰ As we will see, in London *Luisa Miller* was performed for the first time in 1858, two years after *La traviata* (1856), three after *Il trovatore* (1855) and five after *Rigoletto* (1853). Nor was *Simon Boccanegra* (Venice, 1857) performed in London in Verdi's lifetime; according to Basevi, with this opera Verdi attempted a fourth style, which emerged from a closer look at Wagner and the German music drama.²¹ The mismatch between the chronology of Verdi's compositions and that of their London performances gave rise to different interpretations of the models the Italian composer was taking inspiration from. No trace of Basevi's periodisation can be found in the contemporary English press and only occasional reference was made to the manner in which Verdi's operas were reviewed in Paris. As one might expect, Verdi's late operas were often conceptualised in relation to the theories and, to a more limited extent, the works of Richard Wagner. Giacomo Meyerbeer also continued to be cited as an important model for the Italian composer.

Ernani, performed at Her Majesty's Theatre on 8 March 1845, was the first opera bearing the name of Verdi to reach London. *Nabucco* and *I Lombardi* followed in 1846, *I due Foscari* and *I masnadieri* in 1847, *Attila* in 1848. These works triggered quite diverse critical reactions, in a manner similar to what we have observed in Italy. Although it was clear that Verdi possessed a strong dramatic power, not every critic agreed that this feature should be understood as a positive quality. The most conservative commentators attacked the composer and objected to both the librettos he chose and the manner in which he set them to music. The choice of the plays from which Verdi derived his librettos revealed his

---

18   Basevi, pp. 157–58.
19   *Ibid.*, pp. 158–59.
20   *Ibid.*, pp. 230–32.
21   Basevi, p. 265. Rather than agreeing with Basevi on Verdi's different styles, I simply wish to suggest that the different production chronology in London may have led to a different understanding of Verdi's compositional trajectory.

tendency to look to the French Grand Opéra, which was characterised by the crudest passions and the strongest human conflicts. This seemed to explain, at least in part, why such features as melodiousness and melodic ornamentation were no longer to be found in Italian opera. In fact, strong dramas qualified by crude passions and strong human conflicts called for tragical declamation rather than cheerful tunefulness. English critics such as Chorley from *The Athenaeum* and Davison from *The Musical World* conceptualised Verdi's first compositional and dramatic achievements in counterpoint to Rossini and his predecessors, Domenico Cimarosa and Giovanni Paisiello, then considered imperishable classics. In this light, Verdi's passionate compositional style, characterised as it was by a strong preference for declamation—to which proper singing was all too often sacrificed—and a noisy orchestration, was pronounced devoid of any merit. On the other hand, some critics showed signs of sincere appreciation, as *The Herald*, *The Daily News* and *The Post* testified.

On 30 May 1846, *The Illustrated London News* published a portrait of the young Italian composer and acknowledged the prominent position Verdi now held by the side of the beloved Rossini, Bellini and Donizetti.

> We offer to our readers, in the present number, a portrait of the great star of the musical world at this day—Giuseppe Verdi—on whose production the fate of lyrical art would now seem to depend, as the great *maestri* whose works for the last thirty years have had possession of the Italian lyrical stage, Rossini, Bellini, Donizetti, are precluded from any longer wielding the pen for our profit—one by advance of years and exhaustion of mind, the other by premature death, and the third, alas! by a still more terrible fate, loss of reason.[22]

The enthusiastic appreciation in Italy of a composer of Verdi's stamp would appear strange to those who imagined Italian musical taste to be represented by the sickly, sentimental composition until lately classed as "Italian music" *par excellence*. But Verdi's works showed that the 'fatherland of song' had newer and vigorous resources, attributes that promised a brilliant future.

In the late 1840s, Verdi's strong dramatic feeling, energy, passion and exuberant conception prompted words of open hostility from some of the most influential Victorian critics. In the years to come, as Verdi's

---

22 "Verdi," *The Illustrated London News*, May 30, 1846, p. 357.

popular success could be neither denied nor ignored, they mitigated their tone. In the period spanning the years 1849–1852, no new opera bearing the name of Verdi was given in London, despite the fact that four new operas of Verdi premiered in Italy: *La battaglia di Legnano* (Rome, 27 January 1849), *Luisa Miller* (Naples, 8 December 1849), *Stiffelio* (Trieste, 16 November 1850) and *Rigoletto* (Venice, 11 March 1851). In spite of the popular success Verdi had scored in London, it was not until 14 May 1853 that *Rigoletto* was produced at Covent Garden for the first time. Verdi strengthened his position and his operas came to be incorporated into the regular repertoire of both Her Majesty's Theatre and Covent Garden, notwithstanding the repeated attacks of the most hostile music critics.

With *Rigoletto* some commentators referred to what had been said on the continent about Verdi having entered a second, more mature compositional stage. Of course, not everybody agreed and some critics claimed that no sign of such a change could be noticed in his music. The only audible difference consisted in the composer neither overloading the music with trombones and drums nor terminating each act with the usual choirs singing in unison. This change resulted from the different librettos Verdi was setting to music, since they no longer called for strong, noisy effects. When *Il trovatore* was produced at Covent Garden in 1855, even some of the severest critics pronounced much milder judgments. Among them, *The Musical World* expressed a first tentatively positive opinion. In general, Verdi's growing popularity in London was plain and it would have been absurd to deny that he was to some extent gifted; however, the question concerning the basis on which his popularity was founded was still open to debate. More often than not, Verdi was dismissed as a composer devoid of any true merit, while the interpreters were credited with the success of his operas.

With *La traviata*, which premiered in Venice in 1853, it was clear that Verdi was pursuing the dramatic truth even at the expense of the musically beautiful. After the lofty dramas of the early years he was now shifting his attention towards dramatic subjects closer to contemporary everyday life. This explained at least in part the extensive and—according to some—objectionable use Verdi was making of *parlanti*, that is the dramatised style that lies halfway between recitative and proper singing. As previously mentioned, Basevi saw in *La traviata* the rise of a third style in Verdi. The critic lamented that the composer had chosen an immoral subject and argued that under the influence of French literature the notion of true love had now come to justify adultery and concubinage. According to this objectionable tendency, passion if sufficiently spontaneous and sincere might justify any human mistake and redeem any piece of guilt. When applied to marital life this idea could excuse any inconsiderate deviation from the path of virtue.[23]

However, not every critic saw a threat to public morality in the subject of *La traviata*. When in 1856 Alberto Mazzucato reviewed the opera, he ignored that question and instead emphasised what, in his opinion, was one of the composer's highest achievements. Verdi had brought together the dramatic and the musical without mutually sacrificing either; in his opera music and drama were joined in perfect harmony to give rise to moments of intense beauty.[24] Other critics expressed different opinions and some attacked both the composer and the librettist. Carlo Lorenzini, alias Carlo Collodi, deemed the libretto that Francesco Maria Piave had derived from *La Dame aux camélias* by Alexandre Dumas fils an unworthy patchwork made up of bad verses and indecent words. The music, despite some beautiful moments, would never last, owing to a complete lack of dramatic consistency. The moral question, Lorenzini added, was not worth considering since a number of plays of much more dubious morality had long overcrowded the Italian dramatic scene. The morbid reaction exhibited by some members of the female public found no justification in the operatic subject, despite the scandalous text from which it had been derived. According to Lorenzini, a number of reasons could be given to explain why *La traviata* was perfectly harmless. Among them was the role played by the music, to which the text was constantly sacrificed, and the nature of opera as such, which privileges grandiosity and subordinates the meaning of the lyrics to the music.[25]

---

23 Basevi, *Studio sulle opere di Giuseppe Verdi*, pp. 226–28.
24 A. Mazzuccato, "La traviata," *Gazzetta Musical di Milano*, XIV/39, September 28, 1856, pp. 308–09; n. 42, October 19, pp. 329–31. See also Marco Capra, *Verdi in prima pagina*, pp. 65–85.
25 Carlo Lorenzini, "Corrispondenza di Firenze (dove si parla di Livorno)," *L'Italia musicale*, VII/89, November 7, 1855, pp. 353–54. See also Marco Capra, *Verdi in prima pagina*, pp. 103–10.

In 1856 London, *La traviata* triggered a huge discussion and provoked strong reactions. The idea of having a *lorette* on stage was perceived as outrageous and offensive, while the negative influence exerted by French literature was declared deplorable. Of course, not every critic agreed that *La traviata* was immoral, its subject shameful and its music worthless. Nor was it necessarily wrong to disguise corruption by means of beautiful singing. *La traviata*, some critics held, was no less immoral than any other opera of the same kind and, in the end, dealing with morality was still a business of the stage. Even the theatre manager, Benjamin Lumley, had to intervene in the discussion, arguing that the subject was worthy of consideration since it reflected the continuous conflict between good and evil, although in a new shape. The immense popular success *La traviata* scored in London, a success which the moralising positions expressed by the press did much to arouse, also drew the critics' attention to the role played by individual interpreters. Although many a critic agreed that Marietta Piccolomini, the first Violetta in London, was inadequate as a singer, most of them claimed that the enormous success of the opera depended on her dramatic talent. In fact, the composer was confined to a marginal position and *La traviata* was pronounced a success despite Verdi's music.

Luisa Miller was first performed in London in 1858. Little or no attention had been paid to this opera since its premiere nine years earlier. Nor had the debate concerning Verdi's new style found significant resonance in the London press. Furthermore, its success in London was limited and did not add to the composer's fame. But by the late 1850s, *Rigoletto*, *Il trovatore* and *La traviata* had entered the regular operatic repertoire and established themselves as "stock operas" together with *Ernani* and *Nabucco*. A theatre manager could put them on stage at a moment's notice, and rely upon them in order to secure a large audience, all the more so if a cast of cherished interpreters were attached to them. Two singing styles were now generally accepted, depending on the repertoire; while the Rossinian coloratura continued to lie at the foundation of Italian *bel canto*, Verdi's new declamatory manner, no longer condemned as the epitome of a sad state of decadence, came to be considered a more suitable style for modern dramatic operas.

I vespri siciliani reached London in 1859, *Un ballo in maschera* in 1861, *Don Carlos* and *La forza del destino* in 1867. By the end of the 1860s

Verdi was the only living Italian composer enjoying an international reputation. Some London critics still held, however, that this fortunate condition rested less on his artistic merits than on the desperate condition of Italian opera generally. It was felt that although in *Un ballo in maschera* the composer had advanced his dramatic and compositional skills, the attempt to imitate Giacomo Meyerbeer did not result in an improvement, but rather in a reduced effectiveness in the melodies and in a less spontaneous dramatic genius.

In 1862 Verdi's cantata *Inno delle nazioni* was the object of an animated discussion and caused some embarrassment in the press. Having commissioned a march for the inaugural ceremony of the Great London Exhibition, the Royal Commissioners refused to have a cantata performed in its stead, for reasons that were never made entirely clear. Therefore, Verdi's *Inno delle nazioni*, was instead performed on 24 May at Her Majesty's Theatre, upon the conclusion of a performance of *Il barbiere di Siviglia*.

In 1867 *Don Carlos* and *La forza del destino* were given in London. Some critics argued that in *Don Carlos* Verdi had assimilated the lessons of the "German school," although it was unclear how this influence was manifested in his compositional style. Nor was it evident whether by "German school," Wagner's works and theories were meant to be understood. In fact, many critics were still referring to Meyerbeer as Verdi's main reference model.

In 1875, Verdi himself conducted his *Requiem Mass* at the Royal Albert Hall, while in 1876 *Aida* was given at Covent Garden for the first time, featuring Adelina Patti in the title role. In the 1870s, the London musical milieu underwent major changes, mostly due to the prominent position now occupied by Richard Wagner's works and theories. In 1870 *Der Fliegende Holländer* was performed in Italian at Drury Lane, while in 1872 the London Wagner Society was founded. *Lohengrin* and *Tannhäuser* were given at Covent Garden in 1875 and 1876, respectively. Some critics could not resist the temptation to draw a comparison between Verdi and Wagner, and some suggested that while Wagner's lofty theories represented an overwhelming challenge to both the musical cognoscenti and the uneducated operagoers, Verdi's music had a merely entertaining function. *The Times* drew a comparison between the poverty of *Aida's* libretto and the manner in which Wagner's works were characterised by a more stringent sense of dramatic necessity. However, the critic did not agree with those commentators who argued that Wagner's influence was audible in Verdi's music. Although it was not possible to deny that Verdi's style had developed over time, the claim that he was imitating his German colleague was devoid of any concrete justification. Other periodicals acknowledged a change in Verdi's style and suggested that, having abandoned the Italian models, he had begun to found himself upon Meyerbeer and Wagner. The imitation of the first resulted in *Don Carlos*, while the influence of the great prophet of the future was thought evident in *Aida*.

By the time *Otello* and *Falstaff* were performed in London (1889 and 1894), the image of Verdi had undergone a radical change. No longer a young composer to be treated with scorn and contempt, he now commanded respect. The Milan premiere of *Otello* offered itself as an opportunity for the English critics to report on a momentous event in the history of Italian opera. Some of the correspondents published ample retrospectives covering Verdi's career and works, while others indulged in portraying him as a country gentleman, a landed proprietor and successful breeder of horses who now used composition as a means of relaxation. In the 1870s music journalism in London was transformed, largely because a group of well-known personalities passed away and a new generation of young music critics made their appearance. The critics of the young generation treated Verdi with respect, and the hostility that had been meted out to his early operas can no longer be found in the later reviews. Some commentators continued to insist on the relationship between Verdi's late style and Wagner's music-drama. Whether Verdi was considered an imitator of Wagner or not, the compositional technique of the second was constantly hinted at as the benchmark against which the music of the first should be examined. The question concerning the use of *leitmotivs* was often raised, especially when it came to specifying the discriminating factor between Wagner and Verdi. However, no one could deny that with his last operas Verdi had realised two unparalleled masterpieces.

This investigation does not aim at exhaustiveness and four journals occupy a prominent position: *The Athenaeum*, *The Times*, *The Musical World* and *The Musical Times*. Periodicals like *The Illustrated London News*, *The Spectator*, *The Saturday Review*, *The Literary Gazette*, *The Musical Gazette* and *The Leader* have also been taken into consideration in order to reflect the extent to which, on specific occasions, the critical debate could be pervasive. Limited attention has been paid to the figure of George Bernard Shaw, whose complete musical criticism has long been available, selections having also appeared in monographs focusing on specific aspects of his journalistic activity. Although each Victorian periodical followed a slightly different style, with titles often appearing enclosed in quotation marks rather than italicised, the excerpts reproduced in this volume have been standardised according to the current practice. Titles of operas and other long musical compositions or literary works, plays and poems have been italicised, while titles of single arias, scenes, etc. are enclosed in quotation marks. In order to avoid confusion, the names of the characters, which were often italicised in the originals, are reproduced without any typographic emphasis.

1. Music Journalism in Early Victorian London

To describe the conditions of music journalism in Victorian London and define the manner in which Verdi's operas were conceptualised by those critics who attended and reviewed their productions week after week for almost sixty years represents an overwhelming task. Although individual responses can be fruitfully investigated and certain shared tendencies noted, broader generalisations are almost impossible. In Victorian times, around 200 periodicals provided well-informed coverage of music and musical events.[1] Moreover, music journalism underwent a transformation of paramount importance during this period, which involved the rise in the socio-cultural status of journalists and the advance of music criticism from the literary gentlemanly amateurism of an earlier age to a more solid professionalism.[2] However, by 1850 the coverage of music was still uneven in quality and, to make things more complicated, by the end of the century music critics were still publishing anonymously, with one individual often contributing to many different journals.

Four periodicals have particular relevance for this investigation, since they gave uninterrupted coverage to music and musical events between the years 1845 and 1894: *The Athenaeum*, *The Musical World*, *The Times* and *The Musical Times*.

---

1 Leanne Langley, "The Musical Press in Nineteenth-Century England," *Notes* 46/3, Second Series (1990), pp. 583–92.
2 Meirion Hughes, *The English Musical Renaissance and the Press 1850–1914: Watchmen of Music* (Aldershot: Ashgate, 2002), pp. 2–9.

© Massimo Zicari, CC BY 4.0   http://dx.doi.org/10.11647/OBP.0090.01

The *Athenaeum and Literary Chronicle* was one of the most prominent journals in Victorian London. Launched in 1828 by James Silk Buckingham and Henry Colburn, it ran until 1923 and dominated the weekly periodical market; it was considered "an outstanding popular literary journal with mildly liberal principles."[3] Although a literary journal, in January 1834 it assigned a dedicated space to music in the "Music and the Drama" columns. There, Henry Fothergill Chorley, who had joined *The Athenaeum* in 1833, shot his merciless darts. Chorley ruled supreme as the mouthpiece of the journal from the mid-1840s to 1868. A short description of his conspicuous figure has been left by the English writer, politician and *Punch* contributor Rudolph Chambers Lehmann in his *Memories*:

> Of Henry Fothergill Chorley I have a very distinct recollection, though he died thirty-six years ago. He was tall and thin. His eyes blinked and twinkled as he spoke; and his quaint packing gestures and high staccato voice made an impression which caused one of his friends to describe him as the missing link between the chimpanzee and the cockatoo.[4]

Chorley was one of the most influential music critics of his time and was regarded as the most severe, conservative and uncompromising of them all.[5] He disliked Robert Schumann's music and favoured Mendelssohn's, and he was said to have neither the natural gifts nor the education necessary for such a responsible position since, as Lehmann put it, "he took the most violent likes and dislikes; an important matter, seeing that he, so to speak, made public opinion."[6]

As Henry Gay Hewlett was already suggesting in 1873, Chorley's music education was qualified by a tint of amateurism;[7] he nurtured and developed his fervour for music in Liverpool in the 1830s thanks to his intimate friendship with the poetess Felicia Hemans (1793–1835),

---

3 Theodor Fenner, *Opera in London: Views of the Press; 1785–1830* (Carbondale and Edwardsville: Southern Illinois University Press, 1994), p. 45.
4 Rudolph Chambers Lehmann (comp. and ed.), *Memories of Half a Century: a Record of Friendships* (London: Smith, Elder & Co., 1908), p. 230.
5 Robert Terrell Bledsoe, *Henry Fothergill Chorley Victorian Journalist* (Aldershot: Ashgate, 1998), p. 44.
6 Lehmann, *Memories*, p. 228.
7 Henry Gay Hewlett (comp.), *Henry Fothergill Chorley: Autobiography, Memoirs and Letters* (London: Bentley, 1873), I: 82–85.

to whom Chorley would dedicate a biographic essay in 1836.[8] James Z. Hermann, alias Jakob Zeugheer Hermann, conductor of the Liverpool Philharmonic, was his only music teacher; his attendance of the symphonic concerts in Liverpool, together with the composition of small lyric works on texts by Felicia Hemans herself, provided Chorley with the credentials and qualifications necessary to his future career as a critic.

> That he was gifted with a singularly acute ear and retentive memory; that, thanks to his Liverpool teachers, his passionate love of the art was based upon a sound knowledge of the science of music; and that he had acquired a familiarity with the works of its greatest masters that was wide if not profound, are facts about which there can be no dispute. To one thus endowed and informed, a regular course of attendance during several months of the year at the choicest performances of sacred and secular music in London, must of itself have constituted a professional education of no ordinary value.[9]

In addition to its strong tint of conservatism, Chorley's career was characterised by an equally strong commitment to the ethics of art, literature and journalism:

> The whole tenor of his critical career, so far as I have been able to follow it, seems pervaded, and consecrated by a single aim. That Art should be true to herself, her purpose high, her practice stainless, was a creed which he never wearied of preaching. Against any tradition of the past, or innovation of the present, that savoured of falsehood or trick; against all pretenders, who concealed their nakedness by meretricious display or arrogant self-assertion, he ceaselessly protested and inveighed. Alike to the bribery of managers, the venality of journalists and claqueurs, the extravagant assumption of composers, and the insolent vanity of singers and instrumentalists, he showed himself a bitter, almost a remorseless, enemy.[10]

During his lifelong career as a critic Chorley came to be accepted by the best musicians of England and Europe as a thoroughly competent authority, listened to by amateurs with more deference than any other contemporary critic. "In many houses, it has been said, *The Athenaeum*

---

8   Henry Fothergill Chorley, *Memorials of Mrs. Hemans: With Illustrations of her Literary Character from her Private Correspondence* (New York: Sanders & Otley, 1836).
9   Hewlett, *Henry Fothergill Chorley*, 1: 282–83.
10 *Ibid.*, 289–90.

was habitually read solely for the sake of its musical column."[11] However, the extent to which Chorley's criticism could really affect both the general public and the professional musician appears to be problematic, owing to the often excessive quality of his opinions.[12]

In 1830 Charles Wentworth Dilke assumed the editorship of *The Athenaeum*, his involvement with the journal having begun already in the late 1820s.[13] Dilke was strongly committed to the cause of independent journalism and refused to practice puffery, a principle that dovetailed nicely with Chorley's strong sense of professionalism. On this account, Dilke's *Athenaeum* was regarded as a journal of integrity. Upon Chorley's retirement in 1868, it continued to select its music critics on the basis of their competence and experience in the field.[14] Although in the 1870s it developed a more open attitude towards the newest musical ideas and a more lenient position regarding Richard Wagner, it remained a journal of strongly conservative opinions throughout the century.

As suggested by Richard Kitson, *The Musical World* was possibly the only British music journal comparable in quality and authoritativeness to *La Revue et Gazette musicale* (1835–1880), *Die Neue Zeitschrift für Musik* (1834–1909) and the *Gazzetta Musicale di Milano* (1842–1902). Founded by the well-known music publisher Joseph Alfred Novello, it was printed weekly in London from 18 March 1836 to 24 January 1891 and was entirely devoted to music.[15] In 1839, George Alexander Macfarren (1813–1887) took over its editorship. In 1840, Alfred Day (1810–1849) was entrusted with the position of music critic but, his "laconical bitterness" having dissatisfied the editor, James William Davison (1813–1885) was soon asked to take over the role.[16] In 1844 Davison himself announced an important shift; he assumed half proprietorship of the journal and

---

11 *Ibid.*, 184.
12 *Ibid.*, 196.
13 Laurel Brake, Marysa Demoor, *Dictionary of Nineteenth-century Journalism in Great Britain and Ireland* (Gent: Academy Press, 2009), p. 169.
14 Chorley was followed by Campbell Clarke (1868–1870), Charles L. Gruneisen (1870–1879), Ebenezer Prout (1879–1888), Henry F. Frost (1888–1898) John S. Shedlock (1898–1916). See also chapter 18.
15 Richard Kitson, *The Musical World, 1836–1865*, 11 vols. Répertoire International de la Presse Musicale (Ann Arbor: University of Michigan Press, 1996), I: ix–xix.
16 Patricia Collins Jones, "Day, Alfred," *The New Grove Dictionary of Music and Musicians*, 5: 286–87.

became its editor, a position he was to hold until his death.[17] Two years later, in 1846, Desmond Ryan (1816–1888) joined him as sub-editor and contributor.

Fig. 1 James William Davison from a picture reproduced in Joseph Bennett, *Forty Years of Music, 1865–1905* (London: Methuen & Co., 1908).

If Henry Fothergill Chorley reigned supreme as the mouthpiece of *The Athenaeum*, Davison exerted full control over *The Musical World*. His personality was clearly characterised by a strong commitment to the cause of English national music and, even in his earlier career, "he formed one of that group of young men who, about 1835, cherished the idea of a modern native school, an idea for whose maintenance he diligently used his journalistic pen."[18] No less interested in presenting the works of the great modern masters to the general public, he had two maxims that epitomise his thoughts and beliefs: England is not an unmusical country; the people at large can be trusted to appreciate

---

17   *The Musical World*, October 24, 1844, p. 347.
18   Henry Davison, *Music during the Victorian Era. From Mendelssohn to Wagner: Being the Memoirs of J. W. Davison, Forty Years Music Critic of "The Times"* (London: Reeves, 1912), p. 1.

the best music.[19] His knowledge of music was limited to the modern composers and his interest in the music of earlier ages did not go beyond such leading figures as Johann Sebastian Bach and Georg Friedrich Handel. His conservatism regarding artistic matters can be defined in terms of continuity and deference to the masters of past epochs.[20] Francis Burnand, *Punch* contributor for 45 years and its editor for 25, from 1880 until 1906, wrote of Davison that "where his personal likes and dislikes were not concerned, his criticisms were reliable; but where there was a bias, then to read between his lines was an absolute necessity in order to get at anything like the truth."[21] Joseph Bennett, music critic of *The Daily Telegraph* from 1870 and assistant editor of *The Musical World* after Desmond Ryan, entertained a close and long-lasting friendship with Davison. According to Bennett, Davison exerted a strong influence over many colleagues. Among them were Desmond Ryan, long-time critic of *The Standard* and assistant-editor of *The Musical World*; Howard Glover, critic of *The Morning Post* and a respectable composer himself; and Henry Sutherland Edwards, who followed Glover on *The Morning Post* and was a regular contributor to *The Pall Mall Gazette*.[22] Bennett provides us with a detailed account of the peculiar way in which Davison loved to address different issues by assuming fictitious identities and appearing under different pseudonyms collectively called the Muttonians. They were "personal figments of Davison's very quaint and curious intellect— puppets he used for the expression of ideas and sentiments, which through their very plastic individuality, he could represent in the most fantastic forms."[23] The ruling Muttonian, a tall person with a sheep's head and long tapering legs, was Mr Ap Mutton, who stood for Davison himself, but other names, such as Dishley Peters, were also chosen by the critic. Mr Ap Mutton was supported by a council of imaginary figures; behind them a real person was occasionally recognizable (Henry Sutherland Edwards was Shaver Silver, Joseph Bennett was Thaddeus Egg, and Flamborough Head was George Grove), while others were

---

19 *Ibid.*
20 Davison, *Music During the Victorian Era*, p. 70.
21 Francis C. Burnand, *Records and Reminiscences, Personal and General* (London: Methuen, 1904), 2: 277.
22 Joseph Bennett, *Forty Years of Music, 1865–1905* (London: Methuen & Co., 1908), pp. 17–22.
23 *Ibid.*, p. 223.

completely imaginary (Dr Blidge, Dr Grief, Alderman Doublebody, etc.). These figures bear a strong resemblance to Robert Schumann's *Carnival*.

Fig. 2 Mr Ap Mutton, alias James William Davison. Davison loved to address different issues by assuming fictitious identities and appearing under different pseudonyms collectively called the Muttonians. The ruling Muttonian was Mr. Ap Mutton, a tall person with a sheep's head and long tapering legs. From a drawing by Charles Lyall published in Joseph Bennett, *Forty Years of Music, 1865–1905* (London: Methuen & Co., 1908).

Together with important articles and reviews of major musical productions, *The Musical World* included short notices as well as detailed correspondences from the provinces and abroad. The growing concert life in Liverpool, Manchester, Birmingham and Leeds was described in reports from local correspondents; English translations of reviews and articles from the French and German press also made regular appearances, very often reflecting or even supporting the editor's personal inclinations and biases. Authors other than Davison who contributed to *The Musical World* are difficult to identify; since the journal supported the convention of anonymous criticism, most articles appeared unsigned while some bore a pseudonym. This position was overtly advocated in 1859, in contrast with the French system.

> The writers of the London press are at present anonymous, and, according to existing regulations, it is not in their power to print their names if they would. Let us add that in no respectable journal is advantage taken

of the anonymous position. The general public is indeed unacquainted with the names of the persons who contribute so much towards its daily recreation; but all the classes that are immediately affected by criticism can, without the slightest difficulty, point to the critic. Nay the leading actors, musicians, painters—artists, in fact, of all descriptions—are personally acquainted with every writer in the respective departments of the press that concern their interests, and would speak openly if they considered themselves unfairly treated. Far from using the "anonymous" as a shield, the Critic of the press goes to work with the perfect conviction that he will be considered accountable for his opinions to any artist who feels himself unjustly assailed.[24]

As controversial as this position may appear, *The Musical World* reflected the viewpoint of its chief editor, Davison, and never operated as the mouthpiece of any particular party; nor was it the advertising tool of any music publisher.[25] Its orientation was conservative, and its proselytism in favour of English national music stemmed from Davison's personal beliefs; this characteristic resulted in a general hostility towards foreign musicians. Although in the late 1860s its preeminent position was to some extent eroded by *The Musical Times*, *The Musical World* remained a music journal of pivotal importance in Victorian London; it addressed a wide national and international readership that included practicing musicians, both amateurs and experienced professionals. Upon Davison's retirement Joseph Bennett appears to have continued to supervise the journal until 1886, when Francis Hueffer took over. In 1888 the editorship passed into the hands of Edgar Frederick Jacques.

James William Davison also dominated the columns of *The Times*, which he joined in 1846. As the chief music critic of the most prominent and authoritative daily journal in the United Kingdom he exerted an influential role in the English press for over thirty years. However, while as co-proprietor and editor of *The Musical World* he was in a position to trumpet his opinions with no fear of direct consequences, in the capacity of music critic of *The Times* he was expected to express himself in more respectful terms. Because of his aggressive and often overtly biased attitude, he received complaints on more than one occasion during his career, even from the newspaper's editor, John Thaddeus Delane,

---

24 *The Musical World*, July 9. 1859, pp. 441–42.
25 Richard Kitson, *The Musical World, 1866–1891*, 11 vols. Répertoire international de la presse musicale (Ann Arbor: University of Michigan Press, 1996), I: xi.

to whom the journal owed its unprecedented prestige. Therefore, the quality of Davison's writings could be very diverse, mainly depending on the journal he was contributing to. While the reviews he published in *The Times* were usually clear and correct, his vocabulary classical with humorous expressions inserted occasionally here and there, his contributions to *The Musical World* were generally much wittier if not derisive or even blatantly offensive.

Later on in the sixties, while continuing to write for *The Times* and *The Musical World*, Davison started contributing to the *Saturday Review* and the *Pall Mall Gazette*.[26] His leading position granted him the opportunity to attend some of the most relevant musical events of the century, among them the Wagner festival in Bayreuth in 1876, which he recorded as "the triumph of the originator of an artistic cause he regarded as mortally hurtful to Art."[27]

In 1878, upon Davison's retirement, Francis Hueffer was appointed chief music critic of *The Times*. This led to a major shift in the journal's editorial policy for, contrary to his predecessor, Hueffer was a strong supporter of Wagner's music and ideas.[28] After Hueffer, John Alexander Fuller Maitland assumed the position of chief music critic at *The Times* from 1889 until 1911. He was a strong advocate of English music and served the cause of the English Musical Renaissance not only as a critic but also as George Grove's successor on the *Dictionary of Music and Musicians* and as a committed music historian.[29] *The Times* gave ample coverage to music and music events throughout the whole century, never missing a concert or an operatic performance. Its critics seemed to enjoy a certain degree of freedom, and the editor intervened only when the quality of the piece or the position of the critic failed to comply with the journal's editorial policy, as was the case with Davison.

The initial success of *The Musical World* was such that in 1844 its original owner Joseph Alfred Novello decided to get back to the journalistic business and acquire *The Musical Times and Singing Class Circular*. This journal, which had been founded two years before by Joseph Mainzer (1801–1851) in order to promote his teaching system,

---

26 Davison, *Music during the Victorian Era*, p. 275.
27 *Ibid.*, p. 317.
28 Hughes, *The English Musical Renaissance*, p. 21.
29 *Ibid.*, p. 30.

was re-named *The Musical Times* and subsequently published as a monthly under the personal editorship of Novello.[30] Mary Cowden Clarke, Novello's sister, edited the journal from 1853 until 1856, granting ample space for the publication of continental musical treatises (Hector Berlioz, Adolf Bernhard Marx, François-Joseph Fétis and even Leopold Mozart). However, it was not until 1863 that *The Musical Times* achieved prominence, thanks to the work of Henry Charles Lunn. Under Lunn's editorship, which lasted until 1887, not only did the journal increase in size, but it also improved with regard to its "intellectual strength and breadth of interest."[31] After 1870, opera performances received regular notice and particular attention was paid to Verdi's last works (*Requiem*, *Otello* and *Falstaff*). Among its contributors we find the name of Filippo Filippi; editor of the *Gazzetta Musicale di Milano* until 1862 and then critic of the Milan periodical *La Perseveranza* until his death, in 1884 he contributed articles and reviews from Milan.[32] While staff members of the journal did not sign their articles, other external contributors did. Besides Filippo Filippi, the names of Joseph Bennett, George Alexander Macfarren and Edward Holmes are worth mentioning. In 1887 William Alexander Barrett (1834–1891), vocalist, organist, composer and music critic, succeeded Lunn as editor, a position that he kept until his death in 1891.

It has been already pointed out that the quality of the articles published in Victorian London varied. As we shall see, the issue was already raised in the 1890s, when some commentators drew attention to the pitfalls that seemed to be most common in the journalistic profession, all the more so when it came to reviewing a new opera. A certain wariness and a discomforting tendency to be either too superficial or too technical were particularly noticeable. While to be too wary made it impossible for the reader to understand whether the critic liked the opera or not, to indulge in a detailed description of the plot seemed to defy proper

---

30 *Ibid.*, p. 86.
31 Edward Clinkscale, *The Musical Times, 1844–1900*. Répertoire international de la presse musicale (Ann Arbor: University of Michigan Press, 1994), p. ix.
32 Leonardo Pinzauti and Julian Budden, "Filippi, Filippo." *Grove Music Online. Oxford Music Online*. Oxford University Press, accessed June 30, 2014, available at http://www.oxfordmusiconline.com/subscriber/article/grove/music/09638

criticism. Nor did musical parsing lead to a better understanding of the true merits of the composer.

Although it is not entirely true that English music critics were necessarily that cautious when called upon to express their opinion (witness Henry Fothergill Chorley from *The Athenaeum* and James William Davison from *The Times* and *The Musical World*), and even though generalisations are hazardous, it is possible to argue that, at least until the 1870s, Victorian music journalists tended to favour the old and cherish the classics at the expense of everything that sounded threateningly new. This conservative attitude prompted some of them to antagonise modern composers in a language that would be considered unacceptable today. In the 1850s scornful and offensive comments on Verdi, although sporadic, were not entirely absent; occasionally, the most disrespectful critics ended up trivialising the work and scoffing at the composer instead of expressing a genuine, although antagonistic, value judgment. In some cases, as the example of Davison suggests, this attitude was accompanied and reinforced by a strong nationalistic feeling; everything that sounded too new and progressive was understood as dangerous to the cause of English national music. Here and there a certain Philistinism can be also recognised; the idea advocated by Chorley that Art (with a capital A) should be true to herself, her purpose high, and her practice stainless was not devoid of consequences. The resulting hierarchy of the arts, while favouring Mendelssohn's symphonies and oratorios on the one side and Rossini's operas on the other, pushed the modern tendencies of operatic composition down to the lowest position on account of their being either too cumbersome or too trivial. Richard Wagner belonged to the first class, while Giuseppe Verdi was long considered a worthy representative of the second.

What did a music critic's job consist of? As far as opera is concerned, they were expected to review both the newly-composed works that such entrepreneurial managers as Lumley and Frederick Gye brought to London each year and those stock operas that had already entered the regular repertoire and could be mounted at very short notice any time during the season. This resulted in countless reviews appearing especially in daily and weekly newspapers. General magazines and quarterly literary reviews published at a more leisurely pace and included lengthy music analyses and essays addressing larger issues such as compositional style, music aesthetics and even theatrical morality.

More often than not, the review of a newly-composed opera consisted of three main sections. The first introduced the opera to the public in general terms; it touched upon the circumstances leading to its composition, the manner in which it had been received on the continent and the extent to which it could be said to represent a progress in the composer's artistic development. The second section included the analysis of the libretto and the transformation its literary source had undergone in order to achieve the final result; the reviewer indulged in a narrative of the plot and detailed all its intrigues and machinations for the benefit of the uninformed reader. The third and often final section reviewed the quality of the performance and elaborated on the vocal and dramatic skills of the interpreters. Finding faults with a poor voice, an endless tremolo, a fragile intonation and an excessive gesticulation was not uncommon. On the other hand, expressions of enthusiasm and words of strong appreciation were not rare, and personalities like Jenny Lind or Marietta Piccolomini did not pass unnoticed. Their merits were generously scrutinised, and their weaknesses mercilessly pinpointed. In some case, the manner in which Verdi was said to abuse singers and harm their voices prompted expressions of sympathy and concern; then the soloist in question came to be portrayed as the unjustly wronged victim of a progressive composer of unequal competences. Or else, when in 1850s it was no longer possible to argue against Verdi's international prominence, the most reluctant among the critics insisted on crediting only the performers with the success of his works.

Finally, a verdict was pronounced on the true merits of the opera. The work was generally evaluated either with reference to those composers from the past who were said to have established the yet unsurpassed aesthetic canons of the musical art, or to the same composer's earlier achievements. While *Ernani* and *Nabucco* could not bear comparison with Rossini's masterpieces, *Don Carlos* and *Un ballo in maschera* were pronounced Verdi's worst operas when judged against *Ernani* and *Nabucco*. In the 1840s and 1850s Verdi seemed to represent the living evidence that Italian opera was constantly at its lowest ebb.

Once a new opera had successfully entered the regular repertoire the critic's task changed only slightly. It consisted of reminding the reader of the circumstances leading to its composition, drawing attention to the manner in which the London public had already bestowed strong signs of appreciation upon it (perhaps notwithstanding the critic's negative verdict), and reviewing its performance. If a stock opera was staged, the critic focused on the interpreters' merits and drew a comparison between them and those who had already distinguished themselves in the same role.

In fulfilling their task, Victorian critics could rely on and make reference to the verdict their colleagues on the continent had already pronounced; this was especially true when a new opera was put on stage. A case in point is offered by the repeatedly uttered complaints regarding guitar-like rhythmic figures in the orchestral accompaniment, the too numerous unison choruses and the prominence given to the brass instruments that qualify the general critical response to Verdi's operas in London in the late 1840s. These opinions seem to echo the denigrating criticisms uttered by François-Joseph Fétis in the columns of the *Revue et Gazette Musicale de Paris* in the same years.[33] Explicit references to value judgments that had already appeared in the French and German press became more common during the second half of the century. Surprisingly, the same cannot be said about the Italian press. In fact, no explicit indication can be found in the columns of the periodicals taken into consideration that suggests whether the English critics took a real interest in the critical discussion going on among their Italian colleagues. Nonetheless, they seem to have been well informed about the manner in which Italian operatic conventions were evolving, and they were able to make use of the related musical jargon.

But what competences did these music critics possess? If William Ayrton in the monthly *Harmonicum* could assert in 1830 that "not one musical critic in five has the slightest knowledge of the elements or even the language of the art in which he sits on judgment,"[34] the same cannot be said about later generations of critics. Chorley and Davison were not

---

33 Katherin Ellis, *Music Criticism in Nineteenth-Century France* (Cambridge: Cambridge University Press, 1995), p. 197.
34 Theodore Fenner, *Opera in London, Views from the Press, 1785–1839* (Carbondale: Southern Illinois University Press, 1994), p. 4.

the only critics possessed of strong credentials. The German-born Dr Francis Hueffer, from *The Times*, studied philology and music in London, Paris, Berlin and Leipzig, gaining his doctorate in Göttingen for a critical study of the troubadour Guilem de Cabestanh. John Alexander Fuller Maitland, also from *The Times*, entered Trinity College, Cambridge in 1875 and graduated in 1882. While Joseph Bennett was a professional organ player, other representatives of late Victorian music journalism such as Henry Sutherland Edwards (1828–1906) and Hermann Klein (1856–1934) gained prominence on account of their often fertile scholarly production, which included biographies of past composers and essays on opera and music history. Although Victorian music critics possessed competences of different kinds and levels, the amateurism that was said to qualify English music journalism of an earlier era is no longer to be found among the later generations, at least as far as the most prominent music journals are concerned

Not surprisingly, the verdict of the specialist did not necessarily match the response of the general public. Music critics often took it upon themselves to highlight the difference between the abiding and the ephemeral in music matters; whether they were successful or not in fulfilling this task is another question. As was the case with *La traviata* in 1856, the strong objections raised against the immoral quality of the libretto and the triviality of the music could do nothing to dissuade the public from thronging the theatre night after night. The negative verdict of the knowledgeable critic could not affect the enthusiastic response of the unsophisticated.

Finally, an operatic performance in Victorian London was still a fashionable event. The composition of the Victorian public was heterogeneous, with representatives of the old aristocracy occupying their boxes side by side with the members of the new upper middle class. Queen Victoria herself was quite passionate about opera and even took singing lessons from Luigi Lablache; accompanied by Prince Albert, she was often reported to have attended one performance or another. The response of the audience was also habitually recorded in the periodicals; vivid descriptions of the enthusiasm of the public in asking for a certain aria to be encored, in calling for the singers to reappear before the curtain, in throwing bouquets and applauding warmly were common. Some reviewers called attention to the manner in which the vast majority of the subscribers paid less attention to the music than to the interpreter. This was well described by the critic of *The Musical World* in 1845, who argued that "the singers, and not the composers, occupy their thoughts: they think not of what they hear, but of who they hear. An opera, to them, is a species of composition full of delightful solos for the principal vocalists, and the dreary filling up between these solos gives them ample time to look round the house and converse with their friends."[35] While the vast majority of the public idolised the singer, only a select few paid attention to the composer and the score. Therefore, when a cherished star was announced a crowded audience could be easily predicted. The public flocked to the theatre and packed it to the ceiling night after night. Meanwhile, we do not find reviews reporting on singers being hissed or booed by the audience. Strong negative reactions were quite unusual, and it was enough for operagoers to desert the theatre in order to communicate their disapproval, dislike or simple lack of interest. Of course, the audience's behaviour affected the theatre managers' decisions and influenced the composition of the operatic programmes season after season. If a new opera was a failure, the theatre manager was ready to withdraw it after a night or two, and revive an old favourite. If it made a *furore* it was presented over and over again at the expense of the other titles initially announced in the prospectus. Opera in Victorian London was a business strongly dependant on the star system, and music critics could do little or nothing to guide the public response, influence the reception of a new opera or even determine its success.

---

35 *The Musical World*, April 3, 1845, p. 160; also cited in Jennifer Hall-Witt, *Fashionable Acts, Opera and Elite Culture in London, 1780–1880* (Durham: University of New Hampshire Press, 2007), p. 230.

2. *Ernani* (1845)

As early as 1844, Henry Fothergill Chorley, whose tastes and beliefs were marked by a strong tint of conservativism, introduced his readers to the operatic composer who was creating a *furore* all over Europe. The critic, who had not yet had the occasion to hear any of Verdi's works, availed himself of the recent publication in London of some of his operatic airs. Chorley felt obliged to turn his attention to the emerging Italian composer because of his increasing popularity and on account of those recent events that "had called attention of our English public to the modern style, or rather no-style, of Italian singing."[1] Popularity, rather than value, had compelled him to take into account the recent rise of the young Verdi. Chorley's conservative attitude emerges as soon as he sets his aesthetic coordinates and defines the criteria determining success in any operatic undertaking.

> But first, we must remind the reader that the distinctive basis of Italian Opera, from its outset, has been melody—melody in recitative, in air, in concerted piece, and in chorus; the dramatic expression of the moment being largely left to the singer. Even in the German musical drama, though the voice has been often assigned tasks too ungracious to be ever well performed, under the notion of rendering it a mere instrument in the composer's hands, and the adaptation of sound to sense has been more closely studied, still melody has been indispensable to success—in the orchestra if not on the stage.[2]

Chorley defined melody not only as the true foundation of Italian Opera, but also as a condition for success in the more rational German musical

---

1 *The Athenaeum*, August 31, 1844, p. 797.
2 Ibid.

drama where melody, even if associated with the orchestra rather than with the voice, could not be neglected. Dramatic expression was to be understood as an additional ingredient left to the singer's acting skills. In his analysis of the current state of the musical and dramatic arts, Chorley referred to what, in his eyes, appeared to be a widespread tendency all over Europe: getting rid of what was essential, melody, and emphasising what he thought to be of secondary importance, shapeless dramatisation. This lamentable tendency was noticeable also in Hector Berlioz and, more interestingly, in Richard Wagner, whose operas, Chorley held, "we have heard rapturously bepraised, because they contain no tunes which any one can carry away."[3]

Chorley's idea of melody involved form and symmetry, features dear to Rossini but neglected by Bellini and his successors under the pretence of "dramatizing the style." Melodic dramatisation, on the other hand, consisted of vocal passages—shapeless recitatives—which merely functioned as the dramatic expression of the crudest passions and were devoid of any melodic interest. compounding this degradation was the intolerable volume of the orchestra, increased for dramatic effect, which reminded Chorley of the janissary bands, with the strident sound of the wind instruments, the massive boom of the drums and the metallic clash of cymbals. Even when modern composers strove to respect the tenets of canonical composition by adopting symmetrical dispositions of phrases, they failed to reach a sufficient degree of novelty:

> Bellini's successors, less vigorous in invention, have outdone him in renouncing all firmness and ordinance of construction, producing, it is true, tunes in the canonical number of bars required by the poetic ear, but without the slightest novelty of combination or phrase. In short, Italian invention seems fast advancing towards a point at which, whether the idea be old or new it matters little, so that the singer has a *spianato* passage to bawl or to sigh out, either *solus* or in unison with his comrades, a semblance of intensity and contrivance being given by a use of the orchestra, licentious enough to make Cimarosa and Paisiello (those colourists as tender but as consummate in their art as Watteau) turn in their graves.[4]

Having outlined the general framework, Chorley moved on to address Verdi's *Ernani*, which did not belie the general trend: as he could see

---

3   Ibid.
4   Ibid.

from the score, Verdi's work was devoid of any new melody, while the concerted music struck "as a shade worthier and more individual than his songs."⁵ Despite the presence of the much longed-for ordinance in construction and symmetry, this music was likely to produce a peculiarly monotonous effect because of the intrinsic lack of inventiveness that the continuous repetition of the first melodic idea manifested. Verdi's melodies were worn, hackneyed and meaningless, his harmonies and progressions crude, while only his orchestration appeared to have value. Chorley lamented that Verdi's music lacked that fresh and sweet melody which he considered the true foundation of vocal music. However, Chorley's antagonism was tentative, as he had not been afforded the opportunity to attend any of Verdi's operas at that time.⁶

On 17 February 1845, *The Times* announced the programme of the forthcoming ante-Easter opera season at Her Majesty's Theatre: it promised great brilliancy. Giulia Grisi was the *prima donna*, while Napoleone Moriani and Mario, alias Giovanni Matteo De Candia were both engaged as tenors; the tenor Leone Corelli, the inimitable *primo basso* Luigi Lablache and the baritone Luciano Fornasari were also announced. Other names were Marietta Brambilla, Giovanna "Juana" Rossi Caccia, Anaide (Jeanne Anaïs) Castellan, Rita Borio, Felice Bottelli, and Paul-Bernard Barroilhet. Michael Costa would conduct the orchestra. The first opera of the season was *Ernani* by the young composer Giuseppe Verdi, a work that—it was stated—had created a furore on the continent.⁷

A similar announcement was published in *The Athenaeum* on 22 February, an issue which included further previews, among them Verdi's *I Lombardi* and *Nabucco*, Luigi Ricci's *Scaramuccia* and Donizetti's *La favorita*. In conclusion, the piece remarked on the difficulty involved in preparing a successful operatic programme, for the manager must appeal to three different parties: "the fashionable many, who only care for what is the mode of the hour, the amateur few, who are apt to be somewhat impracticable in their requisitions, and the singers, whose name 'as a legion' is Egotism and Indolence."⁸

---

5   Ibid.
6   Robert Bledsoe, "Henry Fothergill Chorley and the Reception of Verdi's Early Operas in England," *Victorian Studies* 28 (1985), pp. 631–55.
7   *The Times*, February 17, 1845, p. 5.
8   *The Athenaeum*, February 22, 1845, p. 204.

Finally, on 8 March, *Ernani* was performed at Her Majesty's Theatre, followed by the ballet *Eoline, ou la Dryade*, taken from Johann Karl August Musäus's *Libussa*. However, as Benjamin Lumley—manager of Her Majesty's Theatre—put it, *Ernani* did not contribute in any marked degree to the theatre's financial prosperity of that year.[9] The London public, before which it was the manager's duty to bring the greatest novelties of the day, reacted with a sense of indifference that was absolutely consistent with its notoriously conservative habits: "That it excited the general enthusiasm awarded to it so lavishly in Italy, cannot be asserted; that it was a failure, may be emphatically denied. The general result of the first introduction of Verdi to the English public was a feeling of hesitation and doubt."[10]

Fig. 3 Benjamin Lumley, in a portrait from the frontispiece of his *Reminiscences of the Opera* (London: Hurst & Blackett, 1864).

---

9   Benjamin Lumley, *Reminiscences of the Opera* (London: Hurst & Blackett, 1864), pp. 103–05. The real author of Lumley's *Reminiscences* has been identified as Harriet Grote (see Jennifer Hall-Witt, *Fashionable Acts*, p. 160).
10 *Ibid.*, p. 103.

Chorley's review of *Ernani*, published on 15 March in the columns of *The Athenaeum*, shows no sign of either doubt or hesitation. His review touched on three issues: the operatic libretto and its dramatic implications; Verdi's musical treatment; the singers and their interpretation. The choice of the libretto showed at first sight that Italians were now looking to the French Grand Opéra for their model of serious musical drama. Both the length of the drama, with its four acts, and its treatment revealed a tendency that seemed to explain, at least in part, why such features as melodiousness and melodic ornamentation were no longer to be found in the Italian operatic music. "Violent passions, elaborate groupings and combinations of incident are treated fearlessly; tragical declamation and situation are obviously now thought to be as necessary as the setting-off the singers."[11]

This new tendency strongly contrasted with the tradition embodied by Domenico Cimarosa, whose *Gli Oriazi e I Curiazi* now seemed to belong to another world, a remote past to look at and long for with a sense of nostalgia.[12] However, although much had been recently achieved with regard to both drama and music, the same could not be said about the vocal art. While drama had gained in force, probability and contrast, and the new school had established greater musical scope, vocal art seemed now to signify what Chorley defined as "arms and legs" gesticulation that left no space for proper vocalisation. Chorley even wondered whether the dramas of Victor Hugo were any better than the less complicated traditional plots of such operas as *Norma* or *La sonnambula*.

The scrutiny of Verdi's compositional achievement was not flattering; the critic accused the composer of plagiarism and was able to point out a good number of passages that supported his claim. On the other hand, Verdi showed "a disposition to study new effects in the concerted music, caused possibly by the present depreciated state of Italian vocal accomplishment, and by the consequent disposition to emulate the energy and grandeur of French theatrical music of combination."[13] The

---

11 *The Athenaeum*, March 15, 1845, p. 275.
12 Cimarosa's *Gli Orazi e i Curiazi* appeared at the King's Theatre in 1805, with nine performances, and in 1806 with eleven. It was revived again in 1814, 1815 and 1829. See Fenner, *Opera in London*, p. 111.
13 *The Athenaeum*, March 15, 1845, p. 275.

tendency to imitate the Grand Opéra depended, to a large extent, on the poor condition of vocal music in what was once the Land of Song. Verdi's choruses were spirited and able to move the audience, and in fact a certain number of pieces were encored; still, Chorley reproached the way Verdi treated the voice:

> Music without uncouthness of interval more ruinous to the voice than Signor Verdi's has, probably, never been produced. The *soprano* part is perpetually above the stave;—requiring, moreover, force and declamation, and not such silvery warblings as Cimarosa and the more considerate elder Italians delighted to allot to the *soprano sfogato*. To make matters worse, the orchestra is for the most part at full strength— very frequently *fortissimo*, leaving the poor *prima donna* no choice, save scream or pantomime.[14]

Again, Chorley longed for those palmy days in which Cimarosa was able to string pearls of flourishing music by accommodating a captivating melody to the natural compass of the voice, in opposition to the ruinous treatment Verdi now reserved for it. Furthermore, the noisiness of the orchestra left singers in a state of exhaustion and frustrated all their efforts to make their voices audible. Chorley's review concluded with a survey of the performers, addressing both the dramatic and vocal skills of each individual and explicitly suggesting that the older school of singing and interpreting had been replaced by that "stout and naked method of the new Italians, which is meant to do duty as grand expression."[15]

Chorley's verdict is consistent with the fears and doubts anticipated in his first scrutiny of the opera Verdi, who belonged to the new Italian school, seemed to favour crude and bloody dramatic plots; his preference for declamation, to which melody was sacrificed, was consistent with that inclination, since the device was particularly effectual insofar as the strongest emotions were involved; his treatment of the voice, now forced to extremes for the sake of dramatic effect, was simply ruinous; the noisiness of the orchestra was such as to force singers to shout and scream all the time; the French model seemed now to prevail upon the Italian classical tradition represented by Cimarosa. So far, Chorley's criticism does not appear to pay particular attention to the reaction

---

14   *Ibid.*
15   *Ibid.*, p. 276.

of the general public: despite his reference to the number of encores allotted to a single aria or duet, and to that feeling of curiosity that he said had accompanied the production of *Ernani* in London, it would be difficult to deduce from his words the extent to which the judgment of the knowledgeable few diverged from that of the fashionable many.

On 25 October 1845, *The Athenaeum* published an article in the columns of the foreign correspondence, calling the reader's attention to the dramatic change taking place in the Italian operatic theatre: a new generation of noisy composers were imposing themselves on those classics among whom Rossini was now to find his place. In that class of newcomers, Verdi's name emerged uncontested although his merits appeared to be highly questionable. The correspondent, in all probability Chorley himself, who was in Florence at that time,[16] having attended a performance of *I Lombardi* at the Teatro dei Solleciti, complained about the disproportion between the orchestral and vocal forces and about the small space in which they were confined. The accomplishments of those new composers who aimed at the dramatic grandeur of the French operas and tried to replicate it in the much smaller Italian theatres, the correspondent held, resulted in an absurd parade. The verdict on Verdi was unequivocal:

> The grand opera of the French must no longer be grumbled at by the Southerns as an arena where fine voices are butchered to make a Paris holiday! Signor Verdi being the most desperate tearer and taxer of his singers who has yet appeared. I think the characteristics of his music are easily mastered; amounting to a certain largeness of outline and *brio* in his slow concerted music,—a picturesque feeling for instrumentation, and a curious absence of fresh melody. Almost all his *cabaletti* proceed by the starts and stops and syncopations, which Pacini introduced so happily, and wore threadbare; since the device,—however effective it sounded in 'I tuoi frequenti palpiti' [*Niobe*, 1826], and 'Lungi dal caro ben' [*La sposa fedele*, 1819]—loses all piquancy, when it becomes an understood thing, that the phrase must begin on the second note of the bar, and the accents fall cross-wise. Then, in the mere filling up of *appoggiatura* and passage, Signor Verdi does not appear to have made the smallest discovery.[17]

In short, Verdi offered a few elements of variety, in a continuous attempt to reach one exaggerated climax after the other; unless he

---
16 Hewlett, *Henry Fothergill Chorley*, 2: 63–64.
17 *The Athenaeum*, October 25, 1845, p. 25.

showed himself capable of composing in a way that would appeal to the educated ear, a short and unsuccessful career would be the result. A similar judgment was presented again in a contribution published in the column "Music and the Drama" on 17 January 1846: *The Verdi-Mania*. The publication of Verdi's *6 Romanze* in London in 1845, by Addison & Hodson, afforded the critic a further opportunity of elaborating on the most popular Italian living composer, even though this effort was a degrading concession. Again, the antagonism between popularity and true value in music was perceived as one of the causes that had led to the disgraceful condition in which musical art currently lay. The verdict was negative—only one of the six vocal pieces was considered acceptable—and failed to conceal the critic's animosity, notwithstanding a final attempt to defend his presumed objectivity.

> Let it not be thought that we have been needlessly severe, or "breaking a butterfly on the wheel." We too often speak in uncompromising phrases of our own young composers striving for popularity to have any excuse, did we spare those who, having obtained it, prove themselves so destitute of sustaining power as Sig. Verdi.[18]

In 1897 Frederick Crowest (1850–1927), author of monographs on *Cherubini* (1890) and *Beethoven* (1903), and of historical essays like *The Great Tone Poets: Being Short Memoirs of the Greater Musical Composers* (1908) and *The Story of the Art of Music* (1912), published his *Verdi: Man and Musician, his Biography with Especial Reference to his English Experiences*. A glance at Crowest's account leads us to suspect that the severity of some critics did not reflect the apparently much more appreciative reaction manifested by the general public.

> The Audience, if not the critics, were delighted with the work [*Ernani*]. The characters so musically individualised, the new and attractive orchestration, the *motive* distinguishing the singer, the perfect *ensemble*, the well-proportioned whole opera—all these thoroughly Verdinian [*sic*] characteristics were seized upon and admired.[19]

Crowest also reproduced a couple of passages taken from *The Illustrated London News* of 15 March 1845, in which an even more enthusiastic report made its appearance: "Encore followed encore from the rising

---

18 *The Athenaeum*, January 17, 1846, p. 73.
19 Frederick F. Crowest, *Verdi: Man and Musician, His Biography with Especial Reference to his English Experience* (London: John Milton, 1897), p. 63.

of the curtain [...] Solos, duets, and trios were applauded with equal fervour, but the concerted pieces created the most surprise and admiration [...] The ensembles possess a novelty and an impassioned fervour unprecedented."[20]

The critic of *The Illustrated London News* had already tried to do full justice to the young composer in the previous issue, where he had acknowledged Verdi's attempt to formulate a new definition of the operatic genre. Even though he was lacking in some of those traditionally cherished qualities that were considered typical of the Italian tradition, the composer was clearly possessed of a true dramatic power. Moreover, the objection raised by some critics, that Verdi was unable to compose nice melodies, was incorrect, for occasional hints of captivating melody were also present in his compositions.

> From the very first bars of this opera [*Ernani*], you feel the power the composer possesses of evoking and describing the deepest sensations of the human breast. There is a massive grandeur in the introduction, followed almost immediately by a spirited chorus, which far surpasses the old form of an overture. Throughout this lyrical composition, the author has principally relied for effect on dramatic situations, combined with concerted pieces. This does not preclude snatches of bewitching melody, which, from time to time, relieve the ear from the pressure of the combined power of voices, whilst each principal singer has assigned to him more than one solo, in which to display the range, the depth, and the fascinating sleights of his voice.[21]

On 15 March the same journal commented positively on the concerted pieces and the marked individuality in the treatment of the voices, and paid the composer a great compliment regarding the distribution of the vocal parts. These, together with the impassioned fervour that characterised the whole composition, were pronounced the composer's best achievements.

> The composer has managed his score in the introductions to his concerted pieces so as to allow each singer in his turn to develop the resources and beauties of his voice—the diversity of feeling by which the personages are agitated is constantly felt, and thus the *ensembles* possess a novelty and an impassioned fervour unprecedented. Verdi has been unusually

---

20 *The Illustrated London News*, March 15, 1845, p. 167.
21 "The Opening of Her Majesty's Theatre," *The Illustrated London News*, March 8, 1845, p. 151.

felicitous in his distribution of the vocal parts. The various characters are so musically individualised, and so peculiarly accompanied by the orchestra, that the voice of the singer becomes as easily recognisable by the *motivi*, as he does by his costume. To secure this is the highest achievement of the dramatic composer.[22]

Later that year the same critic confirmed his judgment. The sad state in which Italian opera lay was to be redeemed by the only living composer of genius.

> A better state of things is, however, we trust, approaching. The appearance of a composer of so much originality of genius as Verdi heralds, it may be hoped, that of a new and more ambitious school, whose masters will not be satisfied with tickling the ear and pleasing the fancy, but will seek for the more permanent and legitimate sources of effect.[23]

The critic restated his opinion in August that year, when he elaborated upon the novelties presented over the past season.

> It [*Ernani*] presents the real type of the lyrical tragedy, where feeling finds its appropriate expression in music. Musical judges allotted to it the palm of sterling merit, but the leaning to public taste was against the probabilities of its obtaining here high favour it has elsewhere enjoyed […] The meretricious sentimental style of the modern school to which, of late years, we have become so accustomed was a bad preparation for the full appreciation of such work as this. *Ernani*, however, at first only half understood, gradually worked its way into the public favour, and was given a greater number of times than any opera of the season; finally, it might be pronounced completely successful.[24]

Even if this attitude, as printed in *The Illustrated London News*, led some to suspect that puffery hid behind such positive judgments, it is possible that the general public, although hesitant and undecided when first exposed to Verdi's new dramatic style, came to accept and even appreciate *Ernani*. Benjamin Lumley's *Reminiscences* call attention to a couple of relevant points. Verdi, who had at his command passion, fire and strong dramatic effect, was confronted with a public that did not seem to be prepared to give its own verdict as to his merits. Widespread feelings of resistance and hostility had qualified the

---
22 *The Illustrated London News*, March 15, 1845, p. 167.
23 *The Illustrated London News*, July 5, 1845, p. 10.
24 "Her Majesty's. Last night.—Retrospect of the Season," *The Illustrated London News*, August 23, 1845, p. 122.

reception of all previous Italian composers when compared with their immediate predecessors. Rossini had been the object of general condemnation when compared with Domenico Cimarosa and Giovanni Battista Pergolesi; Bellini had been condemned when compared with Rossini; Donizetti had been pronounced the unworthy plagiarist of the "now admired" Bellini. Now it was Verdi's turn to be compared with his predecessors and to suffer the consequences of such an unequal confrontation. Verdi's music was promoting novelty to a degree that was guaranteed to provoke the harsh reactions of English classicists, who were distinguished by "a great spirit of opposition to all novelty and an assertion of excellence existing only in the past."[25] According to Lumley, *Ernani* ran for several nights with a moderate degree of success and even such popular favourites as Napoleone Moriani and Luciano Fornasari struggled to gather fresh laurels.

On 10 March 1845 the critic of *The Times*, probably still Charles Lamb Kenney, dedicated a long and articulate piece to the first performance of *Ernani* in London. The critic described Verdi as the most innovative composer of the moment, the one creating a musical epoch, and informed his readers of rumours regarding a new Italian school of opera. The rumours, he maintained, were totally groundless. The reason became evident as soon as one listened to the first air sung by the tenor (the Cavatina "Come rugiada al cespite") which, he wrote, maintained a continuity with any other work heard over the previous years.[26] Then the critic referred to the balance between the voices and the orchestra in terms that sound encouraging, if not positive.

> In his instrumentation he shows himself superior to many of his contemporaries. It is tasteful and judicious, and does not overwhelm the voices, with a hurricane of noise. His concerted pieces are managed with skill, and the septet which occurs in the finale to the first act is one of

---

25 Benjamin Lumley, *Reminiscences of the Opera* (London: Hurst & Blackett, 1864), p. 104. Lumely's analysis was correct; some of Chorley's arguments against Verdi seem to echo the objections Richard Edgcumbe (1764–1839) raised against Rossini in the 1820s. For instance, Edgcumbe expressed his strong dislike of Rossini's noisy orchestration and claimed that he abused the voice: "It is really distressing to hear the leading voice strained almost to cracking in order to be audible over a full chorus and full orchestra, strengthened ofter by trumpets, trombones, kettle-drums and all the noisiest instruments." Richard Edgcumbe, *Musical Reminiscences of an Old Amateur, Chiefly Respecting the Italian Opera in England for Fifty Years, From 1773 to 1823* (London: W. Clarke, 1827), pp. 118–29.

26 *The Times*, March 10, 1845, p. 5.

the best pieces in the opera. His melodies are pleasing, but neither very original nor very striking, and the work is certainly more effective as an *ensemble* than on account of isolated portions.[27]

The review proceeds with a description of the plot, with which some members of the London public would have been already familiar, an English version having been prepared by James Kenney and produced at Covent Garden years before under the title of *The Pledge*. In conclusion, a short review of the performers was provided, giving an account of the quality of the singers involved in the principal roles.

The verdict concerning the quality of Verdi's music was not negative, and it was accompanied by a couple of observations which invited listeners to adopt a more benevolent disposition. The critic intended to draw attention to the significance of the cultural context in which this music originated, and consequently to the critical attitude and aesthetic categories that should be adopted when assessing its value.

> It is by the quality of their melody that the Italian composers must chiefly be judged. To require from them the scientific harmony of Germany, or the dramatic varied expression of France, would be to summon them before a tribunal which they themselves do not recognize; but judging of Verdi by his melody alone, we may fairly say, from the specimen we have heard, that he is not yet equal to the better works of Donizetti. There is in him, however, something of character—as, for instance, in the duet between Silvio and Ernani, when the fatal vow is made which places the life of the latter at the disposal of the former—that gives promise of better things.[28]

A similar notion concerning the kind of cultural relativism that should inform a correct critical approach towards both a composer and his music was presented on the occasion of a later performance of *Ernani*. In our critic's opinion, both composers and music lovers were divided according to geographically-oriented inclinations; among the members of this last group he recognised two distinct classes, "those who reflect upon it [music], and those who regard it as a mere amusement."[29] While the first class admired the works of the Germans, the second, and more numerous, was composed of lovers of the Italian school. But the critic cautioned his readers against a mistake that, presumably, occurred

---

27 Ibid.
28 Ibid.
29 *The Times*, March 17, 1845, p. 4.

often among music lovers and marred the judgment of both amateur and connoisseur.

> The mischief is that there are enthusiasts on both schools, that cannot discover any merit in the compositions of the opposite party, and hence every work is constantly in danger of being judged by a false standard. The fact is that every work ought to be judged from its own point of view, according to the school in which it is composed. If the German taste be applied in judging of the Italian, or the Italian in judging of the German, nothing but fallacy can be the result. In considering the merits of the new composer, Giuseppe Verdi, it is necessary to admit the condition of Italian music, and to wave the contest between rival schools.[30]

The critic was moderately appreciative of *Ernani* but also keen to point out a couple of shortcomings in Verdi's musical treatment of its dramatic subject. The first consisted in a lack of dramatic consistency in the "Scena e terzetto" that precedes the "Finale I," where the three characters sing in unison while expressing different feelings. The second concerned the gap between the dramatic situation and the quality of the music underpinning it in the concluding scene, the "Duetto—Finale Secondo" between Silva and Ernani. However, he ended his review with words of encouragement for the most promising representative of the school of Donizetti. "As a young composer he deserves to be encouraged, rather than to be judged with severity, and from what he has already done, we have a right to hope for something better."[31]

On 22 August the critic of *The Times* took leave of the past opera season with a short summary. This time his comments concerning the degree of novelty introduced by Lumley from Italy are less encouraging; the issue of melodiousness, or the lack thereof, is given as the reason why *Ernani* should not be considered a true, genuine long-lasting success.

> The success of *Ernani* in this country was "fair," but not extraordinary; the "new school," of which Italian journalists had prated so much, proved a mere fiction; and while the skill of the composer was quietly commended, the want of that melody which has contributed so much to the success of all Italian *maestri*, was enough to prevent it from becoming a great favourite. [...] Verdi's name was brought to this country as that of some one very great and original, yet, as we have said, his *Ernani* produced a very trifling effect, and people were glad enough to return

---

30 *Ibid.*
31 *Ibid.*

to the operas to which they had grown accustomed. There is no Italian composer of the present day who makes a stand in this country, with the single exception of Donizetti; and between the *Lucrezia Borgia* (1839) and the *Linda di Chamouni* [sic] (1843) no one operatic novelty that can fairly be called successful has been produced.[32]

When compared to the review that appeared on 17 March, this concluding observation suggests a slight, but still noticeable change in the critic's attitude; now he seems to be less inclined to recognise the composer's value and more prone to evoking Donizetti and the past generation.

As far as the periodicals taken into consideration are concerned, in 1845 Chorley was the only critic who uttered words of strong disapproval, while other commentators offered a range of milder, if not positive, opinions. Verdi's *Ernani* brought a high degree of novelty in both dramatic content and melodic treatment to the London stage, and a sense of amazement was to be expected from those less inclined to welcome novelty in any form. However, the public seem to have responded to Verdi's new opera with unbiased curiosity.

Fig. 4 Giuseppe Verdi in *The Illustrated London News*, 30 May 1846.

---

32   *The Times*, August 22, 1845, p. 5. Donizetti's *Lucrezia Borgia* premiered in Milan in 1833, while *Linda di Chamounix* premiered in Vienna in 1842.

3. *Nabucco* and *I Lombardi* (1846)

Benjamin Lumley opened the opera season at Her Majesty's Theatre on 3 March 1846 with *Nabucco*; *I Lombardi* followed a couple of months later and was performed on 12 May. As Frederick Crowest put it, "the object in presenting this *Nabucco* by Verdi was to afford the English public an opportunity of a further judgment upon the ear-arresting composer of *Ernani*."[1]

In London, *Nabucco* had to be renamed *Nino, Re d'Assyria*, in compliance with a norm that precluded even the slightest hint of a biblical subject in connection to the stage. The change in the title and the plot conformed to this norm, although it was applied with a certain degree of flexibility; in fact "it was possible for religious plays to be granted the Lord Chamberlain's license as long as the directness of the scriptural parallels was obscured sufficiently to satisfy the letter rather than the spirit of the prohibition on scriptural drama."[2] The ban was generally mitigated in so far as an operatic performance in Italian was involved. Since the vast majority of the public did not really understand the lyrics, which were, to some extent, considered complementary to the music, a few changes in the plot and its transposition to a safer historical setting would suffice. The same religious subject which would be banned as a drama was free to be presented in its "musical disguise."

On the occasion of *Nino*'s premiere, both the general public and the critics seemed to divide into two opposing camps: while the first was always keen on novelty, the second tended to reject it entirely in the

---

1 Crowest, *Verdi*, pp. 39–40.
2 John Russell Stephens, *The Censorship of English Drama 1824–1901* (Cambridge: Cambridge University Press, 1980), pp. 101–05.

name of so-called classicism. In a popular sense the opera, conducted by Michael Balfe and interpreted by Luciano Fornasari as Nino, Giulia Sanchioli as Abigail and Amalia Corbari as Fenena, was a success. On the other hand, not all the critics had a high opinion of the artistic value of Verdi's new operas; while Chorley from *The Athenaeum* and Davison from *The Musical World* wrote of Verdi's works in hostile terms, *The Times* and *The Illustrated London News* showed signs of sincere appreciation.

Chorley, whose opinion on Verdi had not improved at all, was among his strongest opponents: "But with every sympathy in favour of a new style, and a new master, our first hearing of the *Nino* has done nothing to change our first judgment of the limited nature of Signor Verdi's resources."[3] Chorley's antagonistic position was founded on two criticisms: lack of melody, to which declamation was preferred, and abundance of noisy effects.

> Signor Verdi's *forte* is declamatory music of the highest passion. In this, never hesitating to force the effect, or to drive the singers to the "most hazardous passes" — he is justified for some extravagance, by an occasional burst of brilliancy, surpassing that of most modern composers [...] But Signor Verdi "is nothing if not noisy;" and, by perpetually putting forth his energies in one and the same direction, tempts us, out of contradiction, to long for the sweetest piece of sickliness which Paisiello put forth long ere the notion of an orchestra had reached Italy, or the singer's art was thought to mean a superhuman force of lungs.[4]

Against these shortcomings lay the figure of Paisiello, whose grace and delicacy were now understood as the vestige of a remote epoch that had gone for ever. In this respect Chorley showed himself to be consisted over time. In fact, quite similar a judgment is to be found in *The Athenaeum* of 16 March, when he reviewed the first performance of *I Lombardi* at Her Majesty's Theatre, featuring Giulia Grisi as Giselda, Mario as Oronte, Luciano Fornasari as Pagano and Leone Corelli as Arvino.

> From the first moment when we examined a portfolio of Sig. Verdi's music [*Ath.* No. 879], we have never seen cause to change the judgment of his claims as a composer then expressed. Nor has the rage for his compositions, since excited in Italy, shaken us. Even the enthusiasts confess them to be meagre in melody — to contain no solitary indication

---

3   *The Athenaeum*, March 7, 1846, p. 250.
4   *Ibid.*

of a new form or manner of *air*, such as gives an individuality to Bellini and Donizetti,—while, to praise their science on the glaring orchestral touches, is to insult the capacities of those who know the meaning of language. There is more science in one of Haydn's minuets to his early quartets, than in all Sig. Verdi's noisy mixtures of ophicleides, *piccoli*, harps, etc. etc.—nay there is a flagrant disregard of science in his music. The vocal composer who writes noisy orchestral parts in *unison* with his singers—who utterly disdain the keeping which allots one order of support and decoration to a *solo*, and another to an assemblage of voices, is bound to show good cause for the reversal of every known principle of common sense, and the sacrifice of every effect. Sig. Verdi is *bizarre* with a vengeance: under the idea of contrast or climax, of dramatic force and passion;—but his science is "to seek"—with his melody;—and unless he take the field under some new form, we cannot believe that his popularity will long survive the discovery of the recipe by which his dash is concocted.[5]

After a detailed analysis of the interpreters' achievements, and despite all his negative remarks, Chorley could not deny that, on the whole, *I Lombardi* was a popular success. However, it was not so popular as to put the beloved classics at risk: "Every one will like to hear it once—but *Il barbiere* and *Otello* will hardly be driven from our stage by the *furore* that it excites."[6]

Of a similar opinion was Davison who, in reviewing *Nabucco* in *The Musical World*, attacked the emerging Italian composer in vehement, nasty terms.

> *Ernani* led us to suspect, and *Nabucco* has certified our suspicion, that of all the modern Italian composers Verdi is the most thoroughly insignificant. We listen, vainly, as the work proceeds, for the semblance of a melody. There is positively nothing, not even a feeling of rhythm—but rather indeed, a very unpleasant disregard for that important element of musical art. The choruses are nothing but the commonest tunes, arranged almost invariably in unison—perhaps because the composer knows not how to write in parts. The concerted music is patchy, rambling and unconnected. The cantabiles are always unrhythmical—and the absence of design is everywhere observable. The harmonies are either the tritest common-places, or something peculiarly odd and unpleasant. Nothing can possibly be more feeble than the orchestration. The employment of

---

5 *The Athenaeum*, May 16, 1846, p. 506.
6 *Ibid.*

the wind instruments is remarkably infelicitous, and all the experiments are failures. The overture is the poorest stuff imaginable, and yet the only glimpses of tune in the opera are comprised within its limits—and these are subsequently employed throughout the work *ad nauseam*. Serious criticism would be thrown away upon such a work. Either "young Verdi" must be a very clever man of business, or he must have come into the world with a silver spoon in his mouth. His popularity in Italy signifies nothing—but the reputation he elsewhere maintains is an enigma. We might overlook his ignorance of all the rules of art, were there in him any indication of natural feeling, or the shadow of inventive power—but alas! No—all is a dead flat—a dreary waste of barren emptiness![7]

There was nothing in Verdi that would call for serious music criticism. The critic also deplored those aspects in Verdi's work that *The Times* had judged more mildly, if not positively: the choirs and the concerted music. One week later, in its *Foreign Intelligence* column, *The Musical World* published a report from Paris, the author of which indulged in a nasty description of Verdi's success in the French capital. Verdi was defined as "a humble imitator of [Pietro Antonio] Coppola, who is a humble imitator of [Luigi] Ricci, who is a humble imitator of [Gaetano] Donizetti, who is a very humble imitator of [Vincenzo] Bellini, who nourished himself on the rinsings of [Gioacchino] Rossini's medicine bottles."[8] His ideas were said to be "scant and vulgar, his instrumentation noisy, unmeaning, and thin, and his general musicianship that of the merest tyro."[9] The reporter, having attended a performance of *Il proscritto* (alias *Ernani*) at the Théâtre-Italien, was in a position to claim that if *Nabucco* was bad, *Ernani* was "decidedly worse."[10] The critic took a stance against his colleagues from the "philosophical *Times*, the sensible *Herald*, the artist-like *Daily News*, and the fashionable *Post*," who were unreasonably exalting this unworthy composer.

When on 12 May *I Lombardi's* was performed at Her Majesty's Theatre, the critic of *The Musical World* decided to defer a critical opinion of its musical merit until the indisposition of Luciano Fornasari

---

7 *The Musical World*, March 7, 1846, p. 105.
8 "Foreign Intelligence," *The Musical World*, March 14, 1846, p. 122. The article is not signed, but the initials "D. B." appear at its end. Unfortunately, the author hiding behind initials has not been identified. See Richard Kitson, *The Musical World 1836–1865*, I: ix–xix.
9 *Ibid*.
10 *Ibid*.

passed; the absence of a single interpreter, the critic wants us to believe, was reason enough to prevent him from forming an opinion about the work at large. However, he felt compelled to give a short summary of the libretto.[11] When reviewing Bellini's *Norma*, given at Her Majesty's Theatre on 2 May, the critic drew a comparison between the young Verdi and his much worthier predecessors Rossini and Donizetti: "The music of Bellini, like that of Donizetti, though pale by the side of the dazzling Rossini, is perfectly refreshing after the stale insipidities and heavy common-places of 'young Verdi.'"[12] Davison shared with Chorley a sentiment of deep appreciation towards Rossini and did not disdain the music of Donizetti and Bellini. Verdi, however, went beyond his forbearance.

Of much milder opinion was the critic of *The Times*, where an ample review of *Nino* made its appearance on 4 March 1846. The critic, perhaps Charles Kenney, reported on the circumstances that had led to the revised libretto and described both the dramatic plot and its musical treatment in quite milder, positive terms. Such adjectives as "beautiful" and "remarkable" were employed repeatedly to define their quality. The review concluded with a final remark suggestive of the favourable reception among operagoers, due especially to the effect produced by the orchestra and the massive choirs.

> The concerted pieces, on which the opera depends more than on the solos, went off remarkably well, and the work was received with a stronger feeling of approbation than has been displayed on the production of any new Italian opera for a long time. The melodies are not remarkable, but the rich instrumentation, and the effective massing of the voices, do not fail to produce their impression, and a "run" for some time may be confidently predicted.[13]

On 13 May, *The Times* published another appreciative review of *I Lombardi*, its critic elucidating the reasons for the opera's international reputation: "While it has all that effective dramatic colouring, that contrasting management of choruses, and that skilful use of his orchestra on which his fame—such as it is—rests, it has much more

---

11   *The Musical World*, May 16, 1846, p. 229.
12   *The Musical World*, May 2, 1846, p. 191.
13   *The Times*, March 4, 1846, p. 5.

striking melody than most of his compositions."[14] After the customary perusal of the dramatic plot, the critic went through each moment of the opera and expressed himself in positive terms with regard to both the music and the performers. In the first act "Giselda (Giulia Grisi) sings (and very charmingly) a beautiful *Preghiera*, lightly accompanied by the orchestra." In the second act "The appearance of Oronte (Giovanni Matteo Mario), the tyrant's son, introduces the 'gem' of the opera, the beautiful song in which the young Turk expresses his love for Giselda, who has been carried off from her father, and is now in Antioch." Later on, the critic notes, "we have a chorus of female voices, with a very pretty accompaniment in the Eastern style, which gives a distinctive character to the piece." In the third act "comes a beautiful duet by Grisi and Mario, which may almost rival Mario's aria in the second," while the "dying scene gives occasion to a most delightful trio, in which the plaintive languid song of Mario and the passionate grief of Grisi combine with exquisite effect." Finally, in the fourth act "the waking Giselda expresses her feelings in a short but effective *scena*" and "a beautiful chorus of Crusaders shortly before the conclusion was an encore."[15] In sum, not a single word of reproach was uttered by the critic of *The Times* with regard to either the music of *I Lombardi* or its composer.

Even more positive were the comments that appeared in *The Illustrated London News*. The critic was far from convinced that the high degree of novelty achieved in both *Nino* and *I Lombardi* should be understood in negative terms; in fact, strong dramatic passion and a marked individuality in the vocal and dramatic treatment of the characters represented progress in the opera. Rather than raising the issue of vocal abuse, he made precise reference to the admirable effect that the voice produced when expressing strong dramatic feelings. Testament to this effect was Giulia Sanchioli's rendition of Abigail in *Nino*, especially in the second scene of the second act, where she pronounced the words "Tutti i popoli vedranno," and in the final duet where "The burst of sound poured forth by Mademoiselle Sanchioli's powerful voice, are admirably expressive of the contrast of feeling between the dethroned monarch."[16] Verdi's most remarkable characteristic, the critic

---

14 *The Times*, May 13, 1846, p. 4.
15 *Ibid.*
16 *The Illustrated London News*, March 14, 1846, p. 175.

maintained, was the manner in which individuality of character was preserved by the music itself. *The Illustrated London News* was by far the most appreciative of the journals: "In fine, in the music of the opera the composer has shown himself possessed of all the legitimate sources of success. It bears the stamp of genius and deep thought, and its effect upon the public proved that its merits were appreciated."[17]

On 16 May, an ample review of *I Lombardi* was published in the columns of the same periodical. Verdi's new opera was immediately pronounced a success "complete and brilliant; and deservedly so, for its beauties are of no common order."[18] Again, the critic acknowledged the degree of novelty involved in the work and invited his readers to think of it as defying the traditional notion of opera. *I Lombardi* should rather be understood as "a lyrical, dramatic, and pictorial poem, illustrating the character, habits, and manners of the first Crusaders, and bringing us on to the deeply interesting scene of their exploits."[19] Instead of entertaining the listener throughout with the hopes and fears, sighs and sobs of a pair of lovers, the opera presented a much more complex dramatic plot. All the *dramatis personae*, with their different personalities, feelings and passions interacted to the best advantage of the music, which changed in character and accommodated itself to the various situations. Later on in the same article, the critic insisted that the audience listen to this opera with different ears, since "a work of this stamp is to the common run of sentimental operas what a novel of Sir Walter Scott would be to a romance of that quondam favourite of school misses, Regina Maria Roche."[20] One single hearing of the opera was not sufficient to appreciate its merits, since the degree of novelty pursued by the composer was such that "the ear needs to become somewhat accustomed to a style so new."[21] Although he did not fail to detect "a somewhat too frequent employment of the brass instruments, and of declamatory phrases," especially in the first two acts, the critic was eager to show that, when the dramataic situation required, the composer was equally capable of assigning beautiful, graceful and

---

17 *The Illustrated London News*, March 14, 1846, also quoted in Crowest, *Verdi*, p. 44.
18 *The Illustrated London News*, May 16, 1846, p. 327.
19 Ibid.
20 Ibid.
21 Ibid.

pathetic melodies to the voices. Hence, such talented interpreters as Grisi and Mario, impersonating Giselda and Oronte, were called upon to express both those stronger emotions, which required adequate vocal power, and those more intimate, sweeter feelings on which the voice could gently rest.

More assertively positive was the judgment expressed by the same critic later on in July when, upon repeated hearings of Verdi's music, he pronounced a more solidly grounded opinion.

> We have again had an opportunity of hearing and judging Verdi's music—two of his operas having been given last week at this [Her Majesty's] Theatre; and with the greater effect that their massive music and splendid harmonies bring into relief the lighter compositions of the school which this composer and his follower bid fair to supplant. Of *Nino*, and *I Lombardi*, our opinion remains unaltered; though to the former composition we must give the palm of superiority, every time we hear it increasing our appreciation of the wonderful imagination and profound science, which characterise this operas as a true form of genius.[22]

The same attitude is visible in a later article, which was published at the conclusion of the opera season, on 15 August.

> To obtain a perfectly correct judgment of the value of a work, and of its materials for lasting fame, we must wait till the first blush of novelty has passed off. Gratified curiosity, surprise, prejudice, and many other extraneous causes, may influence the first reception of any work of art; when these have passed away, it must stand or fall by its own merits.[23]

It was clear that Verdi's opera did not belong to that class of art works which, having outstripped the masterpieces of the greatest composers on first performance, vanished quickly and were soon forgotten. Nor did Verdi's arias sound similar to those bravura pieces that a singer could insert into any opera, so as to show off his or her voice. Verdi was a dramatic composer and his music, as *I Lombardi* demonstrated, was as powerful and strong as a drama by Shakespeare.

> *I Lombardi* is, perhaps, the most essentially dramatic composition of Verdi—it is certainly not, in other respects his best. There are *morceaux* in *Nino* and *Ernani* far surpassing anything in this opera; but *I Lombardi*

---

22 *The Illustrated London News*, July 4, 1846, p. 14.
23 *The Illustrated London News*, August 15, 1846, p. 106.

has the superiority in dramatic power. In this respect, the genius of the composer here stands pre-eminently forward, for the plot on which he was to work is confused and altogether mediocre. He seized upon is redeeming points—its Eastern locality, rich with deeply interesting associations, and the numbers it brought on the stage. Murder, love, revenge, remorse, penitence, zeal—all the passions of the human breast—he has brought into prominence by music eminently calculated to express each in turn, and to contrast them with each other; he threw a rich colouring over the whole, and thus produced a most remarkable work, and one which no doubt enjoy a continued popularity.[24]

The controversial critical attitude that accompanied the reception of both *Nino* and *I Lombardi* was well registered by the manager of Her Majesty's Theatre, Benjamin Lumley, in his *Reminiscences*. In his account of *I Lombardi* he reported that the opera was a great and noisy success, although a doubtful one, in opposition to the relative unanimity of praise with which *Nabucco* had been received. The two opposite parties had confronted each other on the basis of argumentations that were similar in content but opposite in value.

> Whilst, by the Anti-Verdians, *I Lombardi* was declared to be flimsy, trashy, worthless; the Verdi party, and the adherents of the modern school, pronounced it to be full of power, vigour and originality. The one portion asserted that it was utterly devoid of melody—the other, that it was replete with melody of the most charming kind; the one again insisted that it was the worst work of the aspirant—the other, that it was the young composer's *chef-d'oeuvre*.[25]

In the midst of the conflict—Lumley added—the public seemed undecided and wavering, hesitating between novelty and tradition. However, on 13 May 1846 Lumley wrote to Verdi announcing the success of *I Lombardi* in London in unconditional terms, perhaps in the hope that the good news would encourage the composer to undertake the composition of a new opera for his theatre as soon as his health would allow him.

> Je viens vous annoncer que j'ai donné hier *I Lombardi* avec un succès de vrai enthousiasme. Tous les plus grands personnages de l'Angleterre étaient présents, sans excepter la Reine Douairière les Princes et les

---

24 *Ibid.*
25 Lumley, *Reminiscences*, pp. 148–49.

Princesses du sang. Les applaudissements ont été unanimes et je ne doute pas qu'à chaque représentation la vogue augmentera.[26]

Chorley and Davison conceptualised Verdi's first compositional and dramatic achievements in relation to the model provided by Rossini, Cimarosa and Paisiello, whom they now considered as imperishable classics. In Chorley's case, this attitude was consistent with that wider mind-set that led him to prefer Gluck, Mozart, Beethoven and even Weber to Meyerbeer, Berlioz and Schumann. Chorley thought Verdi to be poor in the expression of original and dramatic melody and, like Meyerbeer, to produce effects instead by the "clothing of his thoughts," which was to say by pointless ostentation. He expressed regret for the palmy days of the past and reproach for the unnatural way in which music composition was progressing. Chorley disliked modern bloody plots and showed strong aversion to those fashionable romantic dramas that provided librettists with the unworthy fabric for their scripts. Those music devices now dear to Verdi and his contemporaries, although consistent with the choice of the dramas and the quality of the librettos, involved dramatising the style at the expense of the much cherished *bel canto*. This made the critic long for earlier operas in which the beauty and freshness of genuine melody prevailed over all that was superfluous. Chorley's orientation with regard to Verdi was consistent with his dislike for Berlioz, at whom he had also wagged his finger. Berlioz had failed to continue and develop in the line of his most noble predecessors. In Chorley's eyes, neither Berlioz's nor Verdi's compositional achievements represented progress since, like Schumann, instead of assimilating the models of their greatest forerunners both in the symphonic and the dramatic genres, and instead of continuing to work in the direction they had indicated, all three seemed to have devoted themselves to devising musical ideas of which the most typical feature was awkwardness.

---

26 "I just informed you that yesterday I presented *I Lombardi* to resounding success. All the great figures of England were there, not excepting the Dowager Queen and the Princes and Princesses of royal blood. The applause was unanimous, and I don't doubt that with each performance its popularity will increase." Gaetano Cesari, Alessandro Luzio and Michele Scherillo (eds.), *I copialettere di Giuseppe Verdi* (Milan: Commissione, 1913), pp. 21–22, available at https://archive.org/details/icopialettere00verd

Davison did not fail to seize each and every opportunity to make harsh and gratuitously offensive comments at the expense of the Italian composer in *The Musical World*. He did this to an extent that would be considered intolerable today in a journal claiming credibility and serious commitment. To Davison, Verdi's operas were devoid of any value and did not deserve serious criticism.

At the other end of the scale lay *The Illustrated London News*, whose critic's arguments in favour of Verdi are coloured by a high degree of appreciation, and which seem to reflect more closely the opinion of the general public. *The Times* was also quite positive and the degree of novelty represented by Verdi does not seem to have upset its critic, possibly still Charles Kenney. Positive reviews appeared also in the columns of *The Herald*, *The Daily News* and *The Post*.

However, 1846 witnessed a dramatic change in the critical orientations of *The Times*, for in August of that year James Davison, who had become editor and half proprietor of *The Musical World* in 1844, was appointed chief music critic of the journal.[27] The same person would be called upon to review the same events for two influential journals. This circumstance occasioned texts of quite diverse quality; the gap between the laconic composure that would characterise those which appeared in the columns of *The Times* and the overwhelming acrimony that distinguished the ones published in *The Musical World* is sometimes amazing.

---

27 Henry Davison, *Music during the Victorian Era. From Mendelssohn to Wagner: Being the Memoirs of J. W. Davison, Forty Years Music Critic of "The Times"* (London: Reeves, 1912), p. 64.

4. *I due Foscari* and *I masnadieri* (1847)

In 1846, a series of difficulties between the manager of Her Majesty's Theatre and his star artists resulted in a split or secession, as they called it. The conductor Michael Costa and the three leading singers, Mario, Giulia Grisi and Antonio Tamburini, abandoned Lumley and set out to establish a competing operatic company at Covent Garden.

> The Opera house squabbles of the past season, arising out of Mr Lumley's breach with his musical director, Signor Costa, have grown at length into a great schism, which is beginning to throw the votaries of harmony into a state of the direst discord [...] The rumours which have been current of the establishment of a rival Italian Opera next season, have now assumed an authentic shape; though the formal announcement as to the details of the enterprise, which has for some time been expected, has not yet been issued. In the meantime, however, a sort of demi-official article has appeared in the *Morning Chronicle*, a paper which has distinguished itself by its strong spirit of partisanship in the affair. From this source we learn, that Covent Garden Theatre is to be opened as an Italian Opera house early in 1847; that Signor Costa is engaged as musical director and conductor; that a host of eminent vocalists have been secured; and that almost all the performers of the instrumental orchestra are to follow their late conductor.[1]

Costa, Mario, Grisi and Tamburini, followed by many members of the orchestra, established a rival company led by Giuseppe Persiani in the

---

1 "The Rival Italian Opera," *The Spectator*, September 19, 1846, p. 19. See also Lumley, *Reminiscences*, pp. 156–58.

capacity of manager; on 6 April 1847, they inaugurated a second Italian opera season at Covent Garden with Rossini's *Semiramide*.

In the meantime Lumley had not remained idle and was in fact doubling his efforts to appeal to the London audience, since he was now unable to count on the "old guard." Verdi's international success had convinced Lumley to commission a new opera from the young Italian composer and in the early spring of 1846 he was already advancing this idea. But on 9 April 1845, Verdi informed Lumley that owing to his poor health he would not travel to London, let alone compose a new opera. On 13 May, Lumley again tried to arouse Verdi's interest by informing him that *I Lombardi* had scored a success. This second attempt was also fruitless, for on 22 May Verdi made clear that his mind was unchanged. Things improved in November, when Verdi wrote to Lumley announcing his intention to compose a new opera for London, *Il corsaro*, based on George Byron's poem of the same name. Eventually Verdi decided to set to music a libretto Andrea Maffei had derived from Schiller's *Die Räuber*: *I masnadieri*. Verdi informed Lumley of his new resolution in a letter written on 4 December, where he also stated that, provided that Lumley agreed on having Jenny Lind and Gaetano Fraschini in the cast, he considered the deal sealed.[2] However, another difficulty had to be overcome before *I masnadieri* could be staged. Two years earlier Jenny Lind had signed a contract with Alfred Bunn, manager of the Drury Lane Theatre, which obliged her to make her appearance at his establishment in *Ein Feldlager in Schlesien* (*A Camp in Silesia*), a Singspiel in three acts by Giacomo Meyerbeer. The manager, who had already incurred heavy costs by having the libretto translated into English, threatened Lind with legal action should she not honour the contract.[3] Finally, notwithstanding Bunn's repeated threats, the Swedish Nightingale decided to sing in London as Amalia in Verdi's new opera.[4]

---

2 Charles Osborne (ed.), *Letter of Giuseppe Verdi* (New York: Holt, 1971), pp. 33–39. See also Verdi, *I copialettere*, pp. 30–36.

3 Henry Scott Holland, William Smith Rockstro, *Memoir of Madame Jenny Lind-Goldschmidt: Her Early Art-Life and Dramatic Career, 1820–1851* (London: J. Murray, 1891), I: 232–36, 290–99.

4 Budden, *Verdi*, I: 339–42.

Lumley was doing everything that was in his power to secure the benevolence of the audience, to reward them and to prove that he was able to fulfil his promises, at least to some extent. Among the operas he had pledged to put on were *The Tempest* by Mendelssohn and *Ein Feldlager von Schlesien* by Meyerbeer, which was premiered in Berlin in 1844.[5] Yet neither work, although both were announced at the outset of the season, could be performed. The first was never brought to completion by the composer,[6] while the second had to be cancelled because the composer could not come to London to supervise the rehearsals. At this point Lumley decided to focus on the last novelty announced for the season, *I masnadieri*, for which he had secured both the composer and the star singer.

As a consequence of the intricate events outlined above, Verdi's *I due Foscari* would be produced twice in London in 1847, once by each lyrical establishment. The first performance was on 10 April at Her Majesty's Theatre, the second on 19 June at Covent Garden. On 22 July 1847 Verdi himself was in London to conduct the premiere of *I masnadieri* at Her Majesty's Theatre, featuring Jenny Lind as Amalia.

As chronicled by *The Times*, *The Musical World* and *The Athenaeum*, the premiere of *I due Foscari* at Her Majesty's Theatre had been originally scheduled not for 10 April, but for the subsequent week; an epidemic caused by an unexpected change of weather forced the theatre management to anticipate the production of the new opera and postpone the performance of the already announced *L'elisir d'amore*. The circumstances leading to that hasty alteration were described in detail by *The Times*; Lablache, who was expected to appear as Dulcamara, was affected by a severe cold and unable to sing. But rather than mounting a stock opera, the theatre manager decided to take both the public and his rivals by surprise and present Verdi's new opera.[7] On 10 April, Her Majesty's Theatre opened with *I due Foscari* conducted by Michael Balfe. The cast featured Gaetano Fraschini as Jacopo, Antonietta Montenegro as Lucrezia, Filippo Coletti as the Doge and Lucien Bouché as Loredano.

---

5   Robert Ignatius Letellier, *The Operas of Giacomo Meyerbeer* (Fairleigh: Dickinson University Press, 2006), p. 164.
6   Peter Mercer-Taylor (ed.), *The Cambridge Companion to Mendelssohn* (Cambridge: Cambridge University Press, 2004), p. 217.
7   *The Times*, April 12, 1847, p. 8.

Fig. 5 Scene from *I due Foscari* at the Royal Italian Opera. *The Illustrated London News*, 26 June 1847.

Despite the sudden change, and notwithstanding the risk of compromising the quality of the performance owing to insufficient rehearsals, the critics of *The Musical World*, *The Times* and *The Athenaeum* — possibly Ryan, Davison and Chorley — acknowledged the production as a complete success, at least in popular terms.[8] Chorley complained about the performance, judging it "so little better than a dress rehearsal." Although he felt obliged to admit that the opera had scored a success with the audience, its shortcomings were countless: "*I due Foscari* shared the fate of everything produced at Her Majesty's Theatre, being rapturously received. Yet the performance was most unequal."[9] Chorley objected not only to the quality of the principals, but to that of the chorus and the orchestra also; the first was rough, incorrect and inaudible when called upon to sing behind the scene, while the second was completely detached from the singers. Antonietta Montenegro was judged "feeble,

---

8 Some of the articles that appeared in the columns of *The Musical World* that year bear the initials of Desmond Ryan, who had joined that journal in 1846. As mentioned before, in the meantime Davison had been appointed chief music critic of *The Times*.
9 *The Athenaeum*, April 17, 1847, p. 417.

husky, and uncertain; not disagreeable in *timbre*, but not sufficient for the theatre." Gaetano Fraschini had no expression, and Filippo Coletti was the only attraction; he produced "such forcible and impassioned effects by his voice and his manner, that it is only when measuring him against other contemporaneous that we recollect how little he acts."[10] Chorley insisted on the primacy and superiority of the old classics and expressed his strong dislike for young Verdi.

> In short we can find nothing in the opera to reconcile us to Signor Verdi as *the* Italian composer of the day. There is more fancy in the second act of *Marino Faliero* than in the entire work; and more in any single scene of Rossini's *Otello* than in Donizetti's Venetian tragedy complete. Comparisons are note agreeable; but it is only by comparison that fashionable works can sometimes be distinguished from true treasures of Art.[11]

The Times was of a completely different opinion. Its critic was strongly appreciative of both the music and its rendition. Fraschini never sang so well as in the character of Jacopo; Montenegro, despite some difficulty in the higher compass of her voice, was excellent as an actress and remarkable in the expression of the music; the grand hit of the night was Coletti. His success as the old Doge could without hesitation be called a triumph and the applause of the public was boundless. Despite some mannerisms and the continuous use of the unison in the choir, Verdi's music for *I due Foscari* was deemed an improvement, with such features as melodiousness and tunefulness now playing a greater part.

> We believe we shall express the opinion of the crowded audience of Saturday in saying that this is the most pleasing of Verdi's operas. It has less massiveness in its structure than *Nino,* and less prominence is given to the choruses, which, according to Verdi's manner—we may say, mannerism—are marked by the almost ceaseless employment of the unison [...] Of a flow of melody—of soft airs, followed by agreeable *cabalettas*—in a word, of what are called 'tunes,' there is no lack, and these are generally introduced with a great regard to dramatic effect. For originality they certainly are not remarkable, but they are pleasing throughout, and the manner in which the chorus is frequently brought in, taking up the melody of the principals, is worthy of a composer whose

---

10 *Ibid.*
11 *Ibid.*

> chief object, it is said, is dramatic illustration. On the continent, we believe, *I due Foscari* is esteemed the weakest of all Verdi's operas. This may be the case, and it may have fewer features that would prominently stand out than either *Nino* or *Ernani*, but we must question whether it will not be more popular than the former of those works, and have no doubt whatever that it will be more popular than the latter.[12]

Much more lenient to Verdi and more open to his novelties was the critic of *The Illustrated London News*, whose review of the opera appeared on 17 April.

> The treatment of *I due Foscari* is, in many respects, different from that of the other of his operas (especially *Nino* and *Ernani*) which have been brought out here. The bringing into prominence of the solos and duets, and the consequent diminution of importance of the choruses and concerted pieces, are more in accordance with the general practice of Italian composers, and likely to be more generally popular. For ourselves, though we greatly admire the fine *morceaux* interspersed throughout this opera, we cannot concede that they should take precedence of those masterpieces of composition, the finales and choruses of *Nino* and *Ernani*, in which the genius of the composer has taken its loftiest flight. He has, however, shown in *I due Foscari*, that he possesses genius for the lighter and more popular style of composition, as well as for that generally thought to be his forte; and that he can write *tunes* to compete with any of the Donizettian school. As a dramatic work, *I due Foscari* appears to us far more complete and more impressive than any of the other operas of Verdi's given here.[13]

When compared to Verdi's earlier operas, *I due Foscari* represented a backward step towards a manner of composition that conformed to the Italian *bel canto* tradition, in which nice arias and duets outstripped the concerted pieces in number and relevance. The critic acknowledged Verdi as a composer capable of dealing with either style, and of composing a nice tune as well as a dramatic concertato.

Halfway between the two groups, the hostile and the benevolent, stood the critic of *The Musical World*, whose verdict was extremely favourable towards the interpreters but not towards the composer. Coletti enchanted the audience and was rapturously applauded. Encores and re-calls were countless and the same honours were lavishly

---

12   *The Times*, April 12, 1847, p. 8.
13   *The Illustrated London News*, April 17, 1847, p. 244.

bestowed on the other principals, Fraschini, Bouché and Montenegro. But, the critic held, the performance had been successful despite the music.

> The success of *I due Foscari* must be attributed *entirely* to the principal singers, and to the complete efficiency of Balfe, his band, and his chorus, which came out with unwonted power. The music of Signor Verdi is trash of the flimsiest description—beneath criticism—it offers no one point of musicianship, no one gleam of fancy. To talk of *genius* in reference to such worthless rubbish would be downright impiety. It is utterly destitute of claims to any kind of notice.[14]

Davison continued to express himself in hostile terms despite the success Verdi was enjoying among the common people. This, Davison insisted, was due to the efforts of the talented interpreters, not the merits of the composer.

In his *Reminiscences*, Lumley acknowledges that *I due Foscari* was a partial success at Her Majesty's Theatre, but admits that the production was chosen as a stratagem to keep the audience busy with some novelty while the real attraction of the season, the much awaited Jenny Lind, was not yet in sight.

> In her [Jenny Lind's] continued absence every available resource was put forward. The theatre reopened, as has been stated, on Saturday, the 10th of April. A new opera and a new soprano singer were both forthcoming on the occasion. The opera, given for the first time in this country, the *due Foscari*, of Verdi, and the singer, Madame Montenegro, a Spanish lady of good family, with a clear soprano voice of some compass, and an attractive person, pleased, without exciting any marked sensation.[15]

Despite the tepid terms adopted by the manager, the critics were not in total disagreement, at least as far as the reception of *I due Foscari* among the general public was concerned. *The Athenaeum* judged both the music and the performance in quite negative terms; *The Musical World* maintained that the opera was a success thanks to the quality of the performance and notwithstanding its contemptible music; the critic of *The Times* expressed himself in positive terms about the performance, and judged the music not totally devoid of merits; *The Illustrated London*

---

14   *The Musical World*, April 17, 1847, p. 254.
15   Lumley, *Reminiscences*, p. 180.

News said the opera "more in accordance with the general practice of Italian composers" and not lacking in the dramatic power typically associated with the young composer. These last two journals agreed that in *I due Foscari* Verdi had toned down his dramatic verve and that traditional arias and duets had been restored to their original primacy. All of them found that Giuseppe Verdi's success among operagoers was unquestionable, and his last opera had not failed to appeal to their taste.

Two months later, on 19 June, *I due Foscari* was produced at Covent Garden, featuring three representatives of the old guard: Giorgio Ronconi was the old Doge, Mario was his son Jacopo Foscari and Giulia Grisi was Lucrezia. This time the critic of *The Times* commented on the opera in a manner that strongly suggests a single person now occupied the same position at both *The Times* and *The Musical World*.

> Royal Italian Opera, Covent-Garden. On Saturday Verdi's *I due Foscari* was represented, for the first time at this establishment, with Grisi as Lucrezia, Mario as Jacopo, and Ronconi as the Doge. Our opinion of the music of this opera has already been given, and the present cast, powerful as it is, has not induced us to alter it. The success of *I due Foscari* on Saturday night must, ther, be entirely laid to the merits of the three great artists whose names we have mentioned above, whose genius supplied the grace and feeling that was wanting in the music, and out of a veritable chaos made a world of harmony and truth.[16]

In hinting at the opinion he had previously expressed, Davison seems to confound the content of his contribution to *The Times* with what he had instead published in the columns of *The Musical World*. It was in the second journal that he had pronounced the exact judgment he was now referring to, while in *The Times*, as we have seen, his verdict had been much milder, if not positive. In reviewing this new production of the same opera, he decided not to elaborate further on the poor quality of the music, a few appreciative remarks regarding the principals being more than enough to account for the event.

The article Desmond Ryan contributed to *The Musical World* was much lengthier.[17] It declared Verdi's *I due Foscari*, produced at Covent Garden, to be the most complete success, "a success which, as far as outward demonstrations went, nothing could go beyond, and which

---

16 *The Times*, June 21, 1847, p. 5.
17 His identity is revealed by his initials, D. R. appearing at the end of the review.

must have gratified in no small degree the management as well as the composer, who, we understood, was present in the front of the house."[18] Verdi attended the opera in person; he had joined Emanuele Muzio at the beginning of the month in order to supervise the preparation of his *I masnadieri* and to instruct Jenny Lind in the part. The public showed great excitement at Verdi's presence and bestowed signs of sincere appreciation on the interpreters; not only did Ronconi prove himself great, "but his whole assumption was complete and masterly, and evidenced the subtlest skill combined with real genius."[19] Grisi's Lucrezia was a masterpiece of acting and singing and created as great a *furore* as her Norma, while Mario exhibited to perfection the intense beauty of his voice and method. As the critic put it, the success of the artists, though not of the opera, was immense: every act a re-call, every aria an *encore*. But Desmond Ryan did not show any sign of appreciation towards Verdi or his composition; a first nasty remark detailed the reasons why the composer wrote operas featuring no more than three main personages.

> To a composer of limited genius like Verdi, this custom is of the greatest utility, as it taxes his ingenuity in a small degree, and extenuates him from providing any diversity of effects in his music. Verdi's operas have, evidently, all one grand aim, viz: the development of the higher passions. The means by which this object has been attempted is a source of grievous disputation between the supporters and the opponents of the composer.[20]

It must have been a relief, for so untalented a composer, to have just three characters to work on and one single expressive aim to pursue. In Ryan's opinion, the portrayal of the strongest human conflicts made Verdi "the very antipodes of Mozart and Rossini." Even to have his name mentioned, though in opposition to Mozart and Rossini, the representatives of *classicism* in the opera, was a great compliment to a composer lacking in melodic inventiveness as well as other essential compositional abilities.

---

18 "Royal Italian Opera," *The Musical World*, June 26, 1847, p. 411.
19 *Ibid.*
20 *Ibid.*

> The composer of *I due Foscari* is certainly the most over-rated man in existence. How, without melody, musical knowledge, variety, or even tune, he could have gained his present fame is, to our thinking, a far greater miracle than any of Prince Hoenlowe's—especially as we never believed in *them*; and the means by which his operas continue to receive the approbation of the critics, and the applause of listeners, we can only attribute to some disease in the mind of the age, an epidemic, a monamania [sic], or a visitation akin to that of the potatoes caries, that eats up the vitality and growth of thought. One cause of Verdi's celebrity—and, perhaps, its main cause—is the novelty of his music. It is, indeed, like nothing we ever heard—or, it is, indeed, like nothing [...] This is the principal secret of Verdi's popularity; his music has nothing in common with other music it possesses not the ingredients of other music; it is not grounded on the same principles as other music—in brief, critically speaking, it is not music at all; or it is merely declamatory phraseology.[21]

The final verdict was unequivocal: "The *Due Foscari* is certainly one of the dullest and most unmeaning works we ever heard; there is hardly one tuneable phrase from beginning to end, and the interest is confined exclusively to the artists employed in developing the plot and exhibiting their vocal efforts."[22] Its performance, nevertheless, was a complete and undeniable success, thanks to the value of the artists involved; the insipidity of the music was nullified by the splendour and magnificence of the performance.

As for Chorley, the review published in *The Athenaeum* on 26 June shares his colleagues' opinion with regard to the high merits of the performers as opposed to the inferiority of the music; his judgment on Verdi's compositional skills remained unchanged.

> The puerility of Signor Verdi's instrumentation [...] —the platitude of his melodies—the almost ungrammatical crudity of his modulations, and the total disregard of tone in colouring are too poorly compensated for by the accomplishment of certain effects, to permit us to unsay one word of our former strictures. On the contrary, we were never so aware of the musical worthlessness of Signor Verdi's opera as on the occasion of its performance in the presence of its composer; who, it is more than probable, had never before the opportunity of hearing one of his works given with so signal a perfection.[23]

---

21   *Ibid.*
22   *Ibid.*
23   *The Athenaeum*, June 26, 1847, p. 582.

Chorley took great pains to separate matters that could otherwise be easily confused; he drew a clear line between the music, which was trash as a whole, and the way in which the audience went into raptures over its performance. Although he had to admit that the public had received the opera enthusiastically, still he felt it necessary to urge his readers not to mistake the composition for its rendition. Despite all the shortcomings in the music and notwithstanding the composer's unsuccessful attempts to accomplish certain dramatic effects, the beautiful singing and the impressive acting of the three main interpreters made the opera popular.

The critic of *The Illustrated London News* addressed the importance of the interpreters, especially Mario and Grisi, indulging in a series of unconditionally positive judgments. Such expressions as "transcendent talent," "enormous power of voice," "inexhaustible resources," "divine singing" and "superb acting" were used with some generosity. Verdi could not but benefit from such a powerful cast and, should he consider adopting a milder compositional style, a style more respectful of the singers' voices, he would achieve much better results.

> Verdi's work, therefore, with first rate executants, vocally and instrumentally, and with such a Conductor as Costa, who can develop the *nuances* with such delicacy and precision, will strike the ear of the amateur, more than they will satisfy the judgment of the professor. Verdi has been prodigiously puffed and immensely depreciated; but he is, unquestionably, a man of infinite talent, who may achieve much greater things if he will modify his style—not tax his singers so unmercifully in the declamatory school, and resort to more legitimate means for his effects.[24]

In general, each critic confirmed his previous opinion with regard to the opera while all expressing words of praise and commendation to describe the quality and talent of the members of the "old guard."

The month which elapsed between the production of *I due Foscari* at Covent Garden and the premiere of *I masnadieri* at Her Majesty's Theatre was not uneventful. Lumley was doing his best to raise public expectations and benefit from the presence of his special guest stars. On the one hand, he decided to put Verdi in the limelight by reviving *Ernani* and *I Lombardi*, while on the other he gave Lind the opportunity to shine in all her splendour by appearing in her favourite roles before the debut

---

24 *The Illustrated London News*, June 26, 1847, p. 413.

in *I masnadieri*: *Robert le diable*, *La fille du régiment*, *La sonnambula* and *Norma*.

Ernani was performed again at Her Majesty's Theatre at the end of June — it had been already revived on 3 April. Jeanne Anaïs Castellan, Gaetano Fraschini, Antonio Superchi and Lucien Bouché took the main roles. As *The Musical World* put it, "the opera went off exceedingly well [...] Encores and recalls were as plentiful as blackberries, and bouquets were in extraordinary request."[25] In the same journal Desmond Ryan reviewed a later performance of *I due Foscari* at Covent Garden, an opera which, he suggested, failed to reconcile him to its composer. Instead Ryan decided to record the success of Grisi, Ronconi and Mario: "From scene the first to scene the last the entire performance was a succession of triumphs for the three artists."[26] On 10 July *The Athenaeum* reviewed a revival of *I Lombardi* at Her Majesty's Theatre; the work was so flimsy and so full of pretence that the critic refused to alter his low opinion.[27] The music was bad and its performance even worse; the orchestra was at variance with the choir, and the principal singers struggled to cope with the parts allotted to them.

In the meantime, Jenny Lind was already creating a furore, a fever destined to continue for about three years.[28] Soon after her arrival in London she had made her first public appearance on 17 April when she attended a performance of *I due Foscari* at Her Majesty's Theatre. Her presence had not failed to mesmerise the attention of the entire audience; countless lorgnettes were turned to her small, elegant figure, instead of focusing on the stage.[29] On 4 May, her debut as Alice in Giacomo Meyerbeer's *Robert le diable* at Her Majesty's Theatre (given in Italian as *Roberto il diavolo*) was rapturously applauded and at the end of the performance the opera-house was in a state such as had rarely been witnessed in any London theatre. "The crowded mass, waving hats and handkerchiefs, stamping, knocking, shouting and endeavouring in every possible manner to show their delight, called the vocalist three

---

25 *The Musical World*, July 3, 1847, p. 430.
26 Ibid., p. 432.
27 *The Athenaeum*, July 10, 1847, p. 737.
28 Hermann Klein, *The Golden Age of Opera* (London: Routledge, 1933, reprinted by Boston: Da Capo Press, 1979), xxi.
29 Nathaniel Parker Willis, *Memoranda of the Life of Jenny Lind* (Philadelphia: Peterson, 1851), pp. 34–54.

times before the curtains, with an enthusiasm we have never seen surpassed, and yet which was no more than deserved."[30] Countless encores were demanded at the end of each aria, enriched with all the possible coloraturas she was so famous for, and the stage was literally covered with bouquets. As reported by Lumley, Jenny Lind's debut was a complete, unquestionable triumph from the first moment she opened her mouth to the very end.

> The cadenza at the end of her opening air—the whole of which was listened to with a stillness quite singular—called down a hurricane of applause. From that moment her success was certain. The evening went on, and before it ended Jenny Lind was established as the favourite of the English opera public. Voice, style, execution, manner, acting—all delighted. The triumph was achieved.[31]

After her first appearance as Alice, Jenny Lind was to surpass all previous expectations while singing in *La sonnambula*, as Amina; then in Donizetti's *La fille du régiment* (in Italian as *La figlia del reggimento*), as Maria; and in *Norma*, given by royal command on 15 June. Her exceptionally rapturous reception among the London public was such that 1847 came to be referred to as the year of "the Lind fever."[32] This circumstance impinged not only on the reception of the operas in which she performed, but also of those in which she did not appear. It became usual among some of the critics to distinguish between the Lind nights and the off-Lind nights. For the first a tumult of people literally storming the doors of the theatre was easily predictable, while for the second a sadder, drearier atmosphere was rather to be expected in the opera-house: "The Lind-mania is a new *phobia*, and the rage is fiercer in consequence, like all fevers and plagues that appear for the first time."[33]

At the beginning of July, while Jenny Lind was performing in *La sonnambula* in front of the Royal Couple, Queen Victoria and Prince

---

30   *Ibid.*, p. 42.
31   Lumley, *Reminiscences*, p. 185.
32   Cox, *Musical recollections*, 2: 195.
33   *The Musical World*, July 3, 1847, p. 430. A similar comment on the madness accompanying Jenny Lind's debut can be found in John Desmond Cox's *Musical Recollections*. Unlikely other contemporary commentators, Cox confessed to have been greatly disappointed by the Swedish *prima donna*, who "invariably sang somewhat sharp." John Edmund Cox, *Musical Recollections of the Last Half-Century* (London: Tinsley Brothers, 1872), 1: 194.

Albert—the customary ovations being showered on her by the usual crowd—and *I masnadieri* was in preparation at Her Majesty's Theatre, *Ernani* was produced at the Royal Italian Opera at Covent Garden, featuring Steffanoni in the part of Elvira and Lorenzo Salvi as Ernani. The critic of *The Musical World*, again, singled out a series of shortcomings and drew the readers' attention to the discrepancy between the poor quality of the music and the *furore* created by the interpreters.

> The music of *Ernani* pleases us less than any opera we have heard from the pen of Verdi. None of the situations betray a glimpse of dramatic power. The *finale* to the first act requires but a little less musical depth, and a more thorough non-comprehension of orchestral effects, to render it quite contemptible The unisons, are as lavishly made use of as usual in the composer's score and Verdi's poverty is as conspicuous in the music of *Ernani*, as in any opera of his we have heard. The same mawkishness, the same ultra-sentimentality, the same inanity of melody, or tune prevails throughout We might, perhaps, allow some melodic merit to Elvira's *scena*, "Ernani involami," which has a Paciniish flavour in it, but further concession we could not conscientiously make. The performance of the opera from beginning to end was magnificent, and created an absolute *furore*.[34]

On 20 July, *Robert le diable* was given again in Italian at Her Majesty's Theatre in front of an overflowing audience which, according to *The Musical World*, "paid the Swedish Nightingale all the honours to which she has been accustomed since her visit to England."[35] Finally, two days later *I masnadieri*, the long promised and eagerly expected new opera by Verdi, was premiered at Her Majesty's Theatre, featuring Luigi Lablache as Massimiliano, Italo Gardoni as Carlo, Filippo Coletti as Francesco, Jenny Lind as Amalia, Leone Corelli as Arminio and Lucien Bouché as Moser. Queen Victoria and Prince Albert occupied the royal box and the opera-house was crammed to the ceiling. The work was pronounced a success at least in popular terms: "The opera was highly successful. The talented *maestro*, on appearing in the orchestra to conduct his clever work, was received with three rounds of applause. He was called before the curtain after the first and the third act, and at the conclusion of the opera amidst the most vehement applause."[36]

---

34 *The Musical World*, July 10, 1847, p. 443.
35 *The Musical World*, July 24, 1847, p. 480.
36 *Illustrated London News*, July 24 1847, p. 58.

4. I due Foscari and I masnadieri (1847)

Fig. 6 Jenny Lind (as Amalia) and Luigi Lablache (as Massimiliano) in scene VI from *I masnadieri* at Her Majesty's Theatre. *The Illustrated London News*, 31 July 1847.

The critic of *The Times* expressed himself in the usual terms, staking out a position that might be defined once again as "politically correct." After a lengthy description of the plot and the musical parts of its four acts, a few short remarks were made as to the merits of the main vocalist, Jenny Lind, and the extent to which the opera was a success thanks to her. "The airs sung by Jenny Lind were the most successful in the work, and it is not too much to say that a great portion of their success was due to the fine vocalist."[37] This is despite the fact that Verdi, the critic held, had given no opportunities for individual display and had written more for the ensemble. However, strong signs of appreciation were bestowed by the audience on both the composer and the singer, who received many bouquets. Apart from a couple of observations concerning the extensive use of the choir and the way in which Verdi had illustrated the position of the robbers by a "rough style of music, generally in unison,"[38] little or no attention was paid to his compositional achievements.

---

37 *The Times*, July 23, 1847, p. 5.
38 *Ibid.*

On 24 July, the critic of *The Musical World* declined to express a judgment on the new opera and, while deferring his analysis, gave a detailed account of the ballet in its stead — *Perrot's Pas de Diesses* featuring Fanny Cerrito, Marie Taglioni, Carolina Rosati and Carlotta Grisi. On 31 July, the same journal published a review of *I masnadieri* in which the critic joined the choir of those who, having praised the manager of Her Majesty's Theatre for having secured so great a novelty for his establishment, pronounced the opera a failure in spite of the fact that the composer himself had superintended its preparation. The article at issue represents a interesting case in the history of *The Musical World*, for Davison, the editor of the journal, had failed to complete it. Desmond Ryan had to inform his readers that the fragment published had been left unfinished by the editor who in the meantime had quit town without leaving direction for its completion. The fragment included a few critical remarks about the poor quality of the instrumental overture which, destitute as it was of musical form, was redeemed by the cellist Carlo Alfredo Piatti and his exquisite performance. A short narration of the plot followed, after which the article terminated abruptly. The analysis of the opera was to be deferred until the editor returned but even then, a proper criticism of *I masnadieri* was never published in the columns of *The Musical World*.[39]

The critic of *The Spectator*, who reviewed *I masnadieri* on 24 July, assumed an overtly antagonistic position. Once one had in mind Verdi's previous achievements, the quality of his new work (or lack thereof) could be easily anticipated, however successful it may have been among the public.

> It is Verdi all over; only, we are sorry to say, the tide of his genius has ebbed rather than flowed, and has not reached its high-water mark. His melodies are, to use the French phrase, even paler than usual — weaker in expression and dramatic colouring; while they are liable to the old reproach of triteness, sounding as things long since familiar. Like most of the airs of the modern Italian opera, they are cold, dry outlines; which depend, for richness, beauty, and warmth, entirely on the talents of the singer. The choruses, as in Verdi's previous operas, are in unison. An occasional chorus so constructed may have a peculiar and a happy

---

39   Kitson, *The Musical World, 1836–1865*, I: xiv.

effect; but when we find every chorus so constructed, we must more than suspect a conscious incapacity to deal with great masses of choral harmony.[40]

Furthermore, the performers suffered from the infelicitous parts that the composer forced on their voices. Jenni Lind's unrivalled ability to sing the language of feeling and passion was cramped by the music; Gardoni did his best, although his part was hopelessly cold. Lablache's beautifully pathetic performance was wholly independent of the music; Coletti had to struggle with music which was "either entirely unmeaning or absolutely false in its expression."[41]

On 24 July, Chorley reviewed *I masnadieri* and provided his readers with the usual repertoire of complaints and grumbles. Lumley was to be praised for introducing to English audiences the most recent work of the most popular and fashionable Italian composer and, in doing so, exposing himself to the judgment of the English cognoscenti. Still, *I masnadieri* was Verdi's worst opera: the libretto was gloomy and the music allotted to it could do nothing to improve it; the overture was reduced to a long passage for violoncello solo, while the vocal music exhibited the usual threadbare, hackneyed series of expressive solutions consisting of dotted figures, trills and syncopations. Against all that musical platitude and tameness, only Jenny Lind's cadenzas were pronounced beautiful; that is to say, only those parts of the opera that had not been composed by Verdi were worth listening to. Even the choirs, generally considered Verdi's forte, were strongly criticised for their frivolity and vulgarity. Moreover, the orchestra was almost always offensively noisy at the expense of the voices. Chorley concluded his review of *I masnadieri* by insisting that "the performance must be recorded as a failure of a work which richly deserved to fail—in spite of much noisy applause;" complete oblivion was what the opera deserved. A similar remark made its appearance in *The Athenaeum* on 28 August, when Chorley cast an eye on the past opera season at Her Majesty's Theatre and drew a few conclusive remarks on its artistic merits. Chorley insisted on the failure of Verdi's operas not only among

---

40 *The Spectator*, July 24, 1847, p. 12.
41 *Ibid*.

the critics, but also among the general public. As we have seen, this was a dubious claim.

> One striking peculiarity in the season just over, common to both Operas, has been the absence of much novelty and the failure of the little attempted. Every effort has been made to force upon the public the music of Verdi, as the one composer sought for in Italy; where Pacini and Ricci, and even the more scientific Mercadante, now write without success. But the English will not have Verdi. Our tune-loving play-goers demand fresher and more flattering melodies than he has to bestow. Our severer *dilettanti* refuse to accept his noise for orchestral science—his unisons for choral writings—his outrageous modulations for discoveries.[42]

According to Chorley, the general public, always in search for what was tuneful and pleasantly melodious, had refused to accept the musical modernity forced upon them by the managers of both His Majesty's Theatre and Covent Garden. No matter that this assertion stood in contradiction with what Chorley himself had repeatedly reported, together with his colleagues of *The Times* and *The Musical World*. Words such as success and ovation had been pronounced several times in the previous months when describing the reception of Verdi's works among operagoers. A further note on the poor merits of Verdi, especially when compared with the old classics, made its appearance in *The Athenaeum* on 14 August, when Chorley reviewed a performance of Rossini's *La donna del lago* at Covent Garden. Although the critic described it as a little more than a concert in costume, the second act being merely a pasticcio, still the interest of the work lay in "its being a series of lovely musical pieces—some fresh as Northern spring—some gorgeous as Italian autumn; almost entirely irrespective of any dramatic effect."[43] Contrary to Rossini, Verdi's tunelessness and outrageous instrumentation, even although defended on the score of dramatic effect, were deemed intolerably ugly; in Chorley's conservative opinion, beauty and melodiousness had to prevail over all those dramatic effects to which they were now continuously sacrificed. Even Rossini's

---

42 *The Athenaeum*, August 28, 1847, p. 916.
43 *The Athenaeum*, August 14, 1847, p. 868.

dramatic inconsistencies were to be preferred to Verdi's sense of the drama, if the latter meant a complete lack of musical beauty.

Benjamin Lumley recorded the premiere of *I masnadieri* as a failure, notwithstanding all his efforts.

> The opera was given with every appearance of a triumphant success: the composer and all the singers receiving the highest honours [...] But yet the *Masnadieri* could not be considered a success [...] The interest which ought to have been centred in Mademoiselle Lind was centred in Gardoni; whilst Lablache, as the imprisoned father, had to do about the only thing he could not do to perfection—having to represent a man nearly starved to death.[44]

Interestingly, according to Lumley the reason for the failure lay in the lack of vocal interest allotted to the singer who was supposed to shine most in the delivery of brilliant roulades, virtuoso passages and coloratura ornaments. Despite the enthusiastic expressions used by Emanuele Muzio in a letter written to Antonio Barezzi the day after the premiere, Verdi himself, when writing to Emilia Morosini on 30 July 1847, had to concede that "*I masnadieri*, senza aver fatto furore, hanno piaciuto."[45] The new opera, commissioned explicitly for Her Majesty's Theatre, did not contribute to strengthen the composer's position in front of the critics; Chorley's verdict in this regard admits no doubt:

> *I Masnadieri* turned out a miserable failure, as it deserved to do, since it could but, at all events, as was rightly said, increased Signor Verdi's discredit with every one who had an ear, and was decidedly the worst opera that was ever given at Her Majesty's Theatre, the music being in every respect inferior even to that of *I due Foscari*.[46]

In sum, although it is not entirely true that the opera turned out to be a miserable failure (it was neither booed nor hissed), it is clear that it did not add to the fame of the composer. Nor did it add to the financial prosperity of Her Majesty's Theatre. It ran a few nights and was soon shelved.

---

44 Lumley, *Reminiscences*, pp. 192–93.
45 Cesari and Luzio, *I Copialettere*, p. 461.
46 *The Athenaeum*, July 24, 1847, also cited in Cox, *Musical Recollections*, 2: 195.

By 1847, the severest critics still held that Verdi's compositional skills were rudimentary and his melodies not even worth remembering. That said, his highly dramatic effects and concerted pieces were not entirely contemptible. The popular success he scored was undeniable but this resulted less from the quality of the music than from the talent of the interpreters. Only the critic of *The Illustrated London News* appeared to be entirely appreciative of Verdi, whose dramatic power he was ready to acknowledge.

Fig. 7 Jenny Lind (as Amalia), Italo Gardoni (as Carlo, to the left) and Luigi Lablache (as Massimilano, to the right) in the last scene of *I masnadieri* at Her Majesty's Theatre. *The Illustrated London News*, 31 July 1847.

5. *Attila* (1848)

In the early months of 1848, both London operatic establishments announced seasons full of attractions and presented lists of prominent artists—further evidence of the entrepreneurial attitude underpinning their managers' choices. Benjamin Lumley continued to lead Her Majesty's Theatre, while Edward Delafield and Frederick Gye took over the management of Covent Garden. On either side stars of international reputation were put forward—some already belonging to the London firmament, some completely new—in repeated attempts to whet the public's appetite.

In January, the Royal Italian Opera at Covent Garden announced that the sopranos Angiolina Zoja, from La Scala, and Pauline Garcia Viardot had been secured, in addition to the already well known Giulia Grisi, Giorgio Ronconi, Fanny Persiani, Anaide Castellan etc.[1] In February, the management of Her Majesty's Theatre confirmed the presence of Jenny Lind and announced that the admired soprano Sophie Cruvelli had also been recruited.[2] As Lumley put it, the presence of Jenny Lind "was a tower of strength to the management, since her triumph of the previous year seemed to afford a warrant to her success in the future."[3] But the need for novel attractions to raise expectations and sales was also compelling. Lumley had the chance to hear the young and admired soprano Sophie Cruvelli in Rovigo (Italy), during his usual late autumn scouting tour on the continent in 1847; Cruvelli, then featuring as Odabella in Verdi's *Attila*, was comparatively unknown in London, but her reputation was already

---

1 *The Athenaeum*, January 29, 1848, p. 119.
2 *The Athenaeum*, February 12, 1848, p. 169.
3 Lumley, *Reminiscences*, p. 206.

growing in Italy. As Lumley reports, "overtures were immediately made to her for an engagement for the ensuing season in London."[4] Together with Cruvelli, Lumley had secured a number of prominent artists such as Luisa Abbadia, described as "a Soprano of great reputation from La Scala and other great Theatres of Italy [...] Madlle. Schwartz the eminent Contralto, and established favourite of the Imperial Opera at Vienna [...] Madame Erminia Tadolini of La Scala, Milan; the Carinthia, Vienna; and other great Theatres [...] Signor Cuzzani from La Scala and other great Theatres of Italy [...] Signor Labocetta of the principal theatres of Italy and of the Italian Opera at Berlin [...] Signor Belletti, the admired Baritone, from the Opera la Pergola, at Florence."[5] The promise of a true parade of vocal champions was made to the public. As far as Jenny Lind was concerned, a brilliant success was easily predictable; as the manager reported, upon her arrival in England on 21 April "all London again took up its excitement at same point of 'fever-heat' where it had stood at her departure the previous year."[6] On her first appearance on 4 May she fascinated her "enraptured admirers" in the part of Amina in *La sonnambula*. Again enthusiastic crowds stormed the doors of the theatre, again dresses were torn and hats flung in the air, again the reception was tumultuous, boundless enthusiasm and rapturous acclamations prevailing among the overexcited public. Similar triumphs were chronicled for the subsequent operas in which the Swedish Nightingale made her appearance, her renditions of *La fille du régiment* (given in Italian as *La figlia del reggimento*), *Lucia di Lammermoor*, *Elisir d'Amore*, *Robert le diable* (again given in Italian) being recorded in the same terms. Despite the overwhelming presence of Jenny Lind, Erminia Tadolini, the other *prima donna*, also made a favourable debut in Donizetti's *Linda di Chamounix* and *Don Pasquale*, where her Norina was much applauded. Still, in the London operatic firmament there was limited room for stars and, despite her talent, Tadolini had to settle for a moderate success.

In the battle against the competing operatic establishment at Covent Garden, Lumley was deploying those musical champions most likely to appeal to the largest public: if Jenny Lind was to lead a troop of singers of international prominence, Giuseppe Verdi was undoubtedly

---

4   Ibid., p. 204.
5   *The Athenaeum*, February 12, 1848, p. 169.
6   Ibid., p. 216.

another asset, as the most discussed composer of the moment. Lumley pronounced himself "eager for the fray" and ready to take his position "before the forces of the rival establishment were mustered."[7] As we have seen, Lumley had the chance to attend Verdi's *Attila* in Rovigo in the late autumn of 1847, the opera featuring the young German soprano Sophie Cruvelli, whose rising talent enchanted the manager.[8] The reasons why Lumley took *Attila* into consideration are easily recounted: "None, perhaps, of Verdi's works had kindled more enthusiasm in Italy, or crowned the fortunate composer with more abundant laurels than his *Attila*. Its fame was great in the native land of the composer."[9] In his catering for novelty Lumley had immediately focused on one of Verdi's most popular operas in Italy at that time, and decided to produce it at Her Majesty's Theatre in the hope that it would add to the lustre and splendour of his operatic establishment. *Attila* was meant to become the chief attraction of the ante-Easter opera season at Her Majesty's Theatre, and was premiered on 14 March 1848, with much attention paid to every detail so as to produce it with "great scenic splendour." However, as Lumley reports, the opera was a fiasco.

> But although Verdi had already commenced to make his way to English favour—and this by means of that vigour and dramatic fire which unquestionably belonged to him—the public displayed an unwonted unanimity of sulkiness upon the production of *Attila*. They would have "none of it." Consequently *Attila* proved a failure. Music and *libretto* displeased alike.[10]

It is possible to argue that Lumley was not in a position to either sense or understand those non-musical reasons which lay behind the success of *Attila* in Italy and could not be reproduced in London. In fact, although it would be impossible to demonstrate a direct relationship between Verdi's music and the political unrest that characterised the Italian Risorgimento, "it would be draconian to attempt to deny completely the existence of a relationship between Verdi's music and the political

---

7   Lumley, *Reminiscences*, p. 211.
8   *Ibid.*, pp. 204–14. Lumley's account is inconsistent: he refers first to Rovigo and then to Padua.
9   *Ibid.*, p. 214.
10 *Ibid.*, p. 215.

tenor of the times."[11] The issue has been investigated at length and involves at least three aspects. The first relates to Verdi's commitment to the cause of Italian unification and the extent to which this can be found reflected in his compositional work; the second refers to the potentially subversive content of the libretto; the third involves the manner in which operagoers may or may not have appropriated the political metaphor the lyrics conveyed. In 1848, Verdi expressed his patriotic enthusiasm on many an occasion, as the letters sent to Francesco Maria Piave, Giuseppina Appiani and Giuseppe Mazzini after the Milan revolution testify. Having written to Piave on 21 April to express his patriotic zeal, he wrote to him again from Paris on 22 July, where he had eventually returned, proposing a patriotic opera: "The subject should be Italian and free and, should you fail to find anything better, I would suggest *Ferruccio*, a grand character, one of the great martyrs of Italian liberty."[12] Later on he sent Mazzini, whom he had met in 1847, the music set to a patriotic hymn by Goffredo Mameli which, he suggested, would serve the Italian cause as well as the cannons deployed in the battle field: "may this hymn soon be sung, along with the music of the cannon, in the Lombard plains."[13] However, although Verdi's republican orientation has been established beyond doubt,[14] the extent to which his political commitment translates into his compositional work appears problematic, to say the least. As far as *Attila* is concerned, the information we can glean from the letters written to Francesco Maria Piave in 1845 suggest that Verdi was rather more concerned about the dramatic power of the characters than any political metaphor they might embody. On 12 April, he urged the librettist to study Zacharias Werner's original text in order to get a sense of its dramatic quality; among other characters he mentioned the fierce and vindictive Ildegonda (Odabella in the final version), whose only purpose seems to consist in avenging her father, brothers and lover.[15] Returning to the same subject on 17 November, the

---

11 Roger Parker, *Arpa d'or dei fatidici vati* (Parma: Istituto Nazionale di Studi Verdiani, 1997), p. 29.
12 Giuseppe Verdi, *Lettere*, ed. Eduardo Rescigno (Turin: Einaudi, 2012), p. 195. Verdi refers to Domenico Guerrazzi's *L'assedio di Firenze* (1836), which had scored an immense popular success.
13 Verdi, *Lettere*, p. 199. See also Philip Gossett, "Becoming a Citizen: The Chorus in 'Risorgimento' Opera," *Cambridge Opera Journal* 2/1 (1990): 41–64.
14 Massimo Mila, *L'arte di Verdi* (Turin: Einaudi, 1980), p. 305.
15 Verdi, *Lettere*, p. 116.

composer exhorted Piave to think of Odabella as a woman undecided between her patriotic feeling, her filial affection and her love for Foresto. Upon concluding the letter he referred to what would become the final quartet and urged the librettist to focus on "Passion, whatever passion, but passion!"[16]

Granting that the evidence discussed so far should discourage any attempt to understand the subject of *Attila* as a political metaphor, the relationship between Verdi's operas and the political tenor of the time is still an issue.[17] In fact, despite the intervention of the censors, the libretto of *Attila* includes passages that any contemporary Italian opera goer would have easily understood as an allusion to his own struggle against the foreign invader, regardless of the composer's true intentions. The conflictual dynamics between two antagonistic characters and the subsequent deployment of two rival forces on stage—the first struggling for freedom and independence, the second trying to deprive the first of both—could result in a symbolic, politically-oriented reinterpretation of those dynamics. A diffuse sense of patriotism prompted Italian operagoers to understand the fictional conflict represented in the scene as the symbolic illustration of their own struggle against the foreign oppressor.[18] While Attila, the barbarian of the fifth century, could easily personify the conqueror of Italy in a moment when the country was still to a large extent under the military and political control of Austria and Spain, Odabella, the avenger, could equally be understood as the embodiment of that filial loyalty and family virtue deemed necessary for the fight against enslavement and captivity. This, in a context in which different manifestations of discontent with the Restoration regime would soon lead to a series of riots and revolutions destined to shake the regimes in all Italian states.[19] In the late 1840s, Italian operagoers were more than happy to pick up—or even make up—any political allusion in the libretto, and seize every opportunity that was presented to them

---

16 *Ibid.*, 127.
17 In this regard see also Douglas L. Ipson, "*Attila* takes Rome: The Reception of Verdi's Opera on the Eve of Revolution," *Cambridge Opera Journal* 21/3 (2009): 249–56.
18 Peter Stamatov, "Interpretive Activism and the Political Uses of Verdi's Operas in the 1840s," *American Sociological Review* 67/3 (2002): 345–66.
19 John A. Davis, "Opera and Absolutism in Restoration Italy, 1815–1860," *The Journal of Interdisciplinary History* 36/4, Opera and Society: Part II (2006): 569–94.

to burst into enthusiastic expressions of patriotism, independent of the true intention of either the librettist or the composer.[20] A case in point is offered by the third scene of *Attila*'s Prologo, when Dorabella, questioned by the victorious conqueror, challenges him by expressing her strong patriotic feelings ("Santo di patria indefinito amor" [Holy boundless patriotic love]), and steps forward as the leader of a bunch of women warriors who prefer to engage in battle with the enemy than accept defeat ("Ma noi, noi donne italiche / cinte di ferro il seno / sul fumido terreno / sempre vedrai pugnar" [But you will always see us, Italian women, fight on the foggy ground wearing the iron armour]).[21] Expressions of patriotic feelings such as this one, in combination with the discontent described above, made some of Verdi's operas catalysts for strong patriotic as well as nationalistic reactions, whatever the composer's intention and independent of the intrinsic quality of the music.[22]

The manner in which an opera could assume an overt political function is well suggested by *La battaglia di Legnano*, the only opera Verdi composed to serve the cause of Italian Risorgimento. Written as a commission from the Teatro Argentina in Rome, its successful premiere on 27 January 1849 was accompanied by explicit references to the patriotic feelings that it had ignited among the Roman public. Its enthusiastic reception can be regarded as the culmination of a series of ascending patriotic demonstrations, in a historical moment when the whole country was struggling for independence. On 29 January, the Roman daily journal *Pallade* suggested that Italy, until then indulging in the gentle melodies of the Lombard genius, had now an opportunity to draw from the severity and robustness of this last patriotic work the ardent spark that would rouse and spread national ardour.[23] Similar remarks appeared in the same journal a day later, referring to the *italianissimo valore* of the composer, whose talent in combining patriotic feelings and a deep religious sense had been so much appreciated. Nonetheless, no sooner did the political situation turn against the

---

20 Orazio Mula, *Giuseppe Verdi* (Bologna: Il Mulino, 1999), pp. 86–90.
21 Verdi, *Tutti i libretti d'opera* (Rome: Newton Compton, 2009), p. 193.
22 See also Giuliano Procacci, "Verdi nella storia d'Italia," in *Verdi 2001, Atti del Convegno Internazionale*, ed. Fabrizio della Seta, Roberta Montemorra Marvin and Marco Marica (Florence: Olschki Editore, 2003), pp. 191–204.
23 *Pallade*, January 29, 1849, [n.p.].

Italians, than the enthusiasm raised by the opera waned and *La battaglia di Legnano* was soon put aside.

Lumley did not seem to be aware of these circumstances; nor did those London critics whose reviews of *Attila* made their appearance in 1848. The critic of *The Times*, having narrated the plot, called attention to countless shortcomings in the music; *Attila* appeared to be marked by the same faults as Verdi's former works, without having any of the merits that had made his reputation. The subject, dealing with the violent career of the barbarian conqueror, offered a good number of strong dramatic situations that Verdi had failed to seize. The few effects in the music resulted from an incessant increase in volume, the composer constantly relying upon the unison and showing no skills in the use of counterpoint. His many choruses were less convincing than those in *Nabucco* or even in *I masnadieri*. As for the arias and the treatment of the voice, the usual complaints were put forth; the former were commonplace while the latter strained the singer to the utmost.[24] In short, all applause went to the interpreters, while the music exhibited the usual number of weaknesses and shortcomings.

Fig. 8 Scene from *Attila* at Her Majesty's Theatre, London. *The Illustrated London News*, 15 April 1848.

---

24 *The Times*, March 15, 1848, p. 8.

The critic of *The Musical World* uttered words of the usual unfriendly, unpleasant, openly hostile quality, and concluded his lengthy account by highlighting the only cause of relief in the entire opera: its brevity.

> *Attila* has one merit, which we have found in no other of Verdi's operas; it is short—not sweet, certainly, but short—and that is much when Verdi is at work upon our ears. [...] To sum up, however, which we shall do in a few words:—*Attila* is the worst of all the operas by Verdi that, up to this moment, have been inflicted upon the English public. It is unnecessary to add any thing to this. Reader! Imagine every possible fault in musical composition, and the absence of every possible merit—of beauty, grandeur, simplicity or eleaveness [*sic*]—and you have *Attila*.[25]

Sophie Cruvelli, Italo Gardoni, Giovanni Belletti and Luigi Cuzzani were applauded vehemently and recalled after the curtain fell; Michael Balfe, the conductor, did particularly well with the entire band; Marshall's most admirably-executed scenic effects were of great impact; and, finally, a deep sign of appreciation was bestowed upon Lumley, the spirited director, for producing the opera with such rich a profusion of means. As for the music, the critic hinted at a now well-known repertoire of faults and shortcomings. The orchestration was noisy, the vocal passages were of an unvocal nature, the arias and cabalettas were commonplace, the duets had neither character nor charm, the Finale of Act I consisted of a quantity of "unconnected *remplissage*, wherein the orchestra commenced sundry figures which were never perfected into a phrase."[26]

Again, the merits of the performers, with their vocal and dramatic skills, greatly outweighed those of the composer. Verdi's lack of melodiousness and vocal inventiveness, together with his overzealous care for any type of noisy orchestral effect, resulted in a detrimental impact on the listeners and the critics alike. A note of sorrow was also occasionally addressed to the performers, more and more frequently confronted with Verdi's increasingly overwhelming vocal writing: extreme and awkward melodic contrivances sustained by an exceedingly thunderous orchestration.

---

25   *The Musical World*, March 18, 1848, p. 179.
26   *Ibid.*

The Illustrated London News pointed out that *Attila* resulted from the mixture of positive and negative ingredients now considered most typical of Verdi.

> The work itself possesses the beauties and defects peculiar to Verdi—a certain grandeur of conception and power of dramatic effect is even more striking here than in many other of the *maestro's* compositions. There is a warmth, spirit, and energy in the music which carries away the listener, which excites and inspires; at the same time there is a want of softness and repose which is, in this opera, more than usually perceptible. The too frequent use of the drums and the brass instruments is the great fault we have to find in this work.[27]

The critic returned to the topic in a later issue of the journal when, upon repeated hearings of the opera, he was in a better position to judge it. Furthermore, he addressed the situation of singers now being called upon to master two distinct vocal styles, the lyrical and the dramatic.

> The grandeur of style of this composer is peculiarly suited to the wild, barbarous, highly dramatic character of the subject he has chosen; while its chief interpreters, above all Belletti and Cruvelli, so admirably adapted to their respective parts, give to its performance the utmost effect of which it is capable. Belletti's *Attila* displays the powers of this great artist as a tragedian more fully than any other opera in which we have seen him; and his performance in this and in the *Barbiere* shows him to be possessed of great powers in the most opposite styles of lyrical and dramatic art.[28]

The Athenaeum introduced the newly produced work to its readers by claiming that "it would be difficult to fancy a worse opera even from Verdi." "May we never hear its like again!"[29] was the critic's wish. While the plot was quickly summed up, the music was described as noisy to an outrageous degree; the only portion deserving praise was a symphony descriptive of storm and daybreak in the sixth scene of the Prologue. "In some of the concerted music, too, there is a certain grandeur of climax," the critic maintained, "but the melodies are old and unlovely to a degree

---

27 *The Illustrated London News*, March 18, 1848, p. 185.
28 *The Illustrated London News*, April 8, 1848, p. 238.
29 *The Athenaeum*, March 18, 1848, p. 300.

which is almost impertinent."³⁰ The performance was pronounced good rather than excellent, the interpreters being in general not devoid of merit, regardless of the manner in which their vocal skills were strained to the extreme. Chorley confirmed his hostility to Verdi and pronounced his most recent opera outrageous. To our surprise he had expressed himself in more lenient terms when, not long before, *Ernani* had been revived to open the ante-Easter opera season at Her Majesty's Theatre on 19 February. "Ernani" he wrote on that occasion, "is the new master's best opera—the one which we are most willing to receive in turn with the works of other composers."³¹ Chorley was not changing his mind, nor was he now more inclined to acknowledge Verdi as a composer worthy of his attention. The critic was simply willing to include *Ernani* among the regular operatic repertoire than he had been before. But while *Ernani* could appear side by side with the palmy operas from the past, *Attila* was a confirmation of Verdi's limited talent.

When called upon to review *Attila*, the critic of *The Spectator* joined the choir and expressed himself in terms of scorn and disappointment: "The music is in Verdi's usual manner. His melodies, that is to say, are generally trite, though flowing and sometimes expressive; his choral effects are chiefly produced by masses of unisonous sound; and his instrumentation, on the whole noisy and inartificial, has occasional gleams of grace and delicacy."³² The critic had words of unreserved appreciation only for the singers and the beautiful scenery.

Attila was withdrawn after a few performances but, notwithstanding the ill-favour with which it was received, Benjamin Lumley declared that he had to fall back on Verdi regardless. Therefore, *I due Foscari* was revived on 21 March and *Nino* on 25 March. This could do nothing to mitigate the critics' hostility. According to *The Musical World*, closer familiarity with *Attila* could do nothing to improve its critic's judgment, and a further performance of *I due Foscari*, even though admirable in many ways, "would fail to create any interest for such vapid music as that of Verdi."³³ If one week before the critic had thought *Attila* the

---

30 *Ibid*.
31 *The Athenaeum*, February 26, 1848. p. 226.
32 *The Spectator*, March 18, 1848, p. 16.
33 *The Musical World*, March 25, 1848, p. 198.

feeblest opera he ever attended, now *I due Foscari* was said to usurp its place.

The Athenaeum reviewed *I due Foscari* in the usual manner, the much applauded singers valued for the dramatic acting and declamatory singing now so typical of the so-called new school. Sophie Cruvelli's Lucrezia was said to be "triumphing throughout the opera with the violence of a virago rather than picturing the sorrow of an afflicted noble lady."[34] Chorley continued to long for that vocal delicacy and gentle expression in which he delighted when attending the operas of the past. Now lungs of brass were necessary to sustain the endless screaming required to interpret the modern repertoire, a circumstance that—he claimed—forced operagoers to use cotton pads to protect their ears.

On 27 March, *The Times* reviewed *Nino* and pronounced Coletti's declamatory singing admirable in his rendition of the Assyrian monarch. However, Luisa Abbadia, who made her debut as Abigail, was pronounced "by no means equal to the expectation that had been formed respecting her."[35] Her faults of intonation and other general defects in the execution of her principal aria had occasioned manifest expressions of disappointment among the public. A similar remark on the way in which Abbadia had failed to meet the public's expectations made its appearance on 1 April in *The Musical World*. But, the critic continued, the poor condition of Abbadia's voice, once so stunning, inspired in him "rather a feeling of compassion than of contempt."[36] It was Verdi who should be blamed for her condition. Abbadia, once bestowed with a splendid voice, had to endure the strains forced upon her by a composer whose preference for thunderous effects resulted in devastating consequences for the singers and inflicted endless pain upon the listeners. She had to immolate her voice on the altar of "the new school." Sophie Cruvelli was pronounced the next victim.

> With all our detestation for the so-called music of Verdi, we never commended him and all his operas to the devil with more hearty good will. "This," we inwardly ejaculated," is thy work—thou frothy, impudent nonentity! How many more fresh and beautiful voices wilt thou break upon the wheel of bombast, and utterly annihilate by screaming. Thy

---

34 *The Athenaeum*, March 25, 1848, p. 322.
35 *The Times*, March 27, 1848, p. 5.
36 *The Musical World*, April 1, 1848, p. 211.

next victim, perchance, will be the comely Cruvelli, whose youth is now a shield, and whose stamina will yet resist thy shocking onslaughts; but who cannot long endure if she persist in shouting thy hideous and abominable ravings! Heaven protect her! It would be a good thing were she to fall sick, and be confined to her couch for three years and a day, at the end of which thou wilt have been scouted from the opera boards, thou musty and monotonous mouther! Begone, and afflict us no more with thy plague of screaming. Thou shalt not kill the beautiful; Cruvelli; thou shalt not reduce her to a wreck, and annihilate her with a chronic hoarseness, thou son of a bombshell, as thou hast done with the unfortunate and forlorn Abbadia.[37]

Verdi was the real sinner, the poor singer being just a victim. Chorley was of the same opinion. Reviewing *Nino* from the columns of *The Athenaeum* on 1 April 1848, he referred to Abbadia as an interpreter once appreciated for vocal powers that were no longer to be heard. Of Verdi, Chorley reiterated the well-known refrain that "the faster his operas are produced the sooner will the noise thereof come to an end."[38]

But in 1848 an unprecedented episode occurred in the London press, strongly suggestive of the extent to which the general public disagreed with the critics. On 29 April, referring to the antagonism between Verdi's supporters and detractors, a reader of *The Musical World*, J. De Clerville,[39] defended the Italian composer and the school of which he was said to be the most acclaimed representative from the "repeated maledictions" that appeared in the journal's columns. De Clerville could not subscribe to the expressions of severe censure repeatedly promulgated by the editor of that journal, and in future he would expect more lenient tones with respect to a composer who was also the founder of a new school. Had Verdi failed to satisfy the general expectation of both the public and the critics, he would have at least shown the path along which others might succeed after him. De Clerville also articulated a noteworthy analysis concerning the way in which Verdi's preference for strong effects and dramatic power contrasted with the bias towards elegant vocalisation that was already perceived as old, surpassed and devoid of expressive strength.

---

37 *Ibid*.
38 *The Athenaeum*, April 1, 1848, p. 344.
39 It is difficult to determine the true identity of J. de Clerville. A Jules de Clerville appears as *rédacteur en chef* of the *La Semaine Parisienne* late in the 1870s.

> In my opinion, the tone of operatic music had already begun to show evident symptoms of decrepitude, and was degenerating from the florid to the mawkish and insipid: a more vigorous and healthy tone was desirable to give it due vitality; and if Verdi has done no better service, he has caused a reaction in this respect, and infused spirit and energy into serious dramatic music.[40]

De Clerville warned modern critics not to indulge in those technical sophisms that were so dear to those who had first reviewed the operas of Rossini. Rossini "was coldly welcomed at first, not by the public, but by the critics, as one who departed from received traditions,"[41] and such terms as plagiarist, ignorant, innovator, quack, empiric, etc. which conservative critics had once applied to the Pesarese were now as profusely bestowed upon poor Verdi. De Clerville also pointed out that the mechanisms which lay behind the operatic system in Italy demanded continuous musical as well as dramatic novelty; in fact, theatres in Italy remained open almost throughout the year, and operagoers of diverse social status attended assiduously.

Once he had demonstrated that ample justification for Verdi's innovative orientations was provided by the difficult state in which operatic music lay, the writer then posited that London's two operatic establishments—Her Majesty's Theatre and Covent Garden—were now functioning in complementary fashion, providing their public with operas that reflected two different and opposite attitudes.

> The Covent Garden people are the Conservatives of Music—they almost eschew the productions of the modern Italian school, and have principally directed their attention to the getting-up of operas already known, on a scale of perfection hitherto unattempted. [...] Her Majesty's Theatre, on the contrary, with a few rare exceptions, has turned its attention to the production of modern Italian operas, and in my opinion has thereby gained two objects most desirable in a lyrical establishment: viz. the production of novelty, and the consequent removal of one cause of complaint amongst the subscribers; and a saving of expenditure, in adopting a totally different line of conduct, by which all comparison with its rival is avoided or warded off—a comparison which it would

---

40 J. De Clerville, "Verdi and the Two Operas," *The Musical World*, April 29, 1848, p. 276.
41 *Ibid.*

have been impossible to sustain, considering the present state of the musical market.[42]

Even more interestingly, De Clerville called attention to an issue of extreme significance concerning not only the degree of novelty attained by the composers belonging to the so-called new Italian school, but also the remarkable change in vocal technique that had accompanied it. According to De Clerville, the split between London opera houses in 1846 forced Lumley to recruit his principal singers from interpreters ill at ease with the traditional repertoire; as a consequence, he had to turn his attention towards composers whose music was more suitable to the qualities of the interpreters. Thus, it was the artists recruited by Lumley "with wonderful energy and spirit" who had brought with them their own repertoire—consisting of Verdi, Pacini and Mercadante—and not the other way around.

> Most of the new importations were entirely unknown in Paris and London; and Paisiello, Cimarosa, Mozart, Rossini, were to them a sealed book: they may have heard of such composers, but could not exactly swear as to the age in which they flourished [...] The school of singing was entirely changed; the elegant, serene simplicity of Mozart was to them a dead letter, the charming vocalisation of Rossini beyond their means, an *appoggiatura*, a *cadenza*, a *mordente*, were discarded as superfluous; delicacy and refinement were abandoned for vigour and energy.[43]

The picture drawn by De Clerville appears controversial, for Verdi's *Ernani* was premièred in London in 1845, one year before the split, and early negotiations between the composer and the manager date back to the same year, when Lumley presumably paid a first visit to Verdi to offer him a commission for the summer of 1846. As we have seen, these negotiations were unsuccessful until Verdi decided to compose *I masnadieri*. Furthermore, some of the conditions regarding the interpreters were dictated by Verdi himself, a case in point being that of Jenny Lind and Gaetano Fraschini, the interpreters of *I masnadieri*. Nor could it be alleged that all the singers who had made appearances in Verdi's new operas had no familiarity with the earlier repertoire. However, the writer suggested, and rightly so, that a change had taken

---

42 Ibid.
43 Ibid.

place concerning the development of vocal technique in relation to the renewal of the repertoire. This change was not a degradation caused by a new generation of untalented composers, but the response to a need for novelty, resulting in a new style of singing and dramatic acting. The issue deserves further scrutiny: was it the repertoire that demanded a new vocal technique or the new, wider expressive potential presented by the singers that stimulated a new compositional orientation? De Clerville's letter was followed by a note in which the Editor reiterated his arguments and insisted on his opinion that "Verdi was the greatest impostor that ever took pen in hand to write rubbish."[44]

One week later, on 6 May 1848, an extensive reply to De Clerville's letter appeared in the columns of *The Musical World*, signed by Desmond Ryan, whom the editor had allowed to answer in his stead. Ryan seems particularly interested in the reasons why Lumley turned his attention towards Verdi: "I conscientiously believe," he wrote, "that Mr. Lumley prefers one aria of Rossini to all that Verdi ever fabricated: but having singers in his establishment who would shine more in Verdi than Rossini, he very wisely provided that music in which their talents would be displayed to the greatest advantage. The same feeling actuated the directors of the rival house."[45] It was not Lumley's confidence in the composer's musical value that had led him to produce Verdi's works in his lyrical establishment, Ryan wants us to believe, but rather the attractiveness of the singers who had recently achieved fame thanks to his operas. In that, at least, Ryan's and De Clerville's positions seem to converge, for both misjudged the interest that Lumley had taken in Verdi. However, Ryan insisted, and rightly so, that it was not possible to agree with De Clerville that such high names as Gardoni, Jenny Lind, Cruvelli, etc., had no familiarity with the music of Paisiello, Cimarosa, Mozart or even Rossini. About Verdi, Ryan was categorical: "It is little less than musical blasphemy to bring the names of Rossini and Verdi into juxtaposition."[46] While fertility of imagination, fecundity of thought, novelty of conception, originality of treatment in his ideas and brilliancy in the instrumentation were the talents recognised in Rossini's operas, nothing of that kind could be found in any of Verdi's operatic

---

44   Ibid.
45   Ibid., pp. 289-91.
46   "Verdi and the Two Operas," *The Musical World*, May 6, 1848, pp. 289–91.

achievements. Nothing, apparently, could change the critic's mind. Neither the De Clerville nor Ryan seemed to be able to understand Lumley's straightforward managerial strategy, which consisted in the continuous, strenuous effort to appeal to the public by means of any new vocal attraction as well as any compositional novelty from the continent. However, while De Clerville acknowledged the merits of both a new generation of singers and a young composer, the critic of *The Musical World* refused to admit that Verdi possessed any musical talent.

Finally, the opera season came to its end and some concluding remarks made their appearance in *The Times* and *The Athenaeum*. The critic of *The Times* pronounced the season prosperous, notwithstanding many artistic difficulties; the reappearance of Jenny Lind was marked by the same enthusiasm that had been recorded the previous year, the two new characters she had interpreted having "displayed her talents so favourably that they may be ranked with her best parts of last year."[47] Similarly positive remarks were made with respect to the other novelties brought forward by Lumley; Giovanni Belletti, Filippo Coletti and Sophie Cruvelli were considered to have added to the splendour of that operatic establishment. *Attila*, however, did not raise its composer in public esteem.

> His *Nino* and *Ernani* have gained a permanent place in the musical repertoire of this country, but Verdi does not advance as his compositions increase in number. He lacks melody to allure the ordinary hearer, and science to satisfy the technical judge. In the outline of his conceptions there is something grand and dramatic, but his works are all made after the same model, and what surprises at first loses in effect by repetition.[48]

Despite the milder tones, the critic performed the usual fault-finding and hinted at two frequently abused lines of argument: lack of melodiousness and insufficient musical competence, i.e. in counterpoint.

For his part, in reviewing the past opera season, the critic of *The Athenaeum* showed no leniency. Neither *Attila* nor the interpreters who had made their appearance during the season at Her Majesty's Theatre were addressed in positive terms. The opera was devoid of any merit, while the singers, with only the exception of Belletti, were pronounced

---

47 *The Times*, August 7, 1848, p. 8.
48 *Ibid*.

a failure.[49] To some surprise, Jenny Lind was also deemed a semi-failure. Chorley argued that the three new roles she had interpreted, Adina in *L'Elisir*, Lucia in *Lucia di Lammermoor* and Elvira in *I puritani*, neither added to her fame, nor improved the critic's judgment. He described her as a "songstress of consummate talent, and an actress who knows how to charm within a limited range, equalled in vocal accomplishments and surpassed in dramatic skill by more than one of her contemporaries."[50] Chorley concluded his account of the 1848 opera season at Her Majesty's Theatre in terms more apocalyptic than encouraging: "The year, in brief, in spite of every outward sign of honour and glory, was felt to be virtually one announcing decomposition and embarrassment."[51]

With the performance of *Attila* at Her Majesty's Theatre, the positions established by different critics over the previous few years were generally confirmed. The journalist of *The Illustrated London News* was the only one who expressed himself in favourable terms.

---

49   *The Athenaeum*, August 26, 1848, p. 861.
50   *Ibid.*
51   Chorley, *Thirty Years' Musical Recollections*, 2: 27.

6. Uneventful Years: 1849–1852

If we look at Victorian London operatic life and focus squarely on the production and reception of Verdi's works, the period spanning the years 1849–1852 appears to have been quite uneventful. This impression is reinforced when we consider that, in contrast to London's comparative silence, four new operas bearing the name of Verdi were premiered in Italy during those years: *La battaglia di Legnano* (Rome, 27 January 1849), *Luisa Miller* (Naples, 8 December 1849), *Stiffelio* (Trieste, 16 November 1850), *Rigoletto* (Venice, 11 March 1851). None of them would be performed in London until 14 May 1853, when *Rigoletto* was produced at Covent Garden for the first time.

During these quiet years, however, Verdi strengthened his position in London and his most successful operas continued to make regular appearances at both Covent Garden and Her Majesty's Theatre. On 26 March 1849, the critic of *The Times* reviewed the performance of *Ernani* and, having elaborated only on the interpreters' merits, concluded that "the course of time seems to prove that *Ernani* is the most permanently popular of Verdi's operas."[1] He put aside all pressing questions concerning the value of Verdi's music and admitted that this opera, at least, was now part of the standard repertoire. When the same journal reviewed *I due Foscari* that same year, the critic could not avoid a dig, maintaining that its popular success was due less to the quality of the music than to the opportunity it offered for good baritones to show off.

> Although the music of *I due Foscari* has less to recommend it than that of *Ernani*, and has all the true Verdian want of original melody, it keeps

---

1 *The Times*, March 26, 1849, p. 8.

a position on the stage on account of the good opportunities which the Doge affords to a baritone singer, and of certain effective *morceaux*, which rarely fail to produce an impression.[2]

Reviewing the same performance, *The Athenaeum* also drew the reader's attention to the way in which Van Gelder and Bordas, although liberally applauded, could do nothing to mitigate the pervasive unpleasantness of *I due Foscari*: "the grim, exaggerated, and incoherent music of that opera is beyond the power of any *soprano* or tenor to sweeten or to inform with true expression as distinguished from rant."[3] Chorley simply continued to dislike Verdi and to credit the success of his operas only to their interpreters. *The Musical World* reviewed both the productions of *Ernani* (31 March) and *I due Foscari* (7 April), but focussed uniquely on the performing artists.[4] The rest of the season went smoothly, with no particular mention being made of Verdi's most recent operatic achievements on the continent.

On 12 January 1850, *The Athenaeum* reported a piece of news concerning the production of *Luisa Miller* in Naples, where the success of the opera was said to be dubious and its subject not fitted to the composer.[5] Between February and March, the managers of both Her Majesty's Theatre and Covent Garden were able to issue their official programmes, revealing that four of Verdi's works were to be produced in the course of the ensuing season: *Nino*, *Ernani*, *I Lombardi* and *I due Foscari*.

On 19 March, *Nino* was revived at Her Majesty's Theatre, "chiefly for the purpose of introducing to the public a new baritone, named Lorenzo de Montemerli, but simply styled in the bills Signor Lorenzo."[6] The critic of *The Times* bestowed words of praise on the main interpreters— Lorenzo de Montemerli, Teresa Parodi and Giovanni Belletti were called before the curtain several times during the performance—but failed to express any opinion whatsoever on the true merits of the opera. Two days later, on 21 March, *Ernani* was also revived, this time featuring Sims Reeves; the critic of *The Athenæum* held that "both opera and singers

---

2   *The Times*, April 2, 1849, p. 8.
3   *The Athenaeum*, April 7, 1849, p. 364.
4   *The Musical World*, April 7, 1849, p. 212.
5   *The Athenaeum*, January 12, 1850, p. 51.
6   *The Times*, March 20, 1850, p. 8.

were received with every token of favour and success."[7] However, the critic pointed out that Verdi's music lent itself to a degree of interpretive freedom that he was not inclined to consider appropriate, although it was widely accepted among the public.

> Verdi's music, in its *solo* passages and closes, gives him [Reeves] scope for that slackening of *tempo* and elongation of favourite notes which are considered by "Young Italy" as the style dramatic. But, for the interest of Art—rather than under any hope that our remonstrances will be heard amid so many plaudits—we must point out that Mr Reeves method of producing his tone and phrasing stands in need of refinement and reconsideration,—and that something of facility *must* be acquired by him ere his voice will either blend or *tell* in concerted music.[8]

Similar critical remarks were made with regard to Lorenzo de Montemerli's Carlo Quinto, while more appreciative words were bestowed on Giovanni Belletti's sounder style, noble voice and genuine, unobtrusive musical feeling when interpreting Silva. The critic concluded on a wishful note, declaring his hope that no more of Verdi's music would be heard soon and stating that his popularity in England "was not on the increase."[9] *The Musical World* reviewed both operas on 23 March; the critic introduced the first by stating that "of Signor Verdi's music we have only to say that we dislike it more than ever" and qualified the second as "an event of no ordinary interest."[10] Again, the great expectations for *Ernani* were ascribed less to the artistic value of the opera than to the rentrée of Sims Reeves.[11] The critic also grumbled about Reeves, who had made his reappearance in an opera so poor in melodies and so unvocal.

Later in April of that year, the critic of *The Athenaeum* had to admit that Carlo Beaucardè's success in *I Lombardi*, which was produced on 20 April, was "no less than a triumph,"[12] the tenor possessing the most beautiful voice possible. Again, however, this was despite the fact that the music he had chosen was "of the newest Italian destructives—which, we trust, and believe, will never take root in England."[13]

---

7 *The Athenaeum*, March 23, 1850, p. 320.
8 Ibid.
9 Ibid.
10 *The Musical World*, March 23, 1850, pp. 173–74.
11 Ibid., p. 174.
12 *The Athenaeum*, April 27, 1850, p. 458.
13 Ibid.

On 30 May, *Nino* was again produced in London, this time at the Royal Italian Opera, Covent Garden, under the title of *Anato*. Upon his arrival in England, Giorgio Ronconi had made a public announcement expressing his intention to appear in Verdi's *Nabucco*, a circumstance that prompted the critic of *The Musical World* to utter words of deep, profound disappointment: "highly as we esteem Signor Ronconi's dramatic and lyric genius, we have no desire to witness their exposition through the medium of young Verdi's music."[14] The critic could not comprehend why a vocalist with such large a repertoire should decide to select "the worst opera of the worst composer in Italy."[15] He also wondered why, now that the subscribers of Her Majesty's Theatre were finally repudiating Verdi's music (after having "gorged ad nauseam"), the subscribers of the rival theatre (who had instead been banqueting on Mozart and Rossini) should welcome "Sir Unison and Knight of Pom-Crash."[16]

On 31 May, the critic of *The Times* reviewed the event and took the opportunity to reiterate a series of grumbled variations on his deep longing for those palmy days when *bel canto* really meant beautiful melodies and nice vocalisation. His comments regarding the value of Ronconi, as opposed to the faults of Verdi, epitomise the kind of attitude that the most conservative critics continued to exhibit when referring to Verdi and the sad state of Italian opera.

> He [Ronconi] is, in short a striking example of the most finished school of Italian singing as it existed in those palmy days when Rossini, and not Verdi, was the idol of the Italians. It was to be regretted that Signor Ronconi should find it necessary to make his *rentrée* in one of Verdi's operas, where screaming is so often the substitute for singing, vulgar tunes for graceful melody and mere noise for the rich combinations of choral and orchestral harmony; but his conception of the character of the Assyrian monarch (Anato-Nino-Nabucco) is so fine, and the realization of his conception so masterly, that criticism is disarmed while he is on the stage, and the meagreness of Signor Verdi's invention is lost sight of in the genius of the dramatic artist.[17]

---

14 *The Musical World*, May 18, 1850, p. 303.
15 *Ibid.*
16 *Ibid.*
17 *The Times*, May 31, 1850, p. 8.

The critic clearly favoured a past characterised by "the most finished Italian School of florid singing" to the new manner in which Verdi spoiled the voice by dramatising the style. Further complaints about the noise of the orchestration, the inventionless accompaniments and the commonplace choruses followed in the same article, which also included some remarks on the way in which "even the choral tune 'Va pansiero,' which rarely if ever escapes an encore, on this occasion, although very well sung, passed off with scarcely a hand of recognition."[18] Perhaps, the critic concluded, the English public was finally beginning to realise that Verdi's musical fame was groundless and that Italian music in its present state was degraded. The critic was trying to perform a problematic task, which involved drawing a line between the assumed poverty of the music and the quality of its performance. He insisted on ascribing the popular success of Verdi's works uniquely to the talent of the performers and refused to consider the quality of the music. In his words, *Anato* should be considered a successful music degradation.

On 1 June, the critic of *The Musical World* shot his merciless darts against Verdi's *Anato* and reiterated arguments and objections that strongly suggested the hand of Davison (and demonstrated the role he played at two different journals).

> Thursday was a sad and a joyful night for the Royal Italian Opera. Sad, because it brought us the prince of musical mountebanks, Verdi, the Jew-Peter *tonans*, and joyful, inasmuch as it restored to our longing eyes and wishful ears one of the greatest masters of song that ever adorned the lyric stage.[19]

Ronconi was the musical hero, while *Anato* the utterly ill-constructed opera which was forced upon the public at Covent Garden. The critic insisted on praising the singer for his musical and dramatic merits and on blaming the composer for his absolute lack thereof. Davison's tone was more caustic than colourful:

> Never was a writer of operas so destitute of real invention, so deficient in power, or so wanting in the musician's skill. His sole art consists in weaving ballad tunes—we never find any tune in his songs—into choruses, which sung in unison make an immense noise; or in working

---

18   *Ibid.*
19   *The Musical World*, June 1, 1850, p. 338.

up a finale by means of a tremendous crash of the brass instruments, the drums, and cymbals, and voices screaming at the top of the register. Strip the finales of their noise and nothing remains—absolutely nothing. The instrumentation is thin, insipid and pointless; the colouring overcharged; the construction feeble; the development puerile. He has not a notion of real effect. But let us turn from unsophisticated brass to unadulterated gold—from Verdi to Ronconi.[20]

The usual repertoire of faults and shortcomings was rehearsed by the critic who gave all credit for the success of the performance to the interpreter: "the poverty of the music was completely lost sight of in this [Ronconi's] stupendous exhibition of art."[21] Notwithstanding the poor quality of the music, *Anato* scored a full success with the public. A difficult issue was raised again, concerning the possibility for a critic to discern between the artwork "as such" on the one hand and its rendition on the other, and to acknowledge the quality of the latter despite the worthlessness of the former. The articles published in *The Times* on 31 May and in *The Musical World* one day later seem to have originated from the same pen. They share the same line of arguments and present parallel uses of language, including similar expressions and even wordings. In both, appreciation is bestowed on Ronconi, the finished Italian style (of which Ronconi, again, was the praiseworthy representative) is preferred to the modern style, the choice of Verdi's music is one to be regretted, the usual mistakes and deficiencies are listed and are said to account for the pitiable effect of the music.

One week later, *The Musical World* reproduced a short review from *The Morning Post*, the author of which, in reviewing *Anato*, demonstrated a remarkable degree of wittiness. According to the writer, persons quaintly attired, and not characters, had made their appearance in front of the public, crying and screaming—not singing—for reasons impossible to either understand or decipher.

> A great uproar took place at this establishment last night; several persons attired in quaint costumes appeared upon the stage, and for some reasons which we in vain endeavoured to make out from the business of the scene, or the requirements of the dramatic action, uttered strange cries and piercing screams. The strain upon their pulmonic resources

---

20 *Ibid.*
21 *Ibid.*

appeared to be very great indeed, yet on the whole they did their duty manfully.[22]

The author of this picturesque caricature announced that he had ruminated for some time before finally understanding the philosophy that lay behind these vocal ravings. Whereas a conventional musician would have gone for those musical attributes that characterise the classical simplicity of Mozart and Rossini, Verdi had decided to pursue a much loftier objective.

> But his chief and noblest aim appears to be to show that the human voice, when strained to the utmost, can be made to produce more noise than any combination of instruments whatever, to assert the supremacy of the "voice to Nature," to prove its superiority over mere mechanical inventions and contrivances, even though they be made of brass or sheepskin. Who can deny the elevation of this purpose? Nature *versus* Art! Why should man or woman be out-roared by an ugly trombone, or out-screamed by an impertinent octave flute? To the great object we have mentioned, Verdi has devoted his energies; in the pursuit of it, all smaller considerations to which unphilosophical composers have given their attention, such as melody, harmony, counterpoint, dramatic propriety, originality etc., have appeared to him insignificant and unworthy the attention of a genius.[23]

This critic echoed a well-known repertoire of disapproving phrases, and used all his sarcasm to draw a grotesque picture. Verdi's shortcomings no longer highlighted his lack of inventiveness and poor compositional abilities; instead they revealed a higher purpose, a nobler intention, an attempt to approach music in philosophical terms.

In 1850, the opera season at Her Majesty's Theatre also included *I due Foscari*, the only true novelty being Fromental Halévy's *La tempesta*, which was produced on 8 June and performed six times in succession. Throughout the season it was often reported that the decision to revive such early operas as *Nabucco*, *Ernani* and *I due Foscari* arose from the leading interpreters (Lorenzo de Montemerli, Sims Reeves and Giorgio Ronconi), who had openly manifested their desire to appear in roles that would best fit their dramatic and vocal skills. It was held that neither Lumley nor Gye were particularly interested in Verdi's latest

---

22 "Verdi at the Royal Italian Opera," *The Musical World*, June 8, 1850, p. 350.
23 *Ibid.*, p. 351.

compositional achievements, while increasing attention was paid to the novelties coming from the contemporary French composers. In particular, Lumley's connection with the Théâtre-Italien in Paris seems to have played an important role in determining his more recent managerial decisions.

Cultural life in 1851 London was dominated by one large event, *The Great Exhibition of the Works of Industry of all Nations*, under the patronage of Prince Albert. For this exceptional occasion, a unique and innovative edifice was constructed, the Crystal Palace, designed by Joseph Paxton, the Duke of Devonshire's head gardener. It consisted of a gigantic, temporary structure of glass erected without foundations in Hyde Park.[24]

The critic of *The Musical World* saluted the forthcoming event in quite tepid terms, and expressed moderate expectations only in so far as the invention and manufacturing of new instruments were concerned. While explicit reference was made to the manner in which the Theobald Boehm flute controversy or the innovation of Adolphe Sax instruments might find adequate space for presentation and discussion in the precinct of the Exhibition, limited hope was expressed with regard to pure art, by which the critic meant pure English art. What will the Great Exhibition do for music? What will it do for English music? What will English musicians do for the Great Exhibition? The critic suggested that its influence would turn out to be of immense advantage, for a million or more foreigners were expected to pour into London, eager to see and hear all that the city might offer. The Exhibition provided the English nation with the opportunity to show the true value of its musicians to the rest of the world. Would English musicians take full advantage of this opportunity?

> To the Italian and Frenchman in particular, our composers and players might honourably demonstrate that they did not merit the contempt with which they had been treated. [...] Our singers too could prove to the astonished ears of the French that they have voices; and explain to the Italians how well they can sing much to which the "land of music" is entirely stranger.[25]

---

24 Liza Picard, *Victorian London: The Life of a City 1840–1870* (London: Weidenfeld & Nicolson, 2005), pp. 260–65.
25 *The Musical World*, January 11, 1851, p. 18.

Davison, who was a strong supporter of English musical nationalism, encouraged his colleagues to step forward and advocate the claims of native talents in opposition to those phalanxes of foreign virtuoso players who dominated the London scene. In this respect, the Great Exhibition could do a lot for English music.

Quite predictably, from 1 May, when it was inaugurated, to 15 October, when it closed, the Great Exhibition strongly affected the life of opera theatres and concert venues, for large numbers of foreign as well as local visitors thronged the English capital, visited the Crystal Palace—an attraction in itself—and looked for further fashionable leisure activities to enjoy during their stay. Lumley's response to such a challenge was perfectly consistent with the entrepreneurial attitude he had manifested on previous occasions. Instead of relying uniquely on his already successful repertoire of stock operas, the manager of Her Majesty's Theatre decided to enrich the forthcoming season with as many novelties and attractions as possible. Surprisingly enough, no room was made for a new opera bearing the name of Verdi, a circumstance that prompted some critics to harp on about the sad state of music in Italy and to predict that the supremacy of Italian opera was definitely approaching its end.

On Saturday March 22nd, the ante-Easter season at Her Majesty's Theatre opened with *Lucia di Lammermoor*, featuring Caroline Duprez in the title role, followed by the ballet *L'isle des amours*. On 31 March *The Times* reviewed Daniel Auber's *Gustave III*, as produced at Her Majesty's Theatre, and took this opportunity to assert that its production indicated "the total inability of the Italian stage to furnish pieces for the English metropolis."[26] The choice of a French composer, the critic continued, confirmed that "Verdi's first works were tolerated, but at last he became unendurable; and now it is plainly discovered there is no one whatever but Verdi to be found in the Italian region Italy [sic], as a necessary consequence, is given up altogether."[27]

After the Easter pause both operatic establishments prepared to fight a fierce battle in front of an international, composite public. Among the novelties at Her Majesty's Theatre, *Le tre nozze* was performed, an opera buffa in three acts composed by Giulio Alary (libretto by Arcangelo

---

26 *The Times*, March 31, 1851, p. 5.
27 *Ibid*.

Berrettoni) and first produced at the Théâtre-Italien in Paris that year. Michael Balfe's *I quattro fratelli* (the Italianised version of *Les quatre fils d'Aymon* given at Princess's Theatre in 1844) and Sigismond Thalberg's *Florinda, or the Moors in Spain* followed. All three were pronounced successful, but they were destined for short-lived popularity. Besides some stock operas from Rossini, Bellini and Donizetti, Mozart's *Don Giovanni* was also produced at Her Majesty's Theatre, while *Die Zauberflöte* (given in Italian as *Il flauto magico*) was performed at the Royal Italian Opera. Beethoven's *Fidelio* was performed in both theatres. Besides *Il flauto magico* and *Fidelio*, and in addition to the usual repertoire, the prospectus issued by the manager of the Royal Italian Opera at Covent Garden included six more novelties: Carl Maria von Weber's *Eurianthe*, Louis Spohr's *Faust*, Donizetti's *Les Martyrs*, Gaspare Spontini's *La vestale*, Daniel Auber's *L'enfant prodigue* and Charles Gounod's *Sapho*.[28] It is possible to argue that Lumley and his rival colleague Frederick Gye were trying to appeal less to the local habitués than to the larger international audience gathered in London for the Exhibition, mostly composed of German and French visitors. Verdi's operas, whose reception on the continent had been controversial, were put aside, while precedence was given to lighter works of little consequence (*Le tre nozze*, *I quattro fratelli*), to some of the best-loved Italian classics, to a few German masterpieces (e.g. Mozart and Beethoven) and to some novelties from the modern French school.

Brief mention of Verdi's role among modern operatic composers was made twice in the columns of *The Times*, once in July when Marietta Alboni appeared in her favourite part as Cenerentola, and a second time one month later, when Marianna Barbieri Nini was introduced to the audience on the occasion of her first appearance in Donizetti's *Lucrezia Borgia* at Her Majesty's Theatre. Both the events were reviewed by the critic of *The Times*, who raised the old issue concerning the contemptible condition of modern singing as opposed to the palmy days in which proper vocalisation was sustained by suitable melodies. Alboni was pronounced "the last of a glorious race, the last legitimate singer of the real Italian style, now on the point of dissolution."[29] The dissolution described by the critic had several causes, the chief of which was "the

---

28 *The Musical World*, March 22, 1851, p. 178.
29 *The Times*, July 14, 1851, p. 8.

dearth of composers, which has made the last quarter of a century the most barren in the history of Italian opera."[30] The usual grumble followed, suggesting that the decadence that led from Rossini to Verdi passed through a generation of scanty imitators only to arrive at a rapid, inevitable conclusion.

> The last great genius, the last great composer, of Italy was Rossini. Bellini was a plaintive echo of his saddest strains—Donizetti a vigorous imitator, in whom everything was found but the "divine fire." Rossini, disgusted at the growing apathy for his works in the land of his birth, went to Paris and composed French operas. He altered his style entirely, and gave the death blow to the true Italian school. This was his revenge for the neglect of those who should have cherished him as their only hope. To Rossini, Bellini, and Donizetti succeeded Verdi. Verdi exhibits all the worst faults of his predecessors, exaggerated one-hundredfold, with none of the genius of Rossini, little of the tenderness of Bellini, and less of the facility and *savoir faire* of Donizetti. Nevertheless, Verdi has his merits— viz., occasional felicity of tune, considerable energy, and a dramatic fire that cannot be denied. But these are not enough to sustain a tottering edifice, rapidly crumbling into dust. The Italian school has seen its best days; its decline is near at hand, and it is doubtful whether anything can restore it. *C'en est fini*. There are no composers, no orchestras no chorus, no librettists in Italy.[31]

On 6 August, the same journal published an account of Marianna Barbieri Nini's impersonation of Lucrezia Borgia. "Madame Barbieri Nini owes much of her fame to the operas of Verdi, for which her style and *physique* eminently befit her,"[32] the critic held. He did not intend to pay her a compliment. However beautiful her voice might have been, the *prima donna* who had premiered the female roles of *I due Foscari* and *Macbeth* had "paid the usual penalty entailed upon the exponents of Verdi's music."[33] As a consequence, her rendition of Lucrezia was devoid of all those graceful, sweet and tender touches which are the very essence and soul of the vocal art, such faults as exaggerated accents and caricature of expression substituting for proper vocalisation.

---

30   *Ibid.*
31   *Ibid.*
32   *The Times*, August 6, 1851, p. 8.
33   *Ibid.*

Occasional mention of Verdi's progress was made by the critic of *The Athenaeum*, when reporting from Italy later on that autumn. Chorley took the opportunity to attend a performance of Verdi's new opera *Rigoletto*, which was given in Rome at the Teatro Argentina under the title of *Viscardello* because of Roman censorship. The libretto of *Viscardello* differed slightly from the original, the dramatic action taking place in Boston, the names of the main characters being changed so as to reflect the new setting: the Duke of Nottingham substituted for the Duke of Mantua and Viascardello for Rigoletto. The main interpreters were Carlo Beaucardè, as Il Duca di Nottingham, Filippo Coletti in the title role, Caterina Evers as Gilda, Nicola Benedetti as Sparafucile.[34] The critic reviewed the performance in the usual negative terms, holding that "the opera is by no means its maker's worst,—if only because it is one of Signor Verdi's least noisy operas."[35] Even though the critic was willing to acknowledge that the instrumentation was in some case appropriate and even delicate, while one or two vocal phrases possessed a boldness and a brio worth remembering, he could not help but conclude his review by declaring that "the staleness and commonplace of every motive is only equalled by its ugliness."[36]

The Musical World gave full coverage to the entire 1851 operatic season and reported in detail on the productions and the personalities involved in either establishment. The critic urged his colleagues to seriously consider the sad condition of English music and musicians, and to look to the French to learn how to promote, support and encourage local talent. On 19 July *Ernani* was announced for performance at Her Majesty's Theatre, featuring Sophie Cruvelli as Elvira and Sims Reeves in the title role. *The Musical World* took this opportunity to celebrate the already much celebrated Cruvelli for her excellent rendition of Elvira; after appearing successfully in Ludwig van Beethoven's *Fidelio*, in Vincenzo Bellini's *Norma* and even in Sigismond Thalberg's dubious

---

34 The other interpreters were Calista Fiorio (Maddalena), Vincenza Marchesi (Giovanna), Francesco Giorgi (Il Conte di Mornard), Ettore Mitterpoch (Marnullo), Mariano Conti (Borsa), Achille Biscossi (Il Conte di Gorin), Francesca Quadri (La Contessa), Giuseppe Bazzoli (Scudiero) and Luigi Fani (Paggio). *Viscardello* (Rome: Tipografia Olivieri, 1851).
35 "Foreign Correspondence—Autumn Music in Rome," *The Athenaeum*, October 18, 1851, p. 1097.
36 *Ibid*.

Florinda, Cruvelli further exhibited her superb vocal skills in Verdi's much-to-be-regretted dramatic music. The critic argued that, having entered the innermost recesses of the musical temple when interpreting Beethoven's music, she had gradually moved out of it and was now satisfied to wave her handkerchief on the steps of the porch. Although Verdi's music was not worthy of the temple, it was thanks to Cruvelli that even those already inside it might consider going out to listen to her. After triumphing in Venice in 1847, in London in 1848 and in Paris in 1851, Cruvelli's *Ernani* was once more triumphing over "the convulsive menaces of Signor Verdi's ill-conditioned muse."[37] Quite similar, if not unanimous judgments made their appearance in the columns of *The Times*, *The Morning Post* and *The Morning Herald*, whose critics all rejoiced in the success of the singer, notwithstanding the poor quality of the music. Verdi never appeared to the critics under so favourable a guise.[38] Though Chorley objected to the way in which Cruvelli misused her vocal skills and sacrificed them to her caprice and vagary.[39]

Quite different a position was expressed by the critic of *The Illustrated London News*, who disagreed with his colleagues and took a more detached, neutral stance with regard to the Italian composer's alleged faults. First of all, *Ernani* had been equally successful over the past five years, notwithstanding the different casts that had performed it. This circumstance seemed to provide solid evidence that the success of the opera was not uniquely dependant on the quality of the performers; instead, the "powerful construction of the concerted pieces" represented its main source of attraction. Although a choir of pedantic detractors had raised their voices against all the shortcomings of Verdi's operas, an equal number of qualities were to be found in them, among them skilful dramatic colouring and sensual beauty. It was true that Verdi neglected the art of pure vocalisation, just as it was true that he favoured the expression of violent contrasts in declamatory phrases on the extreme notes of the register; however, this was exactly what the composer wanted for the sake of dramatic effect, and it was just pointless to continue to abuse him and long for the style of the past.[40]

---

37 Ibid.
38 "Crivelli's Elvira," *The Musical World*, July 26, 1851, p. 466.
39 Chorley, *Thirty Years*, II, p. 143.
40 *The Illustrated London News*, July 26, 1851, p. 114.

Mention of Verdi's music was made again in the columns of *The Times* on 14 April 1852, when the production of Rossini's *L'italiana in Algeri* at Her Majesty's Theatre was reviewed. Verdi's music was called instrumental because it destroyed proper vocalisation, a feature typical of Rossini's music.

> The class of opera to which *L Italiana in Algeri* belongs is almost extinct. No composer of the present day attempts it, and it may safely be added that no composer of the present day, in attempting it, would be likely to succeed. For this there are substantial reasons. Singers are educated now in quite a different fashion from that which prevailed in the days of Cimarosa and Paesiello [sic], and in the early times of Rossini. Verdi and his followers have killed the school, without substituting a better. What is chiefly demanded now in a singer is a powerful voice, and a certain amount of dramatic feeling, armed with which he at once launches into the sea of public life. The consequence is inevitable. The majority of singers are quite abroad in one of Rossini's early operas; they have neither the flexibility nor the style; either their voices are stiff and obstinate from want of the necessary training, or impaired, if not altogether destroyed, by "hallooing and singing," not of anthems, like Falstaff, but of Verdi's *cavatinas* and *finales*. We are much mistaken, however, if, some day, the sort of Italian opera of which the one produced last night is so admirable an example be not restored, and the modern specimens, which have really no style whatever, altogether abandoned. Such a result would be well for all parties—for singers, who wish to preserve as long as possible the quality and freshness of their voices, more especially.[41]

Verdi and Rossini represented two worlds, the second composer having killed the school of which the first had been the unsurpassed champion. The very same article was also published in *The Musical World* a few days later, on 17 April, a circumstance strongly suggestive, once more, of the two journals sharing the same critic.[42] In August, the Royal Italian Opera at Covent Garden revived *Norma* featuring as Pollio the tenor Carlo Negrini, who had made his début as a soloist in 1847 as Jacopo in *I due Foscari*. This circumstance once more offered the critic of *The Musical World* the opportunity to expand on the responsibility of Verdi's music for spoiling the singer's voice.

---

41 *The Times*, April 14, 1852, p. 5.
42 *The Musical World*, April 17, 1852, pp. 243–44.

> His reputation has been chiefly acquired in Verdi's operas; and to this may be attributed the fact of what must originally have been a fine and powerful voice, having already deteriorated in quality [...] In his style of singing Signor Negrini betrays an adhesion to that school which, most successful in the boisterous music of Verdi, is most at fault where real vocal expression and legitimate execution are demanded.[43]

The gap between the Rossinian vocal style and the manner in which Verdi mistreated the voice was definitive and irremediable. Not only did the dramatic power required by Verdi's music represent a threat to the voice, it was also an obstacle for those modern singers who, being trained in the modern style, wished to return to the florid vocal style of the past.

When *Ernani* was produced on 8 May 1852 at Her Majesty's Theatre, further comments appeared in *The Times* concerning the extent to which the quality of the interpretation and the merits of the singers outbalanced the scantiness of the music and the limited talent of the composer, a disequilibrium considered crucial to the success of his operas in London.

> *Ernani* was presented on Saturday, for the first time this season. Although Verdi's best work, it is doubtful whether this opera would so long have retained possession of the stage, in a country where the claims of its composer are less easily recognized than on the continent, but for Mdlle. Sophie Cruvelli, who first appeared at Her Majesty's Theatre, in 1848, in the character of the heroine, of which she has since retained almost exclusive possession. On other occasions when *Ernani* has been attempted it has failed. It may therefore be concluded that the part of Elvira, whatever its abstract musical merits, is well suited to Mdlle. Cruvelli, who enters into it with an enthusiasm which savours of evident predilection. A reasonable cause for this may be assigned in the great success she has achieved in *Ernani, Nabucco, Attila,* and other operas of Verdi, at Venice, Genoa, Milan, &c., and more recently at Paris— complacently regarded by Frenchmen as the arbitress and dispenser of musical reputations. Signor Verdi owes a deep debt of gratitude to Mademoiselle Cruvelli; and it is to be hoped this may not be repaid by the ultimate annihilation of her magnificent voice.[44]

---

43 *The Musical World*, August 14, 1852, p. 517.
44 *The Times*, May 10, 1852, p. 8.

This judgment was not shared by the critic of *The Athenaeum*, who considered Cruvelli's force and passion "the mechanical display made by a young and strong person half educated in her profession and prematurely wearied."[45] Not surprisingly, the critic of *The Musical World* fully shared the idea that, despite the limited merit of the composer, *Ernani* was now cherished by the audience uniquely because of the quality of such interpreters as Sophie Cruvelli.

> Verdi owes a large debt of gratitude to Sophie Cruvelli, who, more than fine chivalric story, and the striking character of the music, has helped to elevate and fix *Ernani* in the public mind. We are not of those who scoff and sneer at the scores of young Verdi, because they contain neither the depth of Mozart and Beethoven, nor the inventiveness of Rossini and Auber. He may be not as clever as Donizetti, nor as melodious as Bellini, nor as dramatic as Meyerbeer, nor as overpowering as Halévy; must it therefore follow that he has no merit whatsoever? Far be it from us to affirm any such thing, although, as our readers must be by this time well aware, we are no great lovers of his music. Still he has strong dramatic feeling, and is by no means devoid of energy and passion. If these sometimes degenerate into rant, it proceeds from exuberance, rather than poverty of conception. Be it as it may, there is enough, and unfortunately more than enough in Verdi's music, to show off the capabilities of singers, and with such an artist as Cruvelli, who combines judgment with power, to very great advantage.[46]

Once more, the critic of *The Illustrated London News* was the only one who advocated the merits of the composer and argued that, notwithstanding all the injurious, offensive and hostile opinions directed towards him, his operas were no less successful now than they had been upon their first production. As to the extent Verdi abused the singers' voice, the critic added, it was not a question of the audience or the critic, but of the singers only.

> Verdi has been most outrageously abused since the first introduction of his works into this country but season after season his operas are reproduced, and we never yet have observed the slightest diminution in the interest and effect created by his dramatic power and colouring. There is not the slightest difficulty in pointing out the vices of his school; but it is against the wholesale condemnation of his productions that we

---

45 *The Athenaeum*, May 22, 1852, p. 586.
46 *The Musical World*, May 15, 1852, pp. 312–13.

have always protested and we must continue to protest. The objection that he strains and ruins the voice is, with due submission, the question of the singers, and not that of the audiences, who frequent the theatre for emotions and sensations, and not for the purpose of deciding whether the upper octave of an *artiste's* register can stand the wear and tear of Verdi's vocal writings.[47]

By the end of 1852, the attitude of the critics had remained largely unaltered, at least in so far as the periodicals taken into consideration are concerned. *The Illustrated London News* was the only journal advocating the merits of the composer, against all those who continued to credit only the interpreters with the success his operas continued to score. One new aspect emerged, regarding the antagonistic figure of Richard Wagner. On 25 December 1852, *The Musical World* reported in full a long article from *The Athenaeum* entitled, quite ironically, "The two new (rush) lights to lighten the darkness of the musical Jesuits at Leipzig." *The Athenaeum* described the way in which neither Schumann nor Wagner (the two lights) could really do much to alleviate the darkness in which German music found itself. While lamenting all the faults and shortcomings exhibited by Wagner's operas the critic went as far as to sigh: "How low must the opera goer be brought when he can think of Verdi with complacency and longing!"[48]

---

47   *The Illustrated London News*, May 15, 1852, p. 398.
48   *The Musical World*, December 25, 1852, p. 822.

7. *Rigoletto* (1853)

On 19 March 1853, the directors of the Royal Italian Opera at Covent Garden announced that the opera season would commence on the 29th of that month even though a prospectus had not yet been issued. On the competition's side, in contrast, financial difficulties had imperilled the future of Her Majesty's Theatre. Its doubtful state held the readers' attention, for rumours circulated that Frederick Gye was considering taking over that operatic establishment too.[1] Similar comments made their appearance in March in the columns of *The Times* and *The Athenaeum*, each journal calling the public's attention to the sense of uncertainty and hesitation that the long wait for news had aroused. Eventually, *The Observer* announced that three people had been entrusted with the management of Her Majesty's Theatre: "Mr Nugent, former superintendent of the theatre; Mr Robinson, the late treasurer of the establishment; and Signor Puzzi, the negotiator of engagements with foreign *artistes*, and the caterer of novelites for the theatre for many years."[2] Although there was every reason to believe that the theatre would open in May, this promise remained unfulfilled. Between 1853 and 1856, Her Majesty's Theatre was closed.

The ante-Easter season having passed in silence, on 26 March *The Musical World* informed its readers that the long awaited programme of the Royal Italian Opera at Covent Garden had finally been issued. Gye announced six new operas complementing the regular repertoire: Louis Spohr's *Jessonda*, Verdi's *Rigoletto*, Rossini's *Matilda di Shabran*, Donizetti's *Dom Sébastien* (as Don Sebastian), Vincenzo Bonetti's *Juana*

---

1 *The Musical World*, March 26, 1853, p. 187.
2 *Ibid.*, p. 189.

Shore and Hector Berlioz's *Benvenuto Cellini*. A few words were spent on Berlioz's grand opera and its past fortunes, while nothing could be said of *Rigoletto*, the opera being completely new to both the London public and the critic.³

The season opened with Daniel Auber's *Masaniello* on 2 April, featuring Enrico Tamberlik, Karl Formes and Castellan; stock operas like *Il barbiere di Siviglia*, *L'elisir d'amore*, and *Guillaume Tell* (as *Guglielmo Tell*) followed soon afterwards. On 23 April, it was announced that *Rigoletto* was in rehearsal, and the first performance would take place on 14 May, featuring Angiolina Bosio as Gilda, Mario as Duke of Mantua, Ronconi as Rigoletto, Joseph Tagliafico as Sparafucile and Constance Nantier-Didiée as Maddalena. On the same day of the premiere, a short article was published in the columns of *The Musical World*, announcing Verdi's new opera and hinting at the quality of the interpreters as an easy predictor of its imminent success: "Mario and Ronconi together would render less interesting music than that of Verdi more than tolerable."⁴ However bad the music might be, with such a good cast the opera would easily fulfil the public's (and the critic's) highest expectations. All the more so if the cast included such valued representatives of the old guard as Mario and Ronconi. In the same issue a scornful, derisive caricature of Verdi made its appearance.

> How Verdi Composes. When Verdi has an opera to compose, he waits patiently until the midnight bell has tolled. He then enters his study, in which there is a piano placed between a big drum and cymbals, and seating himself at the piano, he first bangs the drum on the right hand, then crashes the cymbals on the left hand, then thumps the piano in the midst, and while the air is reverberating with the mingled sounds, he commences the first chorus. This is the way Verdi composes. Can anybody have a doubt on the subject?⁵

Although the opera was pronounced a brilliant popular success, the most conservative critics raised the usual objections: it had been warmly welcomed thanks to the splendid interpreters and notwithstanding the poor quality of the music.

---

3   *Ibid.*, p. 187.
4   *The Musical World*, May 14, 1853, p. 305.
5   *Ibid.*

The critic of *The Times* uttered words of deep disappointment and considered Verdi's lack of melodic invention especially evident. In referring to what commentators had been saying on the continent about Verdi entering a second stage of his compositional career and developing a more mature style, the critic held that no sign of advancement could really be found.[6] The only audible difference consisted in the composer neither overloading the music with trombones and drums nor terminating each act with the usual choirs singing in unison. In a way, *Rigoletto* was not even equal to Verdi's previous works, for while in *Ernani* and *Nabucco* it was easy to find stirring melodies, the same could not be said of *Rigoletto*. Again, if possible, the last opera was pronounced the worst.

> In aiming at simplicity, Signor Verdi has hit frivolity. In other operas he has often, with a certain degree of success hidden poverty of idea under a pompous display of instruments; but in the present, abandoning that artifice, and relying upon the strength of his melodic invention, he has triumphantly demonstrated that he has very few ideas that can be pronounced original. In short, with one exception (*Luisa Miller*), *Rigoletto* is the most feeble opera of Signor Verdi with which we have the advantage to be acquainted, the most uninspired, the barest, and the most destitute of ingenious contrivance. To enter into an analysis would be a loss of time and space.[7]

While writing a more detailed analysis of the music would have been a complete waste of time and energy, words of appreciation were generously bestowed upon the interpreters. Ronconi mastered the part of Rigoletto in such a way as to make one regret "that so masterly a performance should occur in an opera which has so little chance of keeping the stage in England."[8] Similar remarks praised Mario's performance as the Duke, whose first aria "Questa o quella" pleased the audience on account of the voice and *abandon* with which the singer invested it and notwithstanding its low musical merit. Despite the poor quality of the melody, both "La donna è mobile" and the quartet "Bella figlia dell'amore" were encored. Madame Bosio's brilliant rendition of Gilda also pleased, although the music allotted to her was "more

---

6 See A. Basevi, *Studio sulle opere di Giuseppe Verdi* (Florence: Tofani, 1859), pp. 156–59.
7 *The Times*, May 16, 1853, p. 8.
8 *Ibid*.

difficult than grateful." In his conclusion the critic could not help but acknowledge the popular success of the opera; however, he insisted that although it had been warmly welcomed by the audience, *Rigoletto* would not last long.

> If encores and recalls of the principal Singers may be taken as an indication of success, *Rigoletto* should be pronounced successful. Unfortunately, however, such conventional compliments no longer signify anything more than good feeling on the part of the audience. We shall be agreeably disappointed, nevertheless, if *Rigoletto* turns out to be an attractive opera, and shall have pleasure in owning that our first impression was a mistaken one.[9]

The same prophetic remark concludes the review that appeared in *The Musical World* on 21 May 1853, where the critic predicted a short and ephemeral life for the opera on account of its poor music and in spite of the highly spirited skills of the interpreters, Ronconi and Mario. "It may flicker and flare for a few nights, fed from the oil of Ronconi's genius, and blown into momentary vitality by the soft breathing of Mario's voice; but it will go out like an ill-wicked rush light, and leave not a spark behind. Such is our prophecy of *Rigoletto*."[10]

Interestingly, the critic failed to articulate the usual hostile attitude to Verdi. Notwithstanding the customary objections to the music, which was characterised by "poverty of ideas, and eternal effort at originality — never accomplished, strange and odd phrases, lack of colouring, and a perpetual swagger in the dramatic effects,"[11] he expressed himself in quite positive, encouraging terms. *Rigoletto* was pronounced inferior to *Ernani*, *I due Foscari* and *Nabucco*, but certainly superior to *I masnadieri*, *I Lombardi* and even to *Macbeth* and *Luisa Miller*, the last two as yet unperformed in London. *Rigoletto*'s music was less offensive to the ear, less loud; it contained melodies capable of charming the general public and airs not entirely devoid of genuine merit. The *canzone* of the Duke of Mantova was pronounced "a very pleasing and catching tune, if not new, and worked out with effect."[12] The aria of Gilda and the duet were agreeable, while the quartet in the last act was said to

---

9   Ibid.
10 *The Musical World*, May 21, 1853, p. 326.
11 Ibid.
12 Ibid.

be "skilfully managed and well voiced," a compliment the critic had never paid to Verdi's music before. Thanks to the wonderful cast, the magnificent scenery and the strong, dramatic plot, the opera had gained a considerable reputation not only on the continent but also in London, where the public had shown clear signs of appreciation. Yet even though *Rigoletto* had scored an undeniable success, the critic was still not inclined to credit the composer with its triumph; instead, he suggested that its celebrity would not be long-lasting. The immediate popularity of *Rigoletto*, however, was confirmed by the fact that the publishers of the score—London, Boosey & Sons—were besieged daily by customers wanting to purchase the piano version of "La donna è mobile," forcing the critic of *The Musical World* to admit that the composer had at least managed one captivating aria.[13]

According to Henry Davison, the son of James William Davison and the compiler of his memoirs, some of the reasons for his father's new lenience towards Verdi lie in events preceding the London premiere of *Rigoletto* by three years. In 1851 Richard Wagner circulated a "communication"[14] to his friends in which he traced the development of his dramatic and musical ideas and expressed his desire to sweep away "a mass of art-encumbering rubbish."[15] This communication triggered a series of strong reactions in England. While some of the most progressive composers saw in Wagner's theories an incentive to pursue their own innovative ideas and their urge for novelty and originality, the most conservative critics considered Wagner's attitude disrespectful and felt threatened by his aggressive claims. One year later, on 23 September 1852, the oratorio *Jerusalem* was performed at the Norwich Festival. Its author was Henry Pierson, a young British composer who, having studied in Germany, was condemned as a mere parasite of the Wagnerian school, even though it was not easy to trace in

---

13 *The Musical World*, May 28, 1953, p. 335.
14 Richard Wagner, "Eine Mittheilung an meine Freunde" (1851) in *Sämtliche Schriften und Dichtungen*, 4: 230–344; English translation by William Ashton Ellis, "A Communication to My Friends," in *Richard Wagner's Prose Works* (London: Kegan Paul, Trench & Trübner, 1895), 1: 267.
15 Henry Davison, *Music During the Victorian Era. From Mendelssohn to Wagner: Being the Memoirs of J. W. Davison, Forty Years Music Critic of "The Times"* (London: Reeves, 1912), p. 139.

his music any affinity with the Bayreuth composer.[16] On that occasion, Davison's conservative inclination prompted him to pronounce Pierson as an admirer of Schumann and a young composer too dangerously influenced by Wagner's false idol. Pierson was a member of the "word-painting" school, something much to be regretted in so talented a musician.[17] Davison's conservatism found in Wagner and Schumann a new source of concern and apprehension; this would turn out to be beneficial to the image of those composers who, like Verdi, appeared less threatening on account of a higher degree of familiarity with their compositional achievements and their complete lack of theoretical formulations.

The critic of *The Athenaeum* shared his colleagues' view with regard to *Rigoletto* and held that the new opera owed its success to any number of reasons apart from the quality of its music.

> But should *Rigoletto* keep our stage for a time, we think that it will be owing partly to the strength of the cast, and the scope afforded by the principal part to Signor Ronconi's acting,—partly to the craft of Mr. Beverley, who made in it his *début* as scene-painter to Covent Garden, and who has produced a pair of night pictures, the first of which is effectively original, the second deliciously beautiful,—partly because the story proves delightful to English play-goers of fashion.[18]

The critic remarked that the peculiarly horrific quality of the plot, as Victor Hugo had conceived it, played an important role in attracting the English public since it appealed to the recent morbid inclination of their imagination. The critic performed the usual fault-finding with Verdi: the composer lacked genuine ideas and skills, especially when called upon to devise proper melodies and sustain them with the appropriate instrumentation. "The music of combination and dramatic action, again, is puerile and queer:—odd modulations being perpetually wrenched out with the vain hope of disguising the intrinsic meagreness of the ideas,—and flutes being used for violins, or *vice versa*, apparently not

---

16 Rosa Harriet Newmarch, "Henry Hugo Pierson" in *Dictionary of National Biography, 1885–1900*, vol. 45, available at Wikisource at https://en.wikisource.org/wiki/Pierson,_Henry_Hugo_(DNB00)

17 *The Times*, September 24, 1852, p. 8. See also Meirion Hughes, *The English Musical Renaissance*, pp. 14–20.

18 "Royal Italian Opera," *The Athenaeum*, May 21, 1853, p. 625.

to charm the hearer, but to make him stare."[19] A different opinion was expressed with regard to the quartet "Bella Figlia," which was deservedly applauded and encored. The critic described it as a gem "founded on a melodious phrase, with clever grouping and neat contrast of the voices,—in which the climax is naturally wrought up, and by which are excited those genial sensations of pleasure which admit of no doubts, and require neither proof nor apology."[20] To our surprise, Chorley was overtly appreciative of the melodious inventiveness that the composer brought to the final quartet; this great achievement should have helped Verdi understand that "thought is not antagonistic to beauty—nor dramatic effect to musical symmetry."[21]

The *Illustrated London News* introduced Verdi's new opera and elaborated on the manner in which his music had been reviewed by most of the London press in quite sardonic terms. While the composer received continuous reprimands from the critics and his name was pronounced as doomed to disappear from the repertoire, his works continued to be successful among the English audience. The reviewer could "recognize in *Rigoletto* a higher order of beauty than struck us even in *Ernani* and the *Due Foscari*, and an abandonment, at the same time, of his most palpable defects. *Rigoletto* cannot be ranked, however, as a masterpiece; it is full of plagiarism and faults, and yet abounds with the most captivating music."[22] The question concerning a second, more mature style was not raised by the critic who rather claimed that although Verdi had not improved in terms of musical construction, he had "skilfully blended with the Italian school the loftiness of declamation and the piquancy of orchestration of the French masters."[23] In the end, the choice of horrific subject matter was not that objectionable, since the general public loved to be ravished by the dramatic power of a plot. It was not so different to the way in which they enjoyed Shakespeare's *Othello* on the dramatic stage. Not a single word was uttered to express regret or complaint for the manner in which the singers' voices were misused or abused. The declamatory style preferred by Verdi when

---

19   Ibid.
20   Ibid.
21   Ibid.
22   *The Illustrated London News*, May 21, 1853, p. 399.
23   Ibid.

called upon to illustrate the dramatic situations of the libretto was particularly congenial to an actor-singer as good as Ronconi, who was particularly esteemed by both the public and the critic. Everything in the performance was a success, notwithstanding the castigating criticisms of the pedants.

The critic of *The Spectator*, having noticed a certain degree of novelty in the music of *Rigoletto*, made no attempt to draw broader generalisations regarding Verdi's alleged new style.

> In the composition of the music, Verdi, like Donizetti in his latest works, has adopted a more solid and operose style than was usual to him; but he has gained in art and elaboration at the expense of freshness. His concerted pieces are more ingeniously wrought, and in his instrumentation he depends less on mere physical strength of sound, than formerly; but in this opera we do not find those simple and natural airs which, in spite of their triteness, give a charm to the *Lombardi* and to *Ernani*.[24]

In London, the opera was received quite warmly thanks to the singers and despite the music but, the critic predicted, its greater success would remain confined to Italy.

In June *Ernani* was revived, followed by Berlioz's *Benvenuto Cellini* and a good number of stock operas: *Les Huguenots*, *Guillaume Tell* (*Guglielmo Tell*), *Don Giovanni*, *Robert le diable* (*Roberto il diavolo*), *Maria di Rohan*, *I puritani*, *Le prophète*, *La favorite* (*La favorita*), *Jessonda*. In August *The Musical World* published a long review of the entire opera season in which its judgment on *Rigoletto* was reiterated. Despite the absurdity of the libretto and notwithstanding the poor quality of the music, the opera had recorded a genuine success thanks to the powerful cast and the manner in which it was staged.

> In short, the true verdict is no more nor less than that Mario, Ronconi, Bosio, Nantier Didée, Tagliafico, Polonini (the old nobleman who curses Rigoletto), Beverley, Costa, orchestra, and chorus, by a very perfect and effective combination of talents succeeded in gaining several favourable hearings for an opera of no great merit, with a drama which, though not devoid of interest, is absurd, and music which, beyond a few pretty

---

24 *The Spectator*, May 21, 1853, p. 8.

tunes, a certain degree of fluency, and one very good quartet, contains really nothing to be praised.[25]

It is quite remarkable that, with the one exception noted before, none of the critics taken into consideration seem to have been concerned about the way in which their continental colleagues had recently conceptualised Verdi's second style. A couple of circumstances regarding the chronology of Verdi's operas in England clarifies how such a meaningful transformation passed unnoticed among the English critics. As Abramo Basevi pointed out in 1859, it was with *Luisa Miller* that Verdi began to show unequivocal signs of change. In his analysis, the Italian critic pointed out that Verdi's first manner—*prima maniera*—was characterised by a certain feeling for the grandiose and the passionate, this last component having led to a general exaggeration of the dramatic sentiment both in the voice and in the orchestra. The voice was used with *slancio* (élan), a particularly energetic impulse to which the traditional notion of melodiousness was sacrificed, while the orchestra was enriched and made particularly loud by an extensive use of the recently developed brass instruments. In Verdi's second manner—*seconda maniera*—the passionate and the grandiose made room for a more moderate, intimate form of expression, with nicer tunes, more gentle sonorities, less passionate singing. Basevi acknowledged that *Luisa Miller* was not only the least noisy of Verdi's operas so far, but also the most skilfully orchestrated.[26]

Similar remarks can be found in the French press, where the issue of Verdi's second phase was raised as soon as *Luisa Miller* was performed. Verdi's *melodrama tragico*, based on Schiller's *Kabale und Liebe*, was premiered in Paris, at the Salle Ventadour du Théâtre-Italien, on 7 December 1852, featuring Sophie Cruvelli in the main role, Constance Nantier-Didiée as Federica Ostheim and Laura, Jémérie Bettini as Rodolfo, and then Ignazio Valli, Fortini and De Susini. The composer himself conducted and the opera was pronounced a success, at least in popular terms; on 19 December the critic of *Le Menestrel* argued that, despite all that had been said about Verdi's new style, it was clear that the composer had simply learned to conform to the dramatic subject.

---

25 *The Musical World,* August 27, 1853, p. 544.
26 Basevi, *Giuseppe Verdi,* p. 157.

> On a dit et répété, à propos de cette partition, qu'elle signalait une transformation complète dans le faire du maître, qu'elle était le point de départ d'une voie nouvelle où il fallait s'engager; il y a, ce me semble, erreur ou du moins confusion dans ce jugement. Verdi n'a pas fait chanter, il est vrai, la petite Luisa comme la superbe Abigaïl; il n'a pu prêter au bonhomme Miller les accents qu'il a mis dans la bouche du doge Foscari; non, sans doute; mais, en cela, il s'est tout simplement conformé à la nature de son sujet; après avoir traité presque exclusivement des drames pompeux et héroïques, il aborde une action bourgeoise; nécessairement et naturellement son pinceau doit recourir plus souvent aux tons simples, naïfs ou gracieux; mais, encore une fois, ce n'est pas là un changement de manière; dans *Luisa*, comme dans les précédents ouvrages, nous retrouvons Verdi tout entier, avec ses qualités, avec ses défauts; avec une propension trop marquée au bruit, aux effets violents; avec des ravissantes et originales mélodies; avec le don précieux de faire vibrer la fibre, et de porter la pathétique au plus haut degré.[27]

Occasional remarks concerning the same issue made their appearance in the following months, the French press being divided in two groups: those who supported Verdi's work and valued the dramatic expression typical of the composer on the one hand, and those who proclaimed him devoid of any true musical talent on the other.

It can be argued that the discussion concerning the composer's second manner, which the performance of *Luisa Miller* had occasioned in Italy and in Paris, did not affect the English press because it was not until 1858 that *Luisa* was produced in London. As previously mentioned,

---

27 "It has been said again and again, on the subject of this score, that it signalled a complete transformation in the master's work, that it was the point of departure for a new way on which it was necessary to embark; there is, it seems to me, error or at least confusion in this judgment. Verdi did not make the little Luisa sing like the superb Abigaïl, it is true; he was unable to lend to the regular guy Miller the accents he put in the mouth of the doge Foscari; no, without doubt; but in that, he merely conformed to the nature of his subject; after having dealt almost exclusively with bombastic and heroic dramas, he is taking on a bourgeois topic; necessarily and naturally, his brush must have more frequent recourse to simple, naïve, or graceful tones; but, again, this is not a change of style; in *Luisa*, as in his previous works, we find again the complete Verdi, with his qualities, with his defects; with a too-marked propensity for no se, for violent effects; with ravishing and original melodies; with the precious gift to make the fibres vibrate, and to raise the pathetic to the highest register." *Le Menestrel*, December 19, 1852, in Hervé Gartioux, *La reception de Verdi en France, Anthologie de la presse 1845–1894* (Weinsberg: Galland, 2001), p. 146.

in 1853 only very feeble echo can be found in the London press of the debate concerning the extent to which Verdi was either progressing towards a new style or simply conforming to the quality of the librettos he was now setting to music.

On 22 October 1853, a few months after *Rigoletto* had premiered at Covent Garden, *The Athenaeum* published a letter from a correspondent who had attended the performance of *Il trovatore* in Florence. The correspondent apologised for his "crudities" with regard to a performance that would have demanded "more critical experience, musical knowledge and presence of mind" than he possessed in order to form anything like a final judgment. Nevertheless, the writer addressed some relevant issues concerning the overall value of the new work.

> I suppose it is unnecessary to state that the opera is by Verdi and equally unnecessary to add that everything that mechanical musical skill can effect has been pressed into his service to supply the place of spontaneous melody and originality. Various tricks of odd keys, and out-of-the-way rhythms are made use of with some success to judge from the applause with which they are received.[28]

The correspondent pronounced *Il trovatore* a great popular success, if the yelling and howling that accompanied the performance were to be understood signs of pleasure and appreciation on the part of the natives, even though, in his eyes, they were more reminiscent of a riot over a contested election. The value of both the libretto and the music was arguable but, the correspondent held, the opera deserved some attention. "You will gather from any description that the whole thing, book and music, is too fragmentary to be an artistic work:—but there is a good deal of interest and more charm in the music, to my thinking, than is usual with Verdi."[29] Again, no mention was made of the recent development in Verdi's compositional work, only an increase in charm and the usual faults.

One year later *Rigoletto* was produced again at Covent Garden, where it scored a second popular success. On 20 May a crowded audience attended its performance, featuring the same cast as the previous year

---

28 "Verdi's *Il Trovatore*," *The Athenaeum*, October 22, 1853, p. 1263.
29 Ibid.

(Ronconi, Mario, Bosio, Nantier-Didiée and Tagliafico). The critic of *The Times* pronounced the opera a popular success but, not surprisingly, ascribed its triumph solely to the merits of the interpreters and the spectacular scenery. This time the critic agreed with his French colleague from *Le Menestrel* about the supposed second style and argued that Verdi had changed his manner only "inasmuch as he has declined every opportunity offered by the situations of Victor Hugo's monstrous but by no means uninteresting drama for constructing elaborate concerted pieces and grand *finales*, and in a great measure eschewed the perpetual noise of brass instruments and obstreperous unisons which characterise the majority of his operas."[30] The critic was also bound to admit that *Rigoletto* would probably remain "a fixture in the repertoire" for some time, for the appreciation shown by the general public was unequivocal, and the approving fiat of the subscribers overruled the judgment of the critics.

While little or no attention was paid to *Rigoletto* in the columns of *The Athenaeum*, the critic of *The Musical World* contented himself with a brief description of the way in which the opera was perfectly cast and powerfully performed, such pieces as "La donna è mobile" or the quartet "Bella figlia dell'amore" being welcomed with a hurricane of applause and then encored.[31] Instead of focusing on Verdi, Davison indulged in a number of lengthy articles detailing the sad state of English music; he advocated the cause of native composers and revived the idea that they should club together, rent the Drury Theatre and organise a true, genuine English opera season.[32] The object in founding an English National Opera was, he argued, to have the works of native composers brought before the English public in the proper style. The scheme did not exclude the possibility of foreign singers participating, but it should not rely on the star-system, for this had already proved fragile and ephemeral. On 20 May, a reader replied to the editor with a long letter sent under the pseudonym of Fiddlestick. He protested quite strongly against the complaints the editor had been uttering on behalf of English musicians, and argued against the idea that foreign music exerted a detrimental influence on the English public. On the contrary,

---

30 *The Times*, May 22, 1854, p. 11.
31 *The Musical World*, May 27, 1854, p. 357.
32 *The Musical World*, May 13, 1854, pp. 316–17.

Italian music had played a special role in pushing local musical drama towards a salutary change and in raising the English public's taste.[33] The picture was not as gloomy and desperate as the editor of *The Musical World* was trying to suggest. Thus a few voices arose that, in expressing their dissent, reveal the extent to which the urge for a national opera was less a shared concern than an individual obsession.

During the 1854 opera season at Covent Garden, alongside the usual stock operas, six works were promised which had never been performed there before: *Oberon, La vestale, Le domino noir* (as *Il Domino Nero*), *Dom Sébastien* (as *Don Sebastian*), *Matilda di Shabran* and *Don Pasquale*. However, only three were finally brought before the public. The season opened on 1 April with Rossini's *Guillaume Tell*, while on 18 April Rossini's comic opera *Matilda di Shabran* was revived, having been shelved for more than 20 years. The critic of *The Times* pronounced the opera the "only one among many instances in which the composer was compelled to derive his inspirations from a jumble of incongruous absurdities,"[34] and took the opportunity to grumble about the way in which the real Italian school of florid singing style had been sadly abandoned by the new generation of composers.

> The music of *Matilda di Shabran* belongs to a school of which there are not many accomplished followers extant. The real Italian *bravura* and the real Italian florid style ceased to exist when Rossini ceased to write for the Italian theatres. The French school of declamation and the ranting system of Verdi and his disciples have usurped its place—whether for the real benefit of the vocal art is a matter for consideration. In the old Italian opera, serious as well as comic, the drama was of no consequence; the music was the chief thing; and until Rossini came the singers were even of more importance than the music. Rossini brought the school to perfection, since he made the singer's display quite as effective as his predecessors, without sacrificing the highest aims of art. Even in *Matilda di Shabran*, one of his highest and most *ad captandum* operas, this is apparent. Without going into detail, the various concerted pieces, so well planned, and in some cases so elaborate and amply developed, are a proof of this. The introduction, the quintet, and the *finale* to the first act (which, by the way, is quite long enough to be divided into two) have

---

33 *The Musical World*, May 20, 1854, pp. 337–38.
34 *The Times*, August 15, 1854, p. 9.

more in them alone of musical idea and musical contrivance than is to be found in half the operas that have recently obtained a standing.[35]

Donizetti's *L'elisir d'amore* was produced on 25 April, followed by Rossini's *Otello* and *Il barbiere di Siviglia*, Beethoven's *Fidelio*, Mozart's *Don Giovanni*, Bellini's *I puritani*, and Verdi's *Rigoletto*, *Norma*, *Lucrezia Borgia*, *Les Huguenots*, *Don Pasquale* and *La favorite* (as *La favorita*). In his final account of the entire opera season, the critic of *The Times* insisted that *Rigoletto* had been particularly cherished by the public, especially on account of the famous quartet.

> We have nothing new to say about this opera, which seems to grow upon the public, except that it contains some of Verdi's most animated music, and has supplied the *orgue de Barbarie* with a tune, in "La donna è mobile," which is retained as soon as it is heard, and, whatever its merit as an original melody, has, somehow or other, acquired universal popularity among the ladies.[36]

In general, the critic did not declare himself entirely dissatisfied, and he pronounced the season not at all unsatisfactory, for even though not all the novelties promised at its commencement had arrived, a strong cast and the appearance of Sophie Cruvelli had secured a large and undeniable success.

---

35 *The Times*, April 19, 1854, p. 7.
36 *The Times*, August 15, 1854, p. 9.

8. *Il trovatore* (1855)

No sooner had 1855 begun than the critic of *The Musical World* engaged in a discussion that challenged his readers and called attention to the works and writings of Richard Wagner. Wagner had been recently invited to succeed Michael Costa as conductor at the Philharmonic Society, and his arrival was imminent. All of musical Europe had reacted badly to his *Judenthum in der Musik*, in which he pronounced the music of Meyerbeer and Mendelssohn a sham; wherever the names of these composers were respected, as a result, Wagner might expect many fierce and vindictive enemies, eager to counterattack. Chorley and Davison, who continued to favour Mendelssohn and value his classical composure, were ready to fight back.[1]

The issue of which conductor would lead the philharmonic concerts resonated in the columns of *The Musical World*, for already in January rumour had it that a decision was almost ready. Hector Berlioz was taken into consideration, but he had already given his word to Henry Wylde, co-founder of the New Philharmonic Society, to appear as conductor of that Society, a circumstance that would prevent him from appearing as the conductor of competing philharmonic concerts. Then Peter von Lindpaintner was asked, but the King of Wurtemburg refused to give him so protracted a leave of absence; Charles Lucas, William Sterndale Bennett, Robert Schumann, Franz Paul Lachner and Ferdinand Hiller were also considered among the possible candidates, but unsuccessfully. In the end, the name of Richard Wagner was announced, "the musician earnestly bent on upsetting all the accepted forms and canons of art,

---

1 Reginald Nettel, *The Orchestra in England, A Social History* (London: Cape, 1948), pp. 183–89.

[…] in order the more surely to establish his doctrines that rhythm is superfluous, counterpoint a useless bore, and every musician ancient or modern, himself excepted, either an impostor or a blockhead."[2] On 20 January it was reported that, according to the latest intelligence, one of the directors of the Philharmonic Society had gone to Zürich to engage the composer of *Tannhäuser* and secure his services for the ensuing season. This information is confirmed in a couple of letters from Wagner to Liszt, both written in January 1855.[3] The agreement reached, on 10 February *The Musical World* took the opportunity to introduce the German composer and conductor to its readers and anticipate the nature of the battle that was to commence.

> Now that the period of Richard Wagner's arrival approaches, it is well for Philharmonic subscribers to make themselves thoroughly acquainted with his art-doctrine, in order that they may easier comprehend his hidden meanings, and appreciate the subtler beauties of his compositions. We shall aid them to the best of our ability, by expounding, on fit occasions, whatever we have the wit to fathom. Our "line," however, not being interminable, there are likely to be many soundings too deep for us to "make"—like Bottom's dream, in Shakespeare, so called because it had "no bottom." In such cases we shall appeal to those, who, having engaged Herr Wagner as Conductor of the Philharmonic Concerts, must be well versed in his philosophy, and steeped by anticipation in the "music of the future."[4]

The tone clearly reveals a vein of sarcasm towards those who, having selected the most troublesome of German conductors, were certainly not sufficiently qualified to extricate themselves from the musical-dramatic entanglement presented by Wagner's theories. The critic begged the directors of the Philharmonic Society to make the composer's esoteric ideas comprehensible and, should they fail to accomplish such a challenging task, suggested the additional service of Dr Franz Liszt, whose efforts to support Wagner and evangelise the crowds were also ridiculed. At Weimar Liszt, who was said to be anxious to hold the torch

---

2   *The Musical World*, January 20, 1855, p. 41.
3   The first letter, although not dated was written presumably in the early weeks of 1855; the second was written on 19 January 1855. Francis Hueffer, *Half a Century of Music in England, 1837–1887. Essays Towards a History* (London: Chapman and Hall, 1889), pp. 43–45.
4   "Reactionary Letters," *The Musical World*, February 10, 1855, pp. 88–89.

"by which the Gospel of St. Richard may be revealed," was certainly willing "to do for Wagner what Proclus did for Plato, Taylor for Aristotle, and St. Thomas Aquinas for the Immaculate Conception."[5] Wagner the messiah needed apostles to enlighten the uninitiated.

Wagner arrived in London on 4 March 1855 and was to conduct eight concerts on the following days: 12 and 26 March, 16 and 30 April, 14 and 28 May, 11 and 25 June. It is unsurprising, therefore, that at the same time a number of articles made their appearance in the columns of *The Musical World*, and raised the issue of Wagner's music and theories.[6] Long before either *Tannhäuser* or *Lohengrin* could be properly performed and listened to in London,[7] the composer was pronounced contemptuous of everybody but himself, devoid of any technical skill and deficient in the treatment of both the orchestra and the voice.[8] Despite the acrimonious attitude exhibited by the editor, however, Wagner was not denied space in the columns of *The Musical World*, and on 24 March his long introductory text to Beethoven's Choral Symphony was published. The editor referred to this text as "an interesting rhapsody," by which he did not intend to pay him a compliment.[9] A few days later, a review of the second concert of the Philharmonic Society (26 March), which included some select pages from *Lohengrin* (Prelude, Procession to the Minster, Wedding March and Bridal Chorus), appeared in the journal's columns and confirmed its scepticism with regard to Wagner's music. Terms such as mysterious, incoherent, abstruse and tone-defying were pronounced, especially to describe the manner in which Wagner seemed to defy the traditional notions of key and key-relation.[10]

Later reviews of the same concert appeared in the columns of *The Musical World*, reproducing what other critics had reported. *The*

---

5 Ibid.
6 Anne Dzamba Sessa, *Richard Wagner and the English* (London: Associated University Press, 1979), p. 18.
7 The first public performance in England of a Wagner composition appears to have been by the Amateur Musical Society on 10 April 1854, when the March from *Tannhäuser* was performed. "Wagner's Music in England," *The Musical Times*, September 1, 1906, p. 589.
8 *The Musical World*, February 17, 1855, p. 99. Since January 1855 a long series of reflections on Wagner's alleged virtues were published in the columns of *The Musical World* under the title "Reactionary Letters."
9 *The Musical World*, March 31, 1855, pp. 177–79.
10 *The Musical World*, March 24, 1855, pp. 200–301.

Spectator pronounced Wagner a conductor capable of holding the orchestra in his hands and realising any desired expressive nuance, in terms of both timing and dynamics. As a dramatic composer, however, the critic declared Wagner different from what he had been led to expect; he was neither obscure nor extravagant, but rather broad and clear, conventional in the treatment of the form and by no means new in melodic invention.[11] The critic of *The Morning Post* shared with his colleague from *The Spectator* a sense of disappointment, for while the theories presented in Wagner's *Das Kunstwerk der Zukunft* were worth the critic's respectful attention, his music, at least as far as the recently performed selection from *Lohengrin* was concerned, showed "no marked individuality of style in the score, no epoch-making innovations, such as the very original literary works of the composer had taught us to look for."[12] For his part, and not surprisingly, Chorley was much less lenient towards Wagner, whom he criticised strongly for a good number of shortcomings. To start with, the conductor had allowed himself to "finish up" Mendelssohn's music and withdraw the *ripieni* instruments from the solos in his Violin Concerto, Henry Blagrove being the soloist. The instrumentation of his own music was particularly objectionable, for Wagner's acute fancies of scoring gave more pain than pleasure; his melodic invention was poor and his music commonplace.[13]

One week later *The Musical World* started publishing the libretto of *Lohengrin* in its columns, to which *Oper und Drama*, translated expressly for that journal, was added on 19 May, thus providing readers with further and more in-depth access to Wagner's theories. In the meantime the season at the Royal Italian Opera commenced on 12 April with Rossini's *Le comte Ory* (as *Il conte Ory*). *Ernani* followed at the end of the month and was repeated three times.[14] While not a single word was uttered on the performance of Verdi's *Ernani*, the third concert of the Philharmonic Society was carefully reviewed and Wagner's conducting was pronounced ' unsatisfactory, full of fits and starts, not always intelligible, sometimes leading to new effects and good effects,

---

11   The opinion appeared in *The Spectator* was also reproduced in *The Musical World*, April 7, 1855, pp. 211–12.
12   *The Musical World*, April 28, 1855, pp. 268–69.
13   *The Musical World*, April 7, 1855, pp. 211–12.
14   *The Musical World*, May 5, 1855, p. 283.

but generally incoherent."[15] The critic disliked the manner in which Wagner invariably took all the second subjects of the symphonic works at a slower pace than the first, and the extent to which *crescendi* and *rallentandi* were abused by the conductor at the expense of the general balance. Despite this, the public was enthusiastic and some of the works were even encored. A further note of regret concerning Wagner's musical art as well as his conducting skills made its appearance in the columns of *The Sunday Times*, whose critic had taken some time to peruse two songs from *Lohengrin* and pronounce his verdict.

> We may not have secured the key to this great music-mystery, or we may be in that state of invincible ignorance impolitely termed obstinacy; but, be it as it may, we are, on the evidence before us, forced to adopt one of two conclusions—either Richard Wagner is a desperate charlatan, endowed with wordly skill and vigorous purpose enough to persuade a gaping crowd that the nauseous compound he manufactures has some precious inner virtue, that they must live and ponder yet more ere they perceive; or else he is a self-deceived enthusiast, who thoroughly believes his own apostolic mission, and is too utterly destitute of any perception of musical beauty to recognise the worthlessness of his credentials.[16]

A detailed analysis of the music in question followed, in which the critic elaborated further on the numerous "stupid and unmeaning oddities" contained in the score. The article concluded with a couple of reflections on the way in which a charlatan composer such as Wagner was harmful to the English nation, in that his music had been imposed on the public so as to mystify them and "still more to divert their attention from the just claims of their artist-countrymen."[17] Speaking of him as a conductor, the critic held that there was little need for him in London, for at least half a dozen Englishmen would have done better: Wagner represented a real threat to the English music. A later review appeared in *The Sunday Times* and called attention to the extreme liberties Wagner took when conducting Beethoven.

> Firstly he takes all quick movements faster than anybody else; secondly he takes all slow movements slower than anybody else; thirdly he

---

15 *Ibid.*
16 "Two Songs by Richard Wagner," *The Sunday Times*, reproduced in *The Musical World*, May 12, 1855, pp. 290–91.
17 *Ibid.*

prefaces the entry of an important point, or the return of a theme—especially in a slow movement—by an exaggerated ritardando; and fourthly, he reduces the speed of an allegro—say in an overture or the first movement—fully one-third, immediately on the entrance of its cantabile phrases.[18]

In the middle of such an animated discussion, *Il trovatore* premiered on 10 May at Covent Garden, featuring Pauline Viardot as Azucena, Jenny Ney as Leonora, Enrico Tamberlik in the title role and Francesco Graziani as the Conte di Luna. W. H. Beverley took care of the unsurpassed scenery while Michael Costa was the conductor. The performers were all positively received, and particular emphasis was bestowed on Viardot's rendition of the main character. With regard to the composer, some of the critics did not spare themselves and insisted on the usual repertoire of recriminations and objections while, to our surprise, much milder judgments were pronounced by some of the severest among them.

The critic of *The Musical World* assumed an ambivalent position, oscillating between the reiteration of a well-known repertoire of faults and a more positive response, possibly owing to the new challenge, present in the background, of Wagner's musical and dramatic achievements. After having described the plot as an accumulation of horrors, and mentioned the extent to which the interpreters should be credited with the success of the performance—Graziani the only exception—the critic pronounced a first tentatively positive judgment.

> Signor Verdi so frequently "surpassed himself," that we looked forward to much more pleasure from the music of *Il Trovatore*, where he is said to have "surpassed himself" once more. It is apparently written with more care than the majority of his works; the unisons are fewer; and the desire to give a true dramatic interest to the scene is more manifest. On the other hand—which surprised us—the tunes are not so frequent as in his former operas. Much of the music of *Il Trovatore*, however, has *character*, is often pleasing, oftener well adapted to the situations, and occasionally in point of freedom and breadth—for example, the air "Ah! Ben mio," in the third act, so magnificently sung by Sig. Tamberlik—worthy of unqualified praise.[19]

Even though the work did not match the critic's expectations, his evocations of fewer unisons, a defined character, a pleasing quality and

---

18 *The Sunday Times*, June 17, 1855, p. 3.
19 *The Musical World*, May 12, 1855, p. 293.

a freedom and breadth worthy of unqualified praise are unprecedented in the earlier issues of *The Musical World*. The critic concluded his first review of *Il trovatore* by promising his readers a more detailed analysis of the music and its performance the following week. On 19 May he fulfilled his promise, elaborated amply on Verdi's last opera and raised a couple of issues of some relevance. First of all, he denied the transformation in Verdi's style that had been postulated on the continent; the new opera exhibited the same faults and shortcomings as the earlier ones. Although he was ready to admit that dramatic power was more present in *Il trovatore* than in any of Verdi's previous operas, he was equally ready to argue that the composer had not improved, for his music was still characterised by want of refinement, coarseness of style and contempt for pure forms.[20] Verdi's growing popularity was unquestionable and it would be absurd to deny that he was to some extent gifted; however, the basis on which his popularity was founded was still open to debate. Bellini and Donizetti were dead and Rossini had also expired, though only musically speaking. Thus Verdi was simply the only living Italian operatic composer. His compositional work was intended for the mob, those common people who were not capable of critical judgment. Verdi was very good at caressing their uneducated ears and at gaining their most deafening applause; he spoke their language and was able to raise their enthusiasm to such an extent as to consign most of his colleagues to neglect. This was his talent. The critic went so far as to draw a comparison between Verdi and those "mundane speculators of the school ironically termed 'fast,' who, incessantly presuming to detect the 'weak side' of humanity, are too intellectually blind to distinguish one side from the other."[21] The critic was referring to Richard Wagner, whose contemptuous sneer towards all his colleagues and whose lofty theories about the music of the future made him the natural antagonist to Verdi as a popular composer. The critic concluded his analysis by inviting Verdi and Wagner to join forces and learn from each other; he suggested that Verdi would particularly benefit from listening to Wagner's *Tannhäuser*. Seen in the light of Wagner's challenging theories and quite unpleasant, if not offensive attitudes, Verdi's way of composing and complying with his

---

20   *The Musical World*, May 19, 1855, p. 313.
21   *Ibid.*, p. 314.

estimators' tastes and orientations was now understood by the critic as talent, something not at all undesirable, even if not entirely satisfactory in terms of pure art.

On 14 May, *The Times* published a detailed review of *Il trovatore* focussing on the way in which the composition appeared to be uneven, even though it exhibited some dramatic power; the habitual list of shortcomings was presented but the general result could not be said to be ineffectual. Although the reviews published in *The Times* and in *The Musical World* a few days later are marked by strong similarities, such wordings as "nonentity," "popular composer" and "the longest opera of the composer" appearing in both, they suggest quite different critical attitudes. While *The Musical World* analysed Verdi's opera in the light of contemporary conversations concerning the future of dramatic music, the critic of *The Times* did not make any similar effort to contextualise. *The Times* pronounced the libretto horrendous, even worse than *Rigoletto*'s, while acknowledging that the music contained some good moments, despite many mistakes. The *canzone* "Stride la vampa," for Azucena, was pronounced "touching and simple" and displaying a "marked character," while the duet between Azucena and Manrico "Mal reggendo all'aspro assalto" offered many points for praise. Of the opera's four long acts, the fourth was pronounced the best, thanks to the scene of the "Miserere" and the subsequent remarkable duet between Count di Luna and Leonora. The performance was exceptionally good, the scenery stunning and the interpreters worthy of praise.[22] Not a single word was offered on the extent to which this last work might represent a progress in Verdi's compositional career, nor did the critic try to draw a comparison between Verdi's unquestionable popularity and Wagner's dubious success.

The critic of *The Athenaeum* pronounced the libretto of *Il trovatore* "a miscellany of forced, yet familiar, melodramatic combinations, owing such little individuality as it possesses to the gipsy troop, who pass through its labyrinths of crime, sorrow, and mystery."[23] The critic was not particularly happy with a libretto that combined dramatic situations of dubious value and limited interest, most of which borrowed from the most hackneyed contemporary French dramas. However, he did

---

22 *The Times*, May 14, 1855, p. 11.
23 *The Athenaeum*, May 12, 1855, p. 539.

not declare himself entirely unsatisfied with the new opera, for Verdi's promise to favour truth and nature over meaningless stage-effects had been fulfilled, at least in part. The "Miserere" was pronounced "effective as a concerted piece being musical and melancholy," while the *terzettino* "Parlar non vuoi?" appeared "a fair specimen of Signor Verdi's desire to produce effect by the combination of different emotions in regular musical form."[24] But, the critic continued, "these gleams of purpose and intelligence" remained isolated against a general background of musical trivialities and countless shortcomings, among them the frequent employment of unison in the main voices. The performance itself was judged excellent in all respects. The following week the critic returned to this topic, for increased acquaintance with *Il trovatore* had put him in a position to elaborate further on both the good and bad points in Verdi's music. The beginning of the second act, the concerted piece at its close and the entire fourth act were said to comprise Verdi's best music, while the rest offered the usual mannerism of phrases and that meagreness and brevity of melodic inspirations that were already known in the composer. Verdi's orchestration showed greater care and delicacy than some of his former operas and in general *Il trovatore* could be listened to "from time to time without repugnance, and the fourth act with pleasure."[25] This was especially true if the opera was performed as well as at Covent Garden. Even more appreciative comments on *Il trovatore* can be found in Chorley's *Musical Recollections*, in which he calls it "the work among his works in which his best qualities are combined, and in which indications scattered throughout earlier productions present themselves in the form of their most complete fulfilment."[26] Chorley insisted that some pieces were particularly effective, among them the "Miserere," and bestowed words of unprecedented praise on Verdi's music, whose personal success as a popular composer was now indisputable in London.

> The mixture of platitude with rugged invention—the struggle to express passion,—the attempt at effect,—in two important points (the "Miserere" one of these) wholly successful,—have been equalled by Signor Verdi in no subsequent opera;—nor did he before, nor has he since, been so

---

24 Ibid.
25 *The Athenaeum*, May 19, 1855, p. 593.
26 Chorley, *Musical Recollections*, 2: 219.

happy in tenderness, in beauty, in melody.—"Il balen" has been the ruling London tune for five years, as undeniably as "Di tanti palpiti" was the tune some forty years ago!—when barrel organs were (and brass bands) as one to ten![27]

The critic of *The Spectator* expressed himself in terms that sound less harsh when compared to his reviews of Verdi's earlier operas; however, he insisted on the composer's weak invention and noisy orchestration.

> In the treatment of this gloomy subject, Verdi has certainly shown greater power than in any of his former works. We find his old addiction to trite phraseology and to noisy and ponderous instrumentation. But we find also melodies of much expression, more solid and satisfactory part-writing, and considerable constructive skill. In this branch of his art he seems to have profited by the works of Meyerbeer; for some of the principal scenes are carried on in concerted music in which the voices of separate groups are combined and blended with that composer's characteristic art.[28]

Even though it cannot be asserted that the number of positive remarks regarding Verdi had increased meaningfully, it can be argued that, by the time *Il trovatore* was produced in London, some of the critics had softened the aggressive edge of their reviews. Those expressions of repugnance and disgust that had accompanied the first appearance of Verdi's music in London are no longer to be found. An increased familiarity with his works, some of which were already part of the regular operatic repertoire at Covent Garden, together with a gradual, but still significant transformation in Verdi's style, however it was defined by contemporary critics, contributed to the improvement of the composer's image among his traditional detractors. As a result, by 1855 milder tones and more appreciative remarks substituted for the scornful expressions typical of the earlier years.

This new understanding of Verdi's music emerges in a review of *Il trovatore* in *The Illustrated London News* of 19 May that year. The critic availed himself of the opportunity to share with his readers a reflection on the common destiny to which, generation after generation, all young composers were subject when compared with the so-called classics.

---

27 Ibid.
28 *The Spectator*, May 12, 1855, p. 11.

Each young generation had to stand comparison with the earlier and suffer from the unequal confrontation. The old classics were inevitably cherished at the expense of the newcomers. Moreover, the critic called attention to the extent to which the judgment of the experts differed from that of the general public, as in the case of Verdi. His operas had continued to score undeniable popular success despite the severe reproach of the learned critics and their repeated attempts to sink him.

> Verdi has long been popular as a dramatic composer; and his popularity has been literal—gained by the voice of the multitude on opposition to that of criticism. While writers learned in musical lore have been labouring to prove that Verdi is a shallow pretender, his operas have been giving delight to thousands in every part of Europe.[29]

The author compared the manner in which Verdi had been treated by critics to the treatment reserved for all of his predecessors. Rossini had been pronounced a shallow pretender when compared to Mozart, Paisiello or Cimarosa, and the same had happened to Donizetti and Bellini when their operas were set against those of Rossini. Sooner or later all those critics who had described the first appearance of a new composer in terms of musical decadence, defining their works as "the spurious claims of charlatans," had been proven wrong. The same was happening now with Verdi.

> They have resisted the general voice as long as they could; and now that they can do so no longer, they are constrained to allow that there must be something in it. Verdi is now talked of, *ex cathedra*, with tolerable respect; and his claims to the character of an artist will at length be admitted, as those of his predecessors have been.[30]

During the last months of the year further discussion was carried out in some journals, addressing both Wagner's objectionable theories and Verdi's popular success. With regard to the first, *The Musical World* reported in August on an article from *The Morning Post* in which it was stated that the German composer's erroneous principles were more harmful to music than his compositions, in the same way that a murderer does less harm to society than the cunning sophist who seeks to justify such a horrendous crime with the blandishment of his words.

---

29 *The Illustrated London News*, May 19, 1855, pp. 495–96.
30 *Ibid.*

> The most hopeless mediocrity—the most insane rhapsodies, might be passed over in silence, or merely provoke a smile; but the dissemination of false theories, rendered still more seductive and dangerous by the brilliant wit, keen satire, imagination, fervid eloquence, and occasional glimpses of truth which this gentleman's literary works include, would require a strong hand to oppose them; and still, in the end, that opposition would prove useless, for the downward course once taken, none but a Sisyphus would attempt to arrest it. Herr Wagner is a necessary devil.[31]

Wagner was a dangerous man and English musicians were cautioned, for while it was clear that Germany was experiencing that moment of decline that inevitably follows the rise of a great culture, England was still in its musical childhood and should steer clear of such cultural degeneration.

On 27 October, a correspondent for *The Athenaeum* reported from Paris on the recent premiere of Verdi's *Les vêpres siciliennes*. He mentioned a number of oddities in the composer's instrumentation—for instance the cellos were now substituting for the violins in singing the melody—but acknowledged "a certain style, evidence of purpose and spirit in the music."[32] Although it was stated that the first success scored by *Les vêpres siciliennes* would not last long, in October the opera, probably also thanks to Sophie Cruvelli's splendid personation of Hélène, was prospering and still attracting the fashionable Parisian public.

---

31 *The Morning Post*, reproduced in *The Musical Times*, August 18, 1855, p. 529.
32 *The Athenaeum*, October 27, 1855, p. 1248.

9. A Moral Case: The Outburst of *La traviata* (1856)

The production of *La traviata* in London in 1856 was preceded by two remarkable events: Her Majesty's Theatre reopened under the leadership of Lumley, and the Covent Garden Opera House was destroyed in a terrible fire. In February, it was rumoured that "the two great establishments in the markets ('Hay' and 'Covent-Garden') would again be striving to outdo each other on Tuesday, Thursday and Saturday, in splendour of pageantry and ruinous superfluity of *prime donne*."[1] On 5 March a fire, whose cause was not possible to ascertain, tore through Covent Garden: "The fire was inexplicable, its progress unexampled, and its ravage incalculable."[2] John Henry Anderson, a magician to whom a short lease had been granted by Frederick Gye, had organised a "Carnival Benefit," a masked ball, which took place on 4 March. At some point between 4 and 5 a.m., the fire began in the carpenter's shop and nothing could be done to extinguish it. The loss was terrible, not only in financial but also in artistic terms. An announcement soon circulated, however, informing the public that Gye had managed to obtain the Royal Lyceum Theatre temporarily and was in a position to confirm the imminent opening of his operatic season there.[3]

Early in April, therefore, the forthcoming Royal Italian Opera season was officially announced by Gye at the Royal Lyceum. Gye had engaged a number of star singers including Marietta Piccolomini, who was

---

1 *The Musical World*, February 2, 1856, p. 73.
2 *The Musical World*, March 8, 1856, p. 152.
3 *The Musical World*, March 29, 1856, p. 201.

expected to make her appearance in Verdi's new opera *La traviata*. In the meantime, the reopening of Her Majesty's Theatre had also been arranged and Lumley had set sail to Paris to organise a new company. On 5 April a short, ironical mention of *La traviata* appeared in *The Musical World*, commenting on Verdi's new opera and prominent position. Since no fewer than three operas belonging to the "Emperor of The Unisons" were promised by Gye, those who cherished Verdi and took delight in his works would be well satisfied.[4]

Later in April Lumley made a public announcement in which he informed his subscribers that Marietta Piccolomini had been secured for his establishment together with Marietta Alboni. On 15 April, meanwhile, Gye opened the Royal Italian Opera season at the Lyceum with *Il trovatore*, featuring the same cast as the year before, Constance Nantier-Didiée, Pauline Viardot and Enrico Tamberlik appearing in the main roles.[5] On 10 May the Italian opera season at Her Majesty's Theatre opened with *La Cenerentola*, featuring Marietta Alboni in the title role, together with Vincenzo Calzolari, Belletti and Zucconi. *Il barbiere di Siviglia* and *La sonnambula* followed immediately thereafter. Finally, on 24 May, while *Rigoletto* was reprised at the Lyceum Theatre, *La traviata* was produced at Her Majesty's Theatre, featuring Piccolomini in the title role, Calzolari as Alfredo and Federico Beneventano as Germont senior.[6] According to Lumley, the enthusiasm the *prima donna* ignited was immense and spread like wildfire. "Once more frantic crowds struggled in the lobbies of the theatre, once more dresses were torn and hats crushed in the conflict, once more a mania possessed the public. Marietta Piccolomini became the rage."[7]

Unlike any other Verdi opera in Victorian London, *La traviata* ignited a debate concerning the immoral nature of its libretto that overshadowed

---

4 *The Musical World*, April 5, 1856, p. 216.
5 *The Musical World*, April 19, 1856, pp. 251–53.
6 Weeks before the premiere at Her Majesty's Theatre was announced the publisher Boosey & Sons was advertising different reductions and arrangements of *La traviata* in the columns of *The Musical World*. In addition to similar arrangements of *Il trovatore* and *Rigoletto*, an unabridged piano reduction of *La traviata*, realised by Rudolf Normann and bearing a portrait of Marietta Piccolomini, was now available, together with a select collection of songs and duets, a *Grand Selection* for military band and an Orchestra suite entitled *La traviata Quadrille and Valse*. Also the English translation of the most celebrated airs was soon made available to the local amateurs.
7 Lumley, *Reminiscences of the Opera*, pp. 375–76.

the discussion of the quality of its music. In the middle lay the figure of Marietta Piccolomini, whose powerful dramatic talent and questionable vocal skills appear to have played a pivotal role in determining the rapturous success of *La traviata* in 1856 London. As many contemporary commentators suggested, she monopolised the audience's attention at the expense of the composer.

In accordance with the Theatre Regulation Act of 1843, every new dramatic piece was to be submitted to the Lord Chamberlain for approval at least seven days before its intended performance. A separate Examiner of Plays appointed specifically for this purpose was responsible for the licensing of any work to be staged, upon the condition that all the necessary emendations be made. Although Alexandre Dumas' *La Dame aux camélias*, from which Francesco Maria Piave had derived the libretto, would be banned twice from the London stage, once in 1853 (under the title *Camille*) and again in 1859, John Mitchell Kemble, the Examiner of the Plays, granted *La traviata* the requested license on 19 May 1856.[8]

As it was generally assumed that audience members understood little or no Italian, and since operagoers were said to bring home just a few nice tunes to hum in their beds—as someone would argue in the course of the ensuing season—censorial interventions consisting in the cutting of entire passages were not frequent with regard to Italian operatic librettos.[9] Furthermore, in an opera the words were considered subsidiary to the music, a circumstance that allowed for greater tolerance on the part of the censorial authority, even when the operatic version of a banned dramatic text was concerned.[10]

The only visible alteration imposed on the libretto of *La traviata* was in Act II, scene 14, where—as reported in *The Times*—the infuriated Alfredo "summons the whole company from the banquet, confesses to them how he has accepted the bounty of Violetta, and by way of repayment flings her portrait at her feet, amid the general indignation of all present, including his own father."[11]

---

8   Roberta Montemorra Marvin, "The Censorship of Verdi's Operas in Victorian London," *Music & Letters* 82/4 (2001): 582–610.
9   *Ibid.*, p. 587.
10 See John Russell Stephens, *The Censorship of English Drama 1824–1901*, p. 83.
11 *The Times*, May 26, 1856, p. 12.

Fig. 9 Scene from *La traviata* at Her Majesty's Theatre. Violetta faints after Alfredo flings her "portrait" at her feet. *The Illustrated London News*, 31 May 1856.

The alteration did not affect the lyrics but rather the stage directions.[12]

Alfredo

Ogni suo aver tal femmina
Per amor mio sperdea
Io cieco, vile, misero,
Tutto accettar potea,
Ma è tempo ancora! tergermi
Da tanta macchia bramo
Qui testimoni vi chiamo
Che qui pagata io l'ho.

Getta con furente sprezzo una borsa ai piedi di Violetta, che sviene tra le braccia di Flora e del Dottore. In tal momento entra il padre

Alfredo

All she possessed, this woman here
Hath for my love expended.
I blindly, basely, wretchedly,
This to accept, condescended.
But there is time to purge me yet
From stains that shame, confound me.
Bear witness all around me
That here I pay the debt

In a violent rage he throws a purse at Violetta's feet—she faints in the arms of Flora and the Doctor. At this moment Alfred's father enters.

---

12 *Verdi's La Traviata: Containing the Italian Text with an English Translation by T.T. Barker; and Music of all the Principal Airs* (Boston: O. Ditson, c. 1888), p. 39.

As we learn from the dialogue between Alfredo and Annina in Act II, scenes 1 and 2, Violetta has been spending all her money to ensure Alfredo's comfortable lifestyle but, after three months, she is running short of money and has been forced to sell her jewels, horses and carriages. Alfredo feels ashamed and when he meets Violetta at the ball in Flora's apartment it is not his intention to insult her by paying her back for her sexual favours; instead, he blames himself for having accepted her generosity and wants to repay the debt. While the words uttered by Alfredo clearly describe the moral obligations that spur him to make amends for his own blindness, none of the audience members would have missed the potentially offensive meaning of his gesture, if he had flung the purse of money as written in the original libretto. Paying Violetta back could have been understood as an explicit reference to her social position and moral condition; this would have shocked the public and offended their sense of decorum.

Notwithstanding this emendation, the effect upon both the public and the critics was enormous and the opera ignited a long-lasting debate. The fear that having a prostitute for a protagonist would encourage immorality, or even enhance the plague of prostitution, played an important role in stirring up the discussion.

Walter E. Houghton argues that, even though a fallen woman was made an outcast by the Victorian code of purity, the difficult living conditions typical of industrial English cities and the extremely low wages at the humblest social level resulted in an enormous number of illegitimate children and fallen women. By 1850 there were at least 50,000 prostitutes in England and Scotland, and 8,000 in London alone, a plague which contemporary commentators called "The Great Social Evil."[13] The Strand, Haymarket and Covent Garden were among the neighbourhoods in London where the phenomenon was most noticeable and pervasive. A police report issued on 20 May 1857 counted 480 prostitutes working in 45 brothels situated in the Covent Garden, Drury Lane and Saint Giles district alone. However, given the difficulty of investigating the underworld outside the already ascertained number of brothels, this figure was said to represent "a conscientious

---

13   Walter E. Houghton, *The Victorian Frame of Mind, 1830–1870* (New Haven and London: Yale University Press, 1957), p. 366.

approximation to the number of street-walkers."[14] As Michael Pearson notes, if the estimate made by the medical journal *The Lancet* in 1857 was correct, it meant that there were roughly 6,000 brothels and 80,000 prostitutes in London alone.[15]

In 1857, the dramatic situation in the theatre district prompted William Acton to coin the expression "Traviata-ism" to suggest a relationship between the objectionable libretto of *La traviata* and the sad spectacle that was forced upon operagoers outside the theatre: "Traviata-ism for ladies may be well enough across the footlights, but a plunge into a hot bath of it on leaving her Majesty's Theatre is a greater penalty than I would impose upon the most ardent admirer of that very popular 'opera without music.'"[16]

Another striking testimony to the manner in which the Strand and Haymarket presented themselves at night is offered by Hippolyte Taine's *Notes on England*.

> Every hundred steps one jostles twenty harlots; some of them ask for a glass of gin; others say, "Sir, it is to pay my lodging." This is not debauchery which flaunts itself, but destitution—and such destitution! The deplorable procession in the shade of the monumental streets is sickening; it seems to me a march of the dead. That is a plague-spot—the real plague-spot of English society.[17]

Prostitution in London was referred to as a plague, and between 1840 and 1850 a long series of publications, books, articles and reports investigated its possible causes and drew attention to its negative consequences on British society.[18] One proposed approach to the problem consisted in banning all the licentious literature that might have endangered the education of young men and women. In 1869

---

14 William Acton, *Prostitution, Considered in its Moral, Social & Sanitary Aspects In London and Other Large Cities* (London: John Churchill, 1857), pp. 16–17.
15 Michael Pearson, *The Age of Consent. Victorian Prostitution and its Enemies* (Newton Abbot: David & Charles, 1972), p. 25.
16 William Acton, *Prostitution, Considered in its Moral, Social & Sanitary Aspects*, p. 118.
17 Hippolyte Taine, *Notes on England* (New York: Holt, 1885), p. 36. Taine's *Notes* were edited in the decade 1861–1871 cfr. p. xxvii).
18 See Michael Ryan, *Prostitution in London, with a Comparative View of that of Paris and New York* (London: Bailliere, 1839); Gustave Richelot, *The Greatest of Our Social Evils: Prostitution*, trans. Robert Knox (London: Bailliere, 1857); James Miller, *Prostitution Considered in Relation to its Cause and Cure* (Edinburgh: Sutherland; London: Simpkin, 1859).

Francis Newman, Professor Emeritus at University College London, expressed himself in the following terms:

> For myself, I am firmly convinced that many things in the school-classics perniciously inflame passion in boys and young men: so do many approved English poems, plays, sculptures and paintings. All such things are a great cruelty to a boy who struggles to keep his imagination undefiled.[19]

Contemporary commentators occasionally referred to the negative influence exerted by French literature upon English society and objected to those modern works of fiction which were "tainted with impurity; borrowing largely, in this, from the French school."[20] Some of them argued that the descriptions of sexuality in which such playwrights as Victor Hugo and Alexandre Dumas indulged were detrimental to the English sense of decorum and contrary to Victorian social values. This issue had already been raised in 1834, when the English poet Robert Southey complained about the immoralities present in the plays of Hugo and the elder Dumas, "which were characterised by a preponderance of adulteresses, prostitutes, seducers, bastards, and foundlings."[21] In 1853 George Henry Lewes made explicit reference to *La Dame aux camélias* and expressed a sense of relief when the Lord Chamberlain refused to license "this unhealthy idealisation of one of the worst evils of our social life." "Paris," he continued, "may delight in such pictures, but London, thank God! has still enough instinctive repulsion against pruriency not to tolerate them." The mistake, Lewes argued, consisted in treating this intolerable "idealisation of corruption" too lightly, a choice that tended to "confuse the moral sense, by exciting the sympathy of an audience."[22]

As we will see, the arguments against Dumas' original drama would be reiterated in the course of the 1856 opera season, when *La traviata* was performed at Her Majesty's Theatre. Interestingly, no trace of this discussion and no reference to the morally questionable subject of

---

19   Francis W. Newman, *The Cure of the Great Social Evil with Special Reference to Recent Laws Delusively Called Contagious Deseases' Acts* (London: Trübner, 1869), p. 26.
20   William Logan, *The Great Social Evil* (London: Hodder and Stoughton, 1871, 1st edn. 1843), p. 232.
21   John Russell Stephens, *The Censorship of English Drama 1824–1901*, pp. 81–83.
22   William Archer and Robert W. Lowe (ed.), *Dramatic Essays: John Forster, George Henry Lewes. Reprinted from the "Examiner" and the "Leader"* (London: Walter Scott, 1896), pp. 240–42.

La traviata can be found in the London periodicals in the month that preceded its first performance. The problem emerged on 28 May, four days after the premiere, when the critic of *The Times*, who had already reviewed *La traviata* two days before, raised the issue of the opera's morality and the extent to which the librettist had been faithful to the original French drama. The commentator went so far as to suggest a way in which the morbidity of the plot might have been attenuated.

> Some means might have been found of preserving the situations of M. Dumas without retaining the social position of the *dramatis personae*. A virtuous young lady who loved devotedly, was insulted at a large party, and ultimately died of consumption, would have served just as well for a heroine as a Parisian *lorette*. At the Theatre du Vaudeville, the lives of people whose existence lies *hors de société*, are found to furnish exceedingly pleasant plots, but London audiences have happily not yet grown used to such society.[23]

The idea of having a *lorette* on stage was perceived as outrageous and offensive, and the negative influence exerted by French literature was deplorable. This opinion reflected the position of those contemporaries who maintained that such a subject was unfit to be brought before "our sisters and wives" and echoed the fear already expressed by George Lewes.

In response to what his colleague at *The Times* had suggested regarding the moral issue, the critic of *The Leader* took a more balanced, unbiased position on 31 May. He did not agree with the *Times* on the benefits of converting the main character into a lady of fashion; that change, he argued, would have failed to result in any moral improvement.

> The critic of *The Times*, who, we observe, has recently taken to the moral as well as the musical sciences, and who has nearly as fine an eye for virtue as ear for Verdi, regrets that the *Traviata* was not converted into a young lady of fashion, broken-hearted by a gay deceiver, in the conventional way of good society. For our own wicked part, we cannot see how that vulgar kind of infidelity in love would be more moral or more affecting than a "lost one" purified by sacrifice and redeemed by death [...] We do not wish to be understood as approving the subject of the *Dame aux Camélias*—in the novel there are incidents that disgust—but we protest against this prudery about the story of a *Traviata* in the thick of our dramatic atmosphere of seductions and adulteries.[24]

---

23 *The Times*, May 28, 1856, p. 5.
24 "Madame Piccolomini—La Traviata," *The Leader*, May 31, 1856, p. 524.

The Athenaeum addressed the subject of *La traviata* in quite negative terms: "the slow pulmonary death of the Lady of Pleasure, when accompanied by an orchestra, is more repulsive to us than when it is gasped, sighed, and fainted to its dying fall."[25] In contrast, *The Illustrated London News* addressed the issue of morality in quite mild terms: although the drama had been censored by the Lord Chamberlain, the opera was more pathetic than outrageous.

> In the Italian opera the groundwork of the story and the principal incidents remain the same; but the details are softened down, and the piece, as it stands, is scarcely more objectionable than others (the *Favorita*, for instance) which pass current on the Opera stage. It is, moreover, irresistibly pathetic, and he must be a stern moralist indeed who can witness unmoved the sorrows of the erring but most interesting heroine.[26]

The critics of *The Literary Gazette* and *Musical Gazette* also joined the choir. They expressed their appreciative and approving opinions with regard to the singer and addressed only in passing the quality of the music.[27] Very little attention was paid to the moral implications involved in the subject of the libretto. In this regard the critic of *The Literary Gazette* held that "the heat and violence of the original" had been "duly abated to suit the more temperate medium of the lyrical stage."[28]

The moral question was also touched upon by the critic of *The Saturday Review*. He argued that the choice of *La traviata* was an instance of bad taste and reiterated the claim made by Lewes. It was against the interest of morality to appeal to the public's sympathetic feelings by putting on stage a character deserving of pity rather than admiration or love. He supported the idea that theatrical representations should benefit public morality and that it was pernicious to make vice appear more fascinating than virtue.

> However we may attempt to disguise the fact—to wrap it up in soft sounding words and high flown phrases—vice is vice, in what light so ever it may appear, and we are sinning against right when we make it seem more fascinating than virtue. If such plots find favour in England, we should at once renounce all hope of seeing public morality in any

---

25 *The Athenaeum*, May 31, 1856, p. 688.
26 *The Illustrated London News*, May 31, 1856, pp. 587–88.
27 "Music and the Drama," *The Literary Gazette: A Weekly Journal of Literature, Science, and the Fine Arts*, May 31, 1856, p. 332.
28 Ibid.

way benefited by the teachings of the stage. At any rate, of *La Traviata* we should be sorry to think that it had made a successful appeal to "the merciful construction of good women."[29]

The critic of *The Morning Post* was of a completely different opinion. He strongly objected to all those prudish commentators who claimed that the subject of *La traviata* was so immoral that it should have been avoided, if not banned. This critic, whose review of *La traviata* was also reproduced in the columns of *The Musical Gazette* on 5 July, held that "The stage, whether it be dramatic or lyric, cannot avoid the exhibition of vice in contrast to virtue any more than a painter can dispense with the shadows which give effect to the lights in his picture."[30] It was a mere absurdity to stage a dramatic fable in which the vices of mankind were not to be touched upon or dealt with. The mistake into which people fell, he argued, was that "they did not sufficiently discriminate between the exposure and the palliation of vice." It was not immoral to deal with vice, but only to treat it lightly or to throw round it an attractive aura. In Violetta's case, it was clear that virtue prevailed over vice; the lost one was understood as the redeemed one, the woman who, having wandered from the path of virtue, showed a stronger sense of honour and virtue than those who abandoned her. Moreover, it was a mistake to confound Dumas' *La Dame aux camélias* with Verdi's *La traviata*, since all that could be perceived as inappropriate and objectionable in the drama had been amended in the opera. *La traviata* was not worse than many other earlier operas.

As these reviews suggest, the issue of the dubious morality of Verdi's most recent opera and the way in which it could be understood as pernicious to the Victorian sense of decorum was raised by many contemporary journals, whose critics joined in a spirited discussion. Notwithstanding the objections to its questionable subject, *La traviata* scored a tremendous success among the public. As was repeatedly emphasised in the press, operagoers thronged the theatre night after night, eager to attend the opera derived from the most controversial drama of an entire epoch. To some extent, the sense of prudery that accompanied the appearance of *La traviata* in London was instrumental

---

29   *Ibid.*
30   "La Traviata," *The Musical Gazette*, July 5, 1856, pp. 285–86 (from the *Morning Post*).

in determining its popular success. This controversy led also to the publication of an anonymous pamphlet, *Remarks on the Morality of Dramatic Compositions with Particular Reference to "La Traviata," etc.* Its author took a stance in defence of the opera and suggested that its popularity was a good sign, since it showed a "tendency to regard mere artificial law-made sins as no sins at all."

> It shows that genuine pity for suffering humanity, ruined and victimized by a hollow and atrocious system of society, animates the bosom of the highest and the fairest in the land. It shows the prevalent disregard for a rotten conventionalism. It shows a growing contempt for the cant of orthodoxy, and the frauds of a gross and withering superstition. It shows that the genuine principles of true morality are recognized, and that there is something in human nature which we could rely on still, and even amidst decomposing institutions, and society in a state of dissolution and collapse is not perhaps the most fallen and debased.[31]

The position expressed by the anonymous author of these *Remarks* invites a reflection on the nature of the discussion that animated the London periodicals soon after the first performance of *La traviata*. Although not every critic shared the same moralising attitude, most of them seemed to agree on the necessity for theatrical performances to treat moral issues with great care. If theatrical representations were to benefit public morality, they had to draw a clear line between what was right and what was wrong; to blur that line by making vice appear more appealing than virtue might have engendered a pernicious confusion in the audience. *La traviata* represented a case in point. The figure of Violetta was surrounded by a positive aura, and the conflicting impressions a spectator might derive from the opposition of her personal dignity to her social condition might also result in that pernicious sympathy to which Lewes had initially referred. Moreover, in *La traviata* the relationship between vice and virtue could have been overturned; Violetta's devotion to Alfredo, her abnegation and her final sacrifice made her a better person than those who looked down upon her with contempt. According to the author of the *Remarks*, while music critics' moralising about *La traviata* showed that they had embraced

---

31 *Remarks on the Morality of Dramatic Compositions: With Particular Reference to "La Traviata," Etc.* (London: John Chapman, 1856), also quoted in Montemorra, pp. 601–02.

the "cant of orthodoxy," the public seemed able to make a distinction between "those genuine principles of true morality" that may be found even in a fallen woman, and the moral stigma that the "atrocious system of society" attached to her. The issue of having a prostitute on stage revealed far more about Victorian class structure and social prejudice than about female immorality.

An even more animated debate concerning the libretto of *La traviata* and its immorality exploded in the Victorian press a few months later. It was triggered by an article published on 2 August in *The Spectator*, in which the critic drew attention to two recent theatrical events which shared the same negative quality: the opera *La traviata* and a play by Tom Taylor, *Retribution: A Domestic Drama in 4 Acts*. Adapted from Charles de Bernard's novel *La loi du tailon*, *Retribution* was given at the Royal Olympic Theatre on 12 May 1856.[32]

The critic agreed with his colleagues that it was Marietta Piccolomini who should be credited with the success of *La traviata*. The young and innocent-looking interpreter had disguised the immoral character of the Parisian courtesan and won the admiration of the public; she had infused Violetta with grace and pathos such as were not to be found in any Parisian *lorette*. The shameful libretto, taken from an infamous modern French novel, had been worthily set to music by Verdi, and the result was simply outrageous. However, the critic regretted that the ladies of the aristocracy seemed to have been neither outraged nor distressed by the vice underlying the opera, since they continued to throng the theatre and crowd their boxes. "But," the critic argues, "these ladies are not exempt from the weakness of slavery to fashion." Then, in order to prevent fashion from prevailing over virtue he envisaged a committee of patronesses whose mission would be to forbid immoral operas from being performed. About *Retribution* the critic was no less lenient, arguing that it was not true that "murder and adultery are the most interesting subjects of dramatic art, for it is not true that the persons guilty of these crimes present the most interesting contrasts of character or the most powerful conflicts of passion."[33] Concluding his review, he claimed that although it was tolerable to "borrow from the

---

32   See Massimo Zicari, "Un caso di moralità: La Traviata nella Londra Vittoriana (1856)," *Musica/Realtà* 103 (2014): 141–57.
33   "Theatrical Moralities," *The Spectator*, August 2, 1856, p. 16.

Italians their mellifluous voices, and from the French their neatness of plot and smartness of dialogue," it was harmful to the moral purity of British society to welcome that "prurient sentiment and melodramatic situation which must be the bane of art." The critic's attitude was consistent with those commentators who considered the influence of foreign literature, especially French, pernicious to the British sense of decorum. He advocated the idea that theatrical representations, whether lyric or dramatic, should reflect the national character and its moral values, whereas the fashion then prevalent in London was to stage more exotic and certainly more immoral works imported from abroad. In this sense the critic was expressing his own nationalistic orientations rather than a concern for the moral function of theatrical performances.

On 4 August, this article was reproduced in the columns of *The Times*, a circumstance that prompted the immediate response of other periodicals and occasioned a discussion in which Lumley eventually intervened in defence of the much discussed opera he had put on stage. In response to *The Times*'s harshly critical article, on 7 August a reader wrote a letter to the editor in which he argued that although it was certainly wrong to make a courtesan the interesting heroine of a drama, incest, murder, rape and many other similar forms of "unbridled debauchery" were common subjects in the opera. *La traviata* was not dissimilar to *Rigoletto*, *Lucrezia Borgia* or even *Don Giovanni*. There was no reason to be so concerned for the British female public, especially because "from the opera they bring away with them but the airs, as from the drama they bring the story."[34] The editor replied by addressing the issue in terms of a "grave question of public morality": while the music was not worth analysing, the libretto was based on a subject that should have never been exhibited on stage in the presence of decent womanhood: "Surely, in order to entertain an English lady it is not necessary to take her for a saunter in the Haymarket at midnight, and to conduct her about 4 a.m. to the consumptive ward of a hospital that she may see a prostitute finish her career."[35]

---

34 "Mademoiselle Piccolomini—The Traviata, to the editor of the Times," *The Times*, August 7, 1856, p. 9.

35 *The Times*, August 7, 1856, p. 8. The reference to Haymarket, where Her Majesty's Theatre was situated, is not accidental: the neighbourhood was notoriously crowded with prostitutes.

Not only was the libretto offensive because of the public representation of prostitution, but also because it called attention to "the brothels and abominations of modern Paris of the Boulevards as they exist in the year 1856." The feeling of deep indignation that characterised the critic's reaction stemmed from the fact that the kind of immorality staged by *La traviata* reflected a problematic aspect of contemporary life instead of some safely remote historical or fictional world. The objection could be extended to many other theatrical pieces whose subjects, be they old or new, were transgressive. It was also argued that, to some extent, such an immoral opera owed its success precisely to the morbid expectations its subject roused among the general public.

In a way, having decided to reproduce the article that appeared in *The Spectator*, the editor of *The Times* seemed to have taken upon himself the responsibility of launching the discussion and supporting the position of those commentators who believed the dramatic performances involved licentious elements harmful to the education of the youth. This finds confirmation in another article appearing on 9 August, in which the critic of *The Times* insisted on the detrimental influence of what he called the "modern school of Satanic writers in Paris." These writers indulged in the representation of those hideous vices which lay in front of anybody who walked the streets of Paris. It was morally wrong to import those French dramas and put them on stage in London; it was wrong to draw the public's attention to harlotry and incest, adultery and seduction; it was wrong to assume that modern English life could offer nothing better than those Parisian vices in which French playwrights took so much interest. In conclusion, the critic apologised to his readers for not having spoken up before but, he held, it had been not his intention to interfere with the profits of managers and actors.

The moralising position of *The Times* prompted the immediate response of the critic of *The Leader*, who commented on the attacks against the management of Her Majesty's Theatre "for producing pieces which turn upon certain vices supposed to be prevalent at the present day,"[36] and ridiculed his colleague for having taken such a prudish position. On 9 August he argued that such aberrations as those present in *La traviata* were "especially the subjects of the dramatic art." In this sense, Verdi's recent achievement was not dissimilar to many other dramatic

---

36 "La Traviata and The Times," *The Leader*, August 9, 1856, p. 757.

as well as operatic works, which did not seem to have provoked such an animated debate. Even though one might question the taste of an artist who selects subjects that are neither powerful nor beautiful, still the stage should be recognised "as the mirror in which society, looking, will see its own defects as well as its beauties." Despite the fact that the editor of *The Times* wanted a mirror in which the distortions and deformities of modern life would be erased, the point in staging *La traviata* was that it presented the old, typical struggle between good and bad, and ended with the expected triumph of good, but in a new shape.

> The march of all these tragedies presents to us invariably the contest between the bad and the good—the peril to which the good is exposed by the bad agency—and, whatever may be the tragic mination [sic], the real triumph of the good. Because in none of these cases does the spirit of the devil gain the victory [...] The class which Violetta la Traviata represents, does exist. It is called into existence by the selfishness and depravity of town-made man; its existence continues unmitigated through the selfish resolve of society to ignore it. But that class consists of some thousands of women—women born to the best qualities of their sex; and these qualities are sometimes so inextinguishable that they remain throughout. If we look gravely into that tragedy, we shall find the same struggle between good and bad, with the same triumph of good. *La Traviata* shows us one instance. After a life of heartless depravity into which she has been led, a natural passion, a genuine affection takes her from it; but she is cast back by the suspicions and repulsions of society.[37]

Although Violetta is condemned by society, her love for Alfredo redeems her for a life of vice. It is Giorgio Germont, Alfredo's father, who asks Violetta to abandon his son. Their debauched relationship will cast a moral shadow on the entire family and especially on Alfredo's sister, whom no decent man will ever marry. It is not until the end of the opera that Violetta's sacrifice is acknowledged, but it is in spite of all social prejudices and moral biases surrounding her. Moreover, the class of women that Violetta embodied in the opera existed in the real world and could be neither ignored nor eliminated. They were victims of the same society to which the audience belonged and in which operagoers saw themselves reflected.

This line of argument was also followed by Lumley, who, in the middle of all this turmoil, felt the urge to make his position clear. In

---

37 *Ibid.*

a letter that appeared in the columns of *The Times* on 11 August the manager stated that it had not been his intention to use a plot of dubious morality for the sole purpose of displaying the vocal and dramatic qualities of the principal artist. Nor would it have been difficult to make those changes in the libretto that might have prevented the critics from reacting so harshly. In arguing against his detractors, Lumley used the very same weapon: the moral nature of the subject.

> As it stands, the melancholy catastrophe illustrates the Nemesis that attends on vice, and that cannot be entirely averted even by the most touching and devoted repentance. Strike out from the character the evil which had blighted it, and the last scene would have offended against the dramatic canon—that suffering should only be exhibited for the purpose of teaching a moral lesson.[38]

According to Lumley teaching a moral lesson was still the purpose of the stage: this goal was achieved by mirroring real life and bringing to the stage subjects that reflected the many possible ways in which the continuous conflict between good and evil was manifested. The moral value of *La traviata* lay in showing the audience that noble feelings could dwell even in the broken heart of a "repentant Magdalena."

In the meantime, the critic of *The Saturday Review* expanded on this issue and called attention to the danger inherent in combining a repulsive plot and a charming actress.

> We cannot but regret that the opera chosen for her *début* was one in which some of the most immoral phases of Parisian life are laid bare before us; but the audience seemed to forget the repulsive nature of the plot in the enthusiasm they felt for the young actress. She looked so pure and innocent that, notwithstanding the truth and fidelity of the impersonation, it was not easy to remember the type of character which she was endeavouring to represent. Herein, however, lies the chief mischief likely to arise from putting such a story on the stage. By the fascination which Mademoiselle Piccolomini throws around the character, and the poetry she infuses into it, the moral sense is deadened, and our perceptions of right and wrong are in danger of becoming misty and confused.[39]

Again, presenting so colourful an instance of the immoral Parisian life, dressed in the clothes of fascination, may have confused the public. The

---

38 "La Traviata. To the Editor of The Times," *The Times*, August 11, 1856, p. 7.
39 *The Saturday Review*, August 9, 1856, pp. 339–40.

charm and allure with which the *prima donna* infused the character may have resulted in a misunderstanding of the plot. One week later the same commentator took a more overtly critical position against the critic of *The Times*, whose behaviour had proven to be neither consistent nor entirely honest. Why had he taken so long to react to the alleged depravity of Dumas's dramatic plot? Did opportunism lie behind such a tardy reaction? Having published a lengthy article on 26 May in which "laudatory criticism" outweighed negative comments and where no mention of the morbidity of the plot was to be found, it was remarkable, the critic of *The Saturday Review* argued, that it took the critic of *The Times* almost three months to express his most profound moral concern. In what now seemed to be rather an attack against *The Times* than a reflection on Verdi's opera, the journalist of the *Saturday Review* now denied that the plot of *La traviata* was immoral, though only one week before he had pronounced it a regrettable circumstance that it displayed the most immoral phases of Parisian life.

> Granting, however, that the literary and dramatic antecedents of the opera inevitably invest it with associations calculated to repel a correct moral taste, we utterly deny that the plot of the piece is in any respect immoral. The moral of *La Traviata*, such as it is, we take to be this—that even in the lowest depths of vice the heart of woman is still capable of being touched by a true and disinterested affection, but that the outraged laws of society forbid her tasting of the unsullied happiness which she has irretrievably forfeited.[40]

To some extent, the power to arouse the audience's repulsion and elicit their strongest reactions was inherent to the operatic genre. But immorality was out of question once Violetta, as also other critics held, was seen as a woman capable of true love but spoiled by our society's false beliefs and moral biases. In this regard, the critic's position was consistent with that of the anonymous author of the *Remarks*, who had argued that it was less a question of female immorality than of social prejudice.

On 16 August, the critic of *The Leader* returned to the issue in terms strongly suggestive of the role *The Times* had played in attracting increasingly larger crowds.

---

40 *The Saturday Review*, August 16, 1856, pp. 352–53.

> The more the *Times* said "Don't go," the more people went; the more it pronounced the performance of the *Traviata* to be unfitted for the presence of ladies, the more ladies were present; for it is a fact that at the additional performances of the opera, the number of women has positively increased in the audience.[41]

The animosity that had characterised the reviews published in the preceding months aroused the public's morbid curiosity. This had induced the audience to respond and contribute, even unintentionally, to the success of the opera; perhaps if *La traviata* had not been a moral case, it would not have drawn so much attention to both its authors and interpreters in London. The issue regarding the dubious moral quality of *La traviata* seemed of less concern to the Victorian female public, who continued to attend its performances and to crowd the opera theatre, than of the male critics, who feared for the negative influence its subject could exert on their wives, sisters, daughters and mothers. The general public seemed to be divided along two distinct orientations: those who looked at prostitution as a social evil and those who sympathised with the sad conditions in which poor young ladies were forced by the unfortunate circumstances of life.[42] As already pointed out, the moralising attitude expressed by the male critics seems to reflect less the issue of female morality than that of the social power structure of Victorian London. Behind this structure lay the belief that women should confine themselves to the domestic dimension, cultivate the ideal of premarital chastity and avoid any exposure to immoral behaviour. This, of course, had little or nothing to do with the real problem of prostitution and its social and economic causes. This dualistic approach is reflected in the repeated references critics made to the repentant Magdalene, a figure evoked to suggest that prostitutes had to repent their own sin despite the fact that, as some Victorian writers had already begun to suggest, they were more often than not "much more sinned against than sinning."[43]

---

41 "La Traviata in the Pulpit," *The Leader*, August 16, 1856, p. 781.
42 Susan Rutherford, "La Traviata or the 'Willing Grisette,' Male Critics and Female Performance in the 1850s," in *Verdi 2001: Atti del convegno internazionale*, ed. Fabrizio Della Seta, Roberta Marvin, and Marco Marica (Florence: Leo S. Olschki, 2003), 2: 585–600.
43 See Deborah Logan, "An 'Outstretched Hand to the Fallen:' The Magdalen's Friend and the Victorian Reclamation Movements: Part I. 'Much More Sinned Against than Sinning,'" *Victorian Periodicals Review* 30/4 (1997): 368–87.

On 23 August, the critic of *The Spectator* returned to this topic and expressed himself in terms consistent with what had been published on 2 August. All the figures involved in the production of theatrical events shared a certain degree of responsibility in the choice of subject matter; among them the press and the general public were to be counted, together with the theatrical manager, the actors, the dramatist and the composer, who were now dragged in front of the tribunal of the press and exposed to public shame. However, the critic insisted that *La traviata* was founded on a licentious novel whose recklessness was neither alleviated nor mitigated by the grace and fascination of Piccolomini's "birdlike voice." On the contrary, it was wrong and even dangerous to push its hideousness into the background and make its allurements more attractive and seductive by means of a fine singer. While the presentation of the morbid anatomy of those vices in which French dramatists like Dumas indulged was in itself deplorable, to have them embodied on stage by a talented singer was detrimental. "But the complete realisation of a scene presented by skilful actors on a modern stage exerts far greater power over the sympathies of an audience, rendered excitable by all the accompaniments of theatrical illusion, and by the contagion of a crowd all sharing the same emotion, than the most powerful writer can exert over his solitary reader."[44] On this account, the critic would not impose on literature the same restrictions he would consider appropriate for stage representations; the alluring, charming qualities of a good actress made of Violetta the object of admiration, and a young lady of weak principles would even envy the grace and gaiety of Violetta, rather than learn the moral lesson imparted by her story.

But if the moral question monopolised the attention of the critics and triggered the curiosity of the public, what was the people's response to the music of *La traviata*? And what role did the main interpreter play in its rapturous success? As Lumley would put it in his *Reminiscences*, "the important problem of permanent success was not completely solved, so far as the season of 1856 was concerned, until the appearance of a young Italian lady of high lineage on the boards of Her Majesty's Theatre."[45] The business of opera was strongly dependent on those international stars whose vocal talent and dramatic power could draw the audience

---
44 *The Spectator*, August 23, 1856, p. 13.
45 Lumley, *Reminiscences of the Opera*, p. 375.

and fill the theatre; whether the critics liked them or not was another question.

At the outset of the season a new rage from Italy had been announced in the columns of *The Musical World*. Marietta Piccolomini was the new star of the operatic firmament; in her country she had caused a frenzy at least equal to that which had accompanied the appearance of Jenny Lind in London a few years before.[46] The descendant of a noble family, Marietta Piccolomini had struggled against her own family to become a singer and devote her life to opera. Having overcome the opposition of her father, she was granted permission in 1852 to appear in public in *Lucrezia Borgia* at the Teatro della Pergola in Florence. The furore she created was soon recorded by the national and international press, and Violetta would become the character she most excelled as. When in 1856 Meyerbeer visited Italy in order to get a sense of the day-to-day practice of contemporary Italian stage music, he made a stop in Siena for the purpose of seeing her Violetta. As the composer noted in his diaries, Piccolomini was "a very significant talent," even though she excelled less in her vocal technique than in her dramatic skills. "Not a big voice, no great singing style, little by way of top notes, but spirit, grace, elegance, fire, important acting ability, peculiarly genial perception of detail; in short she pleases me very much."[47]

Similar opinions about the discrepancy between Piccolomini's small voice and great dramatic talent were expressed by other contemporaries. In 1856 Verdi himself mentioned Piccolomini more than once when discussing the intended composition of *King Lear*; she would be an excellent Cordelia since "her voice is small, but her talent great."[48] Then, it is not surprising that at the beginning of the 1856 opera season both Lumley and Gye were trying to secure Marietta Piccolomini for their operatic establishments. As expected, a true frenzy accompanied her appearance as Violetta in London, even though it did not equal the craze witnessed in Rome, Florence and Turin.

---

46 *The Musical World*, March 29, 1856, p. 200.
47 Robert Ignatius Letellier, ed., *The Diaries of Giacomo Meyerbeer, iii: 1850–1856* (Madison and London: Fairleigh Dickinson University Press, 2001), p. 367.
48 Gaetano Cesari, Alessandro Luzio and Michele Scherillo (eds.), *I copialettere di Giuseppe Verdi* (Milan: Commissione, 1913), pp. 194–197, available at https://archive.org/details/icopialettere00verd

9. A Moral Case: The Outburst of La traviata (1856)   159

Fig. 10 In reporting on Marietta Piccolomini's success, *The London Journal* portrayed her as a real beauty, a charming singer, an impressive actress, and the daughter of a noble family. *The London Journal*, 23 August 1856.

There, it was reported, on many occasions her ardent admirers would have dragged her carriage home, had she not protested against this insane desire. Although the *prima donna* was immediately and almost unanimously credited with the success of the opera, not everybody agreed that she possessed all the vocal as well as dramatic qualities that would justify the unconditional applause that operagoers were bestowing upon her.

> Her voice was a high and pure soprano, with all the attraction of youthfulness and freshness; not wide in range, sweet rather than powerful, and not gifted with any perfection of fluency or flexibility. Her vocalization was far from being distinguished by its correctness or excellence of school. Her acting was simple, graceful, natural, and apparently spontaneous and untutored. To musicians she appeared a clever amateur but never a great artist.[49]

---

49   Lumley, *Reminiscences of the Opera*, pp. 375–76.

According to the critic of *The Times*, the trepidation that accompanied the premiere of *La traviata* in London on 24 May was due to the *début* of Piccolomini rather than to the quality of either the libretto or its music. The new *prima donna*'s rendition of the principal role was declared "the most perfect ever witnessed" and the extensive tribute paid to Piccolomini was instrumental in demonstrating the limits of the music, which "except so far as it affords a vehicle for the utterance of the dialogue, is of no value whatever." It was a "triumph with which the composer has as little to do as possible."[50] The young *prima donna* excelled in those qualities that were related primarily to her histrionic force. She "monopolized to herself all the attention of the public, who contemplating that mute figure forgot the insipid air by which her movements were accompanied."[51] The climax was achieved in the last scene.

> The tottering step with which Mademoiselle Piccolomini endeavoured to reach her chair when the malady was at its height was fine to the highest degree. Every spectator followed her movements with a sort of nervousness, and audibly rejoiced when she was fairly seated, so obvious was the danger that she might fall exhausted in the midst of her efforts.[52]

The *prima donna* left the audience in a state of enthusiastic admiration, which resulted in moments of breathless suspense followed by final stormy applauses and universal calls for her reappearance before the curtain. A couple of days later, *The Times* recorded the resounding success of Piccolomini's second appearance, while still insisting on the poor quality of the music.

> It is Mademoiselle Piccolomini's truthful expression of the sentiments she has to embody, the force of her 'points,' the accurate detail of her by-play, that gain for her the suffrages of her hearers. They applaud lines rather than passages, and regard the music more as a form of elocution than as a specimen of an independent art. An opera in which the composer's work may be set down as nought looks like a sort of solecism, but, nevertheless, that such a thing is to be found, and in a thriving condition, may be ascertained by any one who will witness *La Traviata*.[53]

---

50 *The Times*, May 26, 1856, p. 12.
51 Ibid.
52 Ibid.
53 Ibid.

When on 31 May the critic of *The Musical World* reviewed the premiere of *La traviata*, he drew attention to the triumph of Marietta Piccolomini alone. Her success was certain and the opinion unanimous that "an artist at once original and fascinating had debuted and triumphed."[54] While as a vocal artist Piccolomini revealed her lack of experience and a voice not yet fully trained, in terms of expression and dramatic power she was possessed of great talent and undeniable histrionic art. As far as plot went, the critic referred to what had appeared in the columns of *The Times* regarding the first performance; he deferred the analysis of Verdi's music to a later occasion. On 7 June, he continued to report on the increasing success of Piccolomini and the unprecedented enthusiasm she created but, again, he failed to express an opinion on the musical quality of *La traviata*, or lack thereof.

Fig. 11 Marietta Piccolomini. *The Illustrated London News*, 31 May 1856.

---

54 *The Musical World*, May 31, 1856, p. 346.

On 31 May, *The Illustrated London News* recorded the success of the new opera which, it was argued, belonged entirely to the new *prima donna*. Her qualities as an actress were said to have overshadowed her attributes as a singer, and ample space was dedicated to her noble lineage and struggle to become a singer. Here, Verdi's music was pronounced the weak link; it included some nice melodies, but of a poor quality, while none of the concerted pieces so distinctive of his previous achievements were to be found in *La traviata*.[55] On the same day, *The Saturday Review* pronounced the personal success of Marietta Piccolomini undeniable: "At the end of every act she was loudly called for; her performance was repeatedly interrupted by enthusiastic demonstrations of delight; and when the curtain fell, the audience would not be satisfied until she had three times appeared before them to receive their thanks and plaudits."[56] But, the critic held, Piccolomini's unquestionable success was less dependent on her vocal than on her dramatic skills: "it is as a dramatic *artiste* that she is greatest; and it is principally to her acting that her success is due. Charming as her voice is, the singer was eclipsed by the actress."[57] Having expanded generously on the plot, the critic insisted that the music was not worth discussing: "The fact is, that the latter [the music] is a mere accessory, and that the piece is to be regarded less as an opera than as a powerful drama set to music, of little significance or beauty in itself."[58]

On 2 August, Chorley took the opportunity to recapitulate the achievements of the past season and call attention to the undeserved popularity of Marietta Piccolomini.[59] The critic claimed that "the song of triumph was never louder in misrepresentation of its misdeeds, even in the days that are gone,"[60] by which he intended to illustrate the evident

---

55 *The Illustrated London News*, May 31, 1856, pp. 587–88.
56 *The Saturday Review*, May 31, 1856, p. 104.
57 Ibid.
58 Ibid.
59 In the meantime *Il trovatore* had been produced for the first time at Her Majesty's Theatre, on which occasion Augusta Albertini was also introduced to the London public. At the end of May, while *La traviata* was taking London by storm and Piccolomini was preparing for *La figlia del reggimento*, Johanna Wagner joined the team led by Lumley and made her debut in Bellini's *I Montecchi e I Capuleti* as Romeo. On 26 June, Marietta Piccolomini scored another success as Maria in *La figlia del reggimento*.
60 *The Athenaeum*, August 2, 1856, p. 968.

mismatch between the rage that had accompanied Piccolomini's appearance in London and her true vocal merits. Such expressions as "abuse of fine language" and "mystification of the public" were pronounced by the critic in order to undermine that undeserved chorus of praise. Chorley insisted that Marietta Piccolomini possessed a talent as a dramatic actress but not as a singer. This opinion was also shared by John Edmund Cox, who in 1872 expressed himself in unequivocal terms: "As for singing she had not a idea of what the meaning of that accomplishment really was."[61]

Although not every critic agreed that Marietta Piccolomini was a valuable singer, most of them claimed that she alone was to be credited with the enormous success of the opera. This is confirmed by the countless detailed descriptions of the impressive manner in which she had conveyed the dramatic power of her character to the open-mouthed audience. That she had a small voice seems beyond doubt, but that she could not sing appears to be controversial. The critical opinions that appeared in the London press were to a large extent consistent with those that were to appear in Paris when *La traviata* was given on 6 December 1856. *Le Costitutionnel* pronounced Piccolomini a talent full of grace, originality and surprise, a talent *sui generis*, an artist gifted like nobody else. She could *tell* what other songstresses would *sing*; but she would tell it with such an accent, verve and sentiment that one felt captivated by her charm without realising what the cause might be.[62] *La Patrie* wrote that her success represented the perfect example of a rare dramatic intelligence, though other periodicals expressed doubts about her vocal technique, which appeared to be still undeveloped. Other comments that appeared in the French press later that year confirmed that she was a mesmerising artist whose dramatic talent amply compensated for her untrained vocal technique and feeble voice.

Notwithstanding the hostility shown by the most conservative periodicals, in London *La traviata* continued to be an incontestable success, appealing greatly to the general public. At the end of October, performances resumed at Her Majesty's Theatre; again the opera house

---

61 John Edmund Cox, *Musical Recollections of the Last Half-Century* (London: Tinsley, 1872), p. 301.
62 *Le Costitutionnel*, December 8, 1856. See Hervé Gartioux, *La Réception de Verdi in France*, p. 217.

was besieged by the multitudes, again every box was full, again every single stall was occupied, again Piccolomini was recalled, applauded and covered with bouquets. All those who had prophesied a short and ephemeral success were now proved mistaken. *The Times* recorded once more the triumph of both Piccolomini and the opera:

> Not only was the theatre crammed full as soon as the doors were opened—not only was the standing room in the pit completely choked up by a compact mass of excited humanity, but after this process was accomplished there still remained a crowd outside, anxiously desiring admittance, and refusing to believe that the desire could not be granted. The triumph of the vocalist in every way corresponded to the eagerness of the anticipators. Mademoiselle Piccolomini was watched throughout her exquisite performance with devotional attention, and at the fall of the curtain came those thunders of applause that cannot be imagined by those who have never learned by actual experience what can be done by the lungs of a crowded audience, in a large theatre, raised to the highest pitch of excitement. Then followed 'calls,' each accompanied by a shower of bouquets, and so ended the loud ceremonial.[63]

The critic continued to express strong disapproval for the music, which he considered merely commonplace, and to emphasise the significant gap between the response of the most severe critics and the enthusiasm of the public. While the former referred to the limited resources of the composer and to the consequently low quality of the music, the latter responded to the blandishments of the main vocalist.

> No one pretends to care sixpence about Verdi's music to *La Traviata*; not a single air forming part of it has taken a place among popular tunes, whereas barrel organs have drawn their inspirations from *Don Pasquale* and *La Figlia*. Without Mademoiselle Piccolomini *La Traviata* would probably be unendurable, but *with* Mademoiselle Piccolomini it is one of the 'lions' of 1856, which, universally censured, is universally patronized.[64]

Other contemporary writings seem to confirm the pattern presented thus far: signs of enthusiastic admiration with regard to the main interpreter were frequent, while only moderate and occasional signs of appreciation were expressed for the composer and his music, let alone the libretto.

---

63 "Her Majesty's Theatre," *The Times*, October 27, 1856, p. 10.
64 *Ibid.*, p. 11.

9. A Moral Case: The Outburst of La traviata (1856)   165

In his *Journal of a London Playgoer*, Henry Morley, Emeritus Professor of English Literature at University College London, commented on the way the success belonged to the principal singer only.

> For of *La Traviata*, the opera with which she [Piccolomini] has connected her success, I must say candidly that it is the worst opera by Verdi that has found its way to England, while his very best is, on its own score, barely tolerable to the ears of any well-trained London audience. Generally, too, in each of Verdi's operas there is some one thing that, if not good, may pass for good among the many; there is the "Donna è mobile" in *Rigoletto*, the "Balen del suo sorriso" in the *Trovatore*, or the "Ernani involami" in *Ernani*. In the *Traviata* there is absolutely nothing. Grant a decent prettiness to the brindisi, "Libiamo," and the utmost has been said for an opera very far inferior in value to the worst of Mr. Balfe's. Where the voice of the singer is forced into discords of the composer's making, and the ear is tortured throughout by sounds which the wise man will struggle not to hear, it is obviously impossible to judge fairly of the vocal powers of the *prima donna*.
>
> In spite of bad music, and in spite of a detestable libretto which suggests positions for her scarcely calculated to awaken honest sympathy, in spite of the necessity of labouring with actors who, as actors, can make—and no wonder—nothing at all genuine out of their parts, Mdlle. Piccolomini creates and obtains the strongest interest for a Traviata of her own [...] Mdlle. Piccolomini is the beginning, the middle and the end of the opera, and it is her Traviata that the public goes to see. Her Traviata conquers the libretto to itself; and to a wonderful degree succeeds also in conquering the music and in impressing its own stamp on very much of it.[65]

But what was Verdi's position in London in 1856? How was he conceptualised as an artistic figure? Did the audience really have to endure his music? According to Lumley, "Verdi's music now shared the same fate as its fortunate exponent. It [*La traviata*] pleased—it was run after—it became one of the most popular compositions of the time."[66] In the manager's account, even if the anti-Verdists and the musical purists denounced Verdi's music with the epithets of their stereotyped vocabulary, *La traviata* soon achieved a marked and lasting popularity. Although it was judged "trashy, flimsy and meretricious" by the anti-

---

65   Henry Morley, *The Journal of a London Playgoer from 1851 to 1866* (London: Routledge, 1891), pp. 114–16.
66   Benjamin Lumley, *Reminiscences*, p. 378.

Verdists, among whom a strain of bigotry was pervasive, the dramatic power of the composer impressed the masses. As Frederick Crowest put it, "the popular nature of the music, its freedom from technical and theatrical perplexity, which the public at large is glad to be without, its ever changing colour, variety and expression—all this contributes to the vitality of *La Traviata*."[67] But, as we have seen from the opinions expressed with regard to the main interpreter, little or no attention was paid to the quality of Verdi's music. A first analysis of Verdi's new opera had been carried out by the critic of *The Athenaeum* as early as May, when both Lumley and Gye had promised to produce it.

> It seems written in the composer's later manner,—grouping with his *Rigoletto* and *Trovatore* without being equal to the latter opera,—to demand from its heroine a less extensive *soprano* voice than Signor Verdi usually demands,—to contain in the *finale* to its second act, a good specimen of those pompous slow movements in which the newer Italian *maestro* has wrought out a pattern indicated by Donizetti;—also throughout an unusual proportion of music in triple or waltz *tempo*. If such choice of rhythm have been made in order to represent the festivity of the Parisian scenes through which the consumptive lady of pleasure and her weak, heartbroken lover move, it is as odd an example of disregard to local colouring as was ever produced by artist. In Vienna the *valse* would prevail, in Warsaw the *polonaise* or the *mazurka*, but in Paris, the *gavotte*, the *bourrée*, the *contredanse*, the *galoppe*.[68]

Chorley had taken the opportunity to look over the piano reduction of *La traviata*, so as to draw some possibly premature conclusions. In his opinion, Verdi had mistakenly adopted the triple metre in order to evoke the Parisian scene, instead of considering those genres more typical of French dance music. As a matter of fact, during his visit to Paris in 1847 Verdi had acquired a good knowledge of the Parisian theatrical world, and in a letter to Countess Clara Maffei dated 6 September 1847 he mentioned two plays which were creating a furore in the French capital: Felix Pyat's *Le chiffonnier de Paris*, and Dumas' and Auguste Maquet's *Le Chevalier de Maison-Rouge*.[69] It also seems clear that not only was Verdi well informed about those dramatic novelties

---

67 Crowest, *Verdi*, p. 137.
68 *The Athenaeum*, May 3, 1856, p. 561.
69 Emilio Sala, "Verdi and the Parisian Boulevard Theatre, 1847–9," *Cambridge Opera Journal* 7/3 (1995): 185–205.

depicting poverty and the sordid aspects of Parisian contemporary life, but he also knew about Marie Duplessis' preference for the new waltz dance. Marie Duplessis, the Parisian courtesan after whom Dumas had created Marguerite Gautier, the main character of *La Dame aux camélias*, was keen on waltz, the most fashionable dance in Paris in the late 1840s.[70] Chorley's knowledge of the most recent aspects of Paris social life was probably not up to date, a circumstance that led him to question the suitability of Verdi's choices in that regard. About Verdi's music, Chorley was unequivocal, for he held that "there is, indeed, little in its score to satisfy the mind or to detain the ear." Such a negative verdict would find confirmation in a later article, in which he stated that "the music of *La traviata* is trashy; the young Italian lady cannot do justice to the music, such as it is. Hence it follows that the opera and the Lady can only have established themselves in proportion as Londoners rejoice in a prurient story prettily acted."[71]

Although the Piccolomini rage was much reported in *The Musical World* (on 2 August it published a sonnet that John G. Freeze had dedicated to Marietta Piccolomini) not a word was printed in that journal regarding Verdi's music. As we have seen, *The Illustrated London News* pronounced Verdi's music the weakest part of the performance for, notwithstanding some nice melodies, it included none of those concerted pieces that were to be found in his previous achievements.[72] Other journals had addressed this question only in passing, and judged Verdi's music a mere accessory to the dialogues. *The Times* is a case in point: "We have been thus minute with the plot, because the book is of far more consequence than the music, which, except so far as it affords a vehicle for the utterance of the dialogue, is of no value whatever, and, moreover, because it is essentially as a dramatic vocalist that the brilliant success of Mademoiselle Piccolomini was achieved."[73] When, two days later, the same critic insisted that the public "applaud lines rather than passages, and regard the music more as a form of elocution than as a specimen of an independent art," he was confirming his opinion of the subordinate role played by the music and its limited artistic value.

---

70 Emilio Sala, *Il Valzer delle Camelie* (Turin: EdT, 2008), pp. 53–86.
71 *The Athenaeum*, August 16, 1856, p. 1023.
72 *The Illustrated London News*, May 31, 1856, pp. 587–88.
73 *The Times*, May 26, 1856, p. 12.

La traviata represents an unprecedented case in the reception of Verdi's operas in Victorian London. In 1856, the discussion of the questionable libretto and its moral implications monopolised the attention of the press to such an extent as to relegate the composer to a subordinate role of little influence. Although it was generally argued that dramatic and lyric representations offered themselves as a mirror for the audience's reflection, no sooner was their subject too dangerously close to a problematic aspect of Victorian society, than they were understood as a threat to social respectability and public decorum. What dramatic censors saw on stage did not please them because it challenged those beliefs and convictions that lay at the core of Victorian society as a power system. While some critics objected to the subject of *La traviata* as such, for it was unacceptable to make a French *lorette* the protagonist of an opera, many insisted that it was Piccolomini's "pure and innocent" performance that made its moral character dangerously misty and confusing. It was the seductive power of her acting, the allure of her gestures, the mesmerising quality of her figure that scared the critics. As already suggested, many commentators expressed their strong fear that the positive aura with which she infused the character of Violetta might have a misleading effect on the public, and especially on female operagoers. She made the thin line between right and wrong disappear.

But Marietta Piccolomini also seems to have played a key role in marginalising the figure of the composer. In fact, she was the actress who made people forget about the music or, as some critics suggested, made them wonder whether there was music at all behind the lines she uttered. This balance would be overturned in the following years for, no sooner had Marietta Piccolomini withdrawn from public artistic life, than *La traviata* came to be listened to and appreciated on the basis of its musical and dramatic content.

In Dublin the forthcoming performance of *La traviata*, which was announced for 14 October, provoked reactions similar to those recorded in London. On 11 October John MacHugh, a Catholic chaplain of Dublin, wrote a letter to the Earl of Carlisle, Lord Lieutenant of Ireland, asking for such a dangerous opera to be prohibited in order "to save the public morals of Dublin from such a gross outrage to their Christian and moral feelings.'[74]

---

74   *The Musical World*, October 18, 1856, p. 666.

On 13 April 1857, a "Grand Verdi Festival" was produced at the Exeter Hall and attracted an immense crowd. The festival was reviewed as "a musical entertainment of a novel and varied character [...] for the admirers of Verdi, the popular representative of Young Italy, the concert provided was a real treat, since it comprised a selection of favourite *morceaux* from his three most successful operas—*Il trovatore, La traviata,* and *Rigoletto*."[75] The critic of *The Times* recorded two issues of some importance: first, the Exeter Hall Committee entertained "strong objections to the text of the notorious *Traviata*" and "interdicted the publication of an English translation of the programme in the form of a book of words;" second, an "enormous audience" assembled at the call of Verdi, three-fourths of which "consisted of persons who would on no account have been tempted to visit a theatre, and yet thought it quite legitimate to listen to the words and music of *La traviata* in Exeterhall." The episode is revealing and the way in which it was recorded by *The Times* is even more telling. The idea of producing a "Grand Festival" reflected the extent to which Verdi was appreciated by the general public and demonstrated that his success had unquestionable implications in terms of money-making. To this success, the discussion on the moral quality of *La traviata* had contributed greatly.

By 1857, and despite all negative criticisms, Verdi had established himself as one of the most significant living representatives of Italian opera in London. In the course of the two parallel operatic seasons there, his recent works made their appearance several times, being produced and revived successfully by both operatic establishments. *La traviata* was given at Her Majesty's Theatre on 23 April 1857, featuring Marietta Piccolomini in the title role and Antonio Giuglini in the part of Alfredo, and once more on 18 July, upon conclusion of the entire season. The same opera appeared in the rival season at Covent Garden on 16 May, this time with Angiolina Bosio as Violetta. Her interpretation of the character was distinctly different from that of Piccolomini. Looking more ladylike and refined, in Chorley's eyes, Bosio's Violetta was less offensive, more supportable than Piccolomini's, an opinion shared by some other contemporary commentators.[76] Mario was Alfredo and Francesco Graziani was Germont; the performance, it was said,

---

75 "Exeter-hall," *The Times,* April 14, 1857, p. 10.
76 Susan Rutherford, "La Traviata or the 'Willing Grisette,'" pp. 585–600.

created an unprecedented excitement and *La traviata* filled the theatre for several nights.

On 23 April *Il trovatore* was given at the Royal Italian Opera, featuring Mario as Manrico, with Grisi as Leonora, Nantier-Didiée as Azucena, Graziani as Conte di Luna, Tagliafico as Ferrando. The interpreters were pronounced superb and the opera attracted a crowded audience. The same opera was produced at Her Majesty's Theatre one month later, on 23 May, with Alboni as Azucena, Spezia as Leonora, Giuglini as Manrico, Federico Beneventano as Conte di Luna, Vialetti as Ferrando; again, the opera was a success. On 7 May, Angiolina Bosio was Gilda in *Rigoletto*, and was received with enthusiasm by the crowded audience at the Royal Italian Opera, while on 2 June, *Nino* was produced at Her Majesty's Theatre, featuring the baritone Corsi, who made an impression despite his worn voice.

10. *Luisa Miller* (1858)

On 8 June 1858, *Luisa Miller* had its London premiere. As previously mentioned, little or no attention had been paid to this opera over the past nine years. *Luisa Miller* had been premiered in Naples on 8 December 1849 and produced in Paris, at the Salle Ventadour du Théâtre-Italien, on 7 December 1852. Its first production was briefly refered to in *The Athenaeum*, but its success was considered dubious and its subject unsuitable for the composer.[1] Nor did the debate concerning Verdi's new style resonate in the London press during the ensuing years. Considering the complete oblivion into which *Luisa Miller* had fallen, at least in so far as the London scene was concerned, it may seem surprising that the manager of Her Majesty's Theatre decided to stage it in 1858. His reasons are difficult to ascertain, for no public statement appeared in the press in this regard, and no explicit reference can be found in Lumley's *Reminiscences*. Nevertheless, in emphasising the performers rather than the composers, the theatre manager's account of the season provides us with some clues. The choice of repertoire and the success of the season continued to depend on the vocal and dramatic skills of the star singers. This was especially true at a time when Lumley was facing major financial difficulties and the competing opera house at Covent Garden was again threatening the primacy of Her Majesty's Theatre.

Already in February, Lumley had left London for Vienna, with the intention to recruit Thérèse Tietjens, whose engagement he had unsuccessfully sought the previous year.[2] In Vienna Lumley had a chance to hear Tietjens sing, and the warm applause with which the

---

1   *The Athenaeum*, January 12, 1850, p. 51.
2   Lumley, *Reminiscences*, pp. 428–29.

Viennese public had received her encouraged the manager to hope for a similar, if not better, reception in London. Once back in London he set himself to the planning of the season, challenged by the prospective reopening of the Covent Garden Theatre. Thanks to his efforts, after a short and extraordinary Christmas season that included *Il trovatore*, *La traviata*, *Lucia di Lammermoor* and *La fille du régiment* (in Italian), on 13 April the after-Easter opera season opened at Her Majesty's Theatre. Meyerbeer's *Les Huguenots* was produced on opening night, featuring Thérèse Tietjens as Valentine and Antonio Giuglini as Raoul.[3] In reviewing the event, the critic of *The Musical World* commented on Benjamin Lumley's "proverbial good luck in finding singers at the moment when they are most wanted"[4] and, in so doing, highlighted an aspect of his managerial acumen which was imperative when dealing with productions so strongly affected by the so-called star system. In fact, the name of Thérèse Tietjens followed those of Jenny Lind, Henriette Sonntag and Marietta Piccolomini, whose roles had been of pivotal importance in determining the fortunes of that operatic establishment over the previous years. At the outset of the season Maria Spezia was also claiming her share of notoriety, and for this reason the manager granted her an opportunity by reviving Verdi's *Nino*. Furthermore, Marietta Piccolomini, who was to make her reappearance in *Don Pasquale* as Norina, in Mozart's *Don Giovanni* as Susanna and also in Michael Balfe's *La zingara* (the Italian translation of *The Bohemian Girl*), deserved one more chance "to shine with renewed lustre."[5] Although Lumley' *Reminiscences* provide no further details, it is reasonable to suppose that it was for the sake of Marietta Piccolomini's renewed lustre that a new opera was to be produced, this being the long-forgotten *Luisa Miller* by Giuseppe Verdi.[6]

By the time the extraordinary Christmas operatic programme was presented and the preparation of the regular after-Easter season at Her Majesty's Theatre was in progress, striking news was circulating that the new home of the Royal Italian Opera was rapidly approaching

---

3 *The Musical World*, April 17, 1858, p. 250.
4 Ibid.
5 Lumley, *Reminiscences*, p. 441.
6 Marietta Piccolomini had already appeared in *Luisa Miller* in 1853. See *Teatri Arte e Letteratura*, January 8, 1853, p. 149.

completion. The new theatre at Covent Garden was undergoing major structural changes involving fewer tiers and fewer boxes per tier, an improvement that would afford a more comfortable accommodation to its patrons and attendees, while allowing both the pit and the stage more space. The 300 workers involved were progressing quite rapidly and there were reasons to believe that the theatre might be ready to reopen on 1 May, as planned.[7]

At the end of March Lumley issued the official prospectus and presented a list of *prime donne*, which included the names of Alboni, Ortolani, Spezia, Piccolomini and, of course, Tietjens.[8] On 3 April he announced that *Les Huguenots* would open the season, featuring Tietjens as Valentine and Giuglini as Raoul, while Piccolomini would appear in Verdi's *Luisa Miller*.[9] One week later, Gye issued his prospectus for the forthcoming season at Covent Garden and announced that the new theatre would open on 15 May with *Les Huguenots* (again), featuring almost the same cast as in 1855 (M. Zelger would now substitute for Polonini as St. Bris); Friedrich von Flotow's *Martha* and Ferdinand Hérold's *Zampa* were also included in the prospectus.[10]

Early in May *La traviata* and *Il trovatore* were produced at Her Majesty's Theatre, the first featuring Marietta Piccolomini in the title role, the second featuring Thérèse Tietjens as Leonora; both artists were pronounced successful by the critic of *The Musical World*.[11] On 15 May, while *Il trovatore* was repeated at Her Majesty's Theatre, the Royal Italian Opera at Covent Garden opened with *Les Huguenots*, the two old favourites Giulia Grisi and Mario performing the main roles, a fact that provoked great excitement.[12] In the meantime, looking beyond the two largest operatic establishments in London, the Drury Lane Theatre also opened, offering an Italian opera season that included such hits as *La traviata* and *Rigoletto*. Not every critic welcomed this new enterprise, and *The Musical World* pronounced it "a luxury in the strictest sense of the word."[13] As a matter of fact, the following week saw *La traviata*

---

7 "Royal Italian Opera, Covent Garden," *The Musical World*, January 9, 1858, p. 26.
8 "Her Majesty's Theatre," *The Musical World*, April 3, 1858, p. 218.
9 *The Musical World*, April 10, 1858, p. 226.
10 "Royal Italian Opera," *The Musical World*, April 17, 1858, p. 251.
11 "Her Majesty's Theatre," *The Musical World*, May 8, 1858, p. 298.
12 "Royal Italian Opera," *The Musical World*, May 22, 1858, p. 323.
13 *Ibid.*, p. 324.

performed in three theatres at the same time, each with a different cast, each successfully welcomed by the audience, each a triumph.

Finally, on 8 June 1858 *Luisa Miller* was given at Her Majesty's Theatre, with Piccolomini as Luisa, Marietta Alboni as Duchess Frederica, Antonio Giuglini as Rodolfo, Federico Beneventano as Miller, Vialetti as Walter, Castelli as Wurm, Gramaglia as Laura; Vincenzo Bonetti was the conductor. The opera was repeated two days later for the benefit of Piccolomini, who had been the object of severe criticism, for her vocal style and musical talent did not match her acting skills. Already in May, when she made her appearance in the role of Susanna in Mozart's *Don Giovanni* at Her Majesty's theatre, her intonation had been said to be particularly weak; moreover, the manner in which she had transposed a particular passage and added sundry changes to the aria "Deh vieni non tardar" was considered questionable. As an actress, on the other hand, she was quite charming. [4]

The critics of *The Times*, *The Athenaeum* and *The Musical World* agreed that *Luisa Miller* was (once more) the worst opera Verdi had ever composed. They shared a certain aversion for its dramatic plot and a strong dislike for the manner in which the composer had set it to music. The critic of *The Musical World* held that its music, whose libretto adhered to Schiller's horrible drama *Kabale und Liebe* with tolerable closeness, was "in no respect to be counted among the very best of Signor Verdi's."[15] The first two acts were probably the worst ever, while the third was more dramatic and effective even though it was undermined by an unaccompanied recitative. An analysis of the score was unnecessary. Words of praise were bestowed upon Alboni, whose Duchess Frederica had been quite convincing. One of the best moments in her rendition was the aria "Nozze? [...] con altra donna?" which was not in the original score. Marietta Alboni inserted it, borrowing from Verdi's *Oberto*;[16] its reception was enthusiastic and the singer was very warmly applauded. To this change the omission of the duet scene between Frederica and Rodolfo in Act I was to be added, which included

---

14 "Her Majesty's Theatre," *The Musical World*, June 5, 1858, p. 362.

15 "Her Majesty's Theatre," *The Musical World*, June 12, 1858, p. 378.

16 See the commentary to the critical edition of *Luisa Miller*'s score by Jeffrey Kallberg. Giuseppe Verdi, *Luisa Miller (melodramma tragico in three acts) by Salvadore Cammarano*, ed. Jeffrey Kallberg, ser. 1: *Operas* (Chicago: University of Chicago Press; Milan: G. Ricordi, 1991), p. 6.

the duet "Dall'aule raggianti" and the Cabaletta "Deh! La parola amara." Piccolomini's Luisa was pronounced by the same critic as "her most successful performance, both vocal and histrionic."[17] Giuglini was admirable, Beneventano's Miller would have been better were he not so exaggerated, Vialetti and the others were good as well. The opera was a success, at least in popular terms.

On 14 June, *The Times* pronounced *Luisa Miller* the worst of Verdi's operas, all the more so when one considered the dramatic subject offered by Schiller's *Kabale und Liebe*.

> *Luisa Miller* is the feeblest of Signor Verdi's operas, which is almost as much as to say the feeblest that ever came from the pen of any musician of repute. And yet *Kabale und Liebe*, even after passing through the crucible of one of these ingenious personages who doctor-up *"libretti"* for modern Italian composers, presents incidents and situations of which an earnest labourer in the field of art might have made a great deal."[18]

Instead, Verdi had failed to take advantage of the dramatic content of the libretto and the opera resulted in an endless accumulation of musical platitudes. Not only was *Luisa Miller* lacking in local colour, this being a weakness already well known in the composer, but it also missed those vigorous and strong emotions that were distinctive of the younger Verdi and that were nowhere to be found in this particular opera.

> But in *Luisa Miller* there is nothing of the kind—no trio like that in the last scene of *Ernani*, no finale like that in the second act of *La traviata*, no such lucky hit as the "Miserere" in *Il Trovatore*, no such melodious and well-planned concerted piece, as the quartet in the last scene of *Rigoletto*—nothing, in short, but an uninterrupted series of commonplaces, pale, monotonous, and dreary, which may be fairly symbolized as the sweepings of our composer's study or the rinsings of his wine bottles.[19]

The critic argued that the lack of dramatic vigour in *Luisa* was indicative of the lack of those qualities that had characterised the composer's first appearance in London more than ten years before. While in Europe, the manner in which Verdi had reduced the noisiness in the orchestra

---

17 Ibid.
18 "Music," *The Times*, June 14, 1858, p. 12.
19 Ibid.

and softened the dramatic colour in the voice had been understood as suggestive of a new style, the critic of *The Times* was now grumbling about what he considered a further weakness in the composer's talent, especially when compared to his past achievements. Not a step forward in his compositional development, however defined, but rather a step back to an even lower level of musical artistry. Surprisingly enough, while insisting that *Luisa Miller* was lacking in that dramatic vigour that was so typical of Verdi's earlier works, the critic lamented that Luisa's role represented a case in point in the process of deterioration to which singers' voices were subject. Verdi continued to abuse the voice and none of Piccolomini's efforts could make the declamatory airs allotted to Luisa singable.

The critic of *The Athenaeum* was the least lenient towards the dramatic subject of *Luisa Miller*, for he held that a more distressful drama than Schiller's *Kabale und Liebe* was difficult to find. The reason why a composer like Verdi had chosen it lay exactly in its dreadfulness.

> None in the list [of Schiller's tragedies] is a more cruel tormentor than *Kabale und Liebe*. Perhaps it is for this very reason that Signor Verdi— whose demon seems to demand drama ere it can be made to speak—has selected it as subject for an opera. To ourselves, its absence of local colour and in the monotony of its misery, it appears thoroughly ineligible.[20]

The critic shared with his colleagues a complaint about the lack of local colour and, in terms quite similar to those adopted by his colleague of *The Times*, remarked that the composer had not been able to take advantage of the original drama, which had instead been diluted into a foggy and tearful opera: "The tragedy is shocking,—the opera was lachrymose and tiresome, save when the actors amused us, without meaning to do such harm."[21] About the music, the critic's verdict was unequivocal: "There is little, from first to last, in the music to reconcile us to the composer."[22] The overture, a long monologue on a phrase of four bars, was inexpressive, and the rest of it contained a good amount of platitude. Verdi was not even able to stand comparison with his own former works, let alone those of Rossini and Donizetti; "As regards the

---

20 "Music and the Drama," *The Athenaeum*, June 12, 1858, p. 759.
21 *Ibid.*
22 *Ibid.*

solo music, *Luisa Miller* contains nothing so good as his Settimino or "O sommo Carlo" in *Ernani*,—or his finale in *Nabucco*,—or his quartet in *Rigoletto*, or his "Miserere" in *Il trovatore.*"[23] In his words, everything that was not trite in the score was unpleasant. Again, Verdi had surpassed himself in the worst possible sense:

> The music of *I due Foscari*, was meagre and dismal enough; but the music of *Luisa Miller*, so far as idea is concerned, seems yet more meagre and dismal.—To be just, however, after this wholesale dispraise, we should say, that a disposition may be traced on the composer's part to enrich and to vary instrumentation, leading him in many passages to eccentricity, in some near invention, and in one or two to happy effect.[24]

Given all its faults and shortcomings, the only reason why *Luisa Miller* scored a success in London, the critic concluded, is that it was the only novelty that season.

> Contemporaries state that *Luisa Miller* has succeeded thoroughly. Our explanation of the space devoted to it is, that probably it is the only unfamiliar opera which this season will be produced at either theatre,— further, because Signor Verdi was "the man of this morning," if his late reverses no longer entitle him to bear the title "of the man of to-day,"— lastly, because, as we said a week ago, bad as we hold his music to be, there is attempt at style in it.[25]

The critic confirmed his strong dislike for the *prima donna*; Piccolomini was said to be utterly incompetent and deficient in powers of musical speech, her only talent consisting in a certain dramatic sensibility. She was acceptable as an actress, but doomed to failure as an operatic singer. Alboni sustained the small part of Duchess Frederica with great care; Giuglini was good; Beneventano, as Miller, the sad, serious, soldierly father, was "emphatic in his own way, but that trenched curiously close on the border of grotesque;" Vialetti, as the old Count, was not well played; while Castelli, The Wurm, was quite miscast.

In his *Musical Recollections* Chorley restated his judgment of *Luisa Miller* as the worst opera Verdi ever composed.

---

23 Ibid.
24 Ibid.
25 Ibid.

> It has seemed to me, as one among Signor Verdi's operas, *Luisa Miller*, taken on its own terms, of fire, faggot, and rack, is the weakest of the weak. There are *staccato* screams in it enough to content any lover of shocking excitement; but the entire texture of the music implies (I can but fancy) either a feeble mistake, or else a want of power on the part of an artificer; who, obviously (as Signor Verdi does), demanding situations, and passion, and agony, to kindle the fire under his cauldron—has, also, only one alphabet, one grammar, one dictionary, whatsoever the scene, whatsoever the country—one *cantabile*, one spasmodic *bravura*—one feverish *crescendo*, as the average tools, by pressure of which the stress on the public is to be strained out.[26]

The critic of *The Spectator* agreed to a large extent with his colleagues that the plot was unsuitable, the music unworthy and the performers admirable in their effort to make the best of a score so limited in value. The customary plot involving a young couple whose love was made impossible by a heartless father constituted the subject most typical of Verdi; the composer had set it to music by adopting the usual repertoire of hackneyed solutions.

> As to the music, it is neither better nor worse than that of *Rigoletto* or the *Trovatore*, operas akin to *Luisa Miller* in their black and horrible subjects. Verdi's music has no character of its own. Whatever the subject or the situation, it is equally pretty, trite, and unmeaning, and depends for its effect upon the expression thrown into it by the genius of the performer.[27]

In August *The Musical World* reported an excerpt from *The Leader*, whose opening sentence read "If anything can cure the Verdi fever now raging with unabated virulence among the operatic audiences in this metropolis, it will assuredly be the performance of *Luisa Miller*."[28] The critic commented on Verdi's *Luisa Miller* in terms at least as negative as those used by Chorley in *The Athenaeum*. "Full of sound and fury signifying nothing"[29] was the fitting epitaph for this opera and its production. The fact that Verdi had gained fame and established himself as a composer among the London public signified nothing; the music of *Luisa Miller* was unmitigated trash. "From the first bar to the last, not

---

26 Chorley, *Musical Recollections*, 2: 297–98.
27 "Music," *The Spectator*, June 12, 1858, [n.p.].
28 *The Musical World*, August 14, 1858, p. 523 (from *The Leader*).
29 Ibid.

a glimpse of freshness, not a soupçon of melody, relieves the dreary waste of dullness and unavailing noise.[30]"

The critic found it difficult to believe that this opera might have preceded *Il trovatore*, for while the second was at least full of musical and dramatic vigour, the first was dull and completely devoid of *tunes*. The instrumentation was noisy to the extreme, a continuous clash and clang of the brasses accompanied by an uninterrupted cracking of the strings.

Upon the conclusion of the season, on 10 August, Lumley had to abandon his position and the operatic establishment passed into the hands of his creditor, William Ward, Earl of Dudley.[31]

---

30 *Ibid.*
31 Lumley, *Reminiscences*, p. 446.

11. *I vespri siciliani* (1859)

In 1858, Benjamin Lumley's professioncal career in operatic management terminated, and on 10 August his establishment passed into the hands of Lord William Ward, Earl of Dudley. A long period of financial difficulties preceded this final step. Already in 1852 the financial burden of the enterprise had become too heavy to bear and a committee of noblemen was formed to assist the establishment. Among them, Lord Ward was certainly the most prominent; he soon manifested an intention to purchase the theatre together with Sir Ralph Howard, and by 1856 he became "with a single exception the possessor of every considerable charge on the property."[1] Two years later, upon conclusion of both the official and the "cheap" opera seasons, and at the end of a long legal dispute with Lord Ward, Lumley had to quit.

In February 1859, it was reported that Her Majesty's Theatre had been purchased by a joint-stock company with the intention of converting it into a huge hotel.[2] One month later, on 19 March, Edward Tyrrel Smith, the lessee and director of the Drury Lane Theatre, issued the official programme of his forthcoming Royal Italian Season. As stated in the prospectus, the closing of Her Majesty's Theatre had enabled Smith to avail himself of the services not only of such prominent singers as Tietjens and Giuglini, but also of many other artists previously attached to that operatic establishment. The inaugural night was decided for the 25 April, and *La sonnambula* was chosen for that occasion. A repertoire

---

1   Benjamin Lumley, *The Earl of Dudley, Mr. Lumley, and Her Majesty's Theatre: A Narrative of Facts Addressed to the Patrons of the Opera, His Friends, and the Public Generally* (London: Bosworth & Harrison, 1863), pp. 6–7.
2   *The Musical World*, February 12, 1859, p. 105.

of sixteen stock operas was set forth (including *Ernani, La traviata, Il trovatore* and *Rigoletto*), in addition to which at least five new operas were to be added, among them Verdi's *Macbeth* and *I vespri siciliani*,[3] Mercadante's *Il giuramento*, Rossini's *Guglielmo Tell* and *La gazza ladra*, Friedrich von Flotow's *Martha*, Mozart's *Nozze di Figaro* and Gluck's *Armide*.[4] Not all the promises made at the outset of the season were fulfilled; while *I vespri siciliani* was performed in London on 27 July that year, it was not until 1960 that *Macbeth* could be given in London.

The Royal Italian Opera season at Drury Lane Theatre opened on 25 April with *La sonnambula* conducted by Julius Benedict, while Victoire Balfe (daughter of the conductor Michael Balfe), Cesare Badiali, Castelli and Pietro Mongini played the main characters. The divertissement entitled *Ariadne* (ballet by Petit and music by Adolphe Adam) followed the same night.[5] Great expectations accompanied the opening of the new season, for the theatre had been renovated, cleaned and decorated, allowing for more comfort and a better sight of the stage. The *début* of Victoire Balfe was pronounced successful and, even though Mongini fell ill, the opera went well and was repeated two days later. The production of Donizetti's *La favorite* (as *La favorita*) followed, while *Lucrezia Borgia* served to introduce Tietjens, the star of the season, to the public of the Drury Lane Theatre. Then *Lucia di Lammermoor* was given, followed by *La traviata* featuring Nina Sarolta in the title role and Ludovico Graziani (brother of the baritone) as Alfredo, both in London for the first time. Then it was Enrichetta Weiser's turn to make her appearance in London for the first time as Gilda in *Rigoletto*. Her debut was not well-received and she was replaced by Marietta Brambilla when the opera was reprised, her second chance coming when Mercadante's *Il giuramento* was later produced. Although Weiser sang better, her rendition could do nothing to change the public's opinion of the poor quality of the opera; as a consequence, *Il giuramento* was withdrawn after three performances. *Il trovatore*, *Don Giovanni* and *Les Huguenots* preceded the appearance of Piccolomini in *La traviata*, with Giuglini as Alfredo, which *La fille du régiment* (as *La figlia del reggimento*) followed soon afterwards. On 7 July,

---

3   Since *Les vêpres siciliennes* was given in the Italian translation by Ettore Caimi, the Italian title will be used.
4   *The Musical World*, March 19, 1859, p. 192.
5   *The Musical World*, April 23, 1859, p. 264.

Tietjens was *Norma* for the first time in London and finally, on the 27th, *I vespri siciliani* was produced at Drury Lane.[6]

In the meantime, on 2 April the opera house at Covent Garden opened its Royal Italian Season with *Il trovatore*, featuring the new *prima donna* Marcella Lotti della Santa as Leonora and Achille De Bassini, a baritone new to that theatre, as Conte di Luna. *Il trovatore*, despite some shortcomings in the principals' voices, was well received and repeated twice. After *La sonnambula*, *Maria di Rohan* and *La gazza ladra*, on 2 May Marcella Lotti della Santa appeared as Gilda in *Rigoletto*, accompanied by Mario as the Duke. On 17 May, Rosina Penco, also new to London, made her first appearance as Violetta in *La traviata*. *Don Giovanni*, *I puritani*, *Lucrezia Borgia*, *Norma* and *Otello*—featuring Giulia Grisi, Mario, Ronconi and Enrico Tamberlik—were also produced, followed by Flotow's *Martha* on 31 May and Mercadante's *Il giuramento* on 9 July. A solitary performance of *Il trovatore* was given on 19 July and the season concluded with six performances of Meyerbeer's *Dinorah*. In general, the season was pronounced a success.[7]

This quick summary confirms that by the late 1850s, *Rigoletto*, *Il trovatore* and *La traviata* had entered the regular operatic repertoire in London and had established themselves as "stock operas" in both houses. That is to say, they could be put on stage at a moment's notice, and theatre managers could rely on them to secure a large audience for their establishments; all the more so if a cast of cherished songstresses were attached to them, as was the case with Piccolomini.

This change is also visible in the opinions expressed in the London periodicals; contemporary commentators and music critics were now ready to accept these works as part of the standard operatic repertoire, alongside *Ernani* and *Nabucco*. On 7 May 1859, the critic of *The Musical World* pronounced *Rigoletto* (which had been produced at Covent Garden) the most genial of all the Italian master's works and went so far as to claim that in this opera "the melodies, for the most part, are spontaneous, and dramatic propriety is never once lost sight of."[8] Later on, when *La traviata* was produced at Drury Lane, the critic spared Verdi a few words of praise for the dramatic quality of the final trio, and then

---

6   *The Musical World*, August 6, 1859, pp. 507–08.
7   *The Musical World*, August 20, 1859, p. 540.
8   *The Musical World*, May 7, 1859, p. 297.

focused entirely on the soprano Nina Sarolta and the vocal cast.[9] He was now assessing the performers' vocal skills and dramatic talent on the basis of a repertoire which had come to include *La traviata*, *Rigoletto* and *Il trovatore*. In terms of singing style, two scenarios were now considered acceptable: the first was marked by Rossini's coloratura style while the second was exemplified by Verdi's new declamatory, dramatised manner.

Finally, *I vespri siciliani*, the Italian version of *Les vêpres siciliennes*, was produced on 27 July 1859 at Drury Lane, the libretto having been translated into Italian by Ettore Caimi. The cast saw Tietjens as Hélène, Pietro Mongini as Amigo (Henri), Enrico Fagotti as De Montfort, Vialetti as Procida. The critic of *The Musical World* bestowed words of great praise on Tietjens: "she sang magnificently, and acted with extraordinary vigour and passion."[10] The music was also judged in favourable terms; the beauty of some of the melodies was especially praised as a distinctive feature of this opera, together with the dramatic effect typical of the composer, particularly in the finale.

> The music of *Les vêpres siciliennes* is written with more than usual care, and several of the airs have obtained a well-deserved popularity. As examples we may name the *bolero*, for Hélène in the last act, "Merci, jeunes amies" a florid, brilliant, and effective *morceau*; the romance of Henri, "La brise souffleur loin"—one of the most simple and beautiful melodies Verdi has produced; the air for Montfort, "Au sein de la puissance," introduced into the overture; and the song "Et toi, Palerme," for Procida. In the concerted music too, there are occasionally flashes of genius which show Sig. Verdi at his best. Of course there is one grand finale in which the composer puts forth all his strength. This occurs at the end of the third act, when the conspirators, headed by Hélène and Procida, are foiled in their attempt to assassinate De Montfort, by Henri, who has first discovered his relationship to the governor (his own "governor"). Sig. Verdi has made good use of this situation, and worked it up with dramatic effect. The duet between Montfort and Henri (when the latter learns he is the son of the former, and the former admits he is the father of the latter), is in the popular composer's most telling manner. The quick movement, admirably sung by Signors Mongini and Fagotti,

---

9   *The Musical World*, May 14, 1859, p. 314.
10 *The Musical World*, July 30, 1859, p. 492.

was encored with enthusiasm on Wednesday night. Taken as a whole, the last act of the *Vêpres Siciliennes* is perhaps the best.[11]

Something similar can be observed in *The Times*, whose critic exhibited an even milder attitude towards Verdi's recent achievements than he had done over the previous years. On 5 April, in reviewing Lotti della Santa's second appearance in *Il trovatore* at Covent Garden, he described the music in very positive terms, claiming that this opera "contains some of Signor Verdi's happiest touches and most dramatic writing— the 'Miserere,' the duet with Di Luna, in the course of which Leonora frustrates the ends of her enamoured persecutor by swallowing poison; and the duet with Manrico, which is interrupted by snatches of melody from the sleeping Azucena, and culminates in the death of Leonora."[12] Another favourable review made its appearance in the same journal in May, when the opera was produced at Drury Lane, featuring Tietjens in the main role. While no mention of the quality of the music was made on that occasion, words of praise were generously bestowed on the interpreters and their rendition.[13] On 11 July, when Mercadante's *Il giuramento* was given at Covent Garden, the critic took the opportunity to draw a comparison between the deficiencies present in Mercadante's unsuccessful opera and the charm characteristic of Verdi's music. While a certain degree of novelty and fresh treatment were the reasons for Verdi's undeniable popular success, Mercadante's lack of inventiveness seemed evident in many respects.

> The strongest "cast," the most efficient band and chorus, the most complete and gorgeous stage appointments, would hardly succeed in winning for Signor Mercadante's *Giuramento* even a brief interval of popularity in this country. The drama is prolix; the music, though well written and cleverly instrumented—is dreary, flat, and wearisome, overlaid with tedious recitative and lengthy solo preludes, marked throughout by a certain staleness at once showing the composer barren of invention, and precluding the charm which (as we have seen in Verdi)

---

11   *Ibid.* The reference to the French titles suggests that what the critic had at hand was the original French version and not the Italian translation, which had been also published for that occasion in London, with the English on facing page.
12   *The Times*, April 5, 1859, p. 12.
13   *The Times*, May 20, 1859, p. 8.

invariably attaches to new ideas, however unpretending, and to fresh treatment, however unelaborate.¹⁴

Again, Verdi had finally established himself as a composer worthy of some attention, with some critics referring to his merits as a benchmark against which other composers' achievements should be assessed.

When *I vespri siciliani* was performed at Drury Lane, *The Times* proclaimed it a complete success, fully confirmed by the verdict of the public: "Another remarkable novelty, in the shape of Signor Verdi's grand serious opera, *Les vêpres siciliennes*—under the Italian title of *I vespri siciliani*—was produced last night, for the first time in this country, with incontestable success."¹⁵ The critic was encouraged to predict that this work would definitely maintain its place among Verdi's best operas. The critic called attention to the composer's inventiveness: "though the piece itself, in spite of its melodramatic and spectacular character, appears somewhat heavy and spun out, it is enriched with many of Signor Verdi's happiest thoughts."¹⁶ Many instances of Verdi's resourcefulness, the critic continued, could be found in the incidental ballet, in the choruses and in the lyric moments offered by the duet for Hélène and Henri; the quartet for Hélène, Henri, Procida and De Montfort; and the tenor romance for Henri, "La brezza aleggia" in Act V, whose graceful melody would guarantee future popularity. The interpreters were said to have been brilliant and their success was undeniable as well.

Once more, the most severe of all was the critic of *The Athenaeum*, who showed no more leniency towards Verdi in 1859 than he had done in previous years. While addressing the success of *Il trovatore* at the Royal Italian Opera early in April that year, he reiterated his grievances about the present sad state of the dramatic art, still longing for those palmy days when Rossini was able to pour out work after work, melody after melody for the public to rejoice at. "Those days are over. Signor Verdi is the best—the one—writer of modern Italy—*Il trovatore* is the least bad opera; and, accordingly, *Il trovatore*, given with new singers [...] is, perhaps, not the best, so much as the only card to be played in

---

14   *The Times*, July 11, 1859, p. 9.
15   *The Times*, July 28, 1859, p. 9.
16   *The Times*, August 1, 1859, p. 6.

our weary period of mediocrity."[17] Quite similar remarks made their appearance on 30 April, when the performance of *La gazza ladra* at Covent Garden offered the critic the opportunity to draw an infelicitous comparison between Rossini's masterpiece and Verdi's *Il trovatore*. "There are more ideas in the Introduction to *La Gazza* than in the entire *Trovatore* (in which, by the way, the 'Miserere' might never have been written had not a certain 'Qual mesto gemito,' in *Semiramide*, gone before it."[18] Once more the critic of *The Athenaeum* complained about the sad state of the vocal art, for while Rossini's operas were written for true singers, the most recent ones had to be put in the hands of those "bald, bawling, declamatory people who in Germany and in Italy have tried of late to make sound pass for singing."[19] The critic insisted that the new declamatory style typical of Verdi's operas was the audible consequence of a state of decline. According to Chorley, Mercadante's *Il giuramento* offered itself as another good example of the sad state in which the operatic art lay. Mercadante's uninspired works were all the more lacking when compared to Verdi's. While Verdi's music, despite everything, took off, Mercadante's did not. Even though the critic was ready to acknowledge a few qualities in Mercadante, *Il giuramento*, as well as most of his previous operas, was doomed to a quick, inevitable oblivion. "His voices are carefully handled, his orchestra is discreet, if not inventive; yet there is no denying that his operas 'hang fire,' while those of Signor Verdi 'go off'—and that among the fifty (we believe there are fifty) not one, save perhaps *Elisa e Claudio*, has gained an European reputation."[20]

Upon the season's conclusion, when the critic returned to the premiere of *I vespri siciliani* at Drury Lane, he reiterated a judgment that was consistent with his general critical attitude. Chorley had attended the Paris premiere of *Les vêpres* and already recorded its dubious success on that occasion. Furthermore, that opera had not proven successful in the long run; it had been revived neither in Paris nor in Italy, and it was surprising to see such an unsuccessful opera making its way to the London theatres. Another failure was easy to predict. Chorley

---

17 *The Athenaeum*, April 9, 1859, p. 493.
18 *The Athenaeum*, April 30, 1859, p. 588.
19 *Ibid.*
20 *The Athenaeum*, July 16, 1859, p. 89.

understood *I vespri siciliani* as Verdi's unsuccessful attempt to imitate and emulate the genius of Meyerbeer; the Italian composer had tried to out-do the French, but the results were weak and objectionable. In his effort to follow the French model he had sacrificed his melodic inventiveness to a kind of grandiosity which was not substantiated by adequate musical resources: "The composer is there less catching in his melody than in his other operas, while his attempts at scenic grandeur and orchestral ingenuity betray leanness and want of resource by their noise and eccentricity."[21] The interpreters shared responsibility with the composer for this failure; both Thérèse Tietjens and Pietro Mongini abused their voices by piling up loud sonorities and inappropriate ornaments at the expense of intonation and good taste.

> There can be no question that she [Tietjens] is more zealous in filling the part of the heroine *Helena* than was Mdlle. Cruvelli; there can be no question as to the superb original quality of her voice.—that her voice has gone the wrong way, is partly explained by its owner being German (which implies a false notion of vocal training), partly by the excitement which physical vehemence can always produce among a not very refined audience all the world over. For artists are strong enough to resist this.— The result is shown, in the case of Mdlle. Tietjens, by the incompleteness of every executive passage—by that failure of intonation—which is a disease, not a natural difficulty, with voices so triumphantly firm, so radiantly powerful, as hers has been. To real musicians Mdlle. Tietjens can be no longer the singer of promise that she was. On her arriving here there were hopes in one so magnificently endowed; now, we have small further expectation, except of *fortissimo* laid on *fortissimo*, of false ornament on false ornament, —of decline, in short. Very great is the pity.—Signor Mongini, too, as has been elsewhere said, is doing his worst for himself; and the consequence of such a union betwixt lady and lover was that perpetual exaggeration which is alike fatal and fatiguing.[22]

Chorley's position and line of argument had not changed much. Verdi had not improved, this last opera was possibly his worst, the interpreters were not up to the task. Contrary to his colleague from *The Times*, who

---

21 *The Athenaeum*, August 6, 1859, p. 183. It is worth remembering that Chorley was then working on the English translation of Meyerbeer's *Dinorah*, which was to be produced later on that year for the Royal English Opera at Covent Garden. Chorley was criticised for the quality of his translation by the critic of *The Musical World* (8 October 1859).

22 *Ibid.*

had called attention to Tietjens' splendid dramatic energy and excellent execution, and to the brilliant success scored by Mongini, who had won fresh laurels, Chorley considered neither the composer nor the interpreters worthy of the applause the audience had undeservedly poured on them.

Meanwhile, and to our surprise, the critic of *The Spectator* pronounced *I vespri siciliani* "a ponderous work, in which the composer's own platitudes and commonplaces are blended with laborious endeavours to imitate the depth and solidity of the German school."[23]

---

23 "Music," *The Spectator*, July 30, 1859, p. 19.

12. The Years 1860 and 1861: *Un ballo in maschera*

In 1860 came the last act of the long-running dispute between Lord Ward and Lumley. A legal action of debt for rent was brought by the former against the latter, the plea being "one of accord and satisfaction by giving up possession of the Opera House and cancelling the lease."[1] A verdict for the plaintiff was quickly reached, consisting in damages of £4,560. On 24 February, *The Times* announced that Edward Tyrrel Smith, already manager of the Drury Lane Theatre, had signed an agreement to become the lessee of Her Majesty's Theatre "on a lease of seven, fourteen or twenty-one years."[2] The news was also reported by *The Musical World* on the 25th, and a few weeks later the prospective opening of the Italian opera season at Her Majesty's Theatre gained more coverage. The new manager and lessee was eager to announce that the opera season would commence on 10 April, and that all the necessary arrangements had been completed to guarantee the unsurpassed splendour and prestige for which Her Majesty's Theatre had become deservedly famous the world over. The director had the pleasure to announce that he would "retain the invaluable services of Mademoiselle Tietjens and Madame Alboni, and secure that of Madame Adelaide Borghi Mamo" for his operatic establishment. The conductors Luigi Arditi and Julius Benedict were confirmed, while the names of Pocchini, Ferraris and Cucchi were mentioned in the ballet department.

---

1 *The Musical World*, February 18, 1860, p. 103.
2 James H. Mapleson, *The Mapleson Memoirs, 1848–1888* (Chicago: Belford, Clarke & Co., 1888), 1: 23.

A week later, the list of engagements was enriched by the inclusion of more prominent names, such as Marietta Piccolomini, Maria Brunetti (for the first time in London), Marcella Lotti della Santa and, among the men, Pietro Mongini, Belart, Corsi and Giuglini. It was the director's intention to produce Carl Maria von Weber's *Oberon* and *Der Freischütz*, Gioacchino Rossini's *Otello* and *Semiramide*, Wolfgang Amadeus Mozart's *Le Nozze di Figaro*, Friedrich von Flotow's *Martha*, Donizetti's *La favorite*, and Verdi's *Rigoletto* and *Il trovatore*.[3]

On 31 March, Gye announced that the Italian opera season at Covent Garden would also commence on 10 April with a performance of Meyerbeer's *Dinorah*, featuring Marie Caroline Miolan-Carvalho, Giudita Sylvia, Italo Gardoni, Joseph Tagliafico;[4] Jean-Baptiste Faure, for whom the part was originally composed, would appear in the role of Hoel.[5] Rossini's *La gazza ladra* and *Barbiere di Siviglia*, Mozart's *Don Giovanni*, Meyerbeer's *Les Huguenots*, Beethoven's *Fidelio* and Verdi's *Rigoletto* were among the operas promised in the prospectus, besides which two novelties were also mentioned: Flotow's *Stradella* and Victor Massé's *Les noces de Jeannette*, under the Italian title *Le Nozze di Giannetta*. Costa was confirmed as the conductor and Augusts Harris as the stage manager.

The list of vocal stars presented by both operatic establishments prompted the critic of *The Musical World* to express his concern for the sad state of the Italian vocal art and expand on this issue by raising a critical question: "Does legitimate Italian opera border on dissolution?"[6] Not only did the question address the way in which modern composers had advanced towards a new expressive frontier, but also the extent to which the success of the opera was still dependent on the art of singing: "If Italian opera goes, the art of singing, distinguished from that of vocal declamation, must go with it."[7] On the one hand, there was the vocal declamation so dear to the younger composers, among whom the name of Verdi emerged prominently, while on the other lay the much cherished Rossinian florid style. In advocating the qualities

---

3   *The Musical World*, March 24, 1860, p. 196.
4   *The Musical World*, March 31, 1860, p. 197.
5   *The Musical World*, April 7, 1860, p. 221.
6   *The Musical World*, April 14, 1860, p. 236.
7   Ibid.

of the old method of singing, the critic intended to draw a line between a tradition of uncorrupted vocal mastery and the distasteful fashion brought forward by the new composers. A songstress like Marietta Alboni represented a good case in point.

> It is notorious that those who have been nurtured in the Italian school of singing are also the best interpreters of the classic German models, and equally so that the voices of the Italians of the last and preceding generations were more *enduring*, and preserved their vigour and freshness far longer, than those of the present age. Not to travel, however, from our own time, compare Alboni's execution of the airs in *Figaro* and *Don Giovanni* with that of any singer whose youth and adolescence have been chiefly devoted to the operas of Signor Verdi. The one is even, flowing, well-balanced, natural, and expressive—artistically faultless, in a word; while the other, with here and there a fine point, springing from the successful embodiment of a happy impulse, is unequal, anti-rhythmical, strained, and convulsive.[8]

In our critic's eyes, Rossini's florid music still represented the benchmark against which the performance of individual singers was to be measured. As a consequence, the critic looked with alarm and concern at the process of degeneration that Italian vocal art was undergoing. "The art of singing is no longer taught in Italy; and now even in this vast city of London, where the Italian Opera has flourished for a century and a-half, it seems impossible to obtain a company of *Italian* singers, or to compose a repertory of *Italian* music."[9] To support his claim, the critic drew the reader's attention to the way in which both opera houses in London had put forward a prospectus where German, Belgian and French names outnumbered the Italian among the ranks of the interpreters. The problem arose not only in such new compositions as Flotow's *Martha*, but also in that of *Semiramide*, the most essentially Italian *opera seria* by the most essentially Italian composer: the German soprano Thérèse Tietjens performed Semiramide, Evrard, a Belgian, was Assur and Belart, a Spaniard, was Idreno, while the Frenchman Viallette was Oroe. Even though one might argue that it was not entirely true that Italian singers had disappeared from the international scene, the critic's concern suggests the extent to which a change in the vocal constellation

---

8   Ibid.
9   Ibid., p. 237.

was perceived as capable of threatening or at least destabilising the traditional notion of Italian *bel canto* as it was generally understood.

Later, Verdi's *Il trovatore* (14 April) and *La traviata* (18 April) were produced at Her Majesty's Theatre; the first featured Tietjens, while the second had Piccolomini in the title role. Marietta Piccolomini would give five last farewell performances in her most-cherished role of Violetta. In June *Ernani* and again *Il trovatore* were performed at Her Majesty's Theatre, while on 21 July *Rigoletto* was successfully given at Covent Garden, featuring Mario, Ronconi, Tagliafico, Nantier-Didiée and Miolan-Carvalho. Miolan-Carvalho's rendition of Gilda offered the critic of *The Musical World* the chance to expand further on the issue concerning the modern vocal style. He pronounced the quality of her voice eminently French, by which he meant that it lacked "the rich tone and volume which we are not merely accustomed to find in Italian sopranos almost as a matter of course, but also very frequently in the Germans and English."[10] Unfortunately, Miolan-Carvalho's voice had been enfeebled by the continuous strain put upon the higher notes by performing those vocal parts that had been written by selfish and inattentive young composers. However, the critic was quite appreciative of the music allotted to the character of Gilda and held that the solo air "Caro nome che il mio cor" contained some of Verdi's most genuine melodies and was very much in tune with the sentiment supposed to animate Gilda's young bosom. The critic described Verdi's orchestral accompaniments in positive terms, and pronounced them "the most varied and ingenious to be found in any opera by Signor Verdi."[11]

The 1860 opera season had recommenced under unusually favourable auspices, for the two establishments had been restored to their original splendour and were now again able to compete with each other for supremacy in the lyric art. Smith's effort to take over the management of Her Majesty's Theatre had been successful and the Italian opera season there had resumed the long tradition initiated by Lumley; Covent Garden continued to collect its share of success thanks to Gye's entrepreneurial attitude and his collaborators' skills. In both opera houses, the name of Verdi held a prominent position among those

---

10   *The Musical World*, July 28, 1860, p. 477.
11   *Ibid.*, p. 478.

master composers on whose talents the managers had to rely in order to guarantee their financial health.

At the beginning of 1861, Edward Smith was running two establishments, Her Majesty's Theatre and Drury Lane, and already in January a series of operatic performances in English were given at Her Majesty's Theatre, which included *Il trovatore*, produced in combination with the pantomime *Harlequin and Tom Thumb*. As usual, during the winter months both managers busied themselves undertaking negotiations so as to secure the most cherished artists for their establishments. On 2 February Smith published a short note stating that the rumours suggesting that Tietjens and Giuglini had been engaged for the Royal Italian Opera at Covent Garden were groundless. On the contrary, he was eager to announce that the old cast of Her Majesty's Theatre had been reconfirmed. In the meantime, both theatres continued the by now usual English opera season, consisting of either English operatic works written by local composers (among them Balfe and George Alexander Macfarren), or English translations of stock operas from the Italian (*Il trovatore*) and the French (Auber's *Le domino noir*) repertoire. But when both English opera seasons terminated on 16 March that year, only one Italian opera season could open;[12] in fact, on 6 April 1861 it was positively announced that there would be no performances of Italian opera at Her Majesty's Theatre under the direction of Smith that year.[13] One week later, a short announcement made its appearance in the London press, informing the public that unprecedentedly severe financial losses had led Smith to the inevitable conclusion that, "even with crowded houses night after night, the likelihood of a balance ever being struck to his advantage was far too remote to be taken into account."[14] Once again, the financial burden had played a prominent role in marring the popular success of the operatic season.

On 4 April, the Italian Opera Season at Covent Garden opened with Meyerbeer's *Le prophète*, featuring the same cast as the previous year: Róza Csillag, Amalia Corbari, Enrico Tamberlik and Joseph Tagliafico. This circumstance offered the critic of *The Musical World* the chance to turn his eye again to the change in the repertoire and to the increasing

---

12 *The Musical World*, March 16, 1861, p. 172.
13 *The Musical World*, April 6, 1861, p. 217.
14 *The Musical World*, April 13, 1861, p. 232.

attention the theatre management was paying to the production of French and German operas. "Instead of depending on those composers who created Italian Opera, and infused into it vitality and strength, the director called to his assistance foreign musicians, and entirely changed the nature and character of Italian Opera proper, as far as his theatre was concerned."[15] While the success of French opera at Covent Garden was undeniable, the critic argued that many undeservedly forgotten Italian operas were waiting to be revived. Together with Rossini, whose *L'italiana in Algeri*, *L'inganno felice*, *Il Turco in Italia* and even *Cenerentola* had been long neglected, the names of Domenico Cimarosa, Giovanni Paisiello and Niccolò Piccinni were also mentioned among those whose operas were worth resuming.

When on 9 April, *Rigoletto* was performed again at Covent Garden the critic of *The Musical World* bestowed words of generous appreciation upon the main interpreters, Giorgio Ronconi, in the title role and Marie Caroline Miolan-Carvalho as Gilda. Constance Nantier Didée and Joseph Tagliafico were pronounced effective, natural and picturesque, while Pietro Neri-Baraldi as the Duke of Mantua suffered from the unequal confrontation with a role that had been attached to such an unforgettable interpreter as Mario. *Rigoletto* was said to be Verdi's best opera; the melodies allotted to the jester were pronounced characteristic while Verdi was said to have written nothing more genial and expressive than the music given to Gilda.[16] A couple of months later, Mario's rendition of Rossini's *Barbiere di Siviglia* provided the critic of *The Musical World*, Desmond Ryan,[17] with the opportunity to elaborate once more on the dramatic change in the vocal art that had occurred over the preceding decades. "Such a singer and such music are indeed constituted to uphold genuine Italian vocalisation, in spite of the degenerate influence of Signor Verdi and modern operatic composers."[18] Interestingly, in Ryan's opinion it was not entirely the composer's fault if the Italian vocal art had degenerated into a sad state of decadence, for "when signor Verdi commenced writing for the stage the vocalists in the

---

15   *The Musical World*, April 6, 1861, p. 216.
16   *The Musical World*, April 13, 1861, p. 236.
17   The identity of the critic is clarified by the initial "R" that appears at the end.
18   *The Musical World*, June 8, 1861, p. 360.

legitimate Italian school were extreme rarities."[19] In the critic's analysis, the composer had been compelled to accommodate himself to the limited capacities of those "vociferators" who had substituted for true singers; this circumstance had encouraged poorly skilled interpreters to consider a good voice the only and unique requirement necessary to undertake a successful career in the vocal art, while the severe application necessary to learn proper singing was now dismissed as a tiresome, useless task. The vicious circle thus had inevitable consequences on the repertoire itself, for the lack of good singers now prevented the production of the Rossinian operas: "The school of [Giacomo] David, [Nicola] Tacchinardi, [Manuel] Garcia, [Giovanni Battista] Rubini, [Filippo] Galli, [Antonio] Tamburini and others was gradually dying a natural death, and, as an inevitable consequence, Rossini's music, having nobody to interpret it, was falling into disrepute."[20]

When *Il trovatore* was performed at Covent Garden on 7 May that year, the critic of *The Athenaeum* took the chance to reiterate his usual grievances and express his confidence that finally the public would recognise the poor value of Verdi's most applauded operas.

> The superficial attractions of Signor Verdi's best opera seem to be falling to their true level. The public, we suspect, has had almost enough of the few melodies in the score, too much of its noisy and meagre instrumentation, and to have found out that the extravagance of an opera story may make the whole work as dull as inexpert treatment of an historical anecdote.[21]

The critic put forward the usual arguments: lack of true melodic inventiveness, an excessively noisy instrumentation and a subject not appropriate for dramatic representation. Again, a comparison was drawn between Verdi and Rossini: while the popularity of the first among the public was clearly fading away, the second was still able to appeal to the largest audience by virtue of the intrinsic artistic value of his operas. Unless proven wrong by the success of *Un ballo in maschera*, which was soon to be premiered in London, the critic insisted upon predicting a quick downfall for the composer's undeserved popularity.

---

19   Ibid.
20   Ibid.
21   *The Athenaeum*, May 11, 1861, p. 637.

> The charm of *Rigoletto* and *La Traviata* is already worn out, so that the reign of this music, as intrinsically poor as it is superficially pompous, may possibly be approaching an end in this country, unless it be deferred by some success for *Un ballo in maschera*. Of this music, two contradictory accounts are given; but unless an entire transformation of style has taken place, no well-wisher to composer or to singers will regret if the downfall of a popularity so unmerited should prove to be entire and final. The pleasure in it once exhausted, it is hard to fancy any future race of operagoers returning on Signor Verdi's music.[22]

In the meantime, on 8 June, the Lyceum Theatre opened under the direction of James Henry Mapleson, the late factotum of Smith, and a new Italian opera season was inaugurated with *Il trovatore*, featuring Tietjens as Leonora, Alboni as Azucena, Giuglini as Manrico and Edouard Gassier as Ferrando. The same cast was announced for the performance of Verdi's new opera, *Un ballo in maschera*, which was scheduled for one week later, on 15 June.

As the editor of *The Musical World* testified, the production of Verdi's new opera had been announced by the managers of both Italian theatres in a moment when the prestige of its composer seemed to be on the wane, "when his popularity appeared to totter beneath the new impetus given to good music; when the *Trovatore* was beginning to pall upon the public taste, and the *Traviata* was all but banished from the operatic repertory."[23] Although *Un ballo in maschera* had first appeared among the novelties announced in Gye's prospectus that year,[24] James Henry Mapleson was the first to produce it; *Un ballo in maschera* was given at the Lyceum Theatre on 15 June, and at Covent Garden on 24 June, with a different cast. What is more, the music of Verdi's last opera had already been made familiar to the London public, for it had been performed at two music venues, the Canterbury and the Oxford Music Halls.[25] Given that both music halls offered light entertainments typical of the "song-and-supper rooms," it would be extremely interesting to explore the nature

---

22 *Ibid.*
23 *The Musical World*, June 15, 1861, p. 377.
24 *The Times*, May 29, 1861, p. 8.
25 Both the Music-Halls were run by "the father of the halls," Charles Morton. "Canterbury Music-Hall," in *The Concise Oxford Companion to the Theatre*, edited by Hartnoll, Phyllis, and Peter Found. Oxford University Press, 1996. Available at http://www.oxfordreference.com/view/10.1093/acref/9780192825742.001.0001/acref-9780192825742-e-536

of those changes and adaptations in the music that might have filled the gap between the original operatic product and the expectations of a much larger public. In fact, although the issue concerning Italian opera, and Verdi's works in particular, being burlesqued in Victorian London has been investigated,[26] little attention seems to have been paid to the manner in which Verdi's music was popularised within the province of the music hall during the same years. However, the very fact that Verdi's music was present in venues commonly devoted to light entertainment is a strong sign of his popularity and financial profitability.

In introducing *Un ballo in maschera* to its readers, *The Musical World* pointed out that its subject had been taken from Eugène Scribe's *Gustave III, ou Le bal masqué*, which had already been set to music by Daniel Auber in 1833. Auber's successful opera had been adapted by James Planché as an English melodrama and given at Coven Garden on 13 November 1833, while the Italian translation of the opera was performed in London in 1851.[27] Although Verdi's librettist Antonio Somma had recast the airs, duets and ensembles according to the conventions of the Italian stage, which meant the removal of the first ballet scene and the reduction of the second to a ballroom background, a comparison between Verdi's new opera and its precedents was unavoidable. The Italian composer was now "bringing his music into direct competition with that of one who was a far greater master and more inspired writer than himself."[28] However, the article concluded on a note of optimism, for Verdi was the only living composer from whom not only the general public, but also the qualified critic might expect something sufficiently inspired and dramatically conceived to bear comparison with the French precedent.

> The general public, after all, are not such fools; and Sig. Verdi's long-ending popularity proves incontestably not only that he possesses qualities which no other composer possesses, but that to him belongs the still rarer quality of interesting and exciting in an eminent degree. And so we, too, as well as the *profanum vulgus*, will be right glad to hear a new work which has emanated from his fertile pen.[29]

---

26 Roberta Montemorra Marvin, "Verdian Opera Burlesqued: A Glimpse into Mid-Victorian Theatrical Culture," *Cambridge Opera Journal* 15/1 (2003): 33–66.
27 Edward J. Dent, "Un Ballo in Maschera," *Music & Letters* 33/2 (1952): 101–10.
28 *The Musical World*, June 15, 1861, p. 377.
29 Ibid.

The Musical World devoted ample space to the performance of *Un ballo in maschera* and two different contributions made their appearance in that journal a week later, the first focusing on the music and the second on its performance. The unprecedented situation of two different articles placed in two different columns of the same journal but relating to one and the same musical work can be explained by reference to the recent publication of a series of select piano reductions of vocal airs taken from *Un ballo* by the London publisher Boosey and Sons. This collection was advertised for sale in the same issue of the journal and, as a result, emphatic judgments and flattering remarks characterised both contributions. The first one appeared in the *Reviews* column of *The Musical World* and was to a good extent based on the vocal scores and piano reductions published by Boosey and Sons. The second appeared in the *Operas* column, where the critic reviewed the performance and the interpreters.

As previously mentioned, *Un ballo in maschera* was first performed at the Lyceum Theatre on Saturday 15 June, while the Italian Opera at Covent Garden would present it one week later, on 24 June, after the revival of *Rigoletto*. The success of the opera at the Lyceum, the critic of *The Musical World* held, was undeniable and although different opinions had been expressed in this regard, it was equally undeniable that the opera was full of melodies "likely to fasten on the general ear,"[30] or, to put it in clearer terms, "full of *tune* — of sentimental tune, dramatic tune, and purely *catching* tune."[31] The cavatina for the baritone "Alla vita che t'arride" from Act I, Scene 1 was compared to the insinuating music of Balfe's ballads, while the aria for the soprano "Morrò, ma prima in grazia" from Act III scene 1, or Renato s aria "Eri tu che macchiavi quell'anima" from Act III, Scene 1, provided solid evidence of Verdi's tunefulness. A more promising beginning was not possible and these arias would be rapidly circulating among music amateurs. About the performance the critic was no less enthusiastic and all the performers were pronounced magnificent, unqualified praise being awarded to the whole cast. Giuglini, in the role of Richard, Earl of Warwick, sang with infinite charm and never had to force his voice, while Tietjens, who appeared

---

30 *The Musical World*, June 22, 1861, p. 387.
31 *Ibid.*

"to extraordinary advantage in Verdi's energetic heroine,"[32] outclassed everyone by her tragic abilities. In short, no complaint was expressed by the critic with regard to either the music or its interpretation; no specific reference was made to the loudness of the orchestra or to the coarse treatment of the voices.

One week later, *Un ballo in maschera* was produced at Covent Garden with a different cast (which included Rosina Penco, Marie Miolan-Carvalho, Constance Nantier-Didiée, Francesco Graziani, Mario, Joseph Tagliafico and Zelger) and the same setting adopted in Paris in January of that year. At the Théâtre Italien, Mario had refused to be the Earl of Warwick and to wear the appropriate costume; to accommodate him, the scene was transferred to Naples, and other characters had to be changed to suit the new setting. At Covent Garden the scene was also set in Naples, instead of Boston; Amelia and Oscar had become Adelia and Edgard in Paris and remained unchanged in London, while Samuel and Tom, the two conspirators, were called Armando and Angri at Covent Garden. Mario wore three different costumes, which, *The Times* reported on 1 July, all suited him superbly, especially the picturesque one of a Neapolitan sailor.

When *Un ballo in maschera* was produced at Covent Garden, the critic of *The Musical World* was as appreciative towards the music as he had been on the previous occasion; however he now used different terms to address the question concerning the quality of the voice necessary to perform it. The cast looked powerful but, he held, Verdi's music did not always "suit itself to the means of the best singers."[33] The music demanded an amount of energy and strength of lungs to be found in few singers; while Rosina Penco was admirable in Mozart and Rossini, she was quite inadequate as Verdi's heroine. Francesco Graziani's praiseworthy performance as Renato was judged wanting in dramatic vigour and truth, Mario's impersonation of the Duke being the only performance deserving of unconditional commendation. As already suggested, the critic was now more inclined to accept Verdi among the composers worthy of his admiration; while in previous years he had condemned severely the many shortcomings noticeable in Verdi's treatment of the voice, he now pointed out that singers formed two

---
32   *Ibid.*, p. 390.
33   *The Musical World*, June 29, 1861, p. 407.

different classes. The first included those younger interpreters who were endowed with the necessary skills to perform Verdi's new music, while the second comprised those who, instead, had been trained in the traditional florid style.

The critic of *The Athenaeum* showed no more leniency to *Un ballo in maschera* than he had done with Verdi's previous operas, and he addressed the question concerning the quality of the music and the merits of its composer in the usual negative terms. The fact that Verdi was the only Italian composer enjoying an international reputation did not stem from his artistic merits but, on the contrary, from the sad state of decadence in which Italian opera lay at the moment. Although the composer seemed to have advanced in his dramatic and compositional skills, the attempt to imitate Meyerbeer had not resulted in any improvement, but rather in a reduced effectiveness in the melodies and in a less spontaneous dramatic genius. The idea of setting to music a subject for which Daniel Auber had already written some very beautiful pages was not felicitous, and the result consisted in "many old phrases, with a few new eccentricities of instrumentation."[34] The music in the first act, which takes place in the hut of the sorceress, was pronounced "more tiresome than terrible," Ulrica's *cantabile* was "more peaceful and pretty than appropriate," while nothing could be staler than the Earl of Warrick's *barcarolle*. The second act included the best music in the opera; still, when tested against Meyerbeer's masterwork, it showed its limits. The third act did not improve the general impression: the vocal pieces were poor, while the rest of the music suffered from the infelicitous comparison with Meyerbeer and Auber.

> The end comes in the usual "sound and fury" of screams for the heroine, alternated with sorrowful slow notes for the tenor. To close what has been a long story, though it is one needful to be told, we must state as a conviction that Signor Verdi has not conquered a hair's breadth of new, solid territory in his last opera.[35]

Such a negative criticism was confirmed soon afterwards, when *Un ballo in maschera* was presented at Covent Garden, on the occasion of which the critic of *The Athenaeum* declared himself relieved to be "absolved

---

34 *The Athenaeum*, June 22, 1861, p. 837.
35 Ibid.

from the necessity of returning to the dry and superficial music of this opera, and have only to speak of the cast."[36] However, he took each and every chance to throw his darts against Verdi, whose composition was again made the object of severe criticism. Miolan-Carvalho's personation of Oscar was good, especially considering the talent and skill she had manifested in her Cherubino and the fact that she had "to fight for lean and characterless phrases in place of expressing the beautiful melodies of a great master."[37] Nantier-Didiée was a portentous sorceress, notwithstanding the insignificant music allotted to her character. The final verdict reveals the attitude of the critic at its most characteristic:

> On the whole, though new Italian operas, which any English hearer will admit are scarce, we conceive that Signor Verdi's last will not plant itself on our stage even for such a short and already-exhausted life as that of his *Il Trovatore*. The performance, however, was received with every sign of favour, and—as a performance—deserved to be so received.[38]

The conclusion chimed with that of the previous review, in that both articles insisted on the ephemeral nature of the opera's success and the poor quality of its music. In a way, Chorley shared with his colleague from *The Musical World* the idea that two different singing styles had established themselves among opera singers; the difference was that he continued to treasure the old one and resent the new one unconditionally.

The Times recorded the success scored by Verdi's new opera in terms strongly suggestive of the role a single critic (Davison) was playing in two journals, *The Times* and *The Musical World*. On 10 April 1861, *The Times* reviewed the performance of *Rigoletto*, praising those genial and expressive melodies that Verdi had allotted to the part of Gilda, and indulging in a long and articulate description of Ronconi's dramatic qualities. An identical article was reproduced three days later in the columns of *The Musical World*. The same happened in May, when *Il trovatore* was selected for the first appearance of Penco and Graziani at the Royal Italian Opera, Covent Garden. On 8 May *The Times* reviewed the performance, praising the interpreters for their vocal and dramatic qualities and highlighting the way Signor Tamberlik had "electrified

---

36 *The Athenaeum*, July 6, 1861, p. 25.
37 Ibid.
38 Ibid.

the house, and was twice called before the curtain amid vociferous acclamations for having interpolated, in an unexpected place, his extraordinary high chest C."[39] On 11 May the same review appeared in the columns of *The Musical World*. Again, on 11 June, *The Times* reviewed the performance of *Il trovatore* at the Lyceum Theatre, and the same review appeared in *The Musical World* four days later.[40] On that occasion the critic thought it pointless to elaborate further on the quality of the music, for *Il trovatore* had already proven as enduring as many other undisputed masterpieces from the past (including *Il barbiere di Siviglia* or *Don Giovanni*), able to outlive "the fashion of the period at which it was originally produced."[41] The critic referred to the way in which Verdi had mistreated the singers and abused their voices in quite milder terms. He was ready to acknowledge that even Verdi's music could be properly sung. The point was that only a good singer could "vindicate" Verdi's reputation.

> It has been too persistently maintained that the music given to the Gipsy—that inauspicious and ghastly woman (*vide* English *libretto*)—can only properly be "screamed;" but it is the privilege of Madame Alboni to vindicate the reputation of Signor Verdi by showing that the music of Azucena may be *sung*—and sung, moreover, with as much ease as if it had proceeded straight from the fluent and graceful pen of Rossini himself.[42]

One last reference was made to the quality of the performance when Enrico Delle Sedie's rendition of the character Conte di Luna was reviewed. The critic held that the singer made a good impression "especially in the romance, 'Il balen del suo sorriso,' which, though robbed of its native simplicity by a slight excess of ornament, he sang otherwise remarkably well, amply meriting the encore that, as a matter of course (when was 'Il balen' not encored?), he obtained."[43] The reference to the addition of ornaments is unequivocal and leads us to question whether two vocal styles really coexisted at the time, depending on the repertoire. In fact, even though it is clear that Verdi's

---

39 *The Times*, May 8, 1861, p. 12.
40 *The Musical World*, 15 June 1861, pp. 372–73.
41 *The Times*, June 11, 1861, p. 6.
42 Ibid.
43 Ibid.

vocal writing represents a step forward towards a dramatised style, adding ornaments and replacing written cadenzas was still typical of an uninterrupted tradition that now included Verdi, alongside Bellini, Donizetti and even Rossini.

Finally, on 1 July, *The Times* published a long and articulate review of *Un ballo in maschera* as performed at Covent Garden. Its tone, despite some infelicitous comparison with Auber's precedent, was strongly appreciative. Verdi's music was pure Verdi, "sometimes of Verdi's best, occasionally of a less high standard, but very rarely (if ever) sinking beneath the average Verdi level."[44] Although no technical analysis was necessary, the music revealed its beauties quite naturally and a long-lasting success was easily predicted. The pieces in the first act that demanded attention were immediately individuated by the critic: the Duke's first aria "La rivedrà nell'estasi," thanks to its melodious character, Renato's solo "Alla vita che t'arride," on account of its expressiveness, and the romance of Oscar, "Volta la terrea," because of its sparkling prettiness. Interestingly, the critic drew a comparison between Verdi's felicitous inventiveness and two other composers; while "Alla vita che t'arride" might have passed for one of those insinuating pieces for which Balfe was so much cherished, the sparkling ballade of the Paggio revealed the touch of the late Adolphe Adam. The same remarks had made their appearance in the columns of *The Musical World* on 22 June, suggesting once again that a single person supervised both journals. The solo for Ulrica, "Della città all'occaso," was really beautiful; the trio "Di' tu se fedele" was pronounced tuneful, expressive and full of character; the quintet "E' scherzo od è follia" was the happiest of all the quintets composed by Verdi so far, for the combination of voices was irreproachable and the effect spontaneous. The third act was powerfully set to music, the composer having written no less than four "numbers of which he may reasonably be proud." The air in which Amelia petitions Renato ("Morrà ma prima in grazia") and that in which Renato laments his wife's lost innocence ("O dolcezze perdute") were "both to be admired, the first for its touching pathos, the last for its genuine and expressive melody." Tunefulness, beauty, spontaneity, expressiveness and prettiness were the words chosen by the critic to describe Verdi's

---

44   *The Times*, July 1, 1861, p. 5.

musical accomplishments. However, *Rigoletto, Il trovatore, La traviata,* and even *Nabucco* and *Ernani* were said to include much better and more dramatic pages than this most recent opera.[45]

The critic of *The Spectator* uttered words of cautious optimism and acknowledged the composer's merits despite Verdi's unfortunate decision to set to music a text for which Auber had already written memorable pages.

> But our impression (derived from a single representation) is, that it is equal, if not superior, to any of Verdi's previous operas, especially in the concerted music, where there is a breadth, richness of harmony, and constructive skill, of which this composer has rarely shown himself capable.[46]

With only one exception, in 1861 most of the critics toned down the aggressive reviews that characterised the previous decade and conceptualised Verdi's music in more generous and appreciative terms. While Chorley continued to antagonise Verdi and express his strongly conservative views on melodiousness and inventiveness, the others had come to accept Verdi and the dramatic style typically associated with his operas. The question concerning the vocal technique required to cope with the new style had been also put aside, for it was generally understood that a good singer could master Verdi's dramatic style as well as the traditional florid singing.

In 1861, occasional echoes of the discussion concerning Richard Wagner's recently published "The Music of the Future" reached London from the continent, and articles from the French and the German press were occasionally translated and published in *The Musical World*. When Wagner's *Tannhäuser* was first performed in Paris on 13 March 1861, many reviews from *Die Kölnische Zeitung, Die Niederrheinische Musikzeitung* and *Le Ménestrel* were reproduced in the columns of *The Musical World*, reporting on first the hitches and squabbles that delayed the performance and then on the negative reception scored by its composer.[47] On 23 March, a long report from *Le Ménestrel* (translated and abridged) was included in the columns of *The Musical World*,

---

45 Ibid.
46 *The Spectator*, June 22, 1861, p. 17.
47 *The Musical World*, March 16, 1861, p. 164.

commenting on the hostile reaction of the Paris audience, owing to the unmusical nature of Wagner's music.

> To speak plainly, they were over-excited by an orchestration invariably noisy, by laboured and interminable dissonances; by complications without end as without evident purpose, by superfluous conglomeration of details, by monotonous abuse of the first string of the fiddles, and a superabundance of recitative, tending to produce a dangerous state of turpitude among the audience.[48]

The public, it was suggested, used their silence, their exclamations, their laughter, and occasionally their hisses to condemn the excesses of a musical system that went against the natural categories of good taste, and that only a well-trained specialist might consent to analyse. Similar comments made their appearance in the columns of the *Niederrheinische Musik-Zeitung*, and were reported in *The Musical World*. The critic argued that "the only considerable and determining power which successfully opposed *Tannhäuser* was *French good taste*, which revolted both against the tendentious and supernatural subject of the Legend Drama, and the unmelodious music."[49] The failure of the opera might have been easily predicted, for, in addition to the poor quality of the music, Wagner's conduct, "his boundless self-laudation, his literary self-mirroring, his reformatory bombast, and his revolting degradation of the greatest composers of dramatic music, *obliged* the public to apply a severe standard to his artistic productions, for the purpose of testing what grounds there were for justifying, or ever simply excusing, his wordly bragging."[50]

Similar attention was paid by Chorley to the complete failure of Wagner's *Tannhäuser* in Paris. On 23 March 1861 *The Athenaeum* joined the choir and expressed its verdict on Wagner's new *no-music*.

> No doubt, allowance is to be made for antagonism stirred by Herr Wagner's paraded disdain of the music which preceded his attempts, and by the extravagant ardour of his partisans. But be such allowance greater or less, the work brought to judgment remains intrinsically bad, [...] we are glad, for the sake of Art, that the verdict has been so condemnatory.[51]

---

48   *The Musical World*, March 23, 1861, p. 182.
49   *The Musical World*, April 6, 1861, p. 214.
50   Ibid.
51   *The Athenaeum*, March 23, 1861, pp. 402–03.

13. *Inno delle nazioni* (1862)

In 1862, Verdi's cantata *Inno delle nazioni* was the object of an animated discussion which unfolded in the columns of *The Times*.[1] From 1 May until 1 November 1862, the Great Exhibition, a world's fair, was to be held in London and sponsored by the Royal Society of Arts, Manufactures and Trade. A new gigantic building was constructed to house the fair in South Kensington, and four musicians of international prominence were asked to compose a new work to inaugurate the event. On 6 July 1861, *The Athenaeum* informed its readers that, on the basis of a proposal submitted to the Royal Commissioners by Chorley, an invitation to compose a march for the occasion had been extended to Meyerbeer, Auber and Rossini. Rossini having already declined the invitation, the name of Verdi was offered as a possible substitute, since he was the most popular living Italian composer.[2]

On 28 January 1862, *The Times* announced that important decisions had been taken on the location and decoration of the building that would host the Exhibition, and on the possible avenues by which the public might access it. An additional reference was made to the fast-advancing arrangements concerning the musical portion of the programme, but some confusion arose with regard to the names of the composers who had accepted the Commissioners' invitation. Rossini, Meyerbeer, Auber and Verdi were mentioned, but Verdi, and not Rossini, was said to have declined the invitation.

---

1 Budden, *Verdi*, p. 88.
2 *The Athenaeum*, July 6, 1861, p. 20.

The arrangements for the musical portion of the programme to be gone through at the opening are fast advancing towards completion. It will be recollected that at an early period the Commissioners invited Rossini, Meyerbeer, Auber, and Verdi each to write a march for the occasion, and eventually the invitation was accepted by all but the last-named artist. Dr Sterndale Bennett has been also invited to set to music some words to be written for the occasion by the Poet Laureate. Subsequently, Mr. Costa was invited to undertake the musical arrangements, and to conduct the music at the opening on the 1st of May. Mr. Costa has accepted the invitation of the Commissioners; and since then attention has been given to the extent of the orchestra which would be required to render the opening worthy of the occasion.[3]

William Sterndale Bennett was also invited to contribute to the event, while Michael Costa would supervise it and conduct an impressively large number of performers. "After full consideration it has been determined to employ a musical force of no less than 1800 performers, of whom 400 will be instrumentalists—viz., 240 stringed instruments and 160 wind instruments, the large number of the latter being required for M. Auber's march, which is almost entirely written for wind instruments."[4] The remaining 1400 musicians to be involved were vocalists joining a massive choir. In addition to the initial confusion, on 17 March another report appeared in *The Times* where it was stated that "Rossini, Meyerbeer, Verdi, and Auber have each composed special marches and anthems for this occasion."[5] Not only had Verdi not declined the invitation, but he had already composed a piece to be included in the programme where, surprisingly, the name of Rossini was still mentioned.

On 22 April, a new report was published in the columns of *The Times*, announcing that, since there was no time for more extensive preparation, only three rehearsals had been planned for the inaugural concert, starting on the 29th. About the compositions, it was reported that "Meyerbeer's music has been ready some time, but the score of Auber's great trumpet march, and that of Bennett's cantata only came to hand last week, and Verdi's music has not yet arrived at all."[6] Two days

---

3   *The Times*, January 28, 1862, p. 6.
4   Ibid.
5   *The Times*, March 17, 1862, p. 6.
6   *The Times*, April 22, 1862, p. 7.

later Verdi, who had just arrived in London, wrote a letter which was immediately translated into English by his friend Manfredo Maggioni and sent to the editor of *The Times* in order to clarify his position.[7] It was not true that he had failed to submit his composition on time; the work consisted of a cantata and the decision to compose a vocal piece instead of the requested march resulted from a conversation with Auber, who had already written a march for the same occasion. Verdi also argued that the Commissioners' claim that there was no time to prepare his cantata was unjustified, for a few days would suffice to learn and perform such a short piece. As a matter of fact, the Commissioners refused Verdi's cantata and preparations were soon made to have Auber's, Meyerbeer's and Bennett's compositions performed. On 30 April, another long article was published in the columns of *The Times*, summarising the intricate events that had accompanied the preparation of the inaugural ceremony and describing the magnificence of the forthcoming event. The critic had examined the scores of the three composers now involved (Auber, Meyerbeer and Bennett) and could make a detailed report of the first rehearsal, giving the reader a first rough idea of the unsurpassed pomp that would characterise the opening ceremony. The critic was quite sympathetic to Verdi and, recognising his effort to comply with the commissioners' demands, had to admit that it would be their fault if he could not have his music played.

> Signor Verdi's cantata—but why speak of that which, after having been written in such good faith, and with a feeling not less honourable to its distinguished composer than complimentary to ourselves, has been unceremoniously rejected? We should only be too happy to place on record how worthily Italy—the "Land of Song," the cradle and nursery of music—had done her part in this great festival. But that pleasing task has been denied us—not by Signor Verdi (to his credit be it said), but by Her Majesty's Commissioners.[8]

Apparently, the hitches leading to Verdi's music being refused originated with the director Michael Costa, whose antagonistic attitude towards his colleagues caused a series of difficulties not only with Verdi,

---

7   See Verdi's letter to Arrivabene, 2 May 1862. Alessandro Luzio (ed.), *Carteggi verdiani* (Rome: Reale Accademia d'Italia, 1935–1947).

8   *The Times*, April 30, 1862, p. 5. The same article was published by *The Musical World* on 3 May.

but also with Bennett. In fact, Costa further refused to conduct Bennett's *Cantata*, whose performance had to be entrusted to a second conductor.[9] Because of the nationalistic implications and the patriotic feelings aroused by the possible exclusion of William Sterndale Bennett and the Poet Laureate, Alfred Lord Tennyson, from the opening concert, Costa's contemptible behaviour became the object of further critical discussion. According to *The Musical World*, neither the conduct of Costa nor that of the Commissioners could be considered acceptable, for a private quarrel dating back to 1853 and Costa's consequent vindictive reaction were now interfering with the fulfilment of a public duty.[10] Costa tried to defend himself by sending a letter to the editor of *The Times* (the letter was also reproduced in the columns of *The Musical World*) in which he explained that his refusal to conduct Bennett's compositions had been clear from the very beginning.[11] Not surprisingly, the pending exclusion of Verdi's cantata did not provoke the same reactions in the press or receive the same level of attention. Nevertheless, on 3 May the critic of *The Musical World* published a long article in which he addressed the commissioners' narrow-minded attitude; he described them as "Commissioners of the anti-national Exhibition" and expressed his deep disappointment with the manner in which they had treated the Italian composer.

> But these unfortunate men [the Commissioners] have had a long artistic rope given them, and we are glad to see that they are hanging themselves very fast indeed. Their last movement in this direction has been to reject a *cantata* offered to them in the kindest manner, in the best and most generous spirit, by Sig. Verdi. Some eminent composers, if you asked them for a *cantata*, would give you a march; Sig. Verdi, asked for a march, gives a *cantata*.
> "This is too long," say the Commissioners. "You send us choruses, and even some solo verses to be sung by a man named Tamberlik. You must not trouble us with anything of this kind. Take back your contribution. It is a product of industry for which we can find no place."
> We hope Sig. Verdi will understand the deep disgust which the news of the rejection of his kind, sympathetic co-operation has caused among the musical and general public of London. Our Opera Houses are not

---

9   *The Musical World*, April 19, 1862, p. 248.
10 *The Musical World*, April 26, 1862, pp. 264–65.
11 *The Musical World*, May 3, 1862, p. 279.

endowed with money by the Government, as is the case in many other countries; and Sig. Verdi, however much we may admire his music, could never hope to receive in London anything like the myriads of roubles which the Emperor of Russia gives him, simply as an honorarium, for having written *La Forza del Destino* for the Opera of St. Petersburg. Nor do we imagine that Sig. Verdi attaches any undue importance to such pecuniary trifles. But he probably expected to find the Commissioners of the "Great Exhibition" endowed by Providence with sense, and with some capacity for appreciating art and the intentions of artists. We are sorry for his sake, as the most popular composer in Europe, and for our own as Englishmen, and the compatriots of those disreputable Commissioners, to find that in both these very natural expectations he has been entirely deceived.[12]

The Great Exhibition was granted ample coverage in the London press and its preparation was chronicled in detail with reference to the musical part. Owing to the quality of the rehearsals, a successful opening was anticipated. A shower of praises was bestowed by the critics of *The Times* and *The Musical World* upon both the composers and the performers involved, whose contribution to the success of the forthcoming event was beyond dispute. On 1 May, all expectations were fulfilled and the ceremony was a grand, splendid event, although the queen had decided not to preside over it: she was still mourning for the loss of her beloved husband, Prince Albert, who had passed away on 14 December 1861. After the opening speech delivered by Lord Earl Granville and the reply by His Royal Highness, the Duke of Cambridge, the special musical performances commenced with Michael Costa conducting Meyerbeer's *Ouverture en forme de Marche*. Upon its conclusion, Costa, having refused to conduct Bennett's music, yielded the baton to Prosper Sainton, who conducted Bennett's *Ode* composed on verses written by Tennyson. Then Costa resumed his role and conducted Auber's *March*.[13] Upon the conclusion of the special music, the Bishop of London read a fervent prayer, after which the Duke of Cambridge rose and in a loud voice declared, "By command of the Queen, I now declare the Exhibition open."[14]

---

12 *Ibid.*, pp. 280–81.
13 See also Tal. P. Shaffner and W. Owen, *The Illustrated Record of the International Exhibition of the Industrial Arts and Manufactures, and the Fine Arts, of all Nations, in 1862* (London: London Printing & Publishing Co., 1862), p. 15.
14 *The Times*, May 2, 1862, p. 12.

One week later, the critic of *The Musical World* announced that the production of Verdi's undeservedly rejected cantata had been rehearsed at Her Majesty's Theatre and suggested that justice should be done to one of the greatest living dramatic composers. In his apologetic article, the critic insisted on the manner in which Verdi had been mistreated by the commissioners, whose rejection did not appear to be justified by the claim that the cantata would take too long to rehearse. This decision, as unfair as it appeared to be, roused feelings of sympathy among theatre-goers and music lovers, who now cherished the opportunity afforded to them to attend its performance and judge with their own ears.[15] At this point, the figure of James Henry Mapleson, who in the meantime had taken over management of Her Majesty's Theatre, comes into question, for his testimony about the arrangements leading to the performance of Verdi's cantata seems to match what was reported in the newspapers. In his *Memoirs* Mapleson states that the 1862 operatic season at Her Majesty's Theatre was a complete financial success, not least because of the large audience attracted by the Exhibition. At the end of March, Gye had announced the forthcoming opening of the Royal Italian Opera season at Covent Garden, commencing on 8 April; similarly, Mapleson made his announcement that the opera season at Her Majesty's Theatre would begin on the 26th. The programme announced by Mapleson included Verdi's *Ernani*, *Il trovatore*, *Rigoletto* and *La traviata*, along with the new and successful *Un ballo in maschera*, which would open the season; the part of Renato would feature Leone Giraldoni, the baritone who had created the role in Rome in 1859. At Covent Garden, meanwhile, the same role would be taken by Enrico Delle Sedie, and the programme would include Donizetti's *Dom Sébastien* (as *Don Sebastian*) in addition to the usual repertoire of stock operas.[16]

Based on the manager's reminiscences, it is possible to argue that at the beginning of May he may have considered taking advantage of the incident between the composer and the Commissioners to offer Verdi an alternative location for the performance of his new piece. In his account, Mapleson goes so far as to describe his fortuitous meeting with Verdi, whom he encountered by chance on his way back home, and who expressed his deep disappointment at the treatment he had received at

---

15   *The Musical World*, May 10, 1862, pp. 297–98.
16   *The Times*, March 31, 1862, p. 8.

the hands of the Commissioners. Mapleson, to cheer him up, offered Verdi the opportunity to have his cantata performed at the opera house instead.[17] As a result, Verdi's *Inno delle nazioni*, whose text had been provided by Arrigo Boito, was performed on 24 May at Her Majesty's Theatre, after the *Barbiere di Siviglia* and under the baton of Luigi Arditi. The solo, originally intended for Tamberlik, was successfully performed by Thérèse Tietjens and the whole cantata, *The Times* reported, "by unanimous desire, was given twice from beginning to end, and the composer summoned no less than three times after the first, and twice after the second performance."[18] Verdi was described by *The Times* as a composer whose operas had elicited universal acclaim in England and elsewhere, and it was indisputable that he had achieved another legitimate and brilliant triumph. Again, the review that appeared in *The Times* on 26 May was reproduced in the columns of *The Musical World* a few days later, on 31 May.

The critic of *The Athenaeum* remained unconvinced. He raised a few critical points and argued that Verdi's cantata was unsuitable to the occasion for which it was designed. In fact, the critic held that in advocating the nationalistic claims of a single country, Italy, and in leaving Germany out of the picture, the cantata's text betrayed the spirit of brotherhood that should have informed it. In fact, Verdi's music incorporated three songs, each of them bearing a strongly symbolic value: *God Save the King* represented England, *La Marseillaise* represented France, and *Il Canto degli Italiani*, best known as *Inno di Mameli*, represented Italy. The lyrics mentioned England, "Queen of the Seas," and referred to France, whose military help had been instrumental in the process leading to Italian unification, but failed to include Austria, the eternal enemy. It was thanks to the French military intervention that in 1859 the Sardinian army had defeated Austria and taken possession of the Italian regions until then under the Austrian control.[19] The critic's remark was correct for, in the aftermath of the

---

17   Mapleson, *Memoirs*, p. 43.
18   *The Times*, May 26, 1862, p. 9.
19   After the Austrian defeat in the Second Italian War of Independence in 1859, Giuseppe Garibaldi led an expedition to regain the Kingdom of Naples. In 1861 Victor Emmanuel II was proclaimed King of Italy and Rome, although still under the military and political control of the Pope, was declared capital of the new Kingdom.

Second Italian War of Independence, it was unlikely that Verdi would include Austria in a fraternal, musical embrace. Furthermore, the critic of *The Athenaeum* questioned the quality of the music; the opening chorus was ill-modulated and the long recitative allotted to Tamberlik ineffective, the melody being the only good thing in the whole piece. In the end, the critic declared, the intricate circumstances leading to Verdi's exclusion had been beneficial to the composer, for, had his music been performed alongside that of his French and German contemporaries, he would have suffered from the comparison.[20]

---

20 *The Athenaeum*, May 31, 1862, p 732.

14. *Don Carlos* and *La forza del destino* (1867)

Finally, after five fairly uneventful years, 1867 saw two new operas staged in London that bore the name of the only Italian composer who was able to attract the attention of the international public. On 4 June *Don Carlos* was performed at Covent Garden and conducted by Michael Costa, while on 22 June *La forza del destino* was produced at Her Majesty's Theatre, the conducting duties assumed by Luigi Arditi.

News of the Paris premiere, on 11 March, of Verdi's new grand opera *Don Carlos* began circulating in the London press on the 16th, when an anonymous French correspondent contributed a review to the columns of *The Musical World*.[1] The review was published under the pseudonym of "Figaro" and addressed to Mons. Dishley Peters, one of the pseudonyms used by Davison. As Joseph Bennett testified, this name was frequently used by the editor in a column called "Muttonian." The correspondent expressed himself in terms that were not at all encouraging, declaring himself doubtful as to whether Verdi's most recent opera would establish itself as a long-lasting success. The critic sketched an image of one man who nevertheless embodied two composers of different value: the Verdi who had created such masterpieces as *Ernani*, *Rigoletto*, *Trovatore* and *La traviata*, and the one whose most recent attempts relied on the public's forbearance, for they lacked the necessary dramatic power and therefore failed to convince.

---

1 "Don Carlos, À Mons. Dishley Peters," *The Musical World*, March 16, 1867, p. 161.

Comme je le disais tout à l'heure, il y a deux *Verdi*; l'un, qui fait de quasi chefs-d'œuvre; l'autre, qui illumine une partition tout entière de trois ou quatre morceaux à effet seulement, comptant, pour le reste, sur la longanimité du public. *Don Carlos*, malheureusement, est dû à la plume de ce dernier. Il y a, parbleu! clairsemées çà et là, des pages énergiques, bien vivantes, empruntées, volées même au vrai *Verdi*, mais l'ensemble est boiteux; la griffe du maitre apparait quelquefois, mais ce n'est que par éclairs.[2]

The composer's mistake, the critic continued, lay in his repeated attempt to follow a route that did not belong to him; this he did by imitating Meyerbeer and the French dramatic style. *Don Carlos*'s third act, together with some more isolated pieces, genuinely reflected Verdi's old style, but the rest was quite contemptible. Finally, the French critic suggested that the opera could be improved by shortening it significantly and adding a ballet.

A couple of weeks later, on 30 March, Gye announced the forthcoming season of the Royal Italian Opera at Covent Garden, which would commence on 2 April with the performance of Bellini's *Norma*. Two novelties were included in the prospectus: Verdi's *Don Carlos* and Charles Gounod's *Romeo et Juliette*.[3] On 6 April a similar announcement was made by Mapleson, informing the patrons and subscribers of Her Majesty's Theatre that the Italian opera season there would open on 27 April and include the premiere of Verdi's *La forza del destino*, together with the revival of *I Lombardi*. While the second work was chosen for the opening night, little mention was made of why the production of the first had been delayed for three years. The problem had been finding a tenor equal to the musical requirements of the work; the engagement of Pietro Mongini now removed the difficulty.[4]

---

2   "As I was saying just now, there are two Verdis; the one who creates near-masterpieces; the other who brightens an entire score with three or four pieces for effect only, counting for the rest on the forbearance of the public. *Don Carlos*, unfortunately, is attributable to the quill of the latter. There are, egad!, scattered here and there, pages that are energetic, lively, borrowed, stolen even from the true Verdi, but the whole is lame; the signature of the master appears from time to time, but only in flashes." *Ibid*.
3   *The Musical World*, March 30, 1867, p. 188.
4   *The Musical World*, April 6, 1867, pp. 203–05.

When the critic of *The Musical World* commented on the prospective performance of Verdi's *Don Carlos*, he referred to the "at first doubtful but now apparently unquestioned" success of the opera in Paris, a success due to some of the finest music ever written by its composer.[5] The readers were informed that as the original Paris version was exceedingly long, some judicious cuts would be made by the conductor Michael Costa. The London public would not endure a performance as lengthy as that presented in Paris, and if Rossini, Auber and Meyerbeer had been subject to a similar treatment, it would be "no indignity for Signor Verdi to be submitted to the same indispensable operation."[6] Raising the public's expectations even further, *The Musical World* later published another report from a French correspondent, which included excerpts from the reviews appearing in *Le Moniteur* and *Le Constitutionnel*. The opera was pronounced an unquestionable financial success, as demonstrated by the fact that the theatre continued to fill with audiences. However, its popularity was not due to the compositional style on which the composer's previous successes were based; in fact, a new, completely different style was now recognizable. *Don Carlos* was said to be based on the theories of modern classical music and the figure of Richard Wagner was evoked to suggest the kind of influence that might have played a role in Verdi's development. As the critic of *Le Moniteur* put it, one thing was certain, "namely, that Verdi has completely modified his earlier methods, and adopted principles analogous to those of the German master."[7] Some of the French critics referred to a third style in Verdi but expressed strong doubts as to the extent to which the new phase would please the public and grant the composer a success equal to that obtained by his previous operas. Although the English public had not yet had the opportunity to listen to any of Wagner's dramas, the antagonistic attitude exhibited by the London critics towards the so-called "music of the future" would predictably cast a shadow on the prospective production of Verdi's new opera; at the same time, the parallel drawn between Wagner's controversial theories and Verdi's new style could not but excite general curiosity.

---

5   *Ibid.*, p. 216.
6   *Ibid.*
7   *The Musical World*, April 13, 1867, p. 225.

In the meantime *Un ballo in maschera* was performed at Covent Garden on 23 April, while *I Lombardi* was revived at Her Majesty's Theatre on the 30th. These revivals prompted the critic of *The Musical World* to elaborate on the different qualities of the two operas, especially when compared to the still unheard but already much-discussed new style developed in *Don Carlos*.

> Especially interesting is it to note the distinction in style and method of working between *I Lombardi* and *Don Carlos* — the one full of vulgarities and crudities, but also rich in melody and dramatic power; the other elaborated to an extent that wearies sadly the always expecting and constantly disappointed listener.[8]

For *Un ballo in maschera* the critic again expressed words of strong appreciation, as it contained some of Verdi's best music. "*Don Carlos* has yet to make its appearance among us, and meanwhile the third act of *Un ballo* will rank, in the judgment of English connoisseurs, nearest to the last act of *Il trovatore*, the second *finale* of *La traviata*, and certain scenes in *Rigoletto*, generally accredited as the Bussetese [sic] master's *capo d'opera*."[9] However, the judgment that appeared in the same journal one week later, regarding the qualities and shortcomings of *I Lombardi*, was tepid. The critic dug up some of the grievances that had accompanied its first appearance in London in 1846.

> Though the music has all the crudeness, all the vapour, and much of the empty noise of his earliest style, with little of that strong dramatic feeling and striking melodic invention which have marked his later works, it is still essentially "Verdi," and therefore must interest the many warm admirers of Verdi's genius.[10]

The critic could neither conceal nor deny that Verdi's music contained certain salient qualities, on account of which the composer had become famous not only in his home country but also abroad. The usual grumbles concerning the choral music being almost everywhere in unison, the orchestra for the most part too noisy and the vocal solos excessively strenuous outweighed the critic's sporadically appreciative remarks. A few glimpses of fancy, some occasional true melodic

---

8 *The Musical World*, May 4, 1867, p. 278.
9 Ibid., p. 279.
10 *The Musical World*, May 11, 1867, p. 294.

inventions and dramatic colouring were definitely present in *I Lombardi*. Specific reference was made to the vocal qualities exhibited by Tietjens, who had successfully mastered the "extremely fatiguing, nearly always overstrained, often difficult and rarely effective music of Giselda."[11] The opera, whose score had been subject to some "judicious curtailments" by Arditi, was said to be well worth a hearing but still unlikely to be revived again. The very same article appeared in the columns of *The Times* on 6 May, again suggesting that Davison supervised both periodicals.[12]

One week later, a review of the just-commenced opera season at Covent Garden was published in the columns of the *Saturday Review*, where short mention was made of the repeated performance of *Un ballo in maschera*. It was a shame to see this opera performed again, when other less frequently revived operas were of much greater value. The critic expressed his regret at being obliged to listen to Verdi's rendition of Eugène Scribe's drama, while Daniel Auber's grand opera on the same subject was so much better.

> How deliciously fresh, melodious, and natural is the music of [Auber's] *Fra Diavolo*, from the sparkling overture, with its characteristic drums and trumpets, to the end, compared with that of certain operas we are forced to listen to, and which we would willingly change for some other such comic work from the same prolific pen! For instance, Verdi's *Un ballo in maschera*—which we have had twice already, and which brought back, in the character of Amelia, the heroine, that most uninteresting of *prime donne assolute*, Mdlle. Fricci—might well be laid aside for a season in favour of Auber's *Gustave III*, founded upon the same story, laid out in the same manner, and the music of which is worth all that Verdi ever composed.[13]

Quite similar critical remarks appeared soon afterwards in the same journal, and for analogous reasons, when the critic held that *I Lombardi* should be considered one of Verdi's worst operas.

> When we repeat that *I Lombardi* contains an air for the tenor (Oronte), "La mia letizia," one or two spirited though by no means well-written choruses, short, abrupt, noisy, and generally in unison, a somewhat tortured prayer for Giselda, with occasional passages of less importance,

---

11   Ibid.
12   *The Times*, May 6, 1867, p. 12.
13   *The Musical World*, May 18, 1867, p. 313, from *The Saturday Review*.

we have said all that can justly be said in favour of the music in what is decidedly one of Verdi's worst operas and one of the worst operas ever composed.[14]

On 4 June, the premiere of *Don Carlos* was conducted by Michael Costa at Covent Garden, while, after a revival of *Il trovatore*, *La forza del destino* was in rehearsal at Her Majesty's Theatre. A laconic review of *Don Carlos* made its appearance on 8 June in the columns of *The Musical World*, in which only brief mention was made of the music's value: "As a work of art, *Don Carlos* is, perhaps, the most complete and masterly of Verdi's productions."[15] The critic showed himself to be much more generous when commenting on the excellent quality of the performance and its splendid success among the public. *Don Carlos* was presented in the Italian translation by Achille de Lauzières, and even though Costa had shortened it by eliminating the first act almost completely and by cutting the ballet, its performance was still exceedingly long.[16] It ran for seven performances and was revived the following season, thereafter to be abandoned for 65 years. On 15 June, a more articulate review of the opera was published in the columns of *The Musical World* (the same article had already been published in *The Times* on 10 June), emphasising the extent to which Verdi was indebted to Meyerbeer in both musical and dramatic terms. In spite of all that was indifferent, dull and heavy, Verdi's new opera included some of the finest music he had ever composed. But, the critic suggested, everything that was good in the opera originated from a careful imitation of Meyerbeer's model, and the finale of Act II in the Italian version represented a case in point.

> In the *finale* to what, in the Italian version of the opera, is the second act, he has successfully imitated the vast outline and elaborate details of Meyerbeer, and on a ground, too, where, among recent dramatic composers, Meyerbeer has hitherto stood alone and unapproached. The plan is as broad, the treatment as dramatic, the instrumentation as pompous, and the general effect as bold and imposing as in the *finales* to several of Meyerbeer's operas which we need not stop to signalize by

---

14 *The Musical World*, May 25, 1867, p. 335, from *The Saturday Review*.
15 *The Musical World*, June 8, 1867, p. 376.
16 Harry R. Beard, "'Don Carlos' on the London Stage: 1867 to 1869," in *Atti del II Congresso internazionale di studi verdiani* (Parma: Istituto di Studi Verdiani, 1971), p. 67.

name; and if the *substratum* is not quite original, that is almost the only point of inferiority to be laid to signor Verdi's charge.[17]

In terms of musical-dramatic progress, Verdi seemed faithful to and consistent with his previous works and recent development, a circumstance that led the critic to object to the so-called third style. "What French critics, in speaking of *Don Carlos* call 'Verdi's transformation,' is all 'moonshine.' The music of the new opera is as pure 'Verdi' as anything Verdi ever gave to the world."[18] It was just Verdi, but with a strongly marked tendency for imitating Meyerbeer, a tendency also shared by other contemporary composers. Despite the incongruities in the dramatic plot, for which not only Schiller but also the French librettists were held responsible, and although Verdi's technical ability could not rival Meyerbeer's genius, *Don Carlos* was said to be "crowded with beauties of a more or less elevated order." It was difficult to recall a more remarkable operatic event than its performance at Covent Garden. Having failed to analyse Verdi's score in greater detail, the critic of *The Musical World* returned to that task on 29 June, when an ample, but still incomplete review of the music made its appearance. To start with, the libretto was cumbersome and dull, too heavily reliant on the enthusiastic friendship between Don Carlos and the Marquis de Posa, who continually exchanged vows and embraces. This, together with the illicit love between Don Carlos and the Queen, formed the core business of the entire libretto which, to make things worse, was at variance with the true story of Don Carlos. The transformation in Verdi's style on which the Parisian critics had prated so much, the critic claimed, existed solely in their imagination. "We do not say that he has never been happier than in *Don Carlos*, but we must insist that he was never more emphatically the Verdi we have all long known, the Verdi who for twenty years and more has obtained the willing ear of Europe."[19] The critic called attention to many felicitous moments in the score, notwithstanding some self-borrowing and minor flaws in the treatment of the harmony.

---

17 *The Musical World,* June 15, 1867, p. 387.
18 *Ibid.*
19 "Verdi's 'Don Carlos,'" *The Musical World,* June 29, 1867, pp. 425–27.

Upon conclusion of the London opera season the critic of *The Musical World* referred to Verdi's operas in terms that confirmed the scepticism he had already expressed. Although it was impossible to deny Verdi's international reputation, it rested upon the success of two or three operas out of twenty, among which *Il trovatore* was considered one of the best. For its part, *Don Carlos* showed little chance of surviving a second year, as it lacked those bright melodies and concertato pieces that were characteristic of many of Verdi's previous operas.

> That it contains much of Signor Verdi's most elaborate and carefully-considered music has been asseverated by nine critics out of ten. Nor are we prepared to question the fact. All we wish to say is that it contains not one of those bright melodies that have made the fame of other operas from the same pen—not one concerted piece to rank with the quartet in *Rigoletto* or the quintet in *Un ballo in maschera*, and not one grand *finale* equal in "effect" to the *finale* in *Ernani*, Act III, or the *finale* in *La traviata*, Act II. The piece, moreover, is, for a musical libretto, hopelessly dreary.[20]

The critic was appreciative of the composer's earlier operas on account of a feature, melodiousness, which had once been considered missing, lacking or simply badly executed, sacrificed as it had been to a declamatory style which undermined the Italian vocal tradition and strained the singers' voice. To our surprise, not only was the critic reconsidering the negative judgment he had repeatedly expressed in the past (witness the reviews of *Ernani* and *Nabucco* in 1846, or those of *Rigoletto* in 1853 and *Il trovatore* in 1855), he was also lamenting a lack of melodiousness in Verdi's new style which appeared all the more striking when considered in comparison to the melodiousness of his early operas.

The critic of *The Illustrated London News*, who reviewed *Don Carlos* on 15 June 1867, argued that in this opera Verdi seemed to have assimilated the lesson of the "German school," but was not able to provide evidence to support that claim. It was not clarified how that influence was manifest in Verdi's new compositional style; nor was it sufficiently elucidated whether by "German school" Wagner's works and theories were to be understood. The critic appreciated the turn taken by the Italian composer but doubted whether the more erudite style of Verdi's

---

20   *The Musical World*, August 17, 1867, p. 556.

new opera would continue to fulfil the public's expectations, the implicit assumption being that he was successful as a popular composer.

> His studies in the German school are calculated to increase our respect for his attainments as an artist; but we are not sure that the learned music of this opera will prove as grateful to the popular ear as the familiar melodies of his earlier days. Nor is the subject favourable to popularity.[21]

Verdi's forte lay more in the concertato pieces than in the airs for solo voice; however, he appeared to be a composer of genius. The critic called attention to the quality of the quartet in the third act, "Sia maledetto il rio sospetto," which, he held, "evinces a power of combination worthy of Meyerbeer," and to the finest air in the whole opera, "O mia regina!," which, to his surprise, was not given to the heroine, but to Princess Eboli, a subordinate player.

As usual, the critic of *The Athenaeum* proved to be the least lenient with regard to both the composer and the opera. In his review of *Don Carlos*, appearing on 8 June, he denied that Verdi's compositional style had developed at all, although he appeared to be "more careful in his instrumentation than when he began—more original in combination."[22] Verdi's style was still coarse and harsh and, as a logical consequence, at variance with what was supposedly beautiful in the musical art. The composer was consistent with himself, since *Don Carlos* demonstrated that his preference for morbid, violent, cruel subjects had never really changed. When compared to his previous work, Verdi's latest opera did not really present any sign of genuine improvement, but rather a more mature sense of detachment:

> But the young blood which moved this has apparently chilled; and what we have in its place (to judge from its writer's late operas) is a pretence to accomplishments which he has not yet thoroughly acquired, not relieved by that coarse, spontaneous crudity, or by those occasional glimpses of a more delicate spirit, which, in a period of great, yet not unprecedented decadence (opera having always had its ebbs and flows), seduced the play-going public into the conviction that another great composer had risen above the horizon. There has been no transformation of Signor Verdi's humour,—merely a change from one to another form of it: nothing in any respect analogous to what was done by Signor Rossini

---

21 *The Illustrated London News*, June 15, 1867, p. 606.
22 *The Athenaeum*, June 8, 1867, p. 765.

when, after being the most Italian of opera composers, he wrote his Swiss *Guillaume Tell* for the Grand Opéra of Paris.[23]

Though his initial coarseness had softened, Verdi's compositional skills had not really evolved, nor had he showed a broader expressive palette; his preference for bloody stories and cruel plots was still predominant. *Don Carlos* was pronounced by the critic "a stale, dismal and inflated work," while *Il trovatore* continued to be his best achievement.

In the late 1860s, *The Musical Times* also started reviewing operatic performances in London on a regular basis and on 1 July 1867, it pronounced *Don Carlos* "neither better nor worse than the later productions of this composer."[24] Although infinitely superior to *I Lombardi*, it would not overshadow works like *Trovatore*, *La traviata* or even *Rigoletto*. The model provided by Meyerbeer was mentioned with regard to the great *tableau* concluding the second Act, while Verdi was said to have gained his fame by a "few *cantabile* and catching melodies, interspersed with spasmodic vocal effects and coarse instrumentation."[25] Upon perusal of the score, the critic called attention to some of the most interesting moments in the work and mentioned the "muscular school of writing for which Verdi is so remarkable."[26] The critic could not deny *Don Carlos*'s popular success but had to confess his preference for the composer's earlier works; this new opera was "at least entitled to respect, as the earnest attempt of a composer to escape from a style which his better nature must have whispered to him was inartistic and unreal."[27]

A later article appeared in the columns of *The Musical Times* bearing the signature of Henry C. Lunn, whose nasty attitude towards Verdi in 1867 may remind us of Davison's approach 22 years earlier. When called upon to comment on the London musical season in September that year, he could not avoid lamenting the sad circumstance of being given two new operas to endure, both composed by Verdi.

> We have been so nauseated with Verdi's music lately that it was with dismay that we read the prospectuses of the two Italian Opera-houses for the season just concluded. There could be something worse, we found,

---

23 Ibid.
24 *The Musical Times*, July 1, 1867 p. 97.
25 Ibid.
26 Ibid.
27 Ibid.

than the promise of a new opera by Verdi, and that was the promise of two new operas by Verdi.[28]

With *Don Carlos* a development, or at least a change, in Verdi's style appeared clear even to those critics who were least inclined to acknowledge a true turn towards a third phase. Not even the most reluctant could deny an audible difference between his first accomplishments and the later works. With the one exception of *The Illustrated London News*, none of the critics taken into consideration seemed to agree with their French colleagues on the extent to which Wagner and the so-called German school might have influenced Verdi's recent development. Instead, Meyerbeer was often mentioned when it came to identifying the models from which, according to some, Verdi had taken inspiration. Modern scholars have discussed at length the relationship between Verdi and the French Grand-Opéra and it is clear that the composer was writing for Paris in a tradition that had Meyerbeer for its strongest representative.[29] Whatever the reason why French critics were referring to Wagner, the influence the German composer may have exerted upon the Italian is controversial. In fact, at that time Verdi's knowledge of Wagner's music was limited.[30] Moreover, while *Tannhäuser's* first performance in Paris was given on 13 March 1861 at the Salle Le Peletier of the Paris Opéra, in 1867 London Wagner's music was not really known. The few and far-between performances of single excerpts from Wagner's operas had not left a strong impressions on both London critics and operagoers, and it was not until 1870 that an opera bearing the name of Wagner would be fully performed in London. It was *Der Fliegende Holländer*, given in Italian as *L'Olandese Dannato* at Drury Lane.

In the meantime, the much-talked-of Swedish soprano Christine Nilsson made her first appearance at Her Majesty's Theatre as Violetta in Verdi's *La traviata*, while Clarice Sinico appeared as Leonora in *Il trovatore*. The choice should not surprise us, since it was a common managerial strategy to revive some old operas from the same composer whose most recent accomplishment was in preparation; the older

---

28 "The London Musical Season," *The Musical Times*, September 1, 1867, p. 141.
29 Marcello Conati, "Verdi, Il Grand Opéra ed il 'Don Carlos,'" in *Atti del II Congresso internazionale di studi verdiani* (Parma: Istituto di Studi Verdiani, 1971), pp. 242–79.
30 See Conati, "Verdi, Il Grand Opéra ed il 'Don Carlos,'" p. 271.

operas would market the new one and raise the public's expectations. The announced novelty at Her Majesty's Theatre was, in fact, *La forza del destino*, which would be performed on 22 June. Two days later, *The Times* introduced the new opera to its readers and informed them of the "comparative ill fortune" it experienced on the continent, owing to its extremely intricate plot. The first performance of *La forza del destino* in London featured Thérèse Tietjens, Zelia Trebelli-Bettini, Tom Hohler, Charles Santley, Hans Rokitansky, Edouard Gassier, Pietro Mongini, Baumeister, Foli and Bossi. Such a strong cast was declared a very happy circumstance indeed, since Verdi's music continued to impose unceasing strain upon the singers' voice and not everybody was able to sustain his strongly dramatic roles.[31] A long description of the intricate plot followed, after which the critic indulged in an analysis of the composition: "The music to which Verdi has married this strange galimatias, though very unequal, contains much that is good, some, indeed as good as any he has produced."[32] The overture was pronounced "unimportant and short," the first scene "charming," the duet in the second scene "not very remarkable," Preziosilla's "Canzone" in Act II "rhythmical, spirited, and melodious," Don Carlos' "Ballata" "humorous," the "Miserere" scene a "felicitous masterpiece." The critic suggested that the opera was entirely made up of recitatives, airs, duets and choruses, while the concerted pieces (to which Verdi owed much of his reputation) were entirely missing. Other moments of the opera, although pronounced unimpressive or artificial, were rendered magnificent by the singers impersonating the main characters, while much spirited music was to be found in the choruses and the dance pieces. In general, the opera was pronounced a success, at least in popular terms: "We may return to *La forza del destino*, and meanwhile must conclude with saying that it was received, in spite of the absurd improbabilities and accumulating horrors of the story, with unqualified favour throughout. There were several encores besides the one we have mentioned."[33]

---

31 *The Times*, June 24, 1867, p. 9; the same article appeared in *The Musical World*, June 29, 1867, p. 423.
32 *Ibid.*
33 *Ibid.*

The critic of *The Illustrated London News* seemed to appreciate the opera which, he maintained, was a popular success. With regard to the music, he insisted on the influence of the "German school" being remarkably evident. Verdi was pronounced a real artist and the performance a true accomplishment.

> As a musical work, it is very much in the style which the author has adopted in some of his later productions—a style founded on the German school, and more remarkable for the Teutonic construction of its concerted scenes than for the Italian flow and sweetness of its melodies. There are, however, many powerful as well as beautiful things in the music; and the opera, taken as a whole, is undeniably the work of a real artist. The manner in which it has been produced and is represented entitles the management of the theatre and the performers to the warmest praise.[34]

The Athenaeum, predictably, was particularly hostile and *La forza del destino* was judged inferior even to *Don Carlos*. To start with, the critic agreed with his colleague from *The Times* on the plot being intricate to the extreme.

> [The story] is of the highest extravagance, containing an attempted abduction,—scenes with monks, soldiers, gipsies,—an accidental murder,—and three deaths by duel vengeance and suicide, which close the story in the midst of a thunderstorm. To disentangle all the twistings and windings of such a tale, not too easy to follow, would serve no good purpose.[35]

The music, while lacking in that pure individual melody which one would expect from any Italian composer, had some merit in the orchestral accompaniments (although it was also argued that they were instrumental in concealing the meagreness of the melody). The "quintet" with double chorus, no. 9 in Act II, was the best piece, the "tarantella" was pronounced interesting, while the gypsy's "rataplan" song and chorus were commonplace. Although Verdi was one of the few living composers in Europe in a position to claim critical attention, the critic was no more inclined to accept or get used to those defects

---

34   *The Illustrated London News,* June 29, 1867, p. 655.
35   *The Athenaeum,* June 29, 1867, p. 859.

and extravagances of which the Italian musician was the strongest representative.

Upon the conclusion of the operatic season, *The Musical Times* reviewed *La forza del destino* and drew the reader's attention to the merits of the Swedish *prima donna* Christine Nilsson, a worthy successor of Jenny Lind. The opera proved attractive thanks to the wonderful vocal and dramatic talents exhibited by the singer rather than to the quality of the music itself. The libretto consisted of the usual accumulation of horrors and excesses, but the music showed that the composer had evolved from his earlier style: "The writing is less forced, the melodies, although neither very new nor very striking, seem exactly such as the situations produced without effort in the mind of the composer; and the orchestration has less of that constant straining after glaring effects so observable in most of Verdi's works."[36] The critic argued that although there were many effective moments scattered throughout the work, in so far as the music of the gipsy, Preziosilla, and the "Aria buffa" for Fra Melitone were concerned, the result was disappointing. Instead, the prayer in the second act, the romance "O tu che" for Don Alvaro and the "rataplan" (solo and chorus) were considered worthy of notice, while the duet between Don Alvaro and Don Carlo was declared "unquestionably the best piece of dramatic writing in the opera."[37]

Among the English commentators, the idea of a third style becoming manifest with *La forza del destino* remained questionable, as the critic of *The Musical World* testifies: "Nor can we detect in this opera, any more than in its successor, the change of style with which some critics have recently accredited Signor Verdi—unless, indeed, the change be from a certain sustained brilliancy to a certain elaborate dullness; but this would appear the result of fading invention rather than of deliberate design."[38]

However, not everybody seemed to agree that the recent change in Verdi's style was meaningless or even non-existent. When Frederick Crowest, in his *Verdi: Man and Musician* (1897), commented on the transition to Verdi's third style he argued that the transformation was already manifest in *La forza del destino*.

---

36 "Her Majesty's Theatre," *The Musical Times*, July 1, 1867, p. 97.
37 *Ibid.*
38 *The Musical World*, August 17, 1867, pp. 555–56.

The change of style which was, later on, to show itself so unmistakably in *Aida*, *Otello*, and *Falstaff* was beginning to possess the composer's mind. Sufficient of the new manner oozed out in *La Forza del Destino* for critics and analysts now to point to that opera as the work in which Verdi's third style first begins to be traceable, and it can scarcely be surprising that an unprepared public failed to be impressed with the first hintings at a new style which had yet to be placed before the musical world in a matured and comprehendible state.[39]

39 Crowest, *Verdi*, pp. 148–49.

15. The Late 1860s and Wagner's *L'Olandese dannato* (1870)

The year 1867 came to an end with a terrible catastrophe striking Her Majesty's Theatre: on 6 December, a Friday night, the theatre was totally destroyed by a fire the cause of which was not possible to ascertain.[1] By January 1868, a property fund had already been announced and the patrons of the theatre were invited to subscribe in order to raise the money necessary for a speedy reopening, notwithstanding the dramatic financial losses incurred.[2] In February, rumour had it that the two great opera companies in London were to be united under one management. While Frederick Gye was expected to sell his company and retire, a monopoly regime would be installed under James Mapleson as sole manager. The purported amalgamation of the two operatic enterprises into one "Grand Opera Company" was reported in *The Morning Post* and other London periodicals. On 7 March, Frederick Balsir Chatterton, lessee of Drury Lane, published a communication concerning the consultations he was undertaking with Mapleson. "Negotiations have been on foot between myself, as lessee of Drury Lane Theatre, and Mr. Mapleson, with a view to transferring his enterprise from the no longer existing boards of Her Majesty's to those of Drury Lane Theatre."[3] The negotiations were progressing at such a rapid pace that one week later Mapleson announced that he had secured the Drury Lane Theatre and that his Italian opera season would commence there on 28 March. In

---

1 *The Musical Times*, January 1, 1868, pp. 252–54.
2 *The Musical World*, January 11, 1868, p. 18.
3 *The Musical World*, March 7, 1868, p. 159.

addition to the stock repertoire, the novelties announced by Mapleson included Rossini's *La gazza ladra*, an Italian version of Auber's *Gustave III* and Wagner's *Lohengrin*. At the same time, Gye was also in a position to announce the opening of the forthcoming opera season at Covent Garden, which was scheduled for 31 March.[4] The opera season at Covent Garden was to begin with Rossini's *Le siège de Corinthe* (given in Italian as *L'assedio di Corinto*); Verdi's *Rigoletto* and *Don Carlos* were also included in the prospectus. At Covent Garden, *Rigoletto* was staged on 4 April and repeated on 11, followed immediately by *Don Carlos* on 6 April and *Un ballo in maschera* on 11. At Drury Lane, *La traviata* was produced on the 4th, *Il trovatore* on the 7th and *Rigoletto* on the 18th. Five operas in total, all bearing the name of Verdi.[5]

On 11 April, the critic of *The Musical World*, in reviewing the performances of *Don Carlos* and *Rigoletto* at Covent Garden, confirmed his position and argued that the influence of Giacomo Meyerbeer was evident in Verdi's recent development.

> Nevertheless, the more we know of *Don Carlos*, the more we are disposed to regret that its composer was ever induced to try historical grand opera on the scale and after the manner of the *Huguenots* and the *Prophète*. In his own particular domain—romantic melodrama—Signor Verdi has long been unrivalled; but in *Don Carlos*, despite merits that have been fully avowed and discussed in these columns, he has coped with a giant, and honourably succumbed.[6]

Rigoletto, however, was the work which offered the most genuine proof of Verdi's melodious invention and dramatic power. Verdi's *Un ballo in maschera*, staged at Covent Garden on 11 April, was reviewed one week later by *The Musical World*; the critic confirmed his previous judgment, and pronounced it possibly the composer's best accomplishment after *Rigoletto*.[7] On the other hand, the critic described *Il trovatore*, given at Drury Lane, as "the most hackneyed, if not the best, of all hackneyed operas."[8] After a couple of performances of *La traviata* the name of Verdi

---

4 *The Musical World*, March 14, 1868, p. 171.
5 *The Musical World*, April 4, 1868 p. 227.
6 *The Musical World*, April 11, 1868, p. 245, also published on *The Times*, April 6.
7 *The Musical World*, April 18, 1868, p. 264.
8 Ibid., p. 265.

faded away. Upon conclusion of the opera season at Covent Garden, *The Saturday Review* commented on *Don Carlos*.

> As well might the director of the Royal Italian Opera think to galvanize a corpse as to resuscitate *Don Carlos*, in which the Bussetese musician, instead of depending on means that for nearly thirty years have enabled him to command the ear of Europe, has committed the enormous blunder of imitating Meyerbeer, whose Pegasus he can no more manage than Phaeton could control the horses of Phoebus. Signor Verdi will do wisely in future to refrain from such attempts.[9]

Since it was again Davison working behind the curtain and contributing to both journals, it is not surprising to see how similar the arguments against *Don Carlos* are: in a word, the work was considered an unsuccessful attempt to imitate Meyerbeer's style. Moreover, the critic insisted that Verdi's forte was romantic melodrama, while historical opera lay beyond his grasp. Again, *Rigoletto* was pronounced a relief and *Un ballo in maschera* the opera which ranked best immediately after it.[10]

At this time, the articles that had appeared in the columns of *The Times* were reproduced in the columns of *The Musical World*, a fact suggesting once again that the opinion of a single individual occupied the critical position of both periodicals. In addition to them, Davison also contributed reviews to *The Saturday Review*.

In *The Athenaeum*, Chorley continued to express himself in the usual grumbling terms and, notwithstanding the recent development of Verdi's compositional style, continued to refer to Rossini, whose *Semiramide* was also put on stage that year, as the champion of Italian vocal tradition: "There is more beauty in the first act of that opera (too lengthy though it be, a bad consequence of Signor Rossini's indifference to the arrangement of his *libretti*) than in all Signor Verdi's bombastic productions put together."[11]

---

9   *The Musical World*, June 6, 1868, p. 382, from *The Saturday Review*.

10 *Ibid*. On 15 August a similar opinion made its appearance in the same journal, in a contribution signed under the pseudonym Shaver Silver, behind which the figure of H. Sutherland has been identified. Sutherland was the author of *Rossini and His School* (London: S. Low, Marston, Searle & Rivington, 1881) and *The Lyrical Drama. Essays on Subjects, Composers, & Executants of Modern Opera* (London: W.H. Allen, 1881).

11 *The Athenaeum*, April 11, 1868, p. 533.

Later on that year, while the name of Verdi faded away, the London critics paid more and more attention to those operas by Wagner that were produced on the continent. On 11 July, *The Musical World* published a contribution from the correspondent of the Berlin *Echo*, where Wagner's *Die Meistersinger*, conducted by Hans von Bülow at the Royal Opera Theatre, was said to have "furnished every one with a fruitful theme of conversation."[12] Wagner's score, the critic held, showed that the centre of musical gravity had moved from the singers to the orchestra, a development consistent with the composer's own theories, but at variance with what the critic considered acceptable in operatic matters, especially if one considered the loudness of the orchestra. In August, *The Athenaeum* also devoted a column to the perusal of *Die Meistersinger*, since the publication of the piano version afforded this opportunity. The critic was hostile to the composer and his review was characterised by strong sarcasm. When referring to the music allotted to the tenor, he held that "The vilifier of symmetrical melody, as it has pleased him to be, he can still use it under his own conditions as shamelessly as the veriest tune-spinner of the south."[13]

In September, Chorley was in Germany, whence he reported on the recent musical developments and the role Wagner was playing in the German scene. The attraction there was *Lohengrin* which, conducted by Karl Eckert, opened the opera season at Baden-Baden. The opera was very well performed but, the critic argued, was not worth the enormous effort.

> To us, *Lohengrin* seemed to be the very sublimity of impudence. Of music, in the only sense in which we can understand the term, there is next to none in the entire opera. [...] But the hearing of *Lohengrin* has deepened in us the conviction that if Wagner despises melody, it is because he cannot invent it. He is always earnest and dramatic, but never musical.[14]

Chorley returned to the topic on 19 September, when he tried to elaborate further on the issue of the music of *Lohengrin*.

> I have never received such an impression of haggardness in place of beauty of contour, of bombast thrust forward to do duty for real dignity,

---

12 *The Musical World*, July 11, 1868, p. 489.
13 *The Athenaeum*, August 1, 1868, p. 153.
14 *The Athenaeum*, September 12, 1868, p. 345.

as from *Lohengrin* the other evening. It would be hard to say which was the most noticeable, the poverty of the thoughts, the crudity with which they are set forth, but sparingly relieved by certain ingenious orchestral touches, or the acquiescence of a public, including connoisseurs who have been used to boast their superior depth and far-sightedness in their judgment of music by contempt of all Italian and French ware, and of English pretensions to enjoy and appreciate what is best in music.[15]

The antagonistic opinion expressed on 12 September was confirmed two weeks later when the critic, in reviewing Meyerbeer's *Les Huguenots* as performed at Karlsruhe, drew a comparison between the two and insisted that Wagner's music suffered greatly from the infelicitous comparison.[16]

On 21 November, Chorley announced that Rossini, one of the last men of genius still belonging to the greatest musical period Europe had ever witnessed, had passed away in Paris on 14 November. On the same day a long obituary appeared in the columns of *The Musical World*. Not long afterwards, Chorley informed the readers of *The Athenaeum* that Verdi had suggested to his publisher, Giulio Ricordi, that a Requiem Mass should be expressly written for the first anniversary of Rossini's death, to which the best Italian living composers were called to contribute. Such an idea was pronounced absurd.[17]

As early as February 1869, the news spread again among the London periodicals that the two operatic seasons would soon merge; it was anticipated that the Royal Italian Opera at Covent Garden would open in March and be run by an associated body called "The Directors of the Royal Italian Opera and of Her Majesty's Theatre."[18] As might be expected, some discussion followed and the pros and cons involved in such a change were presented. A monopoly might harm the already poor taste of the London public, since operagoers would no longer be able to choose between two venues. The reason for a coalition management was not made public, but the sad loss of one conductor was lamented as

---

15   *The Athenaeum*, September 19, 1868, p. 378. The article bears the initials of the author, H. F. C.
16   *The Athenaeum*, September 26, 1868, p. 408. The article bears the initials of the author, H. F. C.
17   *The Athenaeum*, December 5, 1868, p. 761.
18   *The Musical World*, March 10, 1869, p. 156. See also *The Athenaeum*, February 27, 1869, p. 315.

one of the first consequences; while Luigi Arditi was retained, Michael Costa would leave his former position. Finally, on 27 March the official prospectus of the Italian Royal Opera at Covent Garden was issued, confirming that the season would commence on 30 March, with Arditi as the conductor. The repertoire, now consisting of 48 stock operas, was to be enriched thanks to the inclusion of Ambroise Thomas' *Hamlet*. Bellini's *Norma* opened the season, followed by *Rigoletto* on 1 April, and Beethoven's *Fidelio* on 3 April.[19]

On 1 April, the critic of *The Musical Times* commented on the opening of the opera season and lamented the loss of Costa, whose valuable work had largely contributed to the success of the Royal Italian Opera over the previous years. A note of scepticism was expressed in regard to the advantages that a united company under a double management would present.[20] On 5 April, *The Times* reviewed the performance of *Rigoletto* under the new management; the American singer Jennie van Zandt, who made her career under the stage name of Madame Vanzini, was Gilda but her voice, although of quite wide range, was said to be neither powerful nor rich;[21] Sofia Scalchi was Maddalena, the Irish bass Allan James Foley (alias Signor Foli) was Sparafucile, Pietro Mongini played the Duke of Mantua, while the role of Rigoletto was assigned to Charles Santley. *Il trovatore* was announced for the same day.[22] The same review was reproduced in the columns of *The Musical World* on 10 April, to which a closing note was added regarding the performance of *Il trovatore*, featuring Thérèse Tietjens as Leonora, Sofia Scalchi as Azucena, Mongini as Manrico, Foley as Ferrando and Charles Santley as Conte di Luna.[23] On 24 April *The Musical World* started the publication of a biographical sketch of Verdi's life signed by "An enthusiastic Verdist."[24] In the meantime, the opera season continued with *Les Huguenots* and *Il flauto magico*, while in May a "New Italian Opera" opened at the Lyceum Theatre, performing *L'elisir d'amore* and *Il barbiere di Siviglia*. In May the Royal Italian Opera season offered *Guillaume Tell* (1 May),

---

19 *The Musical World*, April 3, 1869, p. 231.
20 *The Musical Times*, April 1, 1869, pp. 44–45.
21 Charles Santley, *Student and Singer, the Reminiscences of Charles Santley* (New York, London: Macmillian & Co., 1892), p. 297.
22 *The Times*, April 5, 1869, p. 5.
23 *The Musical World*, April 10, 1869, p. 249.
24 *The Musical World*, April 24, 1869, p. 288.

followed by *Lucia di Lammermoor* (4 May) and *Martha* (6 May), the last featuring Christine Nilsson in the main role.[25] With Christine Nilsson playing Violetta in *La traviata* later in May,[26] on 15 Adelina Patti made her appearance in *La sonnambula*, to which *Lucia di Lammermoor, Don Giovanni*, Antonio Cagnoni's *Don Bucefalo* (first performed in London and immediately withdrawn from the stage) and Gounod's *Faust* (as *Faust e Margherita*) followed over the same month. The season continued in June with *Robert le diable, Il trovatore, Les Huguenots, Faust e Margherita, Il Barbiere, La gazza ladra*, and it reached its climax when the first novelty of the season; Ambroise Thomas' *Hamlet* was given on 19 June. *La fille du régiment* (as *La figlia del reggimento*), *La sonnambula* and *Le prophète* were also performed in July. Upon the conclusion of the opera season, the critic of *The Musical World* confirmed the doubts expressed at its outset and lamented once more the loss of Michael Costa.[27] Similar remarks were made by Henry Lunn in the columns of *The Musical Times* on 1 September, when a review of the London musical season was published.

In 1869 Verdi's compositional work was not subject to any in-depth critical scrutiny, nor was any new opera put on stage that would draw the critics' interest. Instead, considerable attention was bestowed upon Richard Wagner, whose *Das Judenthum in der Musik (Judaism in Music)* had been published in Leipzig. On 17 April *The Musical World* published the English translation of Eduard Hanslick's response to Wagner's attack. To this, more articles followed, focussing on the performance of *Die Meistersinger* at Karlsruhe and the announced production of *Das Rheingold* in Munich on 15 August, granted by permission of the King of Bavaria. Starting on 15 May, the serialised publication of the full text of *Judaism in Music* appeared in the columns of *The Musical World*. Reviews and critical contributions flowed in many a periodical, including *The Pall Mall Gazette* and *The Athenaeum*, which commented quite harshly on Wagner's musical achievements and personal hatred against the Jews. To some extent, the general animosity expressed by the English press was caused by the explicit reference Wagner had made to England, to the religious orientation of the country and to Mendelssohn, one of the country's most cherished musical champions. All this added to the

---

25 *The Musical World*, May 8, 1869, pp. 329–30
26 See *The Times*, May 17, 1869, p. 9 and *The Musical World*, May 22, 1869, pp. 367–68.
27 *The Musical World*, August 21, 1869, p. 588.

already widespread sense of bewilderment that Wagner's theories on musical drama had occasioned among the critics, together with the self-laudatory statements he repeatedly uttered at the expense of his fellow composers.

> The strong point of both these composers [Mendelssohn and Meyerbeer] is public frivolity, encouraged by unreasoning criticism. Mendelssohn has succeeded in England because the English religion inclines more to the Old than to the New Testament, and this may also be the reason why newspaper writers in England are more certain to be Jews than even the newspaper writers of Germany. Meyerbeer, again, owes all his popularity to the fact that the people who go to hear operas are those who want amusement, not those who care for Art.[28]

Wagner's line of argument seemed to lead to some sort of inconclusive syllogism, according to which if all Jews are not able to understand and criticise music, and if all critics who do not like Wagner's music cannot understand and criticise music therefore all the critics who do not like Wagner's music must be Jews. Further reference to the accusations made by Wagner against the English critics appeared one year later in the columns of *The Musical World*, when *Der Fliegende Holländer* was produced at Drury Lane as *L'Olandese dannato*. On that occasion the critic objected to the allegation journalists had kept Wagner out of England, and protested against the claim that it was thanks to the Anglican religion that the Jewish conspiracy and attempt to sabotage Wagner's works had been successful in that country.[29]

The provocative stance taken by Wagner in his writings had ignited strongly antagonistic reactions in the English press. Nevertheless, when called upon to judge his musical dramas not everybody agreed that the German composer was entirely deserving of condemnation. In 1869 an intervention in defence of Wagner appeared in the columns of *The Athenaeum* that is reminiscent of Verdi's experience with *The Musical World* twenty-one years before.[30] On 15 September 1869, Walter Bache, an English pianist and conductor who would distinguish himself for

---

28 "Judaism in Music," *The Athenaeum*, April 24, 1869, p. 578.
29 "Apropos of the Holländer," *The Musical World*, July 30, 1870, p. 506.
30 In 1848 J. De Clerville addressed the manner in which Verdi had been the object of repeated, gratuitous, acrimonious criticisms in the columns of *The Musical World* (29 April 1848), and argued that there could be good reasons why the Italian composer was pursuing an innovative operatic ideal.

his advocacy of Franz Liszt and the so-called New German School in England, wrote a letter to the editor of *The Athenaeum* in which he intervened in the discussion of *Das Rheingold* and pleaded Wagner's cause. He suggested that his works should not be judged by comparison with past composers and argued that "a clear understanding of a Wagner opera must be obtained from an efficient performance of the same."[31] The writer intended to address two issues: the first was the difficulties involved in the performance of Wagner's innovative music, a point upon which Wagner himself insisted whenever he claimed that the tepid reception of his music was due to the poor quality of its performance; the second had to do with the critics who, having perused the score or, even worse, the piano version, were simply not in a position to fully understand and appreciate Wagner's musico-dramatic edifice. In response to this letter, Chorley wrote of Wagner's music in even more contemptuous terms, suggesting that *Das Rheingold* represented a "chaotic monster not meriting the name of a building, in which every accepted law and proportion are reversed or set aside, and in which, failing gold and marble and precious stones, we are bidden to accept, by way of novelty, such rubbish as great artificers of genius have cast aside by reason of its meanness and want of worth."[32]

Although in 1868 Chorley retired from *The Athenaeum*, he continued to contribute articles and reports to the same periodical, now revealing his identity by putting either his name or his initials at their foot. Occasionally, the same writings were reproduced in the columns of *The Musical World*. Chorley's successor as chief music critic of *The Athenaeum* was Campbell Clarke, another conservative critic who loathed modern music and favoured the tradition.[33] After a couple of years, however, Charles L. Gruneisen, whose experience as chief critic on the *Morning Post* dated back to 1844, was appointed in his stead.

Things did not change much in 1870. On 19 March the Italian Opera at Drury Lane, having consolidated its role under the management of George Wood, issued a rich prospectus and began to compete in attractiveness and fashionability with the operatic establishment led by Gye and Mapleson. The Royal Italian Opera season at Covent Garden

---

31 *The Athenaeum*, September 18, 1869, p. 378.
32 *The Athenaeum*, September 25, 1869, p. 410.
33 Hughes, *The English Musical Renaissance and the Press*, p. 72.

(whose conductors were Augusto Vianesi and Enrico Bevignani) commenced on 29 March with *Lucia di Lammermoor*, while Verdi's *Macbeth* was announced among its novelties.[34] The Drury Lane Theatre opened on 16 April with *Rigoletto*, *Der Fliegende Holländer* and *Macbeth* also announced; Luigi Arditi was the conductor.[35] In April the following operas were scheduled for production there: *Lucia di Lammermoor* (18), *Il barbiere di Siviglia* (19), *Faust* (21), *Il flauto magico* (23), *Faust* (25), *Rigoletto* (26), *Le Nozze di Figaro* (28), Weber's operetta *Abou Hassan* (in the Italian version by Salvatore Marchesi) and Mozart's *L'Oca del Cairo* (Italian version by Zaffira) on 30 April.[36] On 23 April, *La traviata* was staged at Covent Garden, featuring Mathilde Sessi in the main role. One week later *The Musical World* pronounced her rendition of the main character closer to that of Angiolina Bosio than to the obtrusively "realistic" performance of Marietta Piccolomini in 1856.[37]

In May Luigi Cherubini's *Medea* was revived at Covent Garden, while Rossini's *Barbiere* introduced Adelina Patti in the part of Rosina together with Mario in that of Count Almaviva. Patti also appeared in *La sonnambula* and *Martha* later that month, while Pauline Lucca was Margherita in Gounod's *Faust* and Leonora in *La favorite*.[38] Thomas' *Hamlet* followed later in May. At Drury Lane, Meyerbeer's *Robert le diable* (as *Roberto il diavolo*) with Christine Nilsson in the part of Alice was the

---

34 *The Musical Times*, May 1, 1870, pp. 458–59.
35 *The Musical World*, March 19, 1870, pp. 192, 198 and 206.
36 *The Musical World*, April 9, 1870, p. 244.
37 *The Musical World*, April 30, 1870, p. 304.
38 Adelina Patti (Madrid, 19 February 1843—Craig-y-Nos Castle, 27 September 1919) won the admiration of the most severe international critics thanks to the quality of her voice, her dramatic talent, and her stylistic versatility. Her repertoire included Rossini's, Donizetti's and Bellini's *bel canto* operas, Mozart's *Don Giovanni* and *Nozze di Figaro* as well as Verdi's *Il trovatore* and *Aida* (see chapter 17), among others. Verdi thought highly of Patti, but she never recorded any of Verdi's arias. She was long considered the most authoritative representative of the *bel canto* and her richly ornamented renditions of the *coloratura* repertoire were much appreciated not only by the public, but also by her colleagues and many contemporary music critics. Patti recorded "Ah non credea mirarti," the aria from the final scene of Vincenzo Bellini's *La sonnambula* (1831), in 1906, at Craig-y-Nos Castle. Her interpretation is characterised by the ubiquitous presence of portamentos (the voice slides up or down before reaching the written note), a few ornaments and a number of ritardandos. Available at https://www.youtube.com/watch?v=w2LY6YLHn7U

main attraction, followed by Gounod's *Faust* and Flotow's *Martha*, in addition to the already announced *Abu Hassan* and *L'Oca del Cairo*.[39]

Finally, on 23 July Wagner's *Der Fliegende Holländer* was produced at Drury Lane as *L'Olandese dannato*, with the Italian version by Salvatore Marchesi. The overture was accompanied by a first burst of applause and an encore was demanded upon its conclusion. The dramatic interest was strong and the public received the novelties in the opera with great enthusiasm: "that every one of the audience felt under the influence of a man who had struck out an original path for himself, and had power enough to make others accompany him, was apparent by the deep interest with which every note was listened to, and the enthusiastic applause with which the various pieces were received."[40] Charles Santley was the Dutchman, Ilma de Murska was Senta, Allan James Foley (Foli) was Daland and Perotti was Erik the Hunter. Luigi Arditi's intelligent conducting contributed to the success of the opera. On 30 July, the critic of *The Athenaeum* reviewed the performance of Wagner's opera and expressed a surprisingly mild opinion, once we consider the tone of the periodical's previous articles. Still, it was claimed, the "music of the future" maintained an uncertain status in England, since *L'Olandese dannato* could not be considered a test of the reception of Wagner's later works.[41] The composition of *Der Fliegende Holländer* dates back to the early 1840s and the composer conducted its premiere at Dresden in 1843. Although Wagner himself considered this work a "decisive turning point" of his career, in 1870 *Der Fliegende Holländer* could not be understood as the best and most up-to-date example of Wagner's evolution towards the so-called "music of the future."[42] Although a milestone in Wagner's compositional development from *Rienzi* (1842), in which the composer followed the model of French Grand Opéra, to his more mature works, *Tannhäuser* (1845) and *Lohengrin* (1850), *Der Fliegende Holländer* was still strongly influenced

---

39 *The Musical Times*, June 1, 1870, p. 489.
40 *The Musical Times*, August 1, 1870, pp. 556–58.
41 "Wagner's 'Fliegende Holländer,'" *The Athenaeum*, July 30, 1870, pp. 153–54.
42 See Richard Wagner, "A Communication to my Friends (1851)," in *Richard Wagner's Prose Works*, translated by William Ashton Ellis (London: Kegan Paul, Trench, Trübner & Co., 1892), 1: 300–09.

by the operatic tradition from which Wagner was then departing. In *L'Olandese*, the critic claimed, Wagner had not violated the laws of operatic tradition, his score being laid out in the conventional form; the overture included the leading themes, while the vocal numbers were divided in the orthodox fashion of recitative and cabaletta. In that regard, the Wagner of *Der Fliegende Holländer* had nothing to do with the much-preached "music of the future." The critic of *The Times* and *The Musical World* held a similar opinion, declaring himself partial to a work which was the least extravagant among others that were formless and contained no genuine music. "Every step since taken in advance of it seems to us a step in the wrong direction."⁴³ The same judgment made its appearance on the very same day in the columns of *The Musical World*, signed by Thaddeus Egg, a pseudonym under which, as we know, the figure of Davison should be recognised. Again, apart from the controversy concerning the English critics opposing Wagner as a reaction to his allegations, *Der Fliegende Holländer* represented a weak starting point for the "music of the future." Wagner himself would have been surprised to see one of his earlier works preferred to the more advanced ones. Still, the critic pointed out that *Der Fliegende Holländer* was "good milk for babes," since the London operagoers' capability to digest more challenging works was yet to develop. In a way, it was a good idea to give the London audience a soft start.

A different issue was raised by the critic of *The Morning Post*, who addressed the degree of novelty offered by Wagner's music when compared to the traditional operatic repertoire and the average taste and expectation of the audience.

> The music with which Wagner has described this story in his opera is of the most remarkable character: utterly unlike any operatic music familiar to the British public, and possessing none of the characteristics of an evanescent popularity, there are few melodies the average London publisher would care to disseminate, because the difficulty of the treatment places them far above the usual style of stuff which the ladies of the present generation have been led by the publishers to believe is taste-improving.⁴⁴

---

43   *The Times*, July 25, 1870, p. 12, and *The Musical World*, July 30, 1870, p. 506.
44   Dennis Arundel, *The Critic at the Opera, Contemporary Comments on Opera in London over Three Centuries* (New York: Da Capo Press, 1980), p. 350. The volume was originally published in London by Benn, 1957.

Although not the most innovative of Wagner's works, the music of *Der Fliegende Holländer* would sound unfamiliar enough to those listeners whose ear had been nurtured in the traditional operatic music of the so-called hackneyed operas. However, the work was performed only twice, a circumstance suggesting that it scored a limited popular success.

The critic of *The Musical Standard* was quite enthusiastic, and pronounced *L'Olandese dannato* the most interesting event of the musical season, an occasion that would convince even the most contemptuous critic of the quality of Wagner's music.[45] In the meantime, having founded the London Wagner Society in 1872, Edward Dannreuther published *Richard Wagner: His Tendencies and Theories* with the purpose of elucidating the composer's ideas for the benefit of the lately arisen curiosity of the English public.[46]

Interestingly, Wagner's controversial position and the hubbub occasioned by the performance of his *L'Olandese dannato* prompted the critic of *The Illustrated Review* to raise one further issue. In commenting on the gradual acceptance of Wagner and the increasing recognition of his artistic value all over Europe, as was suggested by the large number of performances his operas were receiving outside Germany, in 1872 the commentator argued that the troublesome German composer had at least one merit. He had finally shaken the English critics and the public, and woken them from their torpor. Their reaction served to demonstrate that the English composers could not keep up with their French, German and Italian colleagues, and that the English were a "somewhat stolid and unimaginative race." Always too good at criticising and condemning others, they were not as good at creating music worth listening to and speaking of.

---

45 *The Musical Standard*, August 6, 1870, p. 45.
46 Edward Dannreuther, *Richard Wagner: His Tendencies and Theories* (London: Augener, 1873), p. 1.

16. Verdi's *Requiem* and Wagner's *Lohengrin* (1875)

The London opera season of 1875 was full of promise and much attention was paid to the long-awaited performance of Wagner's *Lohengrin* at both theatres: Covent Garden and Drury Lane. The Royal Italian Opera at Covent Garden opened on 30 March with Rossini's *Guillaume Tell*, featuring Victor Maurel in the title role, Marini as Arnold, Bagagiolo as Walter and Bianchi as Mathilde. *Der Freischütz* and *Un ballo in maschera* were announced as coming attractions on 1 and 3 April, respectively. However, the critic of *The Times* remarked on 31 March that the work arousing the most widespread curiosity was unquestionably the much-promised *Lohengrin*, which would feature Emma Albani as Elsa, Anna D'Angeri as Ortrud, Ernest Nicolini as Lohengrin and Victor Maurel as Telramund, as well as Proch and Bagagiolo.[1] Of *Un ballo in maschera*, the same critic reiterated the usual opinion: this opera exhibited Verdi's melodic invention and dramatic force more strikingly than in any of his previous works, *Rigoletto* being the only exception.[2] *Don Giovanni* followed at Covent Garden, while on 10 April the opera season at Her Majesty's Theatre (Drury Lane) opened with Beethoven's *Fidelio*, conducted by Michael Costa and featuring Tietjens in the title role. Among the other novelties promised by the theatre, *Lohengrin* again assumed particular prominence. On 17 April, *Rigoletto* was performed at Her Majesty's Opera (Drury Lane), featuring as Gilda Elena Varesi, daughter of Felice Varesi, the singer for whom *Rigoletto* was first

---

1 *The Times*, March 31, 1875, p. 8.
2 *The Times*, April 5, 1875, p. 7.

conceived, followed by *Le Nozze di Figaro* (22 April) and *Il barbiere di Siviglia* (24 April).

But *Lohengrin* would not be the only musical novelty presented to the London public that year, since on 13 May *The Times* and *The Musical World* announced the forthcoming performance of Verdi's *Requiem Mass* at the Royal Albert Hall, conducted by the composer himself. The idea of a collective *Requiem Mass* celebrating Rossini having failed in 1869, Verdi had resolved to pay his own personal tribute to Alessandro Manzoni, who had passed away on 22 May 1873 and whom he revered. As Verdi mentioned in his letters more than once, he had a true veneration for Manzoni, and his intention to compose a Requiem dedicated to his memory would not have surprised those who knew how passionate he was about him.[3] On the very day that followed Manzoni's death Verdi wrote to Giulio Ricordi informing him that, although he would not attend the funeral, he was already considering a composition dedicated to the great poet. In June, he was discussing a concrete project with the Mayor of Milan, for whom he offered to compose a Requiem Mass to be performed in one year.[4] Negotiations are documented in Verdi's *I Copialettere* and concern Maria Waldmann's participation in its premiere. She was already involved in the performance of *Aida* in Florence and, in order for her to participate in the performance of the *Requiem Mass*, special permission was to be granted by the manager of the Florentine theatre La Pergola. Having overcome the difficulties concerning the singers, the date and the church, Verdi himself conducted the premiere of the *Requiem* at San Marco in Milan on 22 May 1874, the first anniversary of Manzoni's death. Teresa Stolz, Maria Waldmann, Giuseppe Capponi and Ormondo Maini were the four soloists.

In October, the composer wrote to Giulio Ricordi and referred to a tour that would bring the *Requiem* to four European capital cities. In January 1875 another letter to Tito Ricordi suggests that the negotiations were progressing at a rapid pace; the tour could be confirmed and its preparations finalised. A later letter to Giulio Ricordi on 9 February refers to Gye's concern about possible financial losses involved in the

---

3   Barbara Reynolds, "Verdi and Manzoni: An Attempted Explanation," *Music & Letters* 29/1 (1948): 31–43.
4   Michele Scherillo, "Verdi, Shakespeare, Manzoni," *Nuova Antologia* (1912), also quoted in *I Copialettere*, p. 283.

production of the *Requiem* at his theatre and the possibility of having such a composition performed at the Royal Albert Hall instead. Verdi, irritated by all the objections raised by Frederick Gye, closed the letter informing Ricordi that he would not conduct in London.⁵ The obstacles and difficulties were finally overcome, however, and in 1875 the *Requiem* was on tour in Paris, London and Vienna, the originally planned performance in Berlin having been cancelled. The cast was slightly different from the original, for the tenor Angelo Masini and the bass Paolo Medini were now to appear alongside Stolz and Waldmann. The *Requiem* was performed seven times at the Salle Favart (Opéra-Comique) in Paris, between 19 April and 4 May; four times in London, at the Royal Albert Hall, between 15 and 29 May (the first performance was preceded by an open full rehearsal on 12 May); and three times in Vienna (Hofoperntheater) on 11, 12 and 16 June.⁶

As mentioned above, on 13 May the critic of *The Times* and the *Musical World* announced the forthcoming performance of the *Requiem* and reviewed the open rehearsal that had preceded it. The work was presented in appreciative terms and Verdi was referred to as "the most gifted of living Italian musicians," the one who had "charmed the English operatic public with his lyric dramas."⁷ The rehearsal attracted a crowded audience in the recently opened Royal Albert Hall. The orchestra was strong (about 150 members) and the chorus massive, since the Albert Hall chorus, trained by Joseph Barnby, also included members from other choral societies. The open rehearsal having made a deep impression on the selected public and the critics, on 15 May the official performance met general expectations. The same critic reiterated his approval:

> Regard it from what point we may, however, the beauties of the new *Requiem* speak eloquently for themselves, and the intense feeling for which many passages are distinguished cannot but impress all hearers attentively alive to what the composer has to say, and willing to accept it in the belief that he is speaking out his mind with earnest sincerity. Thus considered, the latest emanation from the pen of one to whom we

---

5   Verdi, *I Copialettere*, p. 297.
6   Gundula Kreuzer, "'Oper im Kirchengewande?' Verdi's Requiem and the Anxieties of the Young German Empire," *Journal of the American Musicological Society* 58/2 (2005): 399–450.
7   *The Times*, May 13, 1875, p. 13, and *The Musical World*, May 15, 1875, p. 319.

are indebted for so much that is intrinsically beautiful can scarcely be regarded otherwise than as a model in its style, worthy to rank side by side with the *Stabat Mater* of Rossini.[8]

On 15 May, a similar compliment was paid to the composer by the critic of *The Illustrated London News*, who wrote: "Although it may be admitted that the general style of the music is rather dramatic than solemn, still there is so much of power, skill, and beauty that the work deserves recognition as a remarkable production by a remarkable man."[9]

Probably it was *The Musical Times* that paid the largest attention to the composition of the *Requiem*. A long analysis of the score carried out by Joseph Bennett made its appearance in two issues, on 1 April and 1 May, revealing to the reader the complexities and subtleties of a work which represented a milestone in Verdi's compositional development. A proper review of the performance appeared on 1 June, where the critic admitted that "the presentation of the score to the ear revealed beauties which the eye could scarcely detect, and even those who will insist upon judging this *Requiem* by comparison with other *Requiems*, must admit that it contains much that is thoroughly original, earnest, and effective."[10]

As expected, the critic of *The Athenaeum* was by far the most contemptuous, and his attitude resembles that exhibited by Hans von Bülow one year before in the *Allgemeine Zeitung*.[11] Although the critic argued that it was not "imperatively necessary that in a Requiem the music should be what is called 'religious,'"[12] he made some scornful remarks about the deadly subjects so dear to the composer, and the way in which he seemed to confirm his preference for heroines being killed on stage. A much more serious fault was the lack of a prevalent, distinctive style, for the score was characterised by a marked inequality. "On the one hand, there are passages quite familiar to the ears of those who have heard the services in Italy, Spain, and other countries, where the organist has no fixed faith in any musical *repertoire*; and, on the other,

---

8   *The Times*, May 24, 1875, p. 10, and *The Musical World*, May 29, 1875, p. 358
9   *The Illustrated London News*, May 15, 1875, p. 459
10 *The Musical Times*, June 1, 1875, pp. 109–10.
11 Hans von Bülow, "Musikalisches aus Italien," *Allgemeine Zeitung* (Munich), May 28, 1874, pp. 2293–94, and June 1, 1874, pp. 2351–52; also quoted in Kreuzer, *Oper im Kirchengewande*, p. 399.
12 *The Athenaeum*, May 22, 1875, p. 696.

amazement is raised by the very odd way in which the composer has conceived the meaning of the words."[13] Although the critic objected to the confusion that some contemporary commentators made between the secular and the sacred in music matters, the problem was that, in his *Requiem*, Verdi had brought together expressive devices that were too dissimilar. The mixture resulted from a heterogeneous combination of word painting and church-music-practice reminiscences. Other faults were found with the manner in which Verdi had not mastered the counterpoint and the observed style. That said, the critic admitted that he had been impressed by the "Agnus Dei." He defined it as a gem, vocally and instrumentally, "one of those inspirations which genius alone can produce, and in which the most sublime results are the outcome of simplicity."[14] Furthermore, the critic suggested that the reason why the public had bestowed their unconditional applause upon the *Requiem* lay, at least in part, in the influence of the French press and the puffery which had accompanied its performance in London, by which he probably alluded to the analysis that had appeared in the columns of the *Musical Times* over the previous months.

But in May another long promised and eagerly awaited novelty was in preparation: Wagner's *Lohengrin* was to be performed in London, at both Covent Garden and Drury Lane. As we have seen, it was included in Gye's operatic prospectus, released in March, but early rumour whispered that it would also feature in the season at Her Majesty's Theatre. This circumstance drew the critics' attention, as the number of reviews appearing on that occasion confirm. As *The Illustrated London News* suggested, although no more works from the German composer had been presented on the London stage since the first performance of *Der Fliegende Holländer* in 1870, Wagner's art-principles and music had become the object of a growing interest in the country. The performances of extracts from his operas at the concerts promoted by the recently founded London Wagner Society had contributed to that growing interest, and the fact that both Gye and Mapleson had decided to include *Lohengrin* in their operatic programmes confirmed that the initial reluctance to stage the German composer had finally been overcome.[15]

---

13 *Ibid.*
14 *Ibid.*
15 *The Illustrated London News*, May 15, 1875, p. 459.

In London, *Lohengrin* was given for the first time in Italian at Covent Garden on 8 May 1875. *The Times* reviewed it on 10 May, addressing such relevant issues as Wagner's fascination with myths, the poetical quality of the libretto and the effectiveness of the music. In particular, the music revealed an undeniable poetical tendency, however lofty and pompous the ideas expressed by the composer.[16] One week later, having attended a second performance of *Lohengrin*, the critic of *The Times* argued that "to listen without being deeply impressed by certain passages as, for instance, the duet between Lohengrin and Elsa, after the bridal ceremony, and again the *finale* scene, when the 'Knight of the Swan' takes eternal leave of his disconsolate bride, argues, in our opinion, insensibility to the highest beauty of which musical expression is capable."[17] The critic argued that it was difficult to judge Wagner's music on the basis of isolated hearings of single extracts while only the performance of the entire work would do him full justice. However objectionable his theories may have been, his music was not entirely devoid of interest and beauty.

The critic of the *Daily Telegraph*, whose long and articulate review was reproduced in the columns of *The Musical World*, pronounced it a popular success but expressed strong doubts as to whether it would last long, especially when considering the idiosyncratic nature of Wagner's compositional achievement.

> And now the question arises. Will *Lohengrin* commend itself to the taste of English operagoers, and establish Wagner amongst us? Of its present success we have no doubt. It will be the feature of the season. But how as to future seasons—how as to the theories it illustrates? Can our amateurs transfer their allegiance to music without form; to music as the slave of poetry; to music which is melodious only by snatches, and is charming only in the degree in which it is a violation of Wagner's advanced opinions. They may do so, and it is even possible that Beethoven, Mozart, Rossini, Weber, and the rest may vanish from our lyric stage in favour of an entertainment which dazzles and excites without satisfying the higher faculties of mind and intellect. But success of such a nature could only be temporary. Music is not an affair of declamation, tremolos, trumpets, chromatics, and general swimming about in the vast ocean of tone. Music is tune, form, key-relationship, and adherence to those

---

16 *The Times*, May 10, 1875, p. 10.
17 *The Times*, May 17, 1875, p. 7.

contrapuntal laws which can never be violated with impunity because they spring from a natural necessity. Wagner may triumph awhile, but the masters will return to their old place, and, after all, temporary good fortune means little.[18]

What the critic did not take into consideration was the possibility that, at some point, Wagner would establish himself as a prominent composer alongside the others, and not in their stead; it seemed impossible to have him stand by the side of those figures who represented the pillars of the tradition, as if the acceptance of the one implied the exclusion of the others. On 15 May, *The Athenaeum* published a review of *Lohengrin* and made various critical remarks. To start with, its success in London was dependent less on the quality of the music and the performance than on the magnificent *mise en scène*, a fact which would suggest a short popular life for the opera. The singers in the choir were hopelessly out of tune from beginning to the end, the woodwinds and brasses in the orchestra outbalanced the strings (fifty-four in number), the rendition of the principal singers was characterised by constant tremolo and occasional lack of intonation.

> *Lohengrin* is dependant solely on musical mysticism. The canons of art are discarded, and the leading vocalists are, so to speak, disvoiced. Then arises the question whether there be a public prepared to listen to principals who sing without form, who have phrases in which melody is almost always proscribed, who are used as recitative instruments to sustain the orchestral undercurrent. The representatives of the prominent characters ought to sit in the orchestra, whilst the players should be placed on the stage.[19]

Again, strong doubts were expressed not only with regard to the intrinsic merits of the music, but also about the extent to which the public would be prepared to accept a musical drama that overturned the accepted laws of composition and renounced the conditions that guaranteed long-lasting success. The critic argued that Wagner had not pushed aside any of his colleagues (Verdi among them) and that there could be some place for him in the cohort, under certain conditions; in fact, what was pronounced "good and grand in his opera was to be found where he

---

18 "Lohengrin," *The Musical World*, May 29, 1870, p. 359, from *The Daily Telegraph*.
19 *The Athenaeum*, May 15, 1875, p. 663.

adheres to the forms of his predecessors, while, when he departs from them, he is stilted and passionless, harsh and discordant."[20] The critic of The Morning Post, while referring to Emma Albani's performance as Elsa, raised a question of some relevance; although that part included passages that were beautiful in themselves, they failed to awaken general applause. The endless melodies and uninterrupted orchestral flow made it difficult for operagoers to understand when the moment arrived in which they could express their appreciation: "The restless character of the music and the absence of full closes render it difficult for amateurs to know when they may applaud, and they—probably from fear of interrupting the singer—failed to bestow the plaudits which she [Albani] justly merited."[21]

Contrary to the critic of The Athenaeum, the representative of The Musical Times bestowed words of appreciation not only upon the composer of Lohengrin, but also the singers, even though he considered the choir uncertain and rough.[22] In Wagner's music there was something deep and good and, furthermore, the composer's attempt to improve the audience's behaviour by discouraging or even forbidding the continuous outburst of applause and encores was to be understood as a healthy thing.

Later on that year, much attention was paid by the London periodicals to the announced performance of Wagner's monumental Der Ring Des Nibelungen in Bayreuth, which was already in preparation; the event could not fail to draw the critics' attention and revive the discussion concerning the true merits of the German composer. Reports appeared in the columns of The Athenaeum, The Musical World and The Times regarding the progress of the realisation of Wagner's monumental project, which involved the construction of a newly conceived theatre. The old lateral boxes had been removed and the rows of seats rising in a series of steps represented the most noteworthy novelty. However, when reporting from Bayreuth in September, the critic of The Athenaeum, Gruneisen, expressed strong reservations about the efficacy of the architectural solutions the new auditorium presented, not to speak of the music or its composer.[23]

---

20   Ibid., p. 664.
21   Dennis Arundell, The Critic at the Opera (London: E. Benn, 1857), p. 353.
22   The Musical Times, June 1, 1875, pp. 108–09.
23   The Athenaeum, September 11, 1875, p. 351.

In September, Henry Lunn reviewed the London musical season and argued that, although it was correct to claim that the production of Wagner's *Lohengrin* represented the principal event at both Italian Opera Houses, it would be more correct to say that it was the only event. The season had proved completely destitute of novelty and none of the operas performed would really satisfy and reward the subscribers and patrons of either theatre.[24] Wagner was clearly overshadowing Verdi.

---

24   *The Musical Times*, September 1, 1875, pp. 199–201.

17. Aida (1876)

On 4 March 1876, Gye announced that the opera season at Covent Garden would begin on 28 March with Rossini's *Guillaume Tell*. As usual, the manager was eager to inform the public that he had secured a true parade of star artists for his establishment; this year, the cast included Adelina Patti, Ernest Nicolini and Francesco Tamagno among others. In addition to a selection of works from the traditional repertoire, a couple of novelties were promised that would not fail to attract the public's interest. Verdi's grand opera *Aida*, featuring Adelina Patti in the title role, and Wagner's *Tannhäuser*, with Emma Albani, were announced together with *Lohengrin* and Verdi's most celebrated works: *La traviata, Il trovatore, Rigoletto, Un ballo in maschera, Don Carlos, Ernani* and *Luisa Miller*.[1] Augusto Vianesi and Enrico Bevignani would share conducting duties. After *Guillaume Tell*, which opened the season, *Un ballo in maschera* and *Don Giovanni* were scheduled for early in April, followed by *Les Huguenots, La favorite, Don Pasquale* and *Martha*. A short review of *Un ballo in maschera* appeared in the columns of *The Times*, making a few critical points and referring only to the interpreters. The same thing happened with *La traviata* a couple of weeks later, when *The Times* reviewed the performance and paid particular attention to "Mlle. Rosavella," alias Blanche Roosevelt, the first American female performer to sing Italian operas in London and the author of *Verdi: Milan and 'Othello'* (1887). She was judged a still young soprano from whom perfection could not be expected.[2] On 29 April, Wagner's *Lohengrin* was revived in preparation for the repeatedly announced and long-expected

---

1 *The Times*, March 4, 1876, p. 9.
2 *The Times*, April 17, 1876, p. 7.

Tannhäuser. The critic of *The Times* took this opportunity to utter a few words of appreciation regarding the highly poetical subject of *Lohengrin* and the manner in which the composer had, in many passages, fully realised it in the music.³ Predictably, on 6 May *Tannhäuser* brought an immense crowd to Covent Garden. The overture was repeated and in general the performance was extremely successful, at least in popular terms. Over the same week, *Rigoletto*, *La fille du régiment* (as *La figlia del reggimento*) and *L'elisir d'amore* were also given, while *La sonnambula*, *Lucrezia Borgia*, *Faust* and *Semiramide* were produced at Her Majesty's Opera, Drury Lane.⁴

Fig. 12 Adelina Patti, the first Aida in London in 1876, as seen by the American satirical magazine *Puck* in 1881.

On 16 May, *The Times* announced that *Aida* was in preparation at Covent Garden and likely to be performed early the following month. *Aida* was given in London for the first time on 22 June 1876, and its premiere was preceded by the performance of an orchestral arrangement prepared by Arditi and presented during the promenade concerts at Covent

3   *The Times*, May 2, 1876, p. 8.
4   *The Times*, May 9, 1876, p. 4.

Garden in October 1875. As reported by the *Illustrated London News*, the selection comprised vocal pieces, the instrumental prelude to the opera, ballet and procession music; the orchestra was supplemented by the Coldstream Guards.[5] The sense of anticipation that preceded the performance of Verdi's new opera can be perceived also in a contribution that appeared in the columns of *The Athenaeum* on 29 April 1876, where a review of the Paris premiere of *Aida* on the 22nd of that month was published. The critic described the reception of *Aida* in the French capital as rapturous, and expressed a first opinion on the merits of Verdi's new accomplishment. Although he lamented that the composer continued to revel in the deaths of his principal female personages, the critic had to admit that the strong situations presented in the libretto suited the composer's temperament, and the score included moments that were truly magnificent. The critic found fault with the quality of the melodic ideas, which were judged commonplace, and the manner in which Verdi indulged in their elaboration rather than aiming at concision and brevity. But, the critic continued, notwithstanding these defects, the score offered moments of dramatic inspiration "indicating his individuality and his power, as well as his command of melodious imagery and pathos."[6] Although some duets and romanzas could exemplify the quality referred to by the critic, Verdi's forte lay in the *finales*, where the breadth and grandeur of the ensembles were said to be impressive. As to the extent to which the German school might have exerted its influence over the Italian composer, the critic argued that signs were visible in the treatment of the orchestra; however, he suggested that the model offered by Meyerbeer's music carried more weight than that of Wagner's musico-dramatic works and doctrines. Despite Verdi's tendency to be too loud, the critic acknowledged and appreciated his skills in creating imposing orchestral effects and interesting instrumental solutions.

Another mildly appreciative attitude can be observed in the review that appeared in *The Athenaeum* on 1 July, when *Aida* premiered in London. The critic drew the reader's attention to the line of continuity that connected *Aida* with *La forza del destino* and *Don Carlos* in terms of both form and conception. While the composer's tendency "to note

---

5   *The Illustrated London News*, October 9, 1875, p. 362.
6   *The Athenaeum*, April 29, 1876, p. 608.

human passions in their violence was in no degree modified,"⁷ his style appeared to have developed with regard to the treatment of the orchestra. As already argued in April, it was not Wagner who should be credited for this change, but rather Meyerbeer. Verdi presented an over-intensification of Meyerbeer's model, or, to use the critic's own expression, he had "out-Meyerbeered" Meyerbeer. The Italian composer excelled in those strong human conflicts that had always characterised his dramatic choices, and whenever the expression of extreme emotions was involved, he did not fail to show his dramatic power. The "most telling points and most imposing effects" were to be found in the finale of the second act, but even though the critic argued that none of the duets were either consistent or coherent, he admitted that they contained isolated passages of true beauty. The two duets in the last act (the first between Amneris and Radamès, the second between Aida and Radamès) were pronounced excellent. Adelina Patti's portrayal of Aida was the true attraction of the night, her beautiful voice towering above the *fortissimo* of her colleagues, the orchestra and the chorus. The traditional complaint regarding the manner in which Verdi abused the singers' voices by placing them against the loudest possible orchestral background is no longer to be found among the critic's points. However, while Ernesta Gindele was considered equal to the task allotted to her, the critic held that "the representatives of the male characters were all more or less unfit to meet the calls on their vocal capabilities."⁸ Finally, instead of predicting an ephemeral success, the critic argued that there was no reason why *Aida* should not take a long-lasting place in the repertoire together with Verdi's earlier successes. Notwithstanding the faults and shortcomings evidenced by the critic, the score offered "redeeming features" sufficient to prove that Verdi "still maintains that peculiar ascendency over the sympathies of audiences which asserts itself in striking situations so vividly." "In short," he continued, "Signor Verdi has the faculty, amidst trivialities, of never writing an opera in which there is not some display of emotional and sensational power."⁹ Although Charles Gruneisen shared with his authoritative predecessor a conservative attitude, the way in which he conceptualised Verdi's

---

7   *The Athenaeum*, July 1, 1876, p. 25.
8   Ibid., p. 26.
9   Ibid.

recent compositional achievements was not characterised by the same inflexible, intransigent tone, not to mention the witty language and mocking expressions, typical of Chorley.[10] Verdi, whose operas were included in the regular repertoire and had been appreciated by an international audience for thirty years now, did not need to strive for public recognition or critical consensus. His figure now commanded respect.

A similar impression can be gleaned from the reviews that appeared in the columns of *The Times*. On 23 June, in reporting briefly on the popular success of *Aida*'s first performance, the critic addressed Verdi as the "dramatic composer, who for some 30 years has been one of the chief entertainers of our opera-going public, and whose melodies, through every available source, have long been made universally familiar among us."[11] Even though describing Verdi as "one of the chief entertainers" of opera does not constitute a particularly flattering compliment, such an expression should be understood as a genuine tribute to a composer whose international prominence in 1876 could be neither denied nor ignored. The question arises as to whether or not the reference to his entertaining quality stems from the antagonistic comparison now made with Wagner and his lofty theories on music-drama. In our eyes, the tone adopted by the critic of *The Times* and *The Musical World*, although not apologetic, seems to reveal a new sympathy for the Italian composer. For instance, one of the most common complaints expressed in the mid-1840s concerned the supposed lack of style manifested in his operas, especially when compared to Rossini's masterpieces; this complaint was now replaced by the tribute to "a style of his own." The promises made by the young composer had not remained unfulfilled.

> Although the opinions of connoisseurs differed about the merits of this work, none could dispute the fact that the young musician (Verdi was then in his 30th year) showed real dramatic fire, and—important fact—had a style of his own. How since then he has steadily progressed, furnishing opera after opera, in which more and more original and striking features were recognized, all the world knows; and we believe

---

10 Upon Chorley's retirement Charles Gruneisen took his position as music critic at *The Athenaeum* (see chapter 18).
11 *The Times*, June 23, 1876, p. 9.

that the examples of his genius, from period to period introduced among us, offer a fair test by which to adjudge his absolute merits.[12]

Having narrated the long and intricate plot of *Aida*, the reviewer made some critical remarks and pronounced the story gloomy from first to last. A comparison was drawn between the poverty of *Aida*'s libretto, which was lacking in many respects, and the manner in which Wagner's works were characterised by a more stringent sense of dramatic necessity, thus suggesting that the German composer had now established himself as a benchmark for narrative consistency in operatic matters. However, with regard to the music, the critic could not agree with those commentators who argued that Wagner's influence was audible in Verdi's music. Although it was not possible to deny that Verdi's style had developed over time, the claim that he was imitating his German colleague was unfounded. Verdi had become a cherished figure, one whose music did not represent a threat but instead a tuneful musical cradle in which to rejoice and take delight. He was most admirable owing to his distinct musical identity and, the critic seemed to suggest, he was all the more admirable since he had not embraced the threatening theories of his German antagonist: "Verdi knows better than to dive into unfathomable waters. He is, happily, still the Verdi of our long remembrance, our own Verdi in short; and may he continue to remain so."[13]

Much less critical acumen was displayed by the critic of *The Illustrated London News*, whose review of *Aida* made its appearance on 1 July. The complex questions of a significant change in the composer's style and the alleged influence of Wagner or the so-called German school were addressed in oversimplified terms; the critic suggested that after *Un ballo in maschera*, Verdi seemed to have renounced proper melody for the sake of prolonged declamation, "probably in emulation of Wagner's music."[14] The critic held that the first symptoms of the change in question had become clearer in his recent works, although in *Aida* they had reached an unprecedented level. However, the critic failed to describe in detail what those symptoms consisted of; instead, he insisted on a problematic feature in Verdi's music, declamation, which had been subject to ample

---

12 *The Times*, June 26, 1876, p. 10, and *The Musical World*, July 1, 1876, p. 447.
13 *Ibid.*
14 *The Illustrated London News*, July 1, 1876, p. 22.

scrutiny and severe critical discussion long before either Wagner's music or theories could represent a reference model. Of this gap the critic did not seem to be aware. Having narrated the plot, he then returned to the topic and suggested that the influence of the Wagnerian model was evident in the use of "certain peculiar orchestral devices," both in the prelude and the four acts that follow: what those devices consisted of he was not able to elucidate. As surprising as it may sound, the critic held that even though the music comprised moments that were quite effective, it was "of a sombre tone and rather subordinated to the dramatic action than calculated to interest the hearer apart therefrom."[15] For a moment the critic seems to have forgotten that expressing the dramatic content of the libretto is exactly what music is about in an opera, and that Verdi was particularly keen on emphasising this ability of the music. The performance was good and the public did not spare themselves when the moment arrived to bestow upon the soloists clear signs of unconditional appreciation.

The position expressed by the critic of *The Musical Times* was far more controversial. To start with, he argued that it was possible to acknowledge a certain change in Verdi's style only upon the assumption that he ever had a style—perhaps he had gained in prominence simply by imitating the styles of others. With regard to the various foreign influences, he claimed that no sooner had Verdi abandoned the Italian models, than he had begun to base his work upon Meyerbeer and Wagner. The imitation of the first had resulted in "that pretentious work *Don Carlos*," while the influence of the great prophet of the future was evident "in the Ethiopian Opera *Aida*."[16] Having argued that the production of *Aida* had caused little excitement in both Italy and Paris, he expressed his firm belief that in England it would not obtain a permanent position in the repertoire. Although the critic expressed strong reservations about the manner in which Verdi had captured the true Egyptian local colour, he had a few kind things to say about the concerted pieces and the expression of strong dramatic effects.

> In the impassioned scenes he is certainly most successful, yet in some of his more quiet music—as for instance in the Romance for the tenor,

---

15 Ibid.
16 *The Musical Times*, July 1, 1876, pp. 524–25.

"Celeste Aida" there is much to admire; and in several of the concerted pieces in which the dramatic action is carried on, occasional writing, both for voices and orchestra, occurs which convinces us how legitimately he can command the resources of his art.[17]

However, when the critic turned his attention again to the Wagnerian question, he argued that analysis of the score showed the proposition that *Aida* resembled *Tannhäuser* or *Lohengrin* to be sheer nonsense. "Wagner illustrates his music by a spectacle; Verdi illustrates a spectacle by his music."[18] The music was very loud more often than not, but the interpreters were up to the task assigned to them. The audience itself responded loudly and frantically. One month later Henry Lunn commented on the London musical season of that year from the columns of *The Musical Times* and, to some extent, confirmed the views already expressed. The two most prominent events of the season were Wagner's *Tannhäuser* and Verdi's *Aida*. Of the German composer he claimed that, although a tyrant, he had at least a merit: he taught the singers "their real place in the artistic kingdom,"[19] a quality on account of which he should be forgiven for "a little excess of zeal in carrying out so salutary a reform."[20] On the other hand, the critic addressed Verdi in scornful terms and described *Aida* as "a gaudy spectacle which, as it belongs to no recognised school, we may presume to be Egyptian."[21] Unlike his colleague from *The Times*, Lunn insisted on the impossibility of referring to a precise style when talking of Verdi.

On 24 July, upon the conclusion of the Royal Italian Opera season at Covent Garden, the critic of *The Times* commented on its richness and variety, and provided the reader with a list of composers most in demand, judging by the number of performances of their respective works. Verdi scored highest on the list, with eighteen performances, followed by Donizetti (thirteen), Wagner (eleven), Mozart and Meyerbeer (nine), and Rossini coming in last with seven performances.[22] This confirmed the opinion expressed by the same critic, who pronounced Verdi's

---

17 Ibid.
18 Ibid.
19 *The Musical Times*, August 1, 1876, p. 551.
20 Ibid.
21 Ibid.
22 *The Times*, July 24, 1876, p. 8.

Aida the most successful event of the year, at least in popular terms. In conclusion, although it was impossible to deny that *Aida* represented a significant change in Verdi's compositional style, not everybody agreed on the circumstances leading to that change.

The reviews that made their appearance in the 1870s invite a couple of reflections on the manner in which the changes in Verdi's style had occasioned different reactions among the London critics. However reluctantly, none of the commentators taken into consideration could deny that Verdi's compositional style had developed over the years; signs of this development were evident not only in *Aida*, but also in *Don Carlos* and in other earlier works. Despite the changes, Verdi continued to be Verdi—in some case the cherished Verdi—and it was possible to recognise those features that had come to be associated with him and understood as most typical of his personality; that is to say a preference for strong dramatic situations, an aversion to proper melody—to which declamation was preferred—and a marked talent for the treatment of the *finali*. On the other hand, the composer had toned down some of the undesirable characteristics distinctive of his early operas and, in general, his music had evolved towards greater maturity. The question was what had caused the changes that were now observable, and whether Richard Wagner or the German-born, French-oriented Giacomo Meyerbeer was more responsible for them. A number of contrasting attitudes among the London critics contributes to making this picture all the more intricate. While Verdi had come to represent a familiar figure in the operatic scenario, the recent appearance of Wagner's works in London had caused fear and distress. Compared to Wagner, Verdi the popular composer was a reassuring figure who embodied the Italian tradition, whatever the intrinsic value of his music. Those who feared that Wagner would gain prominence in London took refuge in Verdi and in his unchallenging music. In this light, those critics who recognised in Meyerbeer the model for Verdi's more mature style had caught an essential factor in his recent evolution. In fact, the increasing interest Verdi took in the Paris scene is well documented and echoes of motifs from Meyerbeer's *L'etoile du nord* or *Le prophète* are noticeable in *Les vêpres siciliennes*. While the Paris factor was instrumental in at least some of Verdi's musical choices, the composer always refused to acknowledge any influence whatsoever from Wagner.

On 10 June, *The Times* published a report from its Munich correspondent in which the Wagner Festival in Bayreuth was confirmed and the dates of the performances communicated. During the subsequent months much attention was paid to what was to become the most important musical event of the year. *Der Ring des Nibelungen* was in preparation at Bayreuth. In August ample reports detailed the progress of Wagner's colossal undertaking. A first general comment appearing on 19 August in the columns of *The Times* reassured anxious musicians that the art of music stood in no danger and that "the operatic composers worthy the name, to say nothing of the piping operatic singing birds, who give voice to their melody, can rest in quietude with arms enfolded."[23] The reason was simple. Wagner's work defied the traditional notion of opera; it should be rather considered a play, in which the speeches are declaimed, rather than sung, to an orchestral accompaniment. But it was not even appropriate to define what the orchestra had to play as accompaniment. Therefore, those who continued to busy themselves with the composition of veritable operas had nothing to be worried about.

Fig. 13 Giuseppe Verdi, illustration by Théobald Chartran, *Vanity Fair*, 15 February 1879.

---

23 *The Times*, August 19, 1876, p. 10. The same article were reproduced in the columns of *The Musical World*.

18. Music Journalism in London: The Late 1870s and 1880s

Over the last three decades of the nineteenth century, the musical milieu of Victorian London underwent changes that affected the manner in which Verdi was perceived and his final operas conceptualised. A shift in music journalism took place, leading to a new generation of critics whose minds were more open to the challenges of modern music drama. Not only did Wagner's music come to be generally accepted, but his ideas began to exert an increasingly strong influence over the younger generation. That said, nostalgic commentators continued to lament the sad state of "the Land of Song" and refer to "the palmy days" when describing the glorious past of Italian opera. Eventually, a young generation of Italian composers established themselves as the representatives of a "new school" which attempted to combine the Italian tradition with the Wagnerian musical-dramatic tenets: Pietro Mascagni, Ruggiero Leoncavallo and Giacomo Puccini.[1]

In the 1870s, London music journalism witnessed major changes, at least in part owing to a group of well-known personalities passing away and a new generation of music critics making their appearance. Henry Fothergill Chorley died in 1872. His position at *The Athenaeum* was taken first by Campbell Clarke (1868–1870), who was then followed by Charles L. Gruneisen (1870–1879), Ebenezer Prout (1879–1888), Henry F. Frost (1888–1898) and John S. Shedlock (1898–1916).[2] Campbell

---

1   Massimo Zicari, *The Land of Song* (Bern: Peter Lang, 2008), pp. 91–125.
2   Meirion Hughes, *The English Musical Renaissance and the Press 1850–1914: Watchmen of Music*, p. 66.

© Massimo Zicari, CC BY 4.0   http://dx.doi.org/10.11647/OBP.0090.18

Clarke shared with his predecessor a loathing for modern music, but his contributions to *The Athenæum* were limited by his short tenure. Charles Gruneisen, an experienced journalist from *The Morning Post*, shared his predecessors' conservative attitude and considered Wagner's achievements "illegitimate." Ebenezer Prout and Henry F. Frost were both more progressive and championed Wagner among others, while Shedlock was a conservative who loathed Wagner and opposed his operas. In general, *The Athenæum* continued to be a weekly literary periodical of conservative musical orientation until the end of the century.[3]

James W. Davison withdrew from active professional life in 1879 and died in 1885. His successors at *The Musical World* were Joseph Bennett (1831–1911), whose musical recollections can be found in his *Forty Years of Music 1865–1905* (1908), and Desmond Ryan, along with other promising young British writers. Among them we find T. E. Southgate and Henry Sutherland Edwards (1828–1906); Edwards' interest in opera is well captured by his *Rossini and His School* (1881), *The Lyrical Drama: Essays on Subjects, Composers, & Executants of Modern Opera* (1881) and *The Prima Donna* (1888).[4] After Davison's death, Bennett appears to have continued to supervise *The Musical World*.

Fig. 14 Joseph Bennett, from the frontispiece of his *Forty Years of Music, 1865–1905* (London: Methuen & Co., 1908).

---

3 Ibid.
4 In 1889, Edwards took a special interest in Verdi and contacted him through Boito. See Charles Osborne (ed.) *Letters of Verdi* (New York: Holt, 1971) p. 238.

Appointed music critic by *The Sunday Times* in 1865 and *The Telegraph* in 1870, he contributed extensive music analyses and reports to other periodicals, among them *The Musical Standard* and *The Musical Times* (as we have seen, upon the London premiere of Verdi's *Requiem*, Bennett authored a detailed analysis of Verdi's score).[5] As he narrates in his memoirs, in a few years Bennett established himself as one of the most sought-after pens in London music journalism: "Yet the fact is—so much was a new pen desired that within five years from the appearance of my first concert notice, I became critic of the *Sunday Times*, the *Graphic*, the *Pictorial Times*, and the *Daily Telegraph*, as well as being a regular contributor to the *Musical Standard*, the *Musical World*, and the *Pall Mall Gazette*."[6] From 1886 to 1888 the editorship of *The Musical World* passed to Francis Hueffer, whose appreciative attitude towards Wagner is testified to by his volume *Richard Wagner and the Music of the Future*, published in 1874. Eventually Edgar Frederick Jacques, who was a member of the London Wagner Society (which in 1884 was re-founded as the London branch of the Universal Wagner Society), took command of the journal.[7] Francis Hueffer's work as a music critic was particularly important at *The Times*, where he was appointed chief music critic in 1878. Hueffer opened the columns of the most important daily journal of Victorian London to the advanced ideas and innovative music of Wagner and "used *The Times* in an attempt to channel English music in a progressive, Wagnerite direction."[8] Among the chief critics of *The Times*, the name of John Alexander Fuller Maitland is also worth mentioning, since he distinguished himself as a music historian and as George Grove's successor as the editor of *A Dictionary of Music and Musicians*. He took a deep interest in German music, as his scholarly publications suggest—*Schumann* (1884), *Masters of German Music* (1894), *Joseph Joachim* (1905) and *Brahms* (1911), together with the English translation of Philipp Spitta's biography of J. S. Bach (1899, with Clara Bell)—and he committed himself to the cause of English national music. He used *The Times* to support English composers, and in his *English Music in the XIXth Century* (1902) he drew attention to the so-called "English Musical Renaissance." In describing the Renaissance of English

---

5   Joseph Bennett, *Forty Years of Music*, pp. 9–11.
6   *Ibid.*, p. 27.
7   Richard Kitson, *The Musical World (1866–1891)*, I: xi.
8   Meirion Hughes, *The English Musical Renaissance and the Press 1850–1914*, p. 21.

music he distinguished two phases, one which preceded it and was dominated by foreign musicians, and one in which a group of talented native composers finally gained prominence thanks to the value of their music. These composers were Alexander Campbell Mackenzie (born in 1847), Charles Hubert Hastings Parry (1848), Arthur Gorning Thomas (1850), Frederic Hymen Cower (1852) and Charles Villiers Stanford (1852).[9]

The presence of Henry Lunn at *The Musical Times* had visible consequences upon its output since in the mid-sixties he started including extensive reviews of musical and operatic events in London.[10] Under his leadership (1863), *The Musical Times* eroded the leading position held until then by *The Musical World*. New music journals made their appearance during the second half of the century; among them there were *The Musical Standard* (1862–1893), *The Orchestra* (1864–1887) and *The Monthly Musical Record* (established in 1871 and published until 1960).

A case in point with regard to the development of music journalism in Britain is represented by George Bernard Shaw (1856–1950), one of the most controversial critics of late Victorian London. With reference to the provocative opinions he expressed in the columns of *The World*, he once wrote "I could make deaf stockbrokers read my two pages on music, the alleged joke being that I knew nothing about it. The real joke was that I knew all about it."[11] Shaw was music critic of *The Star* from 1888 to 1890 and *The World* from 1890 to 1894. His reviews written during the first period were collected in *London Music in 1888–1889 as Heard by Corno di Bassetto*, those belonging to the second appeared in *Music in London 1890–94*. To them the well-known writings on Wagner, *The Perfect Wagnerite* (1898), must be added, together with a vast number of reviews written during a lifelong professional career and appearing in different periodicals. Shaw was a witty critic and a brilliant writer who, as he admitted in his *Preface to London Music in 1888–1889 as Heard*

---

9   John Alexander Fuller Maitland *English Music in the XIXth Century* (London: Grant Richards, 1902), p. 184.
10 Nicholas Temperley, "MT and Musical Journalism, 1844," *The Musical Times* 110/1516, 125th Anniversary Issue (1969): 583–86.
11 The complete *opus* is collected in Dan H. Laurence (edited by), *Shaw's Music: The Complete Musical Criticism of Bernard Shaw*, 3 vols. (London: The Bodley Head, 1981), 1: 7.

by *Corno di Bassetto*, treated with contemptuous levity "the pre-Wagner school of formal melody in separate numbers which seemed laid out to catch the encores that were then fashionable."[12] As he put it, all those old-fashioned works were standing in the way of Wagner, the most abused musician then in London. Shaw was an aggressive, violent Wagnerite and participated actively in what he called a blood-thirsty war of religion between Wagner's advocates and detractors. Notwithstanding his attitude towards Wagner and the scornful manner in which he dealt with traditional Italian opera, he was genuinely interested in the younger generation of composers and drew his readers' attention to the works of Mascagni, Leoncavallo and Puccini on many an occasion.[13]

Notwithstanding the increasing attention paid by Victorian periodicals to music and operatic events, and despite the quality of the scholarly contributions which made their appearance in the specialised press over the decades taken in consideration, not everybody agreed on the real value of music journalism in late Victorian London. In 1892, an anonymous contributor to *The Musical Standard* (maybe Joseph Bennett) published a long and articulate analysis of the sad state in which music criticism in London lay at the end of the century. Music journalists were said to be lacking in both solid competence and proper critical acumen, leading either to long and convoluted prose texts indulging in the inessential or to incomprehensible technical analyses of the score, which, by challenging the composer's skills revealed, instead, the critic's own ignorance.

> As to express their opinions and impressions, he [the critic] is generally much to wary a bird to do that. It is, indeed, one of the characteristics of English musical criticism that you may read it through without arriving at any conclusion in your mind as to whether the critic likes or dislikes the work. If it be a new opera, for instance, more than two-thirds of the report will treat of the plot in a descriptive manner, most of which is written beforehand, and the other third will be devoted to the music itself, and to a criticism of the artist. [...] But some of our critics are not content with being so tame, they sometimes think it necessary to speak of the music from a technical point of view, and then it is that their path is strewn with pitfalls; they become modern instances of the truth of the

---

12 Eric Bentley, ed., *Shaw on Music* (New York, London: Applause Books, 1995), p. 30.
13 Massimo Zicari, "Critica musicale e opera italiana a Londra nell'Ottocento: George Bernard Shaw," *Musica e storia* 17/2 (2009): 377–92.

old adage, 'a little learning is a dangerous thing.' Diminished sevenths, consecutive fifths, major, no matter how they might be used ninths, discords, unusual progressions, constant modulations, and especially "ugliness," and "want of melody," are the *bête noire* of those critics who happen to possess a slight smattering of musical knowledge.[14]

A similar point was made by Shaw in the columns of *The World* on 21 October 1891. While referring to the London premiere of *Cavalleria rusticana* (19 October), he called attention to the pitfalls stemming from pointless harmonic analyses of the score.

> Those vivid emotions which the public derive form descriptions of "postludes brought to a close on the pedal of A, the cadence being retarded by four chords forming an arpeggio of a diminished seventh, each grade serving a tonic for a perfect chord," must be sought elsewhere than in these columns. It is perhaps natural that gentlemen who are incapable of criticism should fall back on parsing; but, for my own part, I find it better to hold my tongue when I have nothing to say."[15]

Shaw addressed the question on more than one occasion during his career, and made his point not only with regard to the necessity for a critic to be possessed of solid musical knowledge, but also to be committed to expressing his genuine opinion. This was clearly stated in a contribution appearing in *The World* on 13 June 1894, the title of which read "On Musical Criticism."

> We cannot get away from the critic's tempers, his impatiences, his sorenesses, his friendships, his spite, his enthusiasm (amatory and other), nay his very politics and religion if they are touched by what he criticizes. They are all there hard at work; and it should be his point of honour — as it is certainly his interest if he wishes to avoid being dull — not to attempt to conceal them or to offer their product as the dispassionate dictum of infallible omniscience.[16]

On a later occasion that year Shaw defined the skills necessary to make a good critic, and explained why those who were not possessed of them failed to write good criticism. In "How to Become a Musical Critic," which appeared in *The Scottish Musical Monthly* in December 1894 and

---

14 "Musical Criticism Does it Exist in England?" *The Musical Standard*, November 12, 1892, p. 385.
15 Laurence (ed.), *Shaw's Music*, 2: 431–37.
16 *Ibid.*, 3: 238.

was reprinted in *The New Music Review* in October 1912, he argued that "he [the critic] must have a cultivated taste for music; he must be a skilled writer; and he must be a practiced critic."[17] However, many of those who possessed the first two qualifications were nevertheless poor at their job because, as Shaw maintained, they could not criticise.

> They set to work like schoolmasters to prove that this is "right" and that "wrong;" they refer disputed points to school authorities who have no more authority in the republic of art than the head master of Eton has in the House of Commons; they jealously defend their pet compositions and composers against rival claims like ladies at a musical at-home.[18]

Shaw was addressing a kind of provincialism in music matters that it was now time to dismantle and get rid of. Nor could a patronising tone be considered acceptable in the realm of proper music criticism.

One major factor in the change which music journalism underwent in late Victorian London was the edifice of Wagner's theoretical and dramatic accomplishments, the influence of which is clear from any number of scholarly contributions and reviews that appeared after 1873. The increasing attention paid to the German composer by the press should be understood not only in relation to the ongoing critical discussion at international level, but also as a result of his works being performed in London. As we have seen, in 1855 (long before the first performance of *Der Fliegende Holländer*) the German composer was invited to take the baton laid down by Costa as conductor of the Philharmonic Society; on that occasion, he presented excerpts from *Lohengrin* and the *Tannhäuser* Overture. From 19 May 1855 to 26 April 1856, his *Oper und Drama* was published in the columns of *The Musical World*. After that, and despite no public performances of any of Wagner's music dramas in England in the late 1850s and 1860s, an almost uninterrupted series of contributions, making their appearance particularly in the columns of *The Musical World* and *The Athenaeum*, addressed in more or less critical terms both Wagner's theories and works. In 1870, *Der Fliegende Holländer* was first performed in London as *L'Olandese Dannato*, while in 1872 the London Wagner Society was founded, with Edward Dannreuther assuming a pivotal role. Dannreuther took it upon himself to clarify the composer's

---

17   Ibid., 3: 340.
18   Ibid.

ideas to the English public, a task that he accomplished by publishing the volume *Richard Wagner: His Tendencies and Theories* in 1873. On 19 February 1873, the first concert given by the Wagner Society took place at the Hanover Square Rooms, the programme including the Overture and the Introduction to the Third Act of *Die Meistersinger*, with Dannreuther conducting.[19] In 1875, *Lohengrin* was performed at Covent Garden (in Italian) and at Her Majesty's Theatre, followed by *Tannhäuser* in 1876 (also in Italian) at Covent Garden. In 1877, Wagner paid his third visit to London in order to conduct, together with Hans Richter, a "Wagner Festival" at the Royal Albert Hall, which included six concerts from 7 to 19 May. *Rienzi* was given at Her Majesty's Theatre in 1879 (in English) by the Carl Rosa Company, but it was not until 1882 that the full performance of *Der Ring der Nibelungen* was produced in German at Her Majesty's Theatre and that *Die Meistersinger* and *Tristan und Isolde* were given (in German) at Drury Lane.[20] Likewise, ample coverage was granted by the London press to the performance of Wagner's works on the continent, and special attention was paid to the Bayreuth Festival when it was founded in 1876. Countless reports from Bayreuth made their appearance in the columns of *The Times*, *The Musical World*, *The Athenaeum* and *The Musical Times* on the occasion of the inaugural performance of *Der Ring* in 1876.

As suggested by Hermann Klein in his *Thirty Years of Musical Life in London, 1870–1900* (1903), although Wagner had established himself as a prominent figure on the continent and his works were produced in the main capital cities of Europe, in 1877 London he still met with strong prejudices despite all the efforts of the Wagner Society.

> To make matters clear, I must premise that the adversaries and supporters of Wagnerian art in London were then [in 1877] ranged in three distinct camps. There were (1) those who refused to accept his music under any conditions; (2) those who would accept all he had written down to *Tannhäuser* and *Lohengrin*; and (3) those who worshiped both at the temple and from afar, accepting and rejoicing in everything. The first of these sections was gradually dying out, or was being absorbed by the second, as the beauty of the operas heard in London within the

---

19 F. G. E. "Wagner's Music in England," *The Musical Times*, September 1, 1906, pp. 589–93.
20 *Ibid.*

previous two years slowly but surely forced its way into the heart and understanding of the people. The prejudice against the later works still prevailed, however, and to such an extent that no London impresario yet dreamed of mounting *Tristan*, or *Die Walküre*, or *Die Meistersinger*, despite the success those works were then meeting with in many Continental cities. All one could say was that musicians were beginning to display an interest in the preludes and excerpts occasionally performed in the concert-room; while, as a matter of course, the London Wagner Society was constantly growing in numbers and strength, and working a steady propaganda on behalf of the cause.[21]

Among those who strongly advocated for Wagner's music and ideas, Hueffer played a pivotal role. In his *Richard Wagner and the Music of the Future*, he tried to survey the different stages through which the history of opera had gone, and described the circumstances leading to the reforms that the German composer considered necessary. "For by a rare gift of nature he is endowed with the combined genius of music and poetry, and in him at last we must recognise the reformer who re-unites in the music-drama the two arts of poetry and music, which seemed to be separated by a profound chasm and in reality are one."[22] Hueffer explained the role of Wagner by giving an extensive account of the development of opera, which included a large, although not flattering, paragraph on Rossini and his music.

> Italy, the old cradle of the divine art, was to recover once more her position at the head of musical Europe. Rossini, the most gifted and most spoiled of her sons, sallied forth with an innumerable army of bacchantic melodies to conquer the world, the Messiah of joy, the breaker of thought and sorrow. Europe by this time had got tired of the pompous seriousness of French declamation. It lent but too willing an ear to the new gospel, and eagerly quaffed the intoxicating potion which Rossini poured out in inexhaustible streams. Looking back with calmer eyes at the enormous enthusiasm with which Rossini was received by our grandfathers, we are almost at loss to discern the causes for such an unequalled success. It requires, indeed, all the patience of an English audience to endure nowadays a performance of *Otello*, *Semiramide*, or any of Rossini's serious operas except *Guillaume Tell*. The *recitativo secco*

---

21 Hermann Klein, *Thirty Years of Musical Life in London, 1870–1900* (New York: The Century Co., 1903), p. 67.
22 Fr. Hueffer, *Richard Wagner and the Music of the Future* (London: Chapman & Hall, 1874), p. 49.

is treated by him with all the dryness which this ominous name implies. The melodious structure, mostly founded on dance-like rhythms, verges constantly on the trivial, and wherever Rossini covets the forbidden fruit of counterpoint, his deficiencies become sadly obvious. Only rarely the swan of Pesaro rises with the dramatic power of the situation to a remarkable height of passionate impulse. But Rossini knew his public, and he knew equally well his own resources; prudent, as most Italians are, he did his best to profit by the chances of the situation. What he could do and did admirably well was to open the rich mines of melodious beauty with which nature had endowed him, and which it is so easy to augment and develop in a country whose very language is music, and where the *gondolieri* chant the stanzas of Tasso to self-invented tunes. This principle of absolute melodiousness, as Rossini carried it out to its extreme, combined with the charming freshness of his good-natured humour, was well adapted to silence the objection of graver criticism in the universal uproar of popular applause. The unpleasant fact of a strong family likeness among all these sweet children of song and their common mother the waltz, whether they deplored the sad fate of Desdemona or mimicked the jealous rage of the Seville Dottore, seems to have struck only very few of the enchanted hearers.[23]

Hueffer lamented that Italian opera lay in a state of decadence on account of a compositional style that continued to indulge in separate set pieces and long recitatives at the expense of dramatic truth. In Wagner's dramas, by contrast, one had to "recognise an energetic protest against the established artificialities of a demoralised operatic stage. We have already seen before how the opera itself, based as it was on a misunderstood imitation of the antique drama, had in the course of time completely lost what little there might have been of dramatic economy in its original structure."[24]

Opera came to be perceived as a form of art whose organism was diseased to the core and in which the principles of music and poetry were definitely at variance with each other. This, at least, was the case until Wagner made his appearance.

All this was thoroughly changed by Wagner. He has crushed the hard fetters of petrified formalities in the firm grasp of his hand, remoulding the dead metal by the burning breath of his genius into new shapes of

---

23 *Ibid.*, pp. 37–39.
24 *Ibid.*, p. 74.

harmonious fashion. His operas are no longer a series of separate pieces of music, like duets, arias, and finales, with little reference to the action of the piece, and loosely connected with each other by the weak thread of dry recitativi.[25]

Hueffer's analysis of the manner in which Wagner contributed to the progress of dramatic music also took into consideration some of the criticisms made by hostile contemporary critics. In our eyes, two of them assume particular relevance: the first was the lack of any genuine novelty in the so-called "music of the future," while the second was the alleged absence of true melody in the composer's style. In response to the first point, Hueffer insisted upon the need to distinguish between individual genius and the repertoire of forms and rules that every artist deserving that name should master; however revolutionary and advanced Wagner may have been, he was still deeply rooted in his own time. With regard to the second objection, Hueffer explained that melodiousness only appeared to be lacking in his operas.

> One of these causes is, strange to say, the continuous flow of melodious beauty which characterises our master's creations, and which makes it much more difficult to single out a particular motive in his works, than, for instance, in the Italian opera, where a snatch of fine *cantilena* appears like an oasis in the desert of recitativi secchi. Moreover, in Wagner melody and harmony are so closely connected with the dramatic action, that their separate existence becomes imperceptibly mixed up with the general harmony of the work of art as a whole.[26]

Hueffer's commitment to Wagner's theories and music dramas is also testified to by the writings he contributed to *The New Quarterly Magazine* in April 1875, where he explained the *Ring* and Wagner's use of the sagas, and to the *Examiner* in August 1876, where he returned to the *Ring* and commented on the Bayreuth Festival.[27]

Together with Hueffer and Shaw, the name of William Ashton Ellis, one of Wagner's most faithful champions, is also worth mentioning. The editor of the *Meister*, a quarterly journal published from 1888 to 1895 by the Wagner Society, he wrote *Richard Wagner, a Poet, Musician,*

---

25   Ibid., p. 75.
26   Ibid., pp. 107–09.
27   Sessa, *Richard Wagner and the English*, p. 28.

and Mystic in 1887 and *Wagner's Sketches: 1849, A Vindication* in 1892. Moreover, he took it upon himself to translate Wagner's entire prose works (first edition 1892).[28]

By the mid-1880s an increasingly large number of commentators began to bestow more appreciative judgments upon Wagner and those progressive critics who embraced Wagner's tenets now included his notion of music-drama as one of their main critical criteria. Wagner's idea of dramatic consistency and the newly defined relations between melody and harmony, singer and orchestra, music and drama now informed their value judgments. This involved a change in attitude towards those traditional stock operas on which they now looked down with contempt. Meanwhile, those who still opposed Wagner's theories and disliked his music took refuge in past operas, craving for those "palmy days" when declamation had not yet prevailed over proper singing and the orchestra still played a subordinate role.

A first glance at the notion of palminess is offered to us by Shaw, who addressed the issue in his "Palmy Days at the Opera," which appeared in *The Magazine of Music* in 1886.

> When old-fashioned people deplore the decadence of the modern theatre, and regret the palmy days of the drama, superstitious ones are apt to take the desirability of palminess for granted, without troubling themselves to ascertain the exact conditions which constituted it. On inquiry, we are led to infer that long runs, elaborate scenery and dresses, efficient performance of minor parts, and prose dialogues, are degenerate; but that prompters, changes of program every night, poster playbills printed in blue colour that adheres to everything except the flimsy paper, and "historical costumes—*i.e.* costumes belonging to no known historic epoch—are palmy.[29]

Shaw's sarcastic tone refers to a production system, rather than a repertoire, which implied a changed programme every night and a harried rehearsal every second day. Shaw lamented that those working conditions were insufficient for the actor-singer to prepare his part, and drew attention to the negative results involved in a system that forced the actors into continuous changes of character. "One impersonation is

---

28   *Ibid.*, p. 39.
29   G. B. Shaw, "Palmy Days at the Opera," *The Magazine of Music*, January 1886 (unsigned) in Laurence (ed.), *Shaw's Music*, 1: 432

worth more than many impostures. Long runs mean impersonations: palminess means imposture. Let us rejoice over the departure of the palmy days of the theatre."[30] Shaw clarified his position in a later article, appearing in 1889. In returning to the question, the critic referred to the drawbacks and shortcomings of a system that did not aim at artistic quality on stage.

> The operatic artist of today is a "stock company" artist. He calls himself a *primo tenore* or *basso cantante* instead of a juvenile lead or a first old man; but the difference is only technical. Just as the stock actors could take any part in their line at short notice by learning or recalling the lines, and applying their stage habits to the action; so within one week do the Covent Garden artists contrive to get through *Lohengrin, La Traviata, La Sonnambula, Aida,* and *Le Nozze di Figaro*.[31]

A wider definition of palminess is offered to us by another contemporary commentator, the critic of *The Musical Standard*, who by pronouncing himself a constant admirer of Wagner, took a precise position against the old system.

> We agree with our esteemed friend [of the *Daily Telegraph*] that good vocalization is not to be despised, and that melody, or beautiful tune, is and almost must be a *sine qua non*, whether in the lyrical theatre or the concert room. We also admit, although constant admirers of Wagner, that the music should be secondary, or subsidiary, to the drama of operas. But the age of such works as took the public taste in London some 60 years ago is no longer a "golden" age in many sense of the term. Rossini and his servile imitator, poor Bellini, can no longer command paying audiences. We would, in common with many connoisseurs, rather pay not to sit through such an opera as *Semiramide*, heavy as lead. And the revival of *I Puritani*, by Colonel Mapleson, some ten or eleven years ago, only served to attest the decline and fall of the old system. In 1834 *I Puritani* was in high fashion, and four eminent vocalists formed a fine quartet; but such music is not worthy of the baker's oven. [...] In the opera *Aïda*, again, not to speak of *Otello*, Verdi has adopted, with signal success, Wagner's theory that the opera must combine dramatic action with good music, and not merely serve for a display, before the

---

30 Ibid., 1: 437.
31 G. B. Shaw, "The Opera Season" *The Scottish Art Review*, September 1889, in Laurence (ed.), *Shaw's Music*, 1: 765–66.

footlights, of "walking gentlemen" and well-dressed women with voices above the lines![32]

A certain tunefulness allotted to the voice was no longer sufficient for an old opera to be cherished by the cognoscenti; still, many operagoers seemed to rejoice in an operatic performance simply consisting in a series of nice, melodious arias strung together by means of endless recitatives of no consequence. In that regard the figure of Verdi and the novelty represented by his latest operas provided sufficient evidence that the urge for change was also felt by a composer who was generally perceived as the only living, and thus most authoritative, representative of the Italian operatic tradition. Those progressive critics who had been nurtured in Wagner's theories now craved a music drama that would wed music and text in a coherent way, and opposed those Italian operas from the past which defied this definition of music drama.

A similar position was held by Hermann Klein who, in his *Thirty Years of Musical Life in London*, addressed the issue of the sad state of Italian opera in the following terms: "The history of Italian opera in London during the middle eighties is a history of decline and fall. As the fortunes of English and German opera improved, so did the glorious 'palmy days' of the older school recede deeper and deeper into the shadows of the past."[33]

Although Klein held that the food necessary to resuscitate the dying opera was provided when Arrigo Boito's *Mefistofele* was mounted by James Mapleson at Her Majesty's Theatre in July 1880, it was not until the production of Mascagni's *Cavalleria rusticana* at the Shaftesbury Theatre in 1891 that critics recognised a momentous shift in the history of Italian opera. It is again the critic of *The Musical Standard* who, by providing us with the reasons why Mascagni's opera scored an almost unprecedented success in London, sheds some light on the nature of the change. *Cavalleria rusticana* represented the turning point between the palmy days of the past and a new kind of dramatic work capable of combining Wagner's innovative theories with that vocal style in which the nostalgic public still rejoiced.

---

32 "The Opera Question," *The Musical Standard*, July 30, 1892, p. 85.
33 Klein, *Thirty Years*, p. 152.

Mascagni appeared on the scene at the right time. The public had long outgrown the string of songs which during the early part of this century went by the name of opera. They wanted drama allied to music. Wagner, unfortunately, is beyond the mental grasp of the average operagoer, and Mascagni's opera came as a golden mean between the works of the Bayreuth master and the inanities of the old style of Italian opera.[34]

Of course, the success that accompanied the appearance of Mascagni and the "Young Italian School" was to be understood in relation to the palmy days of Italian opera.

The "palmy days" of the opera have faded away with the popularity of the works themselves. That is not a fact to be regretted, for, indeed, what was the opera house in its "palmy" days, but a social institution, where members of society could outglitter each other in jewels, and where innumerable flirtations progressed with alarming rapidity beneath the combined influences of sentimental songs and dazzling chandeliers? A work of art cannot live in such an atmosphere, and opera was not a work of art, but a peg on which conversation and social intercourse could hang; at best, but a string of lyrical gems, oftener than of paste and glass, strung upon a thread of recitative—in short it was not organic drama, nor did it really aim at anything higher than to give the singers an opportunity of showing off their vocalization. It served its purpose and it has had its day; therefore *requiescat in pace*.[35]

The critic also suggested that, although Wagner had played an important role in the process leading to the change in question, it could not be asserted that he alone had brought that change about. The old-fashioned operas were already fading away and the need for an operatic form that wedded music and drama without renouncing the beauty of melody was already in the air. Furthermore, not only Wagner's theories but also his music were said to be above the heads of the majority of operagoers; they did not attend an operatic performance with the purpose of scrutinising its components through the critical lens of a given theory of drama. Rather, they took delight in listening to something easy enough for them to grasp and bring home humming. The reason why Mascagni was successful lay in the manner in which he had rationalised Italian

---

34 "Why Mascagni is Successful," *The Musical Standard*, November 19, 1892, p. 405.
35 Ibid.

opera by assimilating Wagner's lesson without renouncing the beauties of proper melody.

> In truth, Mascagni's success is due to the fact that he is, in his way, the mouthpiece of the artistic needs of the majority of music lovers; he gives them melody, passion and dramatic interest, and he has absorbed just enough of the modern ideas of music-drama, of which Wagner is the supreme exponent, to hit the popular taste. At any rate, his operas are much more works of art than the majority of those of the old Italian school, and that the public takes an interest in his compositions, is a healthy sign for the future of dramatic musical art. He is the straw that shows which way the wind blows.[36]

Shaw held a similar position. He addressed the issue of the shift in compositional style introduced by the young Italian composers in the last decade of the century on the occasion of the London premiere of Verdi's *Falstaff*. In his "Born-again Italian Opera," which appeared on 23 May 1894 in the columns of *The World*, Shaw described the state of decadence in which Italian opera lay and penned a vivid picture of the affectionate feeling shared by those who believed it was still alive.

> The difficulty was to convince those who had been brought up to believe in it (as I was myself) that it was all over with it: they *would* go on believing that it only needed four fist-rate Italian singers to bring the good old times back again and make the rum-tum rhythms, the big guitar orchestration, the florid cabalettas, the cavatinas in regular four-lines, the choruses in thirds and sixths, and all the rest of it swell out to their former grandeur and sweep Wagner off the boards. [...] But now an unlooked-for thing has happened. Italian opera has been born again. The extirpation of the Rossinian dynasty, which neither Mozart nor Wagner could effect, since what they offered in its place was too far above the heads of both the public and the artists, is now being accomplished by Mascagni, Leoncavallo, Puccini and Verdi.[37]

Shaw adopted an argument already made by the critic of *The Musical Standard*, and claimed that *Tristan* could never kill *L'Elisir*. While imposing new forms of composition could do little or nothing to affect traditional Italian opera, Mascagni and especially Puccini proved able

---

36   Ibid.
37   G. B. Shaw, "Born-again Italian Opera," *The World*, May 23, 1894, in Laurence (ed.), *Shaw's Music*, 1: 214–15.

to develop it from the inside by rationalising it, condensing it and bringing it up to date. The result was amazing and the critic argued that with *Manon Lescaut*, given at Covent Garden on 14 May 1894, a few days before *Falstaff*, "the domain of Italian opera is enlarged by an annexation of German territory."[38]

Although less concerned about Italian opera than English music, Fuller Maitland also took some interest in that moment of artistic decadence to which nostalgic operagoers now referred when evoking the palmy days of Italian opera. When trying to draw the line between the long years of dormant inactivity and the dawn of English native music, in his *English Music in the XIXth Century* (1902), Fuller Maitland devoted an entire chapter to the notion of palminess.

> The Italian opera of the "palmy days," which remained in vogue throughout the greater part of the XIXth century, was an amusement as far removed from the intellectual as could be imagined. From the time when Addison attacked it in the days of Handel to a date within the remembrance of all persons of middle age, a grasp of the action of the piece was not considered an essential part of the evening's enjoyment. Few of the subscribers understood Italian; and from the boxes to the gallery the frequenters of the opera attended the representations, not in order to hear a certain work, but to hear some popular singer in what was called "a favourite part.[39]

Although the general public was attracted by the singers and did not trouble themselves to understand the lyrics, in Maitland's opinion the language in which a given opera was written and performed represented a question of paramount importance. While advocating the cause of native composers he lamented that an English National Opera could not be born as long as the use of foreign idioms on stage continued to prevail over the English tongue. The palmy days of Italian opera were standing in the way of the English National Opera.

Occasional critical notes addressing the lack of dramatic consistency typical of such hackneyed operas as *Lucia di Lammermoor* or *La favorite* continued to make their appearance over the last decade of the century, as testified by the articles that appeared in the columns of *The Musical*

---

38 *Ibid.*, 1: 216.
39 Fuller Maitland, *English Music*, pp. 38–39.

Standard under the pseudonym "R. Peggio."[40] In a way, these articles reveal the extent to which the critics' opinion diverged from the public's orientation; even though the first insisted on the "palmy days of opera" being gone for ever, it was thanks to those stock operas so dear to the nostalgic audiences who crowded the theatres night after night that the operatic business could keep going.

The debate concerning Wagner's drama, the progressive critics' hostility against the notion of palminess, the public's nostalgic longing for the operas of the past, the craving for an English National Opera and finally the appearance of a new group of Italian composers whose dramaturgically consistent work was understood as innovative all contributed to defining the musical milieu of late Victorian London. It was in this renewed context that Verdi's last operas made their appearance.

Fig. 15 This portrait of Giuseppe Verdi was painted by Giovanni Boldini in 1886: a rather tall, gaunt figure, whose long grey hair and wrinkled forehead now commanded respect.

---

40 Zicari, *The Land of Song*, pp. 47–89.

19. *Otello* at the Royal Lyceum (1889)

The Milan premiere of *Otello* offered itself as an opportunity for the English critics not only to report on a momentous event in the history of Italian opera, but also to elaborate on the figure of Verdi as a man and a composer. The content of the London press in 1887 makes clear that he was considered the most authoritative and, in fact, the only living representative of the Italian operatic tradition.[1] Some correspondents published lengthy retrospectives of his industrious career, while others portrayed him as a country gentleman, a landed proprietor and successful breeder of horses who now used composition primarily as a means of relaxation during his leisure hours.[2]

In January 1887, *The Musical World* published a long account of Verdi's career, in which the different stages of his life, from his early steps up to his most recent developments, were described in detail. "Verdiana," as the title of that extensive contribution read, appeared on 8, 15 and 22 January, and was followed by a review of Arthur Pougin's recently published *Verdi, an Anecdotic History of his Life and Works*, translated from the French by James E. Matthew.[3] The review introduced its subject with such words as *giant* and *genius*: "The forthcoming production of *Otello*,

---

1 "Music in 1886," *The Times*, January 4, 1887, p. 3, and "Verdi's New Opera," *The Times*, January 28, 1887, p. 7.
2 A picturesque description of Milan in 1887 and a vivid account of the excitement that preceded the premiere of *Otello* can be found in Blanche Roosevelt, *Verdi: Milan and 'Othello'* (London: Ward & Downey, 1887).
3 Arthur Pougin, *Verdi: Histoire Anecdotique de sa Vie et de ses Œuvres* (Paris: Calmann Lévy, 1886), translated by James E. Matthew, *Verdi, An Anecdotic History of his Life and Works* (London: H. Grevel & Co., 1887).

the favourite child of Verdi's old age, has naturally directed the curiosity of the musical world towards the interesting figure of its author, the last of a race of giants, and the only living composer, perhaps, to whom the word genius may be applied in the proper sense of the much-abused term."[4]

Fig. 16 "Otello in Milan" from Blanche Roosevelt, *Verdi: Milan and 'Othello'* (London: Ward and Downey, 1887), p. 192.

On 1 February, *The Musical Times* published a first long report from Milan informing its readers of the continuous postponements that preceded the premiere of *Otello*. Verdi was described as an artist whose long career had not changed his truest nature, as the fact that he still was a man averse to society and city life clearly demonstrated. The critic bestowed appreciative expressions upon the composer and made reference to the generously informative biography written by Alberto Mazzucato, which had been recently included in George Grove's *Dictionary of Music and Musicians*. Having described Verdi's early style as rugged and passionate, the critic maintained that the composer

---

4 "Some Biographical Works," *The Musical Times*, January 22, 1887, p. 54.

had undergone a long course of changes on account of his extensive experience, clearer perception and a more cultivated artistic nature. Verdi's compositional development led one to hope for further personal accomplishment and a new masterpiece.[5]

On 12 February, *The Spectator* commented on the hubbub accompanying the event in Milan and addressed the different types of expectation it was raising. In referring to three different groups—the old-fashioned operagoers, the Wagnerians and the moderates—the critic distinguished among categories that reflected the changed musical scene not only in Milan, but also in London.

> To old-fashioned operagoers, no matter how deeply they may regret the recent development of his style, he always remains the composer of *Il Trovatore*, *La Traviata*, and *Rigoletto*, and as such will be judged retrospectively, as befits the last representative of the high art of his country. At the other extreme, the Wagnerians, or a certain number of them, point to him with triumph as a distinguished convert to the doctrines, harmonic and dramatic, of their master, and as forecasting the ultimate victory of his principles. Between these two sections, the moderates prefer to regard Verdi as a composer who has marched with the times, and whose work, whether modified by organic development or by external influences, combines at the period of his ripe maturity the intellectuality of the Teuton with the graceful charm of the Italian genius.[6]

In the correspondent's description, it is not difficult to recognise the nostalgic enthusiasts of the palmy days on the one side, and the adherents to the Wagnerian party on the other. In the middle lay the moderates, who seemed ready to welcome Verdi's recent development whatever the causes leading to it. But it was the correspondent of *The Musical World* who assumed the most overtly appreciative position regarding Verdi's most recent accomplishment. The critic called attention to the manner in which Verdi had broken with the past in this last work. None of those forms, devices and expedients were to be found in *Otello* that, being truly distinctive of the Italian operatic tradition, seemed to be conceived exclusively to provoke applause and defy dramatic consistency. Moreover, although the whole opera was dependant on

---

5   "Verdi and his New Opera," *The Musical Times*, February 1, 1887, pp. 73–75.
6   "Verdi," *The Spectator*, February 12, 1887, p. 12.

the "dramatic impulse" and ruled by the "declamatory principle," it abounded with beautiful melodies. This circumstance, the critic held, confirmed "that dramatic truth and abstract musical beauty, so far from being in each other's way, support one another."[7] Verdi should be really congratulated upon this felicitous combination. A short report by Giulio Manzoni followed this contribution, describing the delirious manner in which the public had thronged the theatre to attend the work when it was finally premiered. The frenzied audience bestowed upon both the composer and the interpreters their strong approval and called the composer before the curtains twenty times; encore followed encore and the theatre was really shaken by the crowd gathered for the occasion. Francis Hueffer and Henry Sutherland Edwards were also among the countless journalists who arrived from all over the world to participate in the event. The premiere of *Otello* gained so much international resonance and the press coverage was so large that it could be easily compared to the inaugural performance of Wagner's *Ring* at Bayreuth a few years before.

Then a long report from Milan made its appearance in the columns of *The Times*—it was also reproduced in *The Musical World*—which emphasised the social character of the musical event and described Verdi as a man of genius, an artist possessed of melodic power and purity of aim. Having analysed the remarkable way in which Boito the poet had successfully adapted the original drama to the exigencies of the operatic stage, the critic turned his attention to the music of *Otello*. By renouncing all those forms typical of the Italian operatic tradition (airs, *cabalettas*, set numbers), and by following the dramatic action from beginning to the end, Verdi had shown himself to be able to carry out Wagner's doctrine "with a rigour which would have astonished Wagner himself."[8] This was also evidenced by the fact that even the most beautiful "motive" in the entire opera, that which accompanies the love duet between Otello and Desdemona in the first act, was, according to the critic, not sung at all. It was rather given to the orchestra to interpret. Thus Verdi confirmed that he was "capable of entering into the progressive movement of his time"[9] without renouncing himself. However, the critic held that in one respect

---

7 "Viva Verdi!," *The Musical World*, February 12, 1887, p. 115.
8 "Verdi's *Otello*," *The Musical World*, February 12, 1887, pp. 116–18.
9   Ibid.

Verdi had made a clear mistake. He had decided not to make use of the *leitmotiv* technique, which, as Wagner had amply demonstrated, by serving as a link between the various scenes and the different characters, would have granted the opera a stronger dramatic cohesion while avoiding a certain heaviness in some of its declamatory portions. The critic had learned from Wagner's lesson and was now making use of his doctrines to establish his own criteria for judgment. Wagner's influence is also evident in the wording chosen to describe specific compositional devices, as is clearly the case with "motive" substituting for "melody." *The Musical World* returned to the topic later that year, on 5 March, when a "perplexed in the extreme" correspondent wrote to the editor of that journal arguing against the opinion that Verdi would have written his *Otello* in exactly the same way even if Wagner had written nothing at all. Upon perusal of Verdi's score, the correspondent was able to note a passage in *Otello* that was identical to the opening theme of the *Parsifal* introduction, especially when the bass line and the tremolos in the fiddles were considered. To this correspondence the editor of *The Musical World* replied by advocating respect for the composer's choices and arguing that "A man of Verdi's genius is not likely to borrow his music from other composers."[10] "On the other hand," continued the critic, "it would argue him void of that genius, or even of ordinary intelligence, if he did not perceive that the reformatory efforts of Wagner have brought a complete change over the spirit of modern music."[11] This was well testified by the complete absence of traditional arias and *fioriture,* by the way in which declamation prevailed over melody and by the prominent role assumed by the orchestra.

On 1 March, the correspondent of *The Musical Times* contributed a detailed report from Milan where, insofar as the librettist was concerned, he adopted arguments similar to his colleague. By retaining a good part of the original drama and by giving the opera dramatic unity Boito had proven a good poet and a wise dramatist. The libretto he had prepared for Verdi did not betray Shakespeare's original intention, despite some necessary adaptations. "Given the propriety of choosing *Otello* at all," the critic maintained upon concluding his analysis of the libretto, "then

---

10 "Verdi and Wagner," *The Musical World,* March 5, 1887, p. 175.
11 *Ibid.*

Boito is entitled to well nigh unqualified praise."[12] As for the music, the critic was less inclined than his colleague from *The Musical World* to recognise in Verdi's last work the influence of Wagner's dramatic model. The storm scene at the outset of the opera was declared conventional, still full of energy, a trait that, being typical of his previous operas, Verdi had not lost at all over the years. The two capital numbers "Evviva! Vittoria," and "Fuoco di gioia" were said to be "as formally constructed as any in the master's earlier works," to such an extent that "they could be treated as detached pieces musically complete in themselves." Verdi, the critic maintained, was also a master of musical declamation, a feature that he was very good at combining with traditional melodiousness without renouncing more conventional forms. Surprisingly, the critic expressed an opinion regarding the love duet in the second act that was contrary to that shared by his colleagues: it was rich in pure vocal melody and "set off by richly coloured, yet never obtrusive, accompaniments." The idea that Verdi might have adopted the Wagnerian method by reversing the function of the voice and the orchestra and by allotting the melody to the latter was not shared by the critic of *The Musical Times*, who instead insisted that the Italian composer was and remained simply himself.

> Save for greater freedom of harmonic treatment, we see nothing here inconsistent with the Verdi whom all the world knows. The familiar hand of the master is clearly shown, though the duet undoubtedly exemplifies the liberty of modern practice—liberty, not licence, which Verdi in this case ever avoids.[13]

The manner in which the ensembles were "heavily scored and of strenuous force" was strongly consistent with Verdi's early days, while the true merit of the composer consisted in his taking into consideration dramatic propriety without sacrificing vocal melody. On the use of *leitmotivs*, the critic held that they were nowhere to be seen in *Otello*; occasional repetitions of a single theme here and there were suggestive of a function rather evocative than representative.

On 1 March, *The Monthly Musical Record* published its own ample account of the premiere of *Otello* in Milan. Even if the success of the event was unquestionable, the correspondent reported that quite

---
12 "Verdi's *Otello*," *The Musical Times*, March 1, 1887, p. 149.
13 *Ibid.*

different opinions had been expressed with regard to both the libretto and the music. About the first, although almost unconditional praise was bestowed upon Boito on account of his attempt to be true to Shakespeare's original intentions, some commentators had blamed him for favouring the declamatory style at the expense of true lyricism and, at the same time, for yielding too much to Verdi's demands. But, according to the critic, the most contradictory opinions had been expressed about Verdi's late musical style: those who insisted that Verdi had become a Wagnerian were inaccurate, while those who suggested that he had returned to his early melodic style were simply ridiculous. In the critic's mind the matter was clear; even though Verdi had not become a Wagnerian, his recent development depended on the influence of Wagner's compositional method.

> Since *Aida*, Verdi has made another step in the direction of Wagnerism, for in his latest work the Italian master allows to declamation a preponderating share, gives up to a large extent the old operatic forms, and invests the orchestra with greater importance and significance.[14]

Later that month the London operatic season opened and the critic of *The Musical World*, having drawn attention once again to the recent success of Verdi's opera in Milan, commented on the sad state in which the Italian school of singing lay, and on the critical situation the London theatres were experiencing on account of the rivalry between too many competing impresarios.[15] Together with James Mapleson who, having opened the season at Covent Garden would eventually move to Her Majesty's Theatre, two more figures were now contending for operatic supremacy in the English capital: Joseph Lago, who was expected to take over Covent Garden that year, and Augustus Harris, the manager of the Drury Lane Theatre. Harris eventually rented Covent Garden, and soon gained prominence as the leading operatic manager in London. As a matter of fact, on 5 March Mapleson opened the operatic season at Covent Garden with Verdi's *La traviata*, while *Rigoletto* and *Il trovatore* were to be performed over the subsequent weeks, a circumstance strongly suggestive of the extent to which Verdi's last international success might have influenced the marketing orientation of the manager.

---

14 "Verdi's Otello," *The Monthly Musical Record*, March 1, 1887, p. 49.
15 "Italian Opera," *The Musical World*, March 19, 1887, p. 214.

Furthermore, rumour had it that Harris was already negotiating to have *Otello* in London as soon as possible, though his efforts were not successful. In June, while *Rigoletto* was given again at Covent Garden, Carl Rosa mounted *Lohengrin* in English at Drury Lane. In the meantime *Otello* moved from Milan to Rome, where its success was recorded by the correspondent of *The Musical World* on 28 May.

Notwithstanding its unquestionable success and the rumours concerning Harris' early negotiations, it took more than two years for *Otello* to reach London. Moreover, it would not be given at Covent Garden, but instead at the Royal Lyceum Theatre, where it was mounted on 5 July 1889.[16] Although a detailed scrutiny of the reasons why Harris's attempt to give *Otello* at Covent Garden was unsuccessful would go beyond the scope of this volume, it is still worth investigating the manner in which Victorian journals reported on the circumstances leading to the most important of Verdi's late operas being premiered in a theatre of secondary importance, at least as far as operatic matters were concerned. On 27 April, upon publication of the official prospectus of the Italian opera season at Covent Garden, *The Times* commented on the programme issued by Augustus Harris and argued that, despite the title, Italian operas represented only a minority. In fact, besides Rossini's *Guillaume Tell*, which could not be included for obvious reasons, the number of Italian operas in the prospectus was only six, while six operas belonged to the French repertoire and four to the German, Mozart and Wagner being the only representatives of the latter nation. Among the Italian titles *Lucia* made its appearance, though it was the only one illustrative of the "palmy days" while, on the opposite side, the most advanced and most recent progresses of Italian dramatic composition were represented by Arrigo Boito's *Mefistofele*. In the middle, four of the most popular operas by Verdi were to be counted, *Otello* finding no place in the scheme.[17] The season would commence on 18 May and terminate on 27 July, four attractions having been added to the prospectus of the previous year: Charles Gounod's *Romeo et Juliette* (in

---

16 Further performances were announced on Saturday 6, Monday 8, Thursday 11, Saturday 18, Monday 15, Wednesday 17, Friday 19, Tuesday 23, Wednesday 24, Friday 26, Saturday 27, and a special matinée was also scheduled on Saturday July 20.

17 "The Coming Opera Season," *The Times*, April 27, 1889, p. 12.

French), Giacomo Meyerbeer's *Le prophète*, Wagner's *Die Meistersinger* (in Italian) and Georges Bizet's *Les pêcheurs de perles*. On 25 May, *The Musical World* reviewed the performance of Bizet's *Les pêcheurs de perles* and pronounced it a moderate success, owing to the composer not having developed the dramatic power which had made *Carmen* "so considerable a work."[18] *Les pêcheurs de perles* was repeated only once and abandoned when Gounod's *Faust* was given in its stead. After *Carmen*, Verdi's *Aida* was performed, with Giulia Valda and Francesco d'Andrade as Aida and Radames. Mozart's *Le Nozze di Figaro*, Wagner's *Lohengrin*, Gounod's *Romeo et Juliet*, Meyerbeer's *Les Huguenots* and Verdi's *Rigoletto* followed, leading to what was expected to be the most important enterprise undertaken by Harris that year: Wagner's *Die Meistersinger* in Italian.[19] The translation had been prepared by Alberto Mazzucato, who was to be congratulated upon the difficult task and the brilliant result. The performance, however, was not pronounced satisfactory at all, with many faults and shortcomings listed by the critic of *The Musical World* and blamed on the conductor, Luigi Mancinelli, and the main interpreters.[20]

But Augustus Harris' enterprise was not the only one in London in 1889, since two more operations have to be taken into consideration, that of Mapleson at Her Majesty's Theatre, whose season began next, and that of Marcus L. Mayer at the Lyceum, whose programme started late in the summer and featured one title only: *Otello*.

While Harris' managerial skills were proving extremely successful at Covent Garden, Mapleson was striving to keep his opera season going at Her Majesty's Theatre. He did so by making recourse to some of the old operas from the palmy days.[21] On the other hand, Mayer's enterprise at the Lyceum represents a singular case, since his short summer season relied entirely on one opera. Henry Irving having concluded his dramatic season at the Lyceum Theatre with Shakespeare's *Macbeth*, on 1 July it was announced that Mayer would take over the theatre for a few weeks in order to produce Verdi's *Otello* together with a series

---

18 "Royal Italian Opera," *The Musical World*, May 25, 1889, p. 333.
19 E. D. Parker, *Opera Under Augustus Harris* (London: Saxon, [1900]), pp. 29–30.
20 "*Die Meistersinger* at Covent Garden," *The Musical World*, July 20, 1889, p. 474.
21 Parker, *Opera*, p. 32.

of French plays in which Sarah Bernhardt would appear.[22] Mayer had secured the celebrated La Scala orchestra, conducted by Franco Faccio, and the services of both Victor Maurel,[23] the original Iago, and Francesco Tamagno,[24] the original Otello, Aurelia Cataneó substituting for Romilda Pantaleoni in the role of Desdemona. The minor parts featured Elisa Mattiuzzi as Emilia, Giovanni Paroli as Cassio, Durini as Roderigo, Silvestri as Lodovico and Marini as Montano.

On 6 July, the critic of *The Times* reviewed the event and, having pronounced it "one of the most remarkable productions in dramatic music since *Parsifal*,"[25] immediately addressed the issue concerning

---

22 *The Times*, July 1, 1889, p. 13.
23 Victor Maurel (1848–1923), one of the finest French Baritons of the time, was the first Iago in Verdi's *Otello* in 1887, the first Tonio in Ruggiero Leoncavallo's *Pagliacci* in 1892 and the first Falstaff in Verdi's *Falstaff* in 1893 (see chapter 20). Not only an accomplished singer, he was endowed with rare intelligence and a sharp sense of drama. When reviewing the premiere of *Otello* in Milan in 1887, the critic of *The Times* pronounced Maurel "an artist of the first order." "Maurel," the critic claimed, "realized the character of the plausible villain with a distinctness seldom witnessed, even in the spoken drama. He was 'honest' Iago all over, soft spoken, and looking most innocent when he aimed the most poisonous shafts at the defenceless breast of the Moor" (*The Times*, February 7, 1887, p. 5). On the other hand, George Bernard Shaw voiced a completely different opinion, suggesting that Maurel tended to be illustrative rather than impersonative. Having attended the London performance of *Otello* in 1889, he wrote that Maurel's voice was "woolly and tremolous" and that he acted "quite as well as a good provincial tragedian, mouthing and ranting a little, but often producing striking pictorial effects." Laurence (ed.), *Shaw's Music*, 1: 699. Available at https://www.youtube.com/watch?v=w9DRby0m0kA ("Era la notte," first track).
24 Contrary to Maurel, Francesco Tamagno (1850–1905) was neither a cultivated singer nor a fine dramatic actor. Although he was incapable of conveying the subtleties generally associated with dramatic declamation, he was endowed with a strong and sonorous tenor voice, with which he could easily reach the top notes of the high register. Verdi himself had misgivings about his ability to handle declamation and recitative. When Tamagno performed Otello in Milan the critic of *The Times* wrote: "He is a tenore robusto of the genuine kind and his voice, although without much charm in the middle register, goes up to B flat with perfect ease. His upper notes, indeed, are magnificent, and it is specially worthy of notice that he is a genuine Italian tenor, and not a mere baritone, with some high notes superadded" (*The Times*, February 7, 1887, p. 5). Shaw pronounced his voice "shrill and nasal" but bestowed words of appreciation on his rendition of the character: "Tamagno is original and real, showing you Otello in vivid flashes." Laurence (ed.), *Shaw's Music*, 1: 699. A striking example of Tamagno's vocal skills is offered by the initial scene of *Otello*, when the victorious leader, having defeated the Turkish fleet, reaches Cyprus and, all of a sudden, lets out a scream of exultation ("Esultate") on the upper E sharp and G sharp. Available at https://www.youtube.com/watch?v=qrMl7K6uOdk
25 "*Otello* at the Lyceum Theatre," *The Times*, July 6, 1889, p. 11.

the relationship between Verdi and Wagner. Even though it was not possible to assert that Verdi had adopted Wagner's method, it could not be denied that the latter had exercised a powerful influence upon the former, as even a first superficial hearing would immediately reveal. The critic confirmed the judgment expressed on the occasion of the Milan premiere and maintained that Verdi had clearly renounced all those forms typical of the Italian operatic tradition; had Wagner not contributed to the progress of music-drama, he insisted, this radical change would not have been possible. However, the critic did not share with the partisans of Verdi's new style the impression that none of the composer's melodic inspiration had been lost during the transition from one style to another. He described the *mandolinata* in the second act and the "Ave Maria" in the fourth as the only moments in the opera that would impress the ordinary operagoer; only brief reference was made to the love duet between Otello and Desdemona in the first act, on account of the way in which the "love-motive" was presented again at the close of the opera. The vocal ensembles were particularly noteworthy and some remarks were made with regard to the prominent role given to the orchestra.

A few days later, the critic of *The Athenaeum* congratulated Mayer on his costly enterprise and expressed his gratitude for having granted the London public the opportunity of hearing the most recent work of a justly famous composer. Having bestowed words of appreciation upon the librettist, the critic turned his attention to the music which, he maintained, showed its "essentially modern character combined with its freedom from direct Wagnerian influences."[26] This claim was supported by a first perusal of the score, which showed that the composer had continued to use symmetrically constructed pieces and had not adopted any *leitmotivs*. However, two exceptions to the rule of freedom from Wagner's devices were to be considered: the love duet which concludes the first act, and Iago's "Credo" in the second. The duet, the critic held, "is not formally constructed, and except in the last two bars the voices are kept apart, as in the love duets of the Bayreuth master."[27] Iago's "Credo" was, instead, a clear example of the manner in which declamation prevails in the voice part, while "the orchestra

---

26 *The Athenaeum*, July 13, 1889, [n.p.].
27 Ibid.

comments on the text with a measure of eloquence rarely exceeded even by the Bayreuth master."[23] In general, the critic was tentatively appreciative and, even if he maintained that *Otello* was not the finest of Verdi's operas, it was still a splendid example of the modern Italian art.

Two short notices made their appearance in the columns of *The Musical Times* and *The Musical World* later on, addressing the quality of the performance more than that of the music, to which much attention had already been paid.

Fig. 17 A painting by Achille Beltrame portraying Verdi at the piano in his study at Sant'Agata on his 86th birthday. *La Domenica del Corriere*, October 1899.

---

28 *Ibid.*

20. *Falstaff* at Covent Garden (1894)

As with *Otello* a few years before, Verdi's last operatic achievement drew the attention of the London press long before it reached London. Already in January 1893, correspondents from some of the most prominent English journals were reporting from Milan, where the premiere of *Falstaff* was in preparation. They enriched their accounts by focusing on the figure of the octogenarian composer and the circumstances leading to this last composition. A first glance at the general quality of these articles confirms what we have already observed with regard to *Otello* and suggests the dramatic extent to which the general attitude of the English critics towards Verdi had changed since he first established himself as a young composer of international prominence. Compare the deferential attitude generally exhibited in 1893 to the scornful description of Verdi composing at the piano that appeared in the columns of *The Musical World* on 14 May 1853. A good example of later tendency is offered by an article that appeared in the *Daily Graphic* and was reproduced in *The Musical Standard* on 21 January; in it, a journalist reported on a visit paid to Verdi together with the Italian poet Giosuè Carducci. The old composer was again portrayed as a country gentleman and a landed proprietor who enjoyed gardening and considered music composition a leisure activity. He was no longer a young composer to be treated with contempt, scornfully described while banging on the piano keyboard and other drum instruments. Rather, he was a tall, gaunt figure, whose long grey hair and wrinkled forehead commanded respect.

Upon attending the Milan premiere of *Falstaff* some of the critics raised once more the well-known question of the alleged influence

© Massimo Zicari, CC BY 4.0   http://dx.doi.org/10.11647/OBP.0090.20

exerted by Wagner and his method. For instance, on 18 February the correspondent of *The Musical Standard*, having bestowed upon the composer his appreciative remarks on the spirited music he was still able to write, maintained that the compositional development undertaken by the Italian composer showed that he was in sympathy with Wagner's ideas on music-drama.

> His artistic conscience has naturally accepted, in part, the reforms of the Bayreuth master, and the manner in which the author of *Il Trovatore* has so assimilated, without actually copying, the newer form of music-drama, as shown by his *Otello* and *Falstaff*, places him in the rank of modern composers, in which, had his fame entirely relied on his earlier works, he would have been but a shadow and had lost the name he bears.[1]

It was to Verdi's credit, the correspondent concluded, that he had not stood still. A similar appreciative attitude can be found in the review that made its appearance in the columns of *The Athenaeum* on the same day, where it was held that the steady march of Verdi's genius was the work of a man "who has never swerved from the search after the highest ideal."[2] In this regard, the critic did not share with his colleague from *The Musical Standard* the opinion according to which, in modifying his compositional method, Verdi confessed his conversion to the Wagnerian gospel. *Falstaff* also represented an unprecedented case when compared to Verdi's own works, so remarkable was the gap between this last accomplishment and the previous ones. Boito was congratulated upon the admirably conceived libretto, but it was Verdi's genius that had to be credited for the success of the opera. The irresistible charm of his music came of absolute, humorous simplicity, and was also possibly due to the composer not having had recourse to representative themes.

The Times granted full coverage to the event, which was chronicled in its columns on 10 February a more in-depths analysis of the music making its appearance three days later. However, already on 10 February the critic pronounced *Falstaff* a work "in all respects worthy to rank with the great masterpiece of Verdi's genius, *Otello*, the opera in which the composer proved his power of adaptation to dramatic methods entirely at variance with those he had formerly upheld."[3] The music

---

1 "Verdi," *The Musical Standard*, February 18, 1893, p. 129.
2 "Verdi's *Falstaff*," *The Athenaeum*, February 18, 1893, p. 227.
3 "Verdi's *Falstaff*," *The Times*, February 10, 1893, p. 5.

was said to be original in the highest degree and to show a distinctive character, especially on account of the strong comic element. The work did not present any traditional combinations of recitatives and arias, in the ordinary sense of set pieces, a circumstance granting the opera complete dramatic unity. The critic bestowed words of appreciation upon the interpreters and Victor Maurel was pronounced a wonderful Falstaff both vocally and dramatically.[4]

On 11 February, a short notice was also published which provided the reader with a sense of the boundless enthusiasm ignited by *Falstaff* among the critics.

> The opinion of the musical authorities in general on last night's performance seems united in regarding *Falstaff* as the most masterly of Verdi's works, and as remarkable, not only for its sustained *ensemble*, but for the youthfulness and freshness of its inspiration. Amongst the critical representatives of the foreign Press now here, the enthusiasm approaches extravagance, and there is no appreciable difference of opinion as to the supreme quality of the art of the work.[5]

Finally, on 13 February *The Times* published a more detailed analysis of the opera, where the initial appreciative opinion was confirmed. Verdi was the greatest of modern Italian composers and the most striking characteristic of the opera was the brightness and *vis comica* that permeated it from beginning to end. Granted the radical differences between the two composers, Verdi's *Falstaff* was compared with Wagner's *Die Meistersinger* on account of its freshness and comic cheerfulness, two features which the correspondent insisted upon again at the conclusion of his account. The names of Beethoven and Mendelssohn were also mentioned in order to draw a parallel between the cherished classics and the sparkling inventiveness exhibited by the old Italian composer.

---

4 Ibid. "Rarely has the singer of a part been better fitted for it than is M. Maurel for that of Falstaff, and a welcome freedom from exaggeration characterises both his singing and the style of his make-up, which is an important point and is elaborately contrived to give the necessary effect of enormous girth without overweighting the singer. M. Maurel's delivery of the solo beginning 'L'onore! Ladri' could hardly have been improved, and he received an enthusiastic encore for the charming little passage in the second act beginning 'Quando ero paggio del duca di Norfolk.'" Available at https://www.youtube.com/watch?v=gX-e73R2Kvk

5 "Verdi's *Falstaff*," *The Times*, February 11, 1893, p. 5.

In the following months *The Times* continued to call attention to the opera and reported on its successful reception in Vienna, where it was given twice on 21 and 22 May, and in Berlin, where it had four performances starting in June.[6] The La Scala company was conducted by Edoardo Mascheroni with the original cast, Ramon Blanchart substituting for Victor Maurel in Berlin where, it was reported, he had refused to perform. Two aspects seem to have struck the correspondent regarding the performance in Vienna: the exceedingly high price of the seats and the twofold response of the audience. The public was divided into two classes: those who showed enthusiasm and those who exhibited a "demonstrative coolness," probably less on account of the music than of the high price paid in order to gain admission.[7] At Berlin the public seemed to be taken aback by the high degree of novelty presented by the new opera, which probably needed to be attended more than once before it could be fully understood and appreciated.[8]

On 1 March, Joseph Bennett contributed a long report to *The Musical Times*, whose title read "*Falstaff* and the Land of Song." As he clarified at the end of his extensive text, it had not been his intention to provide the reader with a detailed analysis of Verdi's last accomplishment, but rather to narrate the circumstances leading to its premiere. In fact, upon arriving at Milan after a lengthy journey, the journalist was informed that the performance had to be postponed; this delay offered him the opportunity to attend Alberto Franchetti's *Cristoforo Colombo*, Ambroise Thomas' *Mignon* and Camille Saint-Saëns's *Samson and Delilah*. But the prolonged wait was not an entirely unfortunate circumstance for this had granted him the opportunity to observe the busy life of Milan, and to experience and report on the sense of anticipation so widespread among the people. Everybody seemed to be looking forward to this event, regardless of their social or professional condition.

Finally, *Falstaff* was performed and Bennett chronicled the event in a way strongly suggestive of the high expectations it had raised among both the specialists and the countless enthusiasts who crowded the streets and thronged the theatre. A detailed analysis of the music of

---

6   See also James A. Hepokoski, *Giuseppe Verdi: Falstaff* (Cambridge: Cambridge University Press, 1983), p. 56.
7   "Verdi's *Falstaff* in Vienna," *The Times*, May 23, 1893, p. 3.
8   "Verdi's *Falstaff* at Berlin," *The Times*, June 2, 1893, p. 5.

Falstaff made its appearance in the columns of *The Musical Times* on 1 April and 1 May, enriched with countless musical examples taken from the score and included in the article in order to facilitate the reader's comprehension. The analysis involved an extensive account of all the melodic and harmonic devices chosen by the composer to set to music the different comic situations, and was presented along with a description of the manner in which the story unfolds before the eye of the reader-spectator. Having fulfilled this task only in part, after the description of the first act the critic made a first observation of more general import and hinted at the manner in which Verdi had renounced all the old compositional set forms.

> I have quoted largely from the first part of the opening act in order that some idea as to the character of the music might as soon as possible be obtained, and readers will now understand that, while not employing set musical forms (which no one expected he would do), the composer deals with each sentiment or situation as it arises, unfettered by systems, and that his style and method, though retaining Verdian characteristics, lean towards the clearness and simplicity of older masters in comic opera.[9]

The music, which occasionally reminded the critic of the melodiousness typical of Mozart, included no *leitmotivs* and was always varying depending on the comic situation. It was a modified Verdi, as Bennett maintained, for Verdi's style was tempered, chastened, lightened, but unmistakably recognizable. Upon concluding his analysis the critic pronounced *Falstaff* a dramatic masterpiece and a wonderful proof of artistic vitality in a man of eighty.

One further aspect that emerged on the occasion of the production of *Falstaff* in Milan is the interest English music scholars now took in Verdi, even though no definitive plan had been made to have it performed in London. On 15 April, *The Musical Standard* reported on a lecture that would soon be given at Toynbee Hall[10] by Edward Woodall Naylor[11] on "The Music of the Future." Naylor, as the reporter was in a position to

---

9 "The Music of *Falstaff*," *The Musical Times*, April 1, 1893, p. 203.
10 The Toynbee Hall was founded in 1884 in London's East Side by Samuel Barnett after Arnold Toynbee, the British economic historian. Asa Briggs and Anne Macartney, *Toynbee Hall, The First Hundred Years* (London: Routledge, 1984).
11 Edward Woodall Naylor was the author of *Shakespeare and Music* (London: J. M. Dent & Co., 1896), an essay dealing with the music and the music instrument involved in Shakespeare's works.

anticipate, would argue that the most distinctive aspect of Wagner was the *leitmotiv*, without which there could be no true Wagnerism, and that Verdi, having not adopted it, could not be said to be a follower or even an imitator of the German composer.

Later on in June and July the columns of *The Musical Times* granted ample space to another series of lectures focussing on Verdi's last work, this time the Scottish composer, conductor and music teacher Alexander Campbell Mackenzie being the lecturer. Mackenzie, who was Principal of the Royal Academy of Music, was said to be the most qualified expert to deal with Verdi's music, and his lectures on *Falstaff* at the Royal Institution were meant to raise the curiosity of those who had not yet seen it on the boards.[12] What is more, the musical illustrations were provided by a "number of distinguished artists, including Medora Henson, Herbert Thorndike, Watkin Mills, and David Bispham."[13] Among the many points raised by the scholar, three assume special relevance in our perspective. The first concern was about Verdi having not adopted the *leitmotiv* system; the second involved the manner in which the composer had pursued and happily achieved a high degree of dramatic consistency by way of a "wisely-adopted system of compression and concentration;" the third regarded the melodic charm that prevails over the entire opera. Even if, in the critic's eyes, these three aspects demonstrated how pointless the continuously repeated efforts had been to force the Wagnerian system upon almost every composer in Europe, the question concerning the use of *leitmotiv* shows us the extent to which the Wagnerian model impinged on the reception of any new opera.

The article on Mackenzie's lectures prompted the immediate response of the critic of *The Musical Standard*, who expressed some critical remarks. In his "The Italian School and the Wagnerian System," which made its appearance on 3 June 1893, the critic argued that melodic invention could not be considered in itself a criterion sufficient to make a clear distinction between German and Italian music; in fact, the appreciation of melodic beauty was too strongly influenced by subjective factors such

---

12　Mackenzie's lectures were soon translated and published in Italy: A. C. McKenzie, *Tre letture sopra il Falstaff di Giuseppe Verdi, fatte alla Royal Institution of Great Britain – Traduzione del Maestro P. Mazzoni* (Milan: G. Ricordi and C. Tipografia Edit., 1893)
13　*The Musical Times*, June 1, 1893, p. 330.

as personal taste and individual orientation. Moreover, the ideas that lay at the foundation of the so-called "Wagnerian System" could be as true in any other country, since they were based on the assumption that dramatic consistency should not be sacrificed on the altar of symmetrical melodic phrases and oversimplified orchestral accompaniments. Even though it was true that Verdi had not changed his typically Italian style, the same could not be said of younger Italian composers such as Pietro Mascagni and Ruggiero Leoncavallo, whose *Cavalleria rusticana* and *Pagliacci*, the critic maintained, were "pre-eminently examples of the grafting of the depraved ideas of the Bayreuth composer on the genius of the Italian school."[14] This, the critic concluded, demonstrated how strongly the Wagnerian system had exerted its influence over the younger generation.

Finally, *Falstaff* was put on stage at Covent Garden on 20 May 1894, one month after the Paris premiere, which had taken place on 18 April at the Opéra-Comique in the presence of the composer.[15] On the occasion of the Paris premiere, a French translation of the original libretto had been prepared by Boito himself with the aid of Paul Solanges, and a new French cast was organised around the figure of Victor Maurel; this included Marie Delna as Mrs. Quickly and Edmond Clément as Fenton.[16] The reception of *Falstaff* in Paris was enthusiastic and offered a good preparation for its forthcoming production in London; in fact, as the critic of *The Times* put it, when it was given in London the English cognoscenti immediately "endorsed fully and heartily the verdict of all competent Continental critics concerning Verdi's *Falstaff*, and this masterpiece of comic music was most enthusiastically received."[17] However, the critic suggested that Verdi's new opera represented a challenge, at least in so far as the fashionable audience was concerned. In fact, since the opera contained no dull moments, it allowed no opportunities for social intercourse and agreeable conversation during the performance. Both Boito's libretto and Verdi's music involved a new dramatic style, which was not as easy to grasp at first hearing as the old conventional

---

14 "The Italian School and the Wagnerian System,"*The Musical Standard*, June 3, 1893, p. 425.
15 "Verdi's *Falstaff* in Paris,"*The Times*, April 19, 1894, p. 12.
16 See also Giuseppe Verdi, Arrigo Boito, *The Verdi-Boito Correspondence* (Chicago: University of Chicago Press, 1994), p. 218.
17 *The Times*, May 21, 1894, p. 7.

Italian operas. Arturo Pessina's Falstaff was said to be more genial and more Shakespearian than that presented by Victor Maurel. Emma Zilli's impersonation of Mrs Ford was pronounced "more merriment and sparkling humour than at first," despite a persistent tremolo in the voice, Olga Olghina was barely adequate to the role of Anne Page, while Giulia Ravogli was admirable in her Mrs Quickly. In general, the cast was pronounced good and the performance left nothing to be desired, even though the conductor, Luigi Mancinelli, chose very different tempi from those taken in Milan.[18]

A few days later, the critic of *The Athenaeum* commented on the successful performance of *Falstaff* at Covent Garden and hinted at the most striking characteristic of the entire opera: the endless display of youthful spirit and comic vivacity, which he considered unprecedented, except for Wagner's *Die Meistersinger*. But even though the two composers shared some similarities in the humorous treatment of the comic subject, the differences were not small and concerned the manner in which either composer treated the thematic material. While Wagner made use of the motives in a largely consistent way, Verdi exhibited an unbounded melodic inventiveness, and inserted new themes all the time.[19] Sooner or later, it was impossible not to mention Wagner's compositional technique.

A much more critical opinion was expressed by *The Musical Standard*, whose columnist drew attention to the many shortcomings still present in Verdi's music, especially when compared to Wagner's more consistent compositional system. To start with, a first doubt was raised with regard to the extent to which music as such could be said to be comic at all. Even though the question did not involve Verdi's music alone, the critic wondered whether, given the subject of *Falstaff*, the music could really illustrate and enhance its *vis comica*. While the librettist had successfully understood the characteristics of the original play, the same could not be said of the composer. In fact, the critic suggested, the composer should have reflected in the orchestra the

---

18   The cast included the bass Vittorio Arimondi (1861–1928) as Pistol, a role he had created in Milan in 1893. Thanks to his ponderous bass voice Arimondi enjoyed an international career; among his most celebrated roles there is Jacopo Fiesco in Verdi's *Simon Boccanegra*. Available at https://www.youtube.com/watch?v=ik4TPoom8YU

19   *The Athenaeum*, May 26, 1894, p. 686.

emotional expressions of the characters, instead of keeping it busy with an endless motivic bustle.[20] The critic appeared to be a clear Wagnerite, and expressed his preference for a compositional method that would grant a stronger connection between music and drama. The complete lack of *leitmotivs* in Verdi represented a major flaw.

> Then the bewildering succession of themes, some poor, some much too good to die a sudden death, without any development of them as leit-motiven, gives a want of continuity to the opera, and also a want of definite characterization to the dramatis-personae; so that though the work may charm one at times the effect on the whole is detached and the work arouses not one's interest continuously.[21]

The critic argued that it would have been much better, had the composer adopted Wagner's method *in toto* and used his themes as *leitmotivs*.

> Ready-made melodies, however beautiful (and some in *Falstaff* are indeed enchanting), will not give that continuity without which such a work as *Falstaff* is apt to weary one, unless they are developed and used in illustration of something besides a passing suggestion in the lines of the libretto. And, without this development of themes, how is a work which shall have solid musical interest to be written? The never-ending procession of new themes may be very great proof of the fecundity of a composer's invention, but, when they are only given a passing meaning, they begin to tire the ear and to impart a patchy effect to that which should be a harmonious whole.[22]

However, and notwithstanding some of the usual shortcomings involving the noisy treatment of the orchestra, the score revealed much ingenuity. Although the critic did not share the opinion of those commentators who claimed *Falstaff* to be a musical masterpiece, he could not deny that Verdi had done wonders, especially when one considered his age.

Rather more appreciative was the critic of *The Saturday Review*, whose writing abounded with expressions of praise and commendation. Besides the "Beethovenian" flavour of the first scene, Verdi had proved that it was possible to blend the old and the new, and the results he had achieved were simply marvellous.

---

20 "Verdi's *Falstaff*," *The Musical Standard*, May 26, 1894, p. 431.
21 Ibid.
22 Ibid.

> Here they are in an extraordinary combination of rhythms, there in a most intricate part-writing; here in ravishing freshness of melodic invention, there in the boldness of orchestral figures, and all this without any apparent effort, simply logically, and without interfering for a moment with the continuity of the symphonic wave.[23]

The critic also congratulated the librettist upon the wonderful libretto. Quite a similar appreciative attitude was expressed by the critic of *The Monthly Musical Record* on 1 June. Having defined Verdi's *Falstaff* a masterpiece, he went as far as to mention Mozart, Rossini, Wagner and even Johann Sebastian Bach among the models that the octogenarian had equalled, if not surpassed. This he had achieved by blending together the best methods from the present and the past.

It is possible to observe two aspects emerging from the articles taken into consideration thus far. The first regards the respectful manner in which Verdi was now treated by the English critics, an attitude that ranges from the mildly deferential to the sincerely affectionate. The second regards his compositional style and the extent to which it was conceptualised in reference to Wagner's model. Whether Verdi was considered an imitator of Wagner or not, the compositional technique of the second was constantly hinted at as a benchmark against which the music of the first should be examined. In this regard a prominent position was held by the so-called *leitmotiv* technique, which, according to some, was the clear indicator of any composer's affiliation to the Wagnerian faith; the fact that Verdi did not make use of such a technique was a clear sign of his distinctiveness and autonomy. On the other hand, the declamatory style now so prevalent in Verdi's vocal writing suggested the extent to which the Wagnerian notion of dramatic consistency did inform his compositional approach in a larger sense. All that said, no two critics really shared the same opinion in this regard, especially since no two critics shared the same opinion whether Wagner's model was a good thing.

In general, the Italian opera season at Covent Garden that year was pronounced by the critic of *The Times* a successful one, and the first performance of Verdi's *Falstaff* in London was accompanied by other novelties. The opening work was Giacomo Puccini's *Manon Lescaut*,

---

23 "*Falstaff* at Covent Garden," *The Saturday Review*, May 26, 1894, pp. 552–53.

given on 19 May, which the critic of *The Musical Standard* ascribed to that modern Italian school of which Leoncavallo and Mascagni could be considered the brightest stars.[24] Although the representatives of the so-called Young Italian School could not compare with the old master, a new tendency was manifest in their work; under the influence of Wagner they were now bringing together two different notions, that of opera on one side, and that of music-drama on the other, and their achievement demonstrated that some sort of reconciliation between them was finally possible.

The other novelties put forth during that season were Jules Massenet's *Werther* and *La Navarraise* (which, the critic of *The Times* held, represented the two opposite sides of the same composer's talent), Frederic Cowen's *Signa* and Alfred Bruneau's *L'attaque du moulin*.[25] As a consequence of the extremely successful reception of the novelties presented by Augustus Harris at Covent Garden, the stock operas seemed to come off quite badly.

---

24 *The Musical Standard*, May 19, 1894, p. 419.
25 "The Opera Season," *The Times*, August 2, 1894, p. 3.

Conclusions

By definition, a monograph on the reception history of a given composer will deal less with the musical content of his works than with those conditions that determined their reception in a specific country and over a specific timespan. In fact, the object of reception history does not lie in the artwork as an autonomous and self-contained object, but in the forces that shape its reception, among them those assumptions that underlie the age and country that have been taken into consideration and that define the cultural background.[1] This shifts our focus from the artwork itself to that complex network of cultural relations surrounding it.

Three components are at the heart of this network and its internal processes: the artist, the artwork and the people who receive the artwork. The picture becomes more complex if one looks at what lies behind (or beyond) each of these components. Who is the artist? To what extent can the artist's intentions be found reflected in or expressed through his artistic product? To what extent can the artist's ideas be said to mirror the broad cultural context to which he belongs? Can his art-product be considered the genuine expression of his cultural milieu? What is the nature of the art-product? What other functions did (and does) that artwork have, besides the merely aesthetic one? Do we have enough information to formulate a complete and correct idea of the manner in which it was delivered to the audience? Who sat in the audience? Who reviewed the artwork and its performance? What were the ideas,

---

1   See Carl Dalhaus, *Grundlagen de Musikgeschichte* (Cologne: Musikverlag Hans Gerig, 1977), translated by J. B. Robinson, *Foundations of Music History* (Cambridge: Cambridge University Press, 1983), pp. 150–65.

biases, prejudices, likes and dislikes of those in the audience who were called upon to review these works and assess their aesthetic value? To what extent did the opinion of the critics differ from the response of the audience?

In Italy, the figure of Giuseppe Verdi soon assumed an importance that went beyond the intrinsic value of his music. Whether and to what extent his republican ideas influenced his compositional work, and whether and to what extent his music played a role in the process leading to Italian unification are questions still open to discussion.[2] The possibility of carrying out any in-depth investigation in this regard is highly problematic, given the severe restrictions political authorities, whether Austrian, Bourbon, or papal, imposed on both the operatic performances and the periodicals that reviewed them. Textual censorship covered all those aspects in a libretto which pertained to the political, moral and religious dimensions; a censor could intervene on a single word, a line, a dialogue in a scene, the name of a character and even the title or the subject matter of an entire opera.[3] As we observed with *Attila*, it is impossible to exclude categorically the possibility that Italian operagoers understood its plot as an allusion to their own struggle against the foreign invader. The same can be said of many other operas belonging to Verdi's first period, despite the numerous myths that still need to be debunked by historiography. Severe censorship was also exerted on the press, with the consequence that we cannot expect to find hints or references to the possible political function of these operas in the reviews that appeared in nineteenth-century Italy. All these limitations notwithstanding, how should we understand Verdi's position when considering the events that led to the composition of *La battaglia di Legnano*? And why did Giuseppe Mazzini ask Verdi to set to music a text by Goffredo Mameli that was intended to become the "Italian Marseillaise"?

Production and consumption conditions may also represent an issue, especially when dealing with a music genre such as opera, shaped as it is by the interventions of a number of individuals other than the composer. The discussion triggered by Marietta Piccolomini's portrayal

---

2   See Philip Gossett, "Giuseppe Verdi and the Italian Risorgimento," *Proceedings of the American Philosophical Society*, 156/3, September 2012.
3   See Mario Lavagetto, *Un caso di censura. Il Rigoletto* (Milan: Mondadori, 2010).

of Violetta represents a case in point since, as we have observed, some critics insisted that her dramatic talent was of pivotal importance in determining the popular success of such an unworthy opera as *La traviata*. Different production conditions may have contributed to the response to Italian opera in countries other than Italy. In Italy, even though only large and rich cities could count on first-rate singers and international stars for their prestigious operatic establishments, opera was a pervasive phenomenon and almost every town had a theatre where operatic performances could be given on a seasonal basis. These theatres formed circuits frequented by travelling companies that brought both the most recent novelties and the established repertoire to the remotest provinces of the peninsula. Thanks to its ubiquitous presence across the country, in Italy opera is often said to have played the same role that the literary novel played in France or Victorian England. Moreover, every city could present different performing conditions, depending on the political orientation of the local government—which could impose additional cuts or amendments to the libretto for the sake of public morality, social decorum and political stability—the quality of the local orchestra, the entrepreneurial attitude of the impresario and, not least, the financial prosperity of the theatre. Of course, not all these conditions need apply to the cultural milieu of Victorian London, where other forces led to the reception of a music genre which was still considered a frivolous commodity and an exclusive form of entertainment only occasionally approaching the status of true art.

Finally, an enormous question arises when, in the attempt to reconstruct the reception history of a composer through the countless reviews which appeared in a given country and timespan, one tries to hazard some generalisations. To what extent do these reviews originate from the distinctive personality of single individuals rather than the normative system underlying them? Can we reasonably pursue this task in the hope that the accumulation of data at our disposal will come to form a discernible pattern? Can we strike a balance between the role played by each individual and the commonalities that they all share as members of the same normative system? Shall we ever be able to explain why such a prominent critic as Davison expressed his opinions in the aggressive, often derisory and occasionally offensive manner we have observed? If the fear that foreign musicians might hinder the development of native composers explains, at least in part, Davison's hostility to figures like Verdi, to what extent does this position stem from the same normative system to which Chorley and many other contemporary critics belonged? Can the characteristics of this normative system be described and analysed by reference, for instance, to its Italian and French equivalents? Furthermore, the opinions expressed by the musical cognoscenti, both in Italy and London, should not be confused with the response of the audience; if the opinion of the first is well documented, the reasons why operagoers continued to attend a given opera despite the castigating verdict of the press can be inferred only from scattered and partial evidence.

Despite all the possible differences regarding cultural milieu, production conditions, artistic expectations and consumption habits, some of the arguments presented by the English critics when called upon to review Verdi's works during the second half of the nineteenth century are similar to those made by their Italian colleagues. According to many, Italian opera had developed along a pathway that led from Domenico Cimarosa and Giovanni Paisiello, the founders of *bel canto* but already shelved in the 1840s, to Gioacchino Rossini and his immediate followers, Gaetano Donizetti and Vincenzo Bellini. Upon his arrival, Verdi was often considered as either the youngest exponent of an uninterrupted tradition that was approaching a new frontier, or the unworthy representative of a new type of lyric drama with which the composer had betrayed the very principle that lay at the heart of Italian *bel canto*: melodiousness. This betrayal was evident in the manner in which Verdi sacrificed proper singing to tasteless dramatisation. Still in the 1850s those critics, both Italian and English, who attacked the composer insisted that his oversimplified orchestration, his choirs always in unison and his lack of melodiousness signified his limited talent, despite the popular success some of his operas were enjoying at the international level. In general, a clear perception of the significant gap between what it was possible to listen to at the opera before the mid-1840s and the new dramaturgy proposed by Verdi was widely shared among the critics. What divided them was the manner in which they understood the cause of this gap. Whereas all the critics seemed to recognise the symptoms, not everybody agreed on the diagnosis: a complete lack of compositional skills for some, an innovative attitude that sacrificed traditional melodiousness to more dramatic effects for others. However, what strikes the modern reader when it comes to perusing the reviews that appeared in the London press in the 1840s and 1850s is the offensive quality the most adverse and hostile critics often exhibited. As we have seen, some adopted a language that would be considered unacceptable today, full as it was of scornful, derisive and mocking expressions.

In the years to come even the most hostile critics had to put up with Verdi and accept the idea that at least some of his works were worth listening to on occasion. *Ernani, Nabucco, La traviata, Rigoletto* and *Il trovatore* had been incorporated in the regular operatic repertoire alongside the old classics. Here again, English and Italian detractors shared some similar arguments. For instance, some of them credited only the interpreters with the success of his operas and continued to criticise the composer on account of his numerous shortcomings.[4] However, at some point it became also clear that, whoever was in the cast, operas like *Ernani, Nabucco, La traviata, Rigoletto* and *Il trovatore* continued to be successful. Did their succes depend merely on the interpreters, despite the poor quality of the music?

Morality also represents an issue that many critics raised, whether belonging to Catholic Italy or Anglican England. The subjects of *Il trovatore* and *Rigoletto* were often said to be inappropriate to theatrical representation owing to their unabated viciousness; many wondered what the point might have been in putting on stage a hunchback whose daughter was first raped by a nobleman and then murdered by mistake. Similar objections were raised against the libretto of *La traviata* and critics made repeated reference to Violetta as a revolting Magdalene both in Italy and in London.

By the 1870s, Verdi had consolidated his reputation and in his later years he came to enjoy the comfortable life we found described in the London periodicals when *Otello* was reviewed: a landed proprietor and a breeder of horses. In Italy, he had become a symbol of national identity but music critics, whether Italian, English, French or German, still expressed different opinions as to the value of his music. A common issue was the influence Richard Wagner and certain French composers

---

4 See Pasquale Trisolini, "Il Trovatore a S. Carlo," *Gazzetta Musicale di Napoli*, II/42, October 15, 1853, pp. 333–35, in Marco Capra, *Verdi in Prima Pagina*, pp. 125–31.

may have exerted on him. Over the years the success of Verdi became unquestionable in London too and, as Henry Sutherland Edwards put it in 1881, in England "for the last twelve or fifteen years it has been considered bad taste not to admire Verdi's music."[5] With *Otello* and *Falstaff* the old composer took everybody by surprise, for no one really believed that, given his age, he could still surpass himself and create two masterpieces.

When Verdi passed away on 27 January 1901, in Italy his figure had already risen to the status of myth. With his operas, it was immediately remarked, he had given a voice to the feelings of a populace that had long been fighting for national unification. For instance, on 1 February 1901 *Il Mondo Artistico* published an obituary that suggested his role in the political unrest of the Italian *Risorgimento*:

> We can say that with Giuseppe Verdi one part of the Italian soul fades; that which represented the dreams, the impetuses, the glories, the ideals that led to the formation of our fatherland. The Maestro was, with his vocal music, the wonderful interpreter of the yearnings of our national spirit, struggling between the melancholy of a dark present and a fervour of glory that pressed him bravely towards the future.[6]

We find similar tones in other obituaries published in the Italian press. The image of those martyrs who shed their blood on the altar of national unification is often presented in association with operas like *Nabucco, I Lombardi, Ernani, Attila* and *I vespri siciliani*. Their patriotic music was said to have sparked the heroic feelings of countless citizens, despite the useless efforts of the hated oppressors.[7]

Of course, this tone was not adopted by the London press when the death of Giuseppe Verdi was communicated. 1901 was a sad year for the United Kingdom; Queen Victoria passed away and, as some periodicals quickly reported, an entire epoch had disappeared with her. Queen Victoria's death occurred on 22 January, and that of Verdi followed immediately thereafter, on the 27th. As would be expected, the British periodicals were less interested in a foreign composer, however important in his own country, than in their sovereign, a woman whose

---

5   Henry Sutherland Edwards, *Rossini and his School* (London: Marston, 1881), p. 109.
6   "Verdi," *Il Mondo Artistico*, XXXV, 6–7, February 1, 1901, front page.
7   "Giuseppe Verdi," *Il secolo Illustrato della Domenica* (special supplement), XII/576, February 1901, pp. 34–35, 38–39. See also Capra, *Verdi in Prima Pagina*, pp. 263–76.

death represented a turning point in the history of the United Kingdom and the British Empire. However, Verdi's death provided some of the specialised journals with the opportunity to reflect on him not only as a musician, but also as a man who had distinguished himself for a lifelong career of integrity and uncompromising honesty. A quick look at some of the obituaries that made their appearance soon after the sad news was circulated gives us the opportunity to reflect on the manner in which his figure was now conceptualised retrospectively.

A viewpoint shared among some of the critics involved a limited knowledge of Verdi's earlier works and a declared preference for the later ones. The critic of *The Spectator*, for instance, having called attention to the degree of novelty instigated by Verdi's early operas, a circumstance that encouraged some of the contemporary commentators to talk about a new school being founded, then mentioned their crude, vehement and coarse-fibred quality. It was not until *Aida* that Verdi's compositional development could really reveal the composer's genius, which was fully manifested only in *Otello* and *Falstaff*. A similar position was expressed by the critic of *The Times*, who, having hinted at the alteration in Verdi's dramatic method that appeared in *Rigoletto*, again referred to *Aida* as the moment when a great change in Verdi's compositional style had occurred; this would be fully realised only in his later operas: *Otello* and *Falstaff*. The same happened with the critic of *The Athenaeum*, although he expressed himself in slightly different terms. He insisted on the popularity of Verdi's first operas and suggested that with *Aida* he had evolved towards a more mature style.

> Verdi had, however, acquired fame and fortune with his *Rigoletto* (1851), *Il Trovatore* and *La Traviata* (both in 1853); and in these works, old fashioned as they may now appear, there was individuality and dramatic instinct, the latter quality manifesting itself particularly in the first of the three. It has truly been said that, "if popularity were a sure test of merit, Verdi would indisputably be the greatest operatic composer of the second half of the last century." But early popularity augurs badly for lasting success. In 1871 *Aida* was produced at Cairo, and in this work the composer showed a change of style, one which, as M. Reyer, the French composer and critic, at the time declared, would, if maintained, cause a falling away of some of his partisans, but, on the other hand, would win many to his side. And so it turned out.[8]

---

8 "Verdi," *The Athenaeum*, February 2, 1901, p. 153.

What these three critics had in common seems to have been a limited knowledge of Verdi's early operas and a definite preference for the most recent ones, whose unequivocal success they had personally witnessed. This was the opinion expressed by such a sharp observer and commentator as George Bernard Shaw. In an article that appeared in *The Anglo-Saxon Review* in March 1901, Shaw raised a critical question about his colleagues' true qualifications when it came to discussing Verdi's early operas.

> I have read most of the articles on Verdi elicited by his death, and I have blushed for my species. By this I mean the music-critic species; for though I have of late years disused this learned branch I am still entitled to say to my former colleagues *Anch'io son critico*. And when I find men whom I know otherwise honourable glibly pretending to an intimate acquaintance with *Oberto, Conte di San Bonifacio*, with *Un giorno di regno*, with *La battaglia di Legnano*; actually comparing them with *Falstaff* and *Aida*, and weighing, with a nicely judicial air, the differences made by the influence of Wagner, well knowing all the time that they know no more of *Oberto* than they do of the tunes Miriam timbrelled on the shores of the divided Red Sea, I say again that I blush for our profession, and ask them, as an old friend who wishes them well, where they expect to go to after such shamelessly mendacious implication when they die.[9]

The picture which Shaw illustrated in such vibrant terms resulted, at least in part, from that generational change we have already discussed; between the 1870s and 1880s a new group of critics substituted for those who had witnessed Verdi's first appearance in London in the 1840s. Figures like Chorley and Davison, whose antagonistic positions we have examined at length, had long abandoned the profession, while those younger critics who had taken over their positions in the meantime had grown up in a very different musical milieu. While the old generation had attended the first performances of Verdi's early operas in London and described the manner in which they impinged on the models represented by Rossini, Donizetti and Bellini, the young generation, having Verdi in the background, was confronted with the overwhelming presence of Richard Wagner. Early Victorian critics conceptualised Verdi's *Ernani*, *Nabucco* or *I Lombardi* on the basis of

---

9   G. B. Shaw, "A Word more about Verdi" *The Anglo-Saxon Rivew*, March 1901, in Laurence, *Shaw's Music*, 3: 570.

direct knowledge, whereas the same cannot be said of those younger journalists who were now retrospectively commenting on Verdi's long career. Moreover, some of Verdi's early operas were not revived in London in the second half of the century: while *Il trovatore*, *La traviata* and *Rigoletto* had entered the repertoire and were regularly performed in London, earlier works like *Attila*, *I masnadieri* or *I due Foscari* had been long shelved.

By the mid-fifties, Verdi's most successful operas came to be accepted even by those critics who were averse to his early works, thanks partly to Wagner's controversial positions and threatening figure. In that regard, Verdi the popular composer and Wagner the lofty theoretician were said to hold antagonistic but, to some extent, complementary positions. Gradually, Wagner's music came to be accepted even though his figure continued to suffer from the pompous attitude exhibited in his writings. Eventually, some of the younger Victorian critics, having familiarised themselves with Wagner's music and embraced his theories, could not avoid assessing the value of a newly composed opera through the critical lens of Wagner's doctrines.

It should not surprise us that Shaw argued against the widespread opinion according to which the stylistic gap between works like *Ernani* and *Attila* on the one hand, and *Aida* on the other, depended on the influence of Wagner. Shaw denied Wagner's influence and insisted that when *Aida* was first heard in London it made an impression of "Wagnerism" only because nothing later than *Lohengrin* was then known in the country. On this account, when any recurring theme was erroneously taken for a *leitmotiv*, any unusual or unprecedented compositional device would be understood as "Wagnerian." Instead, Shaw argued that the reason why a change had occurred between *Il trovatore* and Verdi's later operas lay in the manner in which Verdi's creative vein had dried up. His initial spontaneity having died out, he was compelled to search for more sophisticated, more distinguished orchestral solutions. Even though Shaw agreed with his colleagues that Verdi had accomplished this process with *Otello*, he declared the idea that Verdi had been Wagnerised heresy; instead, he suggested that Verdi's genius consisted in expressing "all the common passions with an impetuosity and an intensity which produced an effect of sublimity."[10]

---

10   *Ibid.*, 3: 574.

Finally, a very interesting point was made by Joseph Bennett in the columns of *The Musical Times*; he portrayed in very honest and straightforward terms the acrimonious manner in which for many years Verdi's operas had been attacked and his figure ridiculed by the English press. Bennett was fully appreciative towards Verdi and, in going through the critical positions held by some of his colleagues in the past decades, he insisted that the Italian composer had been repeatedly ill-treated on the basis of many mistaken judgments: "In England, the strenuous, fiery composer, whose music flamed along in such an unmeasured manner, met with strong opposition; in some cases with downright abuse."[11]

Although it was clear that the composer was possessed of "strong dramatic feeling, energy, passion, and exuberant conception," it could not be denied that he was supremely capable of composing beautiful melodies. Bennett compared him to a locomotive whose power and strength not one critic could either resist or oppose. In concluding his contribution, Bennett acknowledged the value of the composer not only in spite of his first detractors' many objections but also in defiance of the apparent popular decline some of his operas were experiencing at the time.

> Writing as above, I have taken no note of the fact that, in England especially, and more or less everywhere, Verdi's operas have gone out of fashion. That does not touch the question of their work; fashions come and go, and neither their coming is evidence for the temporarily favoured nor their going testimony against the cast off. The higher tribunal—the final court of appeal, where sit as judges the wise and prudent of every nation—that alone decides upon value. To those judges, who are unaffected by mere vogue, the position of Verdi among dramatic composers must be committed. They will say of him, or I am miserably mistaken, that not only was he a sincere and devoted musician, but also that he achieved great things, that every note of passion, every shade of sentiment finds in his works true and natural expression. To say this truthfully of any composer is to crown him with unfading laurels.[12]

Finally, any attempt to summarise the reception history of Verdi's operas in Victorian London by suggesting an overarching development from initial hostility to widespread, although still hesitant, acceptance

---

11 "Giuseppe Verdi," *The Musical Times*, March 1, 1901, pp. 153–56.
12 *Ibid.*

may constitute an oversimplification. Despite the apologetic tone adopted by Joseph Bennett and the mild opinion we find expressed in other obituaries, it is difficult for us to determine to what extent in 1901 the initial antagonism to Verdi still remained.[13]

In tracing the trajectory of Verdi's compositional development and in pinpointing the changes in his style, most of the critics still tended to make a distinction between the undeserved popularity of his early operas and the undeniable artistic value of the later achievements (*Otello* and *Falstaff*).

> When one thinks of *Traviata* and *Trovatore*, and the barrel-organs of one's youth, one is tempted to ask whether there is anything quite comparable to this development, this change from being the idol of the mob to the admired of the elect, in the whole history of art,—a change, moreover, that was effected without the aid of a literary propaganda, Verdi Societies, or any of the machinery which contributed so materially to the appreciation of Wagner's commanding genius.[14]

Although nobody could deny Verdi's prominent position at international level, some critics continued to adopt a condescending tone, implying that popularity had nothing to do with artistic value. A case in point is presented by the article that appeared in *The Saturday Review* on 2 February 1901, in which the critic, John F. Runciman, still wondered whether it was really possible to find any beauty in Verdi's melodies and questioned whether his fragile and ephemeral success really meant something, if anything at all, in the end.

> When a really great man goes abroad from this spinning globe one feels at once the difficulty—nay, the impossibility—of summing up his work for many a year to come. No contemporary of Bach could possibly have foretold the meanings Bach's music would have for the nineteenth and twentieth centuries; that Mozart would be placed amongst the immortals would probably have seemed preposterous even to Mozart's most fervent admirers in his own day. Even now there are many who love Wagner and his music, and yet doubt whether he will in the future be regarded as one of the commanding figures of the nineteenth century;

---

13 See Susan Rutherford, "Remembering—and Forgetting—Verdi. Critical Reception in England in the Early Twentieth Century," in *La Critica musicale in Italia nella prima metà del Novecento*, ed. Marco Capra and Fiamma Nicolodi (Venice: Marsilio, 2011), p. 263.

14 "Giuseppe Verdi," *The Spectator*, February 23, 1901, p. 15.

and on the other hand, there are some of us who are perfectly sure that he will be, and in addition know Wagner to contain much that is past our powers of perception, much that will be seen and felt only in a far later time. Has anyone any doubts whatever about Verdi? Does the content of his music overflow the narrow days in which he lived and worked, and stream far away ahead into the centuries not yet born? Will those centuries find in him anything that overshot us, unperceived by us, any new beauty of melody or thought or emotion unfelt by us, and will the people of that time be able to explain to one another why we missed it as we explain to one another why the eighteenth century could not comprehend Bach? The answer must be decisive: No. One knows intuitively and absolutely that there is nothing in Verdi beyond the understanding of this his time. The very fact of his immediate and constant success helps to prove it: he has given the time just as much as it could grasp with nothing baffling or (as the critics said in turn of Mozart, Beethoven, Schumann and Wagner) "obscure" to annoy it. He was not a great creative artist; he was a competent workman and stuck to his job with commendable industry and regularity—not Anthony Trollope was more comically methodical; he knew what the public liked, or perhaps he liked what the public liked, and he gave it to the public, and he had his reward always with promptness. He does not stand amongst the mighty ones; his work, everything he wrote, began to wither from the moment it was first put to paper; and now when he is only dead a few days we can perceive how old-fashioned it is already grown. To set him up as an immortal, to place *Falstaff* and *Otello* with *Don Giovanni*, the *Ring* or *Tristan*, is to Verdi himself a very cruel injustice. Such hasty overpraise cannot but bring about an immediate unjust reaction.[15]

Neither in his early works nor in the last masterpieces, *Otello* and *Falstaff*, could he find a single reason why Verdi's operas should outlive their composer.

---

15   "Verdi and Italian Opera," *The Saturday Review*, February 2, 1901, p. 138.

Appendix I:
Verdi's Premieres in London

1845	*Ernani*, 8 March 1845, Her Majesty's Theatre (Ernani: Napoleone Moriani; Ruy Gomez: Luciano Fornasari; Donna Sol: Rita Borio; Carlo: Felice Bottelli).
1846	*Nabucco* (as *Nino*), 3 March 1846, Her Majesty's Theatre (Nino: Luciano Fornasari; Idaspe: Cerelli; Orotaspe: Felice Bottelli; Abigail: Giulia Sanchioli; Fenena: Amalia Corbari. Conductor: Michael Balfe).
	I Lombardi alla prima crociata, 12 May 1846, Her Majesty's Theatre (Giselda: Giulia Grisi; Oronte: Mario; Pagano: Luciano Fornasari; Arvino: Leone Corelli).
1847	*I due Foscari*, 10 April 1847, Her Majesty's Theatre (Jacopo: Gaetano Fraschini; Lucrezia: Antonietta Montenegro; Doge: Filippo Coletti; Loredano: Lucien Bouché).
	I due Foscari, 19 June 1847, Covent Garden (Lucrezia: Giulia Grisi; Jacopo: Mario; Doge: Giorgio Ronconi).
	I masnadieri, 22 July 1847, Her Majesty's Theatre (Massimiliano: Luigi Lablache; Carlo: Italo Gardoni; Francesco: Filippo Coletti; Amalia: Jenny Lind; Arminio: Leone Corelli; Moser: Lucien Bouché).
1848	*Attila*, 14 March 1848, Her Majesty's Theatre (Attila: Giovanni Battista Belletti; Odabella: Sophie Cruvelli; Foresto: Italo Gardoni; Enzio: Luigi Cuzzani).
1853	*Rigoletto*, 14 May 1853, Covent Garden (Gilda: Angiolina Bosio; Duke of Mantua: Mario; Rigoletto: Giorgio Ronconi; Sparafucile: Joseph Tagliafico; Maddalena: Constance Nantier Didiée).

1855	*Il trovatore*, 10 May 1855, Covent Garden (Azucena: Pauline Viardot; Leonora: Jenny Ney; Manrico: Enrico Tamberlik; Conte di Luna: Francesco Graziani).
1856	*La traviata*, 24 May 1856, Her Majesty's Theatre (Violetta: Marietta Piccolomini; Alfredo: Vincenzo Calzolari; Germont: Federico Beneventano).
1858	*Luisa Miller*, 8 June 1858, Her Majesty's Theatre (Luisa: Marietta Piccolomini; Duchess Frederica: Marietta Alboni; Rodolfo: Antonio Giuglini; Miller: Federico Beneventano; Walter: Vialetti; Wurm: Castelli; Laura: Gramaglia).
1859	*I vespri siciliani*, 27 July 1859, Drury Lane (Hélène: Thérèse Tietjens; Amigo (Henri): Pietro Mongini; De Montfort: Enrico Fagotti; Procida: Vialetti).
1861	*Un ballo in maschera*, 15 June 1861, Royal Lyceum (Richard Earl of Warwick: Antonio Giuglini; Renato: Enrico Delle Sedie; Samuel: Edouard Gassier; Oscar: Josefa Gassier; Amelia: Thérèse Tietjens; Ulrica: Lamaire). *Un ballo in maschera*, 20 June 1861, Covent Garden (Amelia: Rosina Penco; Oscar: Marie Caroline Miolan-Carvalho; Ulrica: Constance Nantier-Didiée; the Duke: Mario; Renato: Francesco Graziani; the Chief Conspirators: Joseph Tagliafico and M. Zelger).
1867	*Don Carlos*, 4 June 1867, Covent Garden (Elisabeth de Valois: Pauline Lucca; Princess Eboli: Antonietta Fricci, Don Carlos: Emilio Naudin; Rodrigo: Francesco Graziani [Marquis de Posa]; Philip II: Petit; Grand Inquisitor Enrico Bagagiolo). *La forza del destino*, 22 June 1867, Her Majesty's Theatre (Leonora: Thérèse Tietjens; Baumeister; Don Carlo: Charles Santley; Alvaro: Pietro Mongini; Preziosilla: Zelia Trebelli-Bettini; Trabuco: Tom Hohler; Padre Guardiano: Hans Rokitansky; Melitone: Edouard Gassier; Foley, Bossi).
1875	*Requiem*, 15 May 1875, Royal Albert Hall (Teresa Stolz, Maria Waldmann, Angelo Masini and Paolo Medini; Conductor: Verdi).
1876	*Aida*, 22 June 1876, Covent Garden (Aida: Adelina Patti; Amneris: Ernesta Gindele; Radames: Ernest Nicolini; Amonasro: Francesco Graziani; Ramphis: Giuseppe Capponi; King of Egypt: Federico Feitlinger).

1889	*Otello*, 5 July 1889, Royal Lyceum (Desdemona: Aurelia Catanéo; Otello: Francesco Tamagno; Cassio: Giovanni Paroli; Iago: Victor Maurel).
1894	*Falstaff*, 20 May 1894, Covent Garden (Meg: Aurelia Kitzu; Dame Quickly: Giulia Ravogli; Anne Page: Olga Olghina; Alice: Emma Zilli; Falstaff: Arturo Pessina; Bardolph: Pellegalli-Rosetti; Pistol: Vittorio Arimondi; Dr Caius: Armandi; Ford: Antonio Pini-Corsi; Fenton: Umberto Beduschi).

Appendix II: Verdi and Wagner in London

Year	Verdi	Wagner
1845	*Ernani* at Her Majesty's Theatre	
1846	*Nabucco, I Lombardi* at Her Majesty's Theatre	
1847	*I due Foscari, I masnadieri* at Her Majesty's Theatre	
1848	*Attila* at Her Majesty's Theatre	
1853	*Rigoletto* at Covent Garden	
1855	*Il trovatore* at Covent Garden	Wagner is appointed Conductor of the London Philharmonic Society
1856	*La traviata* at Her Majesty's Theatre	
1858	*Luisa Miller* at Her Majesty's Theatre	
1859	*I vespri siciliani* at Drury Lane	
1861	*Un ballo in maschera* at the Royal Lyceum	

1867	*Don Carlos* at Covent Garden; *La forza del destino* at Her Majesty's Theatre	
1870		*Der Fliegende Holländer* in Italian as *L'Olandese Dannato* at Drury Lane
1872		The London Wagner Society is founded
1875	*Requiem* at Royal Albert Hall	*Lohengrin* (in Italian) at Covent Garden
1876	*Aida* at Covent Garden	*Tannhäuser* (in Italian) at Covent Garden
1877		Wagner conducts the Wagner Festival at Royal Albert Hall, from 7 to 19 May, together with Hans Richter.
1879		*Rienzi* at Her Majesty's Theatre
1882		*Der Ring der Nibelungen*, at Her Majesty's Theatre *Die Meistersinger* and *Tristan und Isolde* at Drury Lane.[*]
1889	*Otello* at Royal Lyceum	
1894	*Falstaff* at Covent Garden	

---

[*] F.G.E. "Wagner's Music in England," *The Musical Times*, September 1, 1906, pp. 589–93.

Appendix III: The Periodicals

The Athenaeum (weekly)

1830   Charles Wentworth Dilke assumes the editorship of the journal

1833   Henry F. Chorley joins the journal as music critic

1868   Campbell Clarke (critic)

1870   Charles L. Gruneisen (critic)

1879   Ebenezer Prout (critic)

1888   Henry F. Frost (critic)

1898   John S Shedlock (critic until 1916)

The Musical World (weekly)

1836   Joseph A. Novello founds the journal

1839   George Alexander Macfarren takes over the editorship

1840   James William Davison becomes music critic, soon after Alfred Day

1844   Davison becomes half-proprietor of the journal

1846   Desmond Ryan is appointed assistant editor

1868	Joseph Bennett becomes assistant editor after Ryan's death (his name as a Muttonian was "Thaddeus Egg") and chief editor after Davison's death in 1885
1886	Francis Hueffer (critic)
1888	Edgard Frederick Jacques (critic until 1891)

The Musical Times (monthly)

1842	*The Musical Times and Singing Class Circular* is founded by Joseph Mainzer
1844	Joseph A. Novello acquires the journal, whose title is changed to *The Musical Times*, and assumes its editorship
1853	Mary Cowden Clarke, Novello's sister, edits the journal
1864	Henry Charles Lunn is editor of the journal; contributors to the journal in the 1870s and 1880s include Filippo Filippi, Joseph Bennett, George Alexander Macfarren and Edward Holmes
1887	William Alexander Barrett succeeds Lunn as editor, a position he keeps until his death
1891	Edgard Frederick Jacques becomes editor

The Times (daily)

1846	Charles Kenney falls ill and James William Davison is appointed chief music critic
1878	Upon Davison's retirement Francis Hueffer is appointed in the same capacity
1889	John Alexander Fuller Maitland assumes the position until 1911

Select Bibliography

Acton, William. *Prostitution, Considered in its Moral, Social & Sanitary Aspects in London and Other Large Cities, with Proposals for the Mitigation and Prevention of its Attendant Evils.* London: John Churchill, 1857. http://dx.doi.org/10.1192/bjp.4.24.276

Arundel, Dennis. *The Critic at the Opera.* New York: Da Capo Press, 1980. First published London: E. Benn, 1957.

Balthazar, Scott L., ed. *The Cambridge Companion to Verdi.* Cambridge: Cambridge University Press, 2004. http://dx.doi.org/10.1017/ccol9780521632287

Basevi, Abramo. *Studio sulle opere di Giuseppe Verdi.* Florence: Tofani, 1859.

Beard, Harry R. "'Don Carlos' on the London Stage: 1867 to 1869," in *Atti del II Congresso internazionale di studi verdiani*, 59–69. Parma: Istituto di Studi Verdiani, 1971.

Bennett, Joseph. *Forty Years of Music, 1865–1905.* London: Methuen & Co., 1908.

Bentley, Eric, ed. *Shaw on Music.* New York, London: Applause Books, 1995.

Bledsoe, Robert Terrell. "Henry Fothergill Chorley and the Reception of Verdi's Early Operas in England." *Victorian Studies* 28/4 (1985): 631–55.

— *Henry Fothergill Chorley Victorian Journalist.* Aldershot: Ashgate, 1998.

Boito, Arrigo. *The Verdi-Boito Correspondence.* Chicago: University of Chicago Press, 1994.

Brake, Laurel, and Demoor, Marysa. *Dictionary of Nineteenth-Century Journalism in Great Britain and Ireland.* Gent: Academy Press, 2009.

Briggs, Asa, and McCartney, Anne. *Toynbee Hall, The First Hundred Years.* London: Routledge, 1984. http://dx.doi.org/10.4324/9780203127742

Budden, Julian. *The Operas of Verdi.* Oxford: Clarendon Press, 1992.

— *The Master Musicians: Verdi.* London: Dent, 1985.

Burnand, Francis C. *Records and Reminiscences, Personal and General.* London: Methuen, 1904.

Capra, Marco. *Verdi in prima pagina. Nascita, sviluppo e affermazione della figura di Verdi nella stampa italiana dal XIX al XXI secolo.* Lucca: Libreria Musicale Italiana, 2014.

— "'Effekt, nicht als Effekt.' Aspekte der Rezeption der Opern Verdis in Italien des 19. Jahrhunderts" in *Giuseppe Verdi und seine Zeit*, edited by Markus Engelhardt, 117–42. Laaber: Laaber Verlag, 2001.

Cesari, Gaetano, Luzio, Alessandro and Scherillo, Michele (eds.), *I copialettere di Giuseppe Verdi* (Milan: Commissione, 1913), available at https://archive.org/details/icopialettere00verd

Chorley, Henry Fothergill. *Memorials of Mrs. Hemans: with Illustrations of her Literary Character from her Private Correspondence.* New York: Sanders & Otley, 1836.

— *Music and Manners in France and Germany: A Series of Travelling Sketches of Art and Society.* London: Longman, 1841.

— *Modern German Music: Recollections and Criticisms.* London: Smith, 1854.

— *Thirty Years' Musical Recollections* London: Hurst & Blackett, 1862.

Clinkscale, Edward. *The Musical Times, 1844–1900.* Répertoire international de la presse musicale. Ann Arbor: University of Michigan Press, 1994.

Cox, John Edmund. *Musical Recollections of the Last Half-Century.* London: Tinsley Brothers, 1872.

Crowest, Frederick James. *Verdi: Man and Musician, His Biography with Especial Reference to his English Experiences.* London: John Milne, 1897.

Davison, Henry. *Music During the Victorian Era. From Mendelssohn to Wagner: Being the Memoirs of J. W. Davison, Forty Years Music Critic of "The Times."* London: Reeves, 1912.

Dent, Edward J. "Un Ballo in Maschera." *Music & Letters* 33/2 (1952): 101–10. http://dx.doi.org/10.1093/ml/xxxiii.2.101

Edgcumbe, Richard. *Musical Reminiscences of an Old Amateur Chiefly Respecting the Italian Opera in England for Fifty Years, from 1773 to 1823.* London: Clarke, 1827.

Edwards, Henry Sutherland. *Rossini and his School.* London: Sampson Low, Martson & Co., 1881.

— *The Lyrical Drama. Essays on Subjects, Composers, & Executants of Modern Opera.* London: Allen & Co., 1881.

Ellis, Katherine. *Music Criticism in Nineteenth-Century France.* Cambridge: Cambridge University Press, 1995. http://dx.doi.org/10.1017/cbo9780511470264

Fenner, Theodore. *Opera in London: Views of the Press 1785–1830.* Carbondale and Edwardsville: Southern Illinois University Press, 1994. http://dx.doi.org/10.5860/choice.32-6143

Gartioux, Hervé. *La reception de Verdi en France*. Weinsberg: Galland, 2001.

Gossett, Philip. "Becoming a Citizen: The Chorus in 'Risorgimento' Opera." *Cambridge Opera Journal* 2/1 (1990): 41–64. http://dx.doi.org/10.1017/s0954586700003104

— "Giuseppe Verdi and the Italian Risorgimento," in *Proceedings of the American Philosophical Society* 156/3 (2012).

Hall-Witt, Jennifer. *Fashionable Acts, Opera and Elite Culture in London, 1780–1880*. Durham: University of New Hampshire Press, 2007.

Hartnoll, Phyllis, and Found, Peter, ed. *The Concise Oxford Companion to the Theatre*. Oxford: Oxford University Press, 1996. http://dx.doi.org/10.1093/acref/9780192825742.001.0001

Harwood, Gregory W. "Verdi's Reform of the Italian Opera Orchestra," in *19th Century Music* 10/2 (1986): 108–34. http://dx.doi.org/10.1525/ncm.1986.10.2.02a00020

Hepokoski, James A. *Giuseppe Verdi: Falstaff*. Cambridge: Cambridge University Press, 1983.

Hewlett, Henry G. comp. *Henry Fothergill Chorley: Autobiography, Memoir and Letters*, 2 vols. London: Richard Bentley, 1873.

Houghton, Walter E. *The Victorian Frame of Mind, 1830–1870*. New Haven and London: Yale University Press, 1957.

Hueffer, Francis. *Richard Wagner and the Music of the Future*. London: Chapman and Hall, 1874. http://dx.doi.org/10.1017/cbo9780511703577

Hughes, Meirion. *The English Musical Renaissance and the Press 1850–1914: Watchmen of Music*. Aldershot: Ashgate, 2002.

Kitson, Richard. *The Musical World (1836–1865)*. Répertoire international de la presse musicale. Ann Arbor: University of Michigan Press, 1996.

— *The Musical World (1866–1891)*. Répertoire international de la presse musicale. Ann Arbor: University of Michigan Press, 2006.

Klein, Hermann. *Musical Notes 1889*. London: Novello, 1890.

— *Thirty Years of Musical Life in London*. New York: The Century Co., 1903.

— *The Golden Age of Opera*. London: Routledge, 1933.

Kreuzer, Gundula. "'Oper im Kirchengewande?' Verdi's Requiem and the Anxieties of the Young German Empire." *Journal of the American Musicological Society* 58/2 (2005): 399–450. http://dx.doi.org/10.1525/jams.2005.58.2.399

— *Verdi and the Germans*. Cambridge: Cambridge University Press, 2010.

Ipson, Douglas L., "Attila Takes Rome: The Reception of Verdi's Opera on the Eve of Revolution." *Cambridge Opera Journal* 21/3 (2009): 249–56. http://dx.doi.org/10.1017/s0954586710000157

Izzo, Francesco. "I cantanti e la recezione di Verdi nell'Ottocento: trattati e corrispondenza," in *Verdi 2001: Atti del convegno internazionale*, ed. Fabrizio Della Seta, Roberta Marvin, and Marco Marica, 1: 173–87. Florence: Leo S. Olschki, 2003.

Langley, Leanne. "The Musical Press in Nineteenth-Century England." *Notes* 46/3 (1990): 583–92. http://dx.doi.org/10.2307/941425

Laurence, Dan H., ed. *Shaw's Music The Complete Musical Criticism of Bernard Shaw*. London: The Bodley Head, 1981.

Lavagetto, Mario. *Un caso di censura Il Rigoletto*. Milan: Mondadori, 2010.

Lehmann, Rudolf Chambers, comp. and ed. *Memories of Half a Century: A Record of Friendships*. London: Smith, Elder & Co., 1908. http://dx.doi.org/10.2307/906975

Loewenberg, Alfred. *Annals of Opera*. London: Calder, 1978.

Logan, William. *The Great Social Evil*. London: Hodder and Stoughton, 1871.

Lumley, Benjamin. *Reminiscences of the Opera*. London: Hurst & Blackett, 1864.

— *The Earl of Dudley, Mr. Lumley, and Her Majesty's Theatre: A Narrative of Facts Addressed to the Patrons of the Opera, his Friends, and the Public Generally*. London: Bosworth and Harrison, 1863.

Mackenzie, Alexander Campbell. *Tre letture sopra il Falstaff di Giuseppe Verdi, fatte alla Royal Institution of Great Britain – Traduzione del Maestro P. Mazzoni*. Milan: G. Ricordi and C. Tip. Edit., 1893.

Maitland, John Alexander Fuller. *English Music in the XIXth Century*. London: Grant Richards, 1902.

Mapleson, James Henry. *The Mapleson Memoirs, 1848–1888*. Chicago: Belford, Clarke & Co., 1888.

Martin, George Whitney. *Verdi in America: Oberto through Rigoletto*. Rochester: University of Rochester Press, 2011.

Mazzini, Giuseppe. "Filosofia della musica," in *Scritti editi ed inediti*, 94 vols. Imola: Cooperativa tipografico-editrice Paolo Galeati, 1906–1943.

Mila, Massimo. *L'arte di Verdi*. Turin Einaudi, 1980.

Miller, James. *Prostitution Considered in Relation to its Cause and Cure*. Edinburgh: Sutherland; London: Simpkin, 1859.

Monaldi, Gino. *Verdi e Wagner*. Rome: Civelli, 1887.

Montemorra Marvin, Roberta. "The Censorship of Verdi's Operas in Victorian London" *Music & Letters* 82/4 (2001): 582–610. http://dx.doi.org/10.1093/ml/82.4.582

— "Verdian Opera Burlesqued: A Glimpse into Mid-Victorian Theatrical Culture." *Cambridge Opera Journal* 15/1 (2003): 33–66. http://dx.doi.org/10.1017/s0954586703000338

Morley, Henry. *The Journal of a London Playgoer from 1851 to 1866.* London: Routledge, 1891.

Mula, Orazio. *Giuseppe Verdi.* Bologna: Il Mulino, 1999.

Nettel, Reginald. *The Orchestra in England, A Social History.* London: Cape, 1948.

Newman, Francis W. *The Cure of the Great Social Evil with Special Reference to Recent Laws Delusively Called Contagious Diseases' Acts.* London: Trübner, 1869.

Osborne, Charles, ed. *Letters of Giuseppe Verdi.* New York: Holt, 1971.

Parker, E. D. *Opera Under Augustus Harris.* London: Saxon, 1900.

Parker, Roger. *Arpa d'or dei fatidici vati.* Parma: Istituto Nazionale di Studi Verdiani, 1997.

Picard, Liza. *Victorian London: The Life of a City 1840–1870.* London: Phoenix, 2006.

Pougin, Arthur. *Verdi: Histoire Anecdotique de sa Vie et de ses Oeuvres.* Paris: Calmann Lévy, 1886. Translated by James E. Matthew. *Verdi: An Anecdotic History of his Life and Works.* London: H. Grevel & Co., 1887.

Procacci, Giuliano. "Verdi nella storia d'Italia," in *Verdi 2001, Atti del Convegno Internazionale* edited by Fabrizio della Seta, Roberta Montemorra Marvin, Marco Marica, 1: 191–216. Florence: Olschki Editore, 2003.

Remarks on the Morality of Dramatic Compositions: With Particular Reference to "La Traviata," etc. London: John Chapman, 1856.

Reynolds, Barbara. "Verdi and Manzoni: An Attempted Explanation." *Music & Letters* 29/1 (1948): 31–43. http://dx.doi.org/10.1093/ml/xxix.1.31

Richelot, Gustave. *The Greatest of Our Social Evils: Prostitution.* Translated by Robert Knox. London: Bailliere, 1857.

Roosevelt, Blanche. *Verdi: Milan and "Othello."* London: Ward and Downey, 1887.

Ryan, Michael. *Prostitution in London, with a Comparative View of that of Paris and New York.* London: Bailliere, 1839.

Rutherford, Susan. "La Traviata or the 'Willing Grisette,' Male Critics and Female Performance in the 1850s," in *Verdi 2001: Atti del convegno internazionale*, ed. Fabrizio Della Seta, Roberta Marvin, and Marco Marica, 2: 585–600. Florence: Leo S. Olschki, 2003.

— "Remembering—and Forgetting—Verdi. Critical Reception in England in the Early Twentieth Century," in *La Critica musicale in Italia nella prima metà del Novecento*, ed. Marco Capra and Fiamma Nicolodi, 263–82. Venice: Marsilio, 2011.

Sala, Emilio. *Il Valzer delle Camelie.* Turin: EdT, 2008.

— "Verdi and the Parisian Boulevard Theatre, 1847–9." *Cambridge Opera Journal* 7/3 (1995): 185–205. http://dx.doi.org/10.1017/cbo9780511920615.003

Santley, Charles. *Student and Singer, the Reminiscences of Charles Santley.* New York, London: Macmillian & Co., 1892. http://dx.doi.org/10.1017/cbo9781107775497

Scherillo, Michele. "Verdi, Shakespeare, Manzoni. Spigolature nelle lettere di Verdi." *Nuova Antologia di Lettere, Scienze ed Arti* 47 (1912): 193–225.

Sessa, Anne Dzamba. *Richard Wagner and the English.* Cranbury, London: Associated University Press, 1979.

Shaffner, Taliaferro Preston, and Owen, W. *The Illustrated Record of the International Exhibition of the Industrial Arts and Manufactures, and the Fine Arts, of all Nations, in 1862.* London: London Printing & Co., 1862. http://dx.doi.org/10.1017/cbo9781107238916

Stamatov, Peter. "Interpretive Activism and the Political Uses of Verdi's Operas in the 1840s." *American Sociological Review* 67/3 (2002): 345–66. http://dx.doi.org/10.2307/3088961

Steffan, Carlida, ed. *Rossiniana: Antologia della critica nella prima metà dell'Ottocento.* Pordenone: Edizioni Studio Tesi, 1992.

Stephens, John Russell. *The Censorship of English Drama 1824–1901.* Cambridge: Cambridge University Press, 1980.

Taine, Hippolyte. *Notes on England.* New York: Holt, 1885.

Verdi, Giuseppe. *Lettere.* Edited by Eduardo Rescigno. Turin: Einaudi, 2012.

— *Tutti i libretti d'opera.* Rome: Newton Compton, 2009.

Verdi, Giuseppe, and Boito, Arrigo. *The Verdi-Boito Correspondence.* Chicago: University of Chicago Press, 1994.

Richard Wagner. "Eine Mittheilung an meine Freunde." 1851 in *Sämtliche Schriften und Dichtungen,* 4: 230–344. English translation by William Ashton Ellis. *A Communication to My Friends* in *Richard Wagner's Prose Works.* London: Kegan Paul, Trench & Trübner, 1895.

Wiebe, Heather. "Spectacles of Sin and Suffering: La Traviata in Victorian London." *Repercussions* 9/2 (2001): 33–67.

Willis, Nathaniel Parker. *Memoranda of the Life of Jenny Lind.* Philadelphia: Peterson, 1851.

Zicari, Massimo. "Un caso di moralità: La Traviata nella Londra Vittoriana (1856)." *Musica/Realtà* 3/103 (2014): 141–57.

— "Verdi and Wagner in Early Victorian London: The Viewpoint of *The Musical World.*" *Studia Musica* 59/1 (2014): 51–64.

— "La prima recezione di Giuseppe Verdi a Londra: Henry Fothergill Chorley e l'Athenaeum." *Schweizer Jahrbuch für Musikwissenschaft,* 31 (2011): 27–60.

— "Nothing but the Commonest Tunes:" The Early Reception of Verdi's Operas in London, 1845–1848.' *Dissonance*, 114 (2011): 44–49.

— "Critica musicale e opera italiana a Londra nell'Ottocento: George Bernard Shaw," *Musica e storia* 17/2 (2009): 377–92.

— *The Land of Song*. Bern: Peter Lang, 2008.

Index

6 *Romanze* by Verdi 38
Abbadia, Luisa 78, 87, 88
Abou Hassan by Carl Maria von Weber 242, 243
A Camp in Silesia. See Ein Feldlager in Schlesien
Acton, William 144
Adam, Adolphe 182, 205
Addison 38, 283
Aida by Verdi 12, 231, 248, 257, 258, 259, 261, 262, 263, 264, 265, 279, 291, 293, 315, 316, 317, 322, 326
Alary, Giulio 103
Albani, Emma 5, 247, 254, 257
Alboni, Marietta 104, 140, 170, 173, 174, 177, 191, 193, 198, 204, 322
Anato. See Nabucco
Anderson, John Henry 139
Appiani, Giuseppina 80
Arditi, Luigi 191, 215, 217, 221, 238, 242, 243, 258
Ariadne by Adolphe Adam 182
Arimondi, Vittorio 323
Armandi 323
Armide by Gluck 182
Arrivabene, Opprandino 1
Attila by Verdi 7, 77, 79, 80, 81, 82, 83, 84, 85, 86, 92, 93, 109, 310, 314, 317, 321, 325
Auber, Daniel 103, 104, 110, 114, 195, 199, 202, 205, 206, 209, 210, 211, 213, 219, 221, 234
Ayrton, William 27

Bache, Walter 240
Bach, Johann Sebastian 20, 269, 306, 319, 320
Badiali, Cesare 182
Bagagiolo, Enrico 247, 322
Balfe, Michael 46, 59, 63, 84, 104, 165, 172, 182, 195, 200, 205, 321
Balfe, Victoire 182
Barbieri Nini, Marianna 104, 105
Barezzi, Antonio 75
Barnby, Joseph 249
Barrett, William Alexander 24, 328
Barroilhet, Paul-Bernard 33
Basevi, Abramo 4, 5, 6, 7, 9, 121
Baumeister 228, 322
Beaucardè, Carlo 97, 106
Beduschi, Umberto 323
Beethoven, Ludwig van 38, 54, 104, 106, 107, 110, 126, 129, 131, 192, 238, 247, 252, 299, 320
Belart 192, 193
bel canto 2, 11, 54, 62, 98, 194, 312
  declamatory singing 2, 8, 9, 11, 32, 36, 46, 51, 66, 67, 87, 107, 119, 125, 176, 184, 187, 192, 224, 252, 262, 265, 275, 278, 288, 289, 290, 291, 295, 306
  florid singing 8, 99, 109, 125, 192, 193, 202, 206, 282
Bell, Clara 269
Belletti, Giovanni Battista 78, 84, 85, 92, 96, 97, 140, 321

Bellini, Vincenzo 1, 2, 3, 4, 8, 32, 41, 47, 48, 49, 104, 105, 106, 110, 126, 133, 137, 205, 218, 238, 279, 312, 316
Benedetti, Nicola 106
Benedict, Julius 182, 191
Beneventano, Federico 140, 170, 174 175, 177, 322
Bennett, Joseph 20, 22, 24, 28, 217, 250, 268, 269, 271, 300, 301, 318, 319, 328
Bennett, William Sterndale 127, 210 211, 212, 213
Benvenuto Cellini 114, 120
Berlioz, Hector 24, 32, 54, 114, 120, 127
Bermani, Benedetto 4
Bernard, Charles de 150
Bernhardt, Sarah 294
Berrettoni, Arcangelo 104
Bettini, Jémérie 121
Beverley 118, 120, 132
Bevignani, Enrico 242, 257
Bianchi 247
Bispham, David 302
Bizet, Georges 293
Blagrove, Henry 130
Blanchart, Ramon 300
Boehm, Theobald 102
Boito, Arrigo 215, 280, 288, 289, 290, 291, 292, 298, 303
Bonetti, Vincenzo 113, 174
Bordas 96
Borghi Mamo, Adelaide 191
Borio, Rita 33, 321
Bosio, Angiolina 114, 115, 120, 123 169, 170, 242, 321
Bossi 228, 322
Bottelli, Felice 33, 321
Bouché, Lucien 59, 63, 68, 70, 321
Brahms, Johannes 269
Brambilla, Marietta 33, 182
Bruneau, Alfred 307

Brunetti, Maria 192
Buckingham, James Silk 16
Bülow, Hans von 236, 250
Bunn, Alfred 58
Burnand, Francis 20
Byron, George Gordon 58

Cabestanh, Guillem de 28
Cagnoni, Antonio 239
Caimi, Ettore 184
Calzolari, Vincenzo 140, 322
Camille. See *La Dame aux camélias*
Cammarano, Salvatore 4
Capponi, Giuseppe 248, 322
Carducci, Giosuè 297
Carmen by Bizet 293
Castellan, Anaide (Jeanne Anaïs) 33, 68, 77, 114
Castelli 174, 177, 182, 322
Catanéo, Aurelia 294, 323
Cavalleria rusticana by Mascagni 272, 280, 303
Cerrito, Fanny 72
Chatterton, Frederick Balsir 233
Cherubini, Luigi 38, 242
Chorley, Henry Fothergill 8, 16, 17, 18, 19, 25, 27, 31, 32, 33, 35, 36, 37, 44, 46, 47, 49, 54, 60, 61, 66, 67, 73, 74, 75, 86, 87, 88, 93, 96, 106, 107, 119, 127, 130, 135, 162, 163, 166, 167, 169, 177, 178, 187, 188, 189, 203, 206, 207, 209, 235, 236, 237, 241, 261, 267, 312, 316, 327
Cimarosa, Domenico 8, 32, 35, 36, 41, 54, 90, 91, 108, 137, 196, 312
Clarke, Campbell 241, 267, 268, 327
Clément, Edmond 303
Colburn, Henry 16
Coletti, Filippo 59, 61, 62, 70, 73, 87, 92, 106, 321
Coppola, Pietro 2, 48
Corbari, Amalia 46, 195, 321
Corelli, Leone 33, 46, 70, 321

Corsi 170, 192
Costa, Michael 33, 57, 67, 120, 127, 132, 192, 210, 211, 212, 213, 217, 219, 222, 238, 239, 247, 273
Covent Garden Theatre 6, 9, 12, 42, 57, 58, 59, 64, 67, 68, 70, 74, 77, 78, 89, 95, 96, 98, 99, 104, 108, 113, 118, 123, 125, 132, 135, 136, 139, 143, 169, 171, 172, 173, 183, 185, 187, 192, 194, 195, 196, 197, 198, 200, 201, 202, 203, 205, 214, 217, 218, 220, 221, 222, 223, 234, 235, 237, 238, 241, 242, 247, 251, 252, 257, 258, 259, 264, 274, 279, 282, 291, 292, 293, 297, 303, 304, 306, 307, 321, 322, 323, 325, 326
Cowden Clarke, Mary 24, 328
Cowen, Frederic Hymen 270, 307
Cox, John Edmund 163
Cristoforo Colombo by Franchetti 300
Crowest, Frederick 38, 45, 166, 230
Cruvelli, Sophie 5, 77, 78, 79, 84, 85, 87, 88, 91, 92, 106, 107, 109, 110, 121, 126, 138, 188, 321
Csillag, Róza 195
Cucchi 191
Cuzzani, Luigi 78, 84, 321

d'Andrade, Francesco 293
D'Angeri, Anna 247
Dannreuther, Edward 245, 273, 274
Das Kunstwerk der Zukunft (The Music of the Future) 130, 206, 243, 244, 269, 275, 277, 301
Das Rheingold by Wagner 239, 241
David, Giacomo 197
Davison, James William 8, 18, 19, 20, 21, 22, 23, 25, 27, 46, 47, 49, 54, 55, 60, 63, 64, 72, 99, 103, 117, 118, 124, 127, 203, 217, 221, 226, 235, 244, 268, 311, 312, 316, 327, 328
Day, Alfred 18
De Bassini, Achille 183
De Clerville, J. 88, 89, 90, 91, 92

Delafield, Edward 77
Delane, John Thaddeus 23
de Lauzières, Achille 222
Delle Sedie, Enrico 204, 214, 322
Delna, Marie 303
Der Fliegende Holländer (L'Olandese dannato) by Wagner 12, 227, 240, 242, 243, 244, 245, 251, 273, 326
Der Freischütz by Weber 192, 247
Der Ring Des Nibelungen by Wagner 254, 266, 274, 326
De Susiri 121
Die Meistersinger by Wagner 236, 239, 274, 275, 293, 299, 304, 326
Die Räuber 58
Die Walküre by Wagner 275
Die Zauberflöte (Il flauto magico) by Mozart 104, 238, 242
Dilke, Charles Wentworth 18, 327
Dinorah by Meyerbeer 183, 192
Dom Sébastien (Don Sebastian) by Donizetti 1, 113, 125, 214
Don Bucefalo by Cagnoni 239
Don Carlos by Verdi 11, 12, 13, 26, 217, 218, 219, 220, 222, 223, 224, 225, 226, 227, 228, 229, 234, 235, 257, 259, 263, 265, 322, 326
Don Giovanni by Mozart 104, 120, 126, 151, 172, 174, 182, 183, 192, 193, 204, 239, 247, 257, 320
Donizetti, Gaetano 1, 2, 3, 4, 7, 8, 33, 41, 42, 43, 44, 47, 48, 49, 61, 69, 78, 104, 105, 110, 113, 120, 126, 133, 137, 166, 176, 182, 192, 205, 214, 264, 312, 316
Don Pasquale by Donizetti 1, 78, 125, 126, 164, 172, 257
Don Sebastian. See Dom Sébastien
Drury Lane Theatre 12, 58, 143, 173, 181, 182, 183, 184, 185, 186, 187, 191, 195, 227, 233, 234, 240, 241, 242, 243, 247, 251, 258, 274, 291, 292, 322, 325, 326

Dumas, Alexandre, fils 10, 141, 145, 146, 148, 155, 157, 166, 167
Duplessis, Marie 167
Duprez, Caroline 103
Durini 294

Eckert, Karl 236
Edwards, Henry Sutherland 20, 28, 268, 288, 314
Ein Feldlager in Schlesien (A Camp in Silesia) by Meyerbeer 58, 59
Ellis, William Ashton 277
Eoline, ou la Dryade by Cesare Pugn 34
Ernani by Verdi 6, 7, 11, 26, 31, 32, 33, 34, 35, 37, 38, 39, 40, 41, 42, 43, 44, 45, 47, 48, 52, 62, 67, 68, 70, 86, 90, 92, 95, 96, 97, 101, 106, 107, 109, 110, 115, 116, 119, 120, 130, 165, 175, 177, 182, 183, 194, 206, 214, 217, 224, 257, 313, 314, 316, 317, 321, 325
Euryanthe by Weber 104
Evers, Caterina 106
Evrard 193

Faccio, Franco 294
Fagotti, Enrico 184, 322
Falstaff by Verdi 6, 13, 24, 231, 282, 297, 298, 299, 300, 301, 302, 303, 304, 305, 306, 314, 315, 316, 319, 320, 323, 326
Faure, Jean-Baptiste 192
Faust by Spohr 104
Faust (Faust e Margherita) by Gounod 239, 242, 243, 258, 293
Feitlinger, Federico 322
Ferraris 191
Ferruccio 80
Fétis, François-Joseph 2, 24, 27
Fidelio by Beethoven 104, 106, 126, 192, 238, 247
Filippi, Filippo 5, 24, 328
Florinda, or the Moors in Spain by Thalberg 104, 107

Flotow, Friedrich von 173, 182, 183, 192, 193, 243
Foley, Allan James, alias Foli 228, 238, 243, 322
Formes, Karl 114
Fornasari, Luciano 33, 41, 46, 48, 321
Fortini 121
Franchetti, Alberto 300
Fraschini, Gaetano 58, 59, 61, 63, 68, 90, 321
Freeze, John G. 167
Fricci, Antonietta 221, 322
Frost, Henry F. 267, 268, 327

Galli, Filippo 197
Garcia, Manuel 77, 197
Gardoni, Italo 70, 73, 75, 84, 91, 192, 321
Gassier, Edouard 198, 228, 322
Gindele, Ernesta 260, 322
Giraldoni, Leone 214
Giuglini, Antonio 169, 170, 172, 173, 174, 175, 177, 181, 182, 192, 195, 198, 200, 322
Gli Oriazi e I Curiazi by Cimarosa 35
Glover, Howard 20
Gluck, Christoph Willibald 54, 182
God Save the King 215
Gounod, Charles 104, 218, 239, 242, 243, 292, 293
Gramaglia 174, 322
Graziani, Francesco 132, 169, 170, 201, 203, 322
Graziani, Lodovico 182
Great Exhibition 102, 103, 213
Grisi, Carlotta 72
Grisi, Giulia 33, 46, 50, 52, 57, 64, 65, 67, 68, 77, 170, 173, 183, 321
Grove, George 21, 23, 269, 286
Gruneisen, Charles L. 241, 254, 260, 267, 268, 327
Guglielmo Tell. See Guillaume Tell
Guillaume Tell (Guglielmo Tell) by Rossini 114, 120, 125, 182, 226, 238, 247, 257, 275, 292

Gustave III, ou Le bal masqué by Auber 103, 199, 221, 234
Gye, Frederick 25, 77, 101, 104, 113, 139, 140, 158, 166, 173, 192, 194, 198, 214, 218, 233, 234, 241, 248, 249, 251, 257

Halévy, Fromental 101, 110
Hamlet by Thomas 238, 239, 242
Handel, Georg Friedrich 20, 283
Harlequin and Tom Thumb 195
Harris, Augustus 192, 291, 292, 293, 307
Haydn, Franz Joseph 47
Hemans, Felicia 16, 17
Henson, Medora 302
Her Majesty's Theatre 7, 9, 12, 33, 34, 45, 46, 48, 53, 57, 59, 60, 63, 67, 68, 70, 72, 73, 75, 77, 79, 86, 89, 92, 93, 95, 96, 98, 101, 103, 104, 106, 108, 109, 113, 139, 140, 145, 152, 157, 163, 169, 170, 171, 172, 173, 174, 181, 191, 194, 195, 214, 215, 217, 218, 220, 222, 227, 233, 237, 247, 251, 274, 280, 291, 293, 321, 322, 325, 326
Hermann, Jakob Zeugheer 17
Hérold, Ferdinand 173
Hewlett, Henry Gay 16
Hiller, Ferdinand 127
Hofoperntheater (Vienna) 249
Hohler, Tom 228, 322
Holmes, Edward 24, 328
Howard, Ralph 20, 181
Hueffer, Francis 22, 23, 28, 269, 275, 276, 277, 288, 328
Hugo, Victor 35, 118, 124, 145

I due Foscari by Verdi 7, 57, 59, 60, 61, 62, 63, 64, 66, 67, 68, 75, 86, 87, 95, 96, 101, 105, 108, 116, 119, 122, 177, 317, 321, 325
Il barbiere di Siviglia by Rossini 12, 47, 85, 114, 126, 140, 192, 196, 204, 215, 238, 242, 248
Il Canto degli Italiani by Verdi 215

Il conte Ory. See *Le comte Ory*
Il corsaro by Verdi 58
Il domino nero. See *Le domino noir*
Il flauto magico. See *Die Zauberflöte*
Il giuramento by Mercadante 182, 183, 185, 187
I Lombardi alla prima crociata by Verdi 7, 33, 37, 45, 46, 47, 48, 49, 50, 51, 52, 53, 58, 67, 68, 96, 97, 116, 218, 220, 221, 226, 314, 316, 321, 325
Il proscritto. See *Ernani*
Il trovatore by Verdi 7, 9, 11, 123, 127, 132, 133, 134, 135, 136, 140, 165, 166, 169, 170, 172, 173, 175, 177, 178, 179, 182, 183, 184, 185, 186, 187, 192, 194, 195, 197, 198, 203, 204, 206, 214, 217, 220, 222, 224, 226, 227, 234, 238, 239, 257, 287, 291, 298, 313, 315, 317, 319, 322, 325
Il Turco in Italia by Rossini 196
I masnadieri by Verdi 7, 57, 58, 59, 65, 67, 68, 70, 72, 73, 74, 75, 83, 90, 116, 317, 321
Inno delle nazioni by Verdi 12, 209, 215
I puritani by Bellini 93, 120, 126, 183, 279
I quattro fratelli. See *Les quatre fils d'Aymon*
Irving, Henry 293
I vespri siciliani. See *Les vêpres siciliennes*

Jacques, Edgar Frederick 22, 269, 328
Jessonda by Spohr 113, 120
Joachim, Joseph 269
Juana Shore by Bonetti 114
Judaism in Music. See *Judenthum in der Musik*
Judenthum in der Musik (Judaism in Music) 127, 239

Kabale und Liebe 121, 174, 175, 176
Kemble, John Mitchell 141
Kenney, Charles Lamb 41, 49, 55, 328
Kenney, James 42

King Lear 158
Kitzu, Aurelia 323
Klein, Hermann 28, 274, 280

La battaglia di Legnano by Verdi 9, 82, 83, 95, 310, 316
Lablache, Luigi 28, 33, 59, 70, 73, 75, 321
La Cenerentola by Rossini 104, 140, 196
Lachner, Franz Paul 127
La Dame aux camélias 10, 141, 145, 146, 148, 167
La donna del lago by Rossini 74
La favorita. See *La favorite*
La favorite (La favorita) by Donizetti 33, 120, 126, 182, 192, 242, 257, 283
La figlia del reggimento. See *La fille du régiment*
La fille du régiment (La figlia del reggimento) by Donizetti 68, 69, 78, 162, 172, 182, 239, 258
La forza del destino by Verdi 11, 12, 213, 217, 218, 222, 228, 229, 230, 231, 259, 322
La gazza ladra by Rossini 182, 183, 137, 192, 234, 239
Lago, Joseph 74, 291
La loi du tailon 150
La Marseillaise 215, 310
Lamperti, Francesco 5
La Navarraise by Massenet 307
La sonnambula by Bellini 35, 68, 69, 78, 140, 181, 182, 183, 239, 242, 258, 279
La sposa fedele by Guglielmi 37
L'assedio di Corinto. See *Le siège de Corinthe*
L'assedio di Firenze by Guerrazzi 80
La tempesta by Halévy 101
La traviata by Verdi 7, 9, 10, 11, 28, 139, 140, 141, 144, 145, 147, 148, 149, 150, 151, 152, 153, 154, 155, 156, 157, 160, 161, 162, 163, 164, 165, 166, 167, 168, 169, 172, 173, 175, 182, 183, 184, 194, 198, 206, 214, 217, 220, 224, 226, 227, 234, 239, 242, 257, 279, 287, 291, 311, 313, 315, 317, 322, 325

L'attaque du moulin by Bruneau 307
La vestale by Spontini 104, 125
La zingara. See *The Bohemian Girl*
Le Chevalier de Maison-Rouge 166
Le chiffonnier de Paris by Pyat 166
Le comte Ory (Il conte Ory) by Rossini 130
Le domino noir (Il domino nero) by Auber 125, 195
Lehmann, Rudolph Chambers 16
leitmotiv 13, 289, 290, 295, 301, 302, 305, 306, 317
L'elisir d'amore by Donizetti 59, 78, 93, 114, 126, 238, 258, 282
L'enfant prodigue by Auber 104
Le nozze di Giannetta. See *Les noces de Jeannette*
Leoncavallo, Ruggiero 267, 271, 282, 303, 307
Le prophète by Meyerbeer 120, 195, 234, 239, 265, 293
Les Huguenots by Meyerbeer 120, 126, 172, 173, 182, 192, 234, 237, 238, 239, 257, 293
Le siège de Corinthe (L'assedio di Corinto) by Rossini 4, 234
Les Martyrs by Donizetti 104
Les noces de Jeannette (Le nozze di Giannetta) by Massé 192
Les pêcheurs de perles by Bizet 293
Les quatre fils d'Aymon (I quattro fratelli) by Balfe 104
Les vêpres siciliennes (I vespri siciliani) by Verdi 11, 138, 181, 182, 183, 184, 186, 187, 188, 189, 265, 314, 322
L'etoile du nord by Meyerbeer 265
Lewes, George Henry 145, 146, 147, 149
Libussa by Musäus 34
Linda di Chamounix by Donizetti 78

Lind, Jenny 26, 58, 59, 63, 65, 67, 68, 69, 70, 71, 73, 75, 77, 78, 90, 91, 92, 93, 158, 172, 230, 321
Lindpaintner, Peter von 127
L'inganno felice by Rossini 196
L'isle des amours 103
Liszt, Franz 128, 241
L'italiana in Algeri by Rossini 108, 196
L'Oca del Cairo by Mozart 242, 243
Lohengrin by Wagner 12, 129, 130, 131, 234, 236, 237, 243, 247, 248, 251, 252, 253, 254, 255, 257, 264, 273, 274, 279, 292, 293, 317, 326
L'Olandese dannato. See Der Fliegende Holländer
Lorenzini, Carlo (alias Collodi) 10
Lotti della Santa, Marcella 183, 185, 192
Lucas, Charles 127
Lucca, Pauline 242, 322
Lucia di Lammermoor by Donizetti 78, 93, 103, 172, 182, 239, 242, 283, 292
Lucrezia Borgia by Donizetti 44, 104, 105, 126, 151, 158, 182, 183, 258
Luisa Miller by Verdi 6, 7, 9, 11, 95, 96, 115, 116, 121, 122, 171, 172, 173, 174, 175, 176, 177, 178, 257, 322, 325
Lumley, Benjamin 11, 25, 34, 40, 41, 43, 45, 53, 57, 58, 59, 63, 67, 69, 73, 74, 75, 77, 78, 79, 83, 84, 86, 90, 91, 92, 101, 102, 103, 104, 139, 140, 151, 153, 154, 157, 158, 165, 166, 171, 172, 173, 179, 181, 191, 194
Lunn, Henry Charles 24, 226, 239, 255, 264, 270, 328
Lyceum Theatre 139, 140, 198, 200, 204, 238, 285, 292, 293, 322, 323, 325, 326

Macbeth by Verdi 6, 105, 116, 182, 242, 293
Macfarren, George Alexander 18, 24, 195, 327, 328
MacHugh, John 168

Mackenzie, Alexander Campbell 270, 302
Maffei, Andrea 58
Maffei, Clara 166
Maggioni, Manfredo 211
Maini, Ormondo 248
Mainzer, Joseph 24, 328
Maitland, John Alexander Fuller 23, 28, 269, 283, 328
Mameli, Goffredo 80, 215, 310
Mancinelli, Luigi 293, 304
Manon Lescaut by Puccini 282, 306
Manzoni, Alessandro 248
Manzoni, Giulio 288
Mapleson, James Henry 198, 214, 215, 218, 233, 234, 241, 251, 279, 280, 291, 293
Maquet, Auguste 166
Marchesi, Salvatore 242, 243
Maria di Rohan by Donizetti 1, 120, 183
Marini 247, 294
Marino Faliero by Donizetti 61
Mario, alias Giovanni Matteo De Candia 33, 46, 50, 52, 57, 64, 65, 67, 68, 114, 115, 116, 120, 123, 169, 170, 173, 183, 194, 196, 201, 242, 321, 322
Marshall 84
Martha by Flotow 173, 182, 183, 192, 193, 239, 242, 243, 257
Marx, Adolf Bernhard 24
Masaniello by Auber 114
Mascagni, Pietro 267, 271, 280, 281, 282, 303, 307
Mascheroni, Edoardo 300
Masini, Angelo 249, 322
Massenet, Jules 307
Massé, Victor 192
Matilda di Shabran by Rossini 113, 125
Matthew, James E. 285
Mattiuzzi, Elisa 294
Maurel, Victor 247, 294, 300, 303, 304, 323

Mayer, Marcus L. 293, 294, 295
Mazzini, Giuseppe 2, 3, 80, 310
Mazzucato, Alberto 2, 3, 4, 10, 286, 293
Medea by Cherubini 242
Medini, Paolo 249, 322
Mefistofele by Boito 280, 292
Mendelssohn, Felix 16, 25, 59, 127, 130, 239, 240, 299
Mercadante, Saverio 1, 2, 3, 74, 90, 182, 183, 185, 187
Meyerbeer, Giacomo 7, 12, 13, 54, 58, 59, 68, 110, 127, 136, 158, 172, 183, 188, 192, 195, 202, 209, 210, 211, 213, 218, 219, 222, 223, 225, 226, 227, 234, 235, 237, 240, 242, 259, 260, 263, 264, 265, 293
Mignon by Thomas 300
Mills, Watkin 302
Miolan-Carvalho, Marie Caroline 192, 194, 196, 201, 203, 322
Mongini, Pietro 182, 184, 188, 189, 192, 218, 228, 238, 322
Montemerli, Lorenzo de 96, 97, 101
Montenegro, Antonietta 59, 61, 63, 321
Moriani, Napoleone 33, 41, 321
Morley, Henry 165
Morosini, Emilia 75
Mosè in Egitto by Rossini 4
Mozart, Leopold 24
Mozart, Wolfgang Amadeus 54, 65, 90, 91, 98, 101, 104, 110, 126, 137, 172, 174, 182, 192, 201, 242, 252, 264, 282, 292, 293, 301, 306, 319, 320
Murska, Ilma de 243
Musäus, Johann Karl August 34
Muzio, Emanuele 65, 75

Nabucco (Anato; Nino, Re d'Assyria) by Verdi 1, 2, 3, 4, 7, 11, 26, 33, 45, 46, 47, 48, 49, 50, 52, 53, 61, 62, 83, 86, 87, 88, 92, 96, 98, 99, 100, 101, 109, 115, 116, 170, 172, 177, 183, 206, 224, 313, 314, 316, 321, 325

Nantier-Didiée, Constance 114, 120, 121, 123, 140, 170, 194, 196, 201, 203, 321, 322
Naudin, Emilio 322
Naylor, Edward Woodall 301
Negrini, Carlo 108, 109
Neri-Baraldi, Pietro 196
Newman, Francis 145
Ney, Jenny 132, 322
Nicolini, Ernest 247, 257, 322
Nilsson, Christine 227, 230, 239, 242
Nina, o sia La pazza per amore by Paisiello 3
Nino, Re d'Assyria. See *Nabucco*
Niobe by Pacini 37
Norma by Bellini 35, 49, 65, 68, 69, 106, 108, 126, 183, 218, 238
Novello, Joseph Alfred 18, 23, 24, 327, 328
Nozze di Figaro by Mozart 182, 192, 193, 242, 248, 279, 293
Nugent 113

Oberon by Weber 125, 192
Oberto, Conte di San Bonifacio by Verdi 3, 174, 316
Olghina, Olga 304, 323
Oper und Drama 130, 273
Ortolani 173
Otello by Rossini 47, 61, 126, 183, 192, 275
Otello by Verdi 13, 24, 231, 279, 285, 286, 287, 288, 289, 290, 292, 293, 295, 296, 297, 298, 313, 315, 317, 319, 320, 323, 326
Othello 119

Pacini, Giovanni 2, 37, 74, 90
Pagliacci by Leoncavallo 303
Paisiello, Giovanni 3, 8, 32, 46, 54, 90, 91, 137, 196, 312
Pantaleoni, Romilda 294
Parodi, Teresa 96
Paroli, Giovanni 294, 323
Parry, Charles Hubert Hastings 270
Parsifal by Wagner 289, 294

Patti, Adelina 12, 239, 242, 257, 260, 322
Paxton, Joseph 102
Pellegalli-Rosetti 323
Penco, Rosina 183, 201, 203, 322
Pergolesi, Giovanni Battista 41
Perotti 243
Persiani, Fanny 77
Persiani, Giuseppe 57
Pessina, Arturo 303, 323
Piatti, Carlo Alfredo 72
Piave, Francesco Maria 10, 80, 81, 141
Piccinni, Niccolò 196
Piccolomini, Marietta 11, 26, 139, 140, 141, 150, 154, 157, 158, 160, 161, 162, 163, 164, 165, 167, 168, 169, 172, 173, 174, 175, 176, 177, 182, 183, 192, 194, 242, 310, 322
Pierson, Henry 117, 118
Pini-Corsi, Antonio 323
Planché, James 199
Pocchini 191
Polonini 120, 173
Pougin, Arthur 285
Prince Albert 28, 70, 102, 213
Proch 247
Prout, Ebenezer 267, 268, 327
Puccini, Giacomo 267, 271, 282, 306
Puzzi, Giovanni 113
Pyat, Felix 166

Queen Victoria 28, 69, 70, 314

Ravogli, Giulia 304, 323
Reeves, Sims 96, 97, 101, 106
Requiem by Verdi 12, 24, 237, 247, 248, 249, 250, 269, 322, 326
Retribution 150
Reyer, M. 315
Ricci, Federico 2
Ricci, Luigi 2, 33, 48, 74
Richter, Hans 274, 326
Ricordi, Giulio 237, 248
Ricordi, Tito 248
Rienzi by Wagner 243, 274, 326

Rigoletto (Viscardello) by Verdi 7, 9, 11, 95, 106, 113, 114, 115, 116, 117, 118, 119, 120, 123, 124, 126, 134, 140, 151, 165, 166, 169, 170, 173, 175, 177, 178, 182, 183, 184, 192, 194, 196, 198, 200, 203, 206, 214, 217, 220, 224, 226, 234, 235, 238, 242, 247, 257, 258, 287, 291, 293, 313, 315, 317, 321, 325
Risorgimento 79, 82, 314
Robert le diable (Roberto il diavolo) by Meyerbeer 68, 70, 78, 120, 239, 242
Roberto il diavolo. See Robert le diable
Robinson 113
Roche, Regina Maria 51
Rokitansky, Hans 228, 322
Romeo et Juliette by Gounod 218, 293
Ronconi, Giorgio 64, 65, 68, 77, 98, 99, 100, 101, 114, 115, 116, 118, 120, 123, 183, 194, 196, 203, 321
Roosevelt, Blanche 257
Rosa, Carl 274, 292
Rosati, Carolina 72
Rossi Caccia, Giovanna 33
Rossini, Gioacchino 1, 2, 3, 4, 7, 8, 25, 26, 32, 37, 41, 48, 49, 54, 58, 61, 65, 74, 89, 90, 91, 98, 101, 104, 105, 108, 110, 113, 125, 126, 130, 133, 137, 176, 182, 184, 186, 187, 192, 193, 196, 197, 201, 204, 205, 209, 210, 219, 225, 234, 235, 237, 242, 247, 248, 250, 252, 257, 261, 264, 268, 275, 276, 279, 292, 306, 312, 316
Royal Albert Hall 12, 248, 249, 274, 322, 326
Royal Opera Theatre (Berlin) 236
Rubini, Giovanni Battista 197
Runciman, John F. 319
Ryan, Desmond 19, 20, 60, 64, 65, 68, 72, 91, 92, 196, 268, 327, 328

Sainton, Prosper 213
Saint-Saëns, Camille 300
Salle Favart (Paris) 249
Salle Le Peletier (Paris) 227

Salvi, Lorenzo 70
Samson and Delilah by Saint-Saëns 300
Sanchioli, Giulia 46, 50, 321
Santley, Charles 228, 238, 243, 322
Sapho by Gounod 104
Sarolta, Nina 182, 184
Sax, Adolphe 102
Scalchi, Sofia 238
Scaramuccia by Ricci 33
Schiller, Friedrich 58, 121, 174, 175, 176, 223
Schumann, Robert 16, 21, 54, 111, 118, 127, 269, 320
Scott, Walter 51
Scribe, Eugène 199, 221
Semiramide by Rossini 58, 187, 192, 193, 235, 258, 275, 279
Sessi, Mathilde 242
Shakespeare, William 6, 52, 119, 128, 289, 291, 293
Shaw, George Bernard 14, 270, 271, 272, 273, 277, 278, 279, 282, 316, 317
Shedlock, John S. 267, 268, 327
Signa by Cowen 307
Silvestri 294
Simon Boccanegra by Verdi 7
Sinico, Clarice 227
Smith, Edward Tyrrel 181, 191, 194, 195, 198
Solanges, Paul 303
Somma, Antonio 199
Sonntag, Henriette 172
Southey, Robert 145
Southgate, T. E. 268
Spezia, Maria 170, 172, 173
Spitta, Philipp 269
Spohr, Louis 104, 113
Spontini, Gaspare 104
Stabat Mater by Rossini 250
Stanford, Charles Villiers 270
Steffanoni 70
Stiffelio by Verdi 9, 95
Stolz, Teresa 248, 249, 322

Superchi, Antonio 68
Sylvia, Giudita 192
Tacchinardi, Nicola 197
Tadolini, Erminia 78
Tagliafico, Joseph 114, 120, 123, 170, 192, 194, 195, 196, 201, 321, 322
Taglioni, Marie 72
Taine, Hippolyte 144
Tamagno, Francesco 257, 294, 323
Tamberlik, Enrico 114, 132, 140, 183, 195, 203, 212, 215, 216, 322
Tamburini, Antonio 57, 197
Tannhäuser by Wagner 12, 128, 129, 133, 206, 207, 227, 243, 257, 258, 264, 273, 274, 326
Taylor, Tom 129, 150
Teatro Argentina (Rome) 82, 106
Teatro dei Solleciti (Florence) 37
Teatro della Pergola (Florence) 158
Tennyson, Alfred Lord 212, 213
Thalberg, Sigismond 104, 106
The Athenaeum 8, 13, 15, 16, 18, 19, 31, 33, 35, 37, 38, 46, 47, 59, 60, 63, 66, 68, 73, 74, 75, 77, 78, 85, 86, 87, 88, 92, 93, 96, 97, 106, 110, 111, 113, 118, 123, 124, 134, 135, 138, 147, 162, 166, 167, 171, 174, 176, 178, 186, 187, 188, 197, 202, 203, 207, 209, 215, 216, 225, 229, 235, 236, 237, 239, 240, 241, 243, 250, 253, 254, 259, 260, 261, 267, 268, 273, 274, 295, 298, 304, 315, 327
Théâtre-Italien (Paris) 48, 102, 104, 121, 171
The Bohemian Girl (La zingara) by Balfe 172
The Illustrated London News 8, 13, 38, 39, 40, 44, 46, 50, 51, 52, 55, 60, 62, 64, 67, 71, 76, 83, 85, 93, 107, 110, 111, 119, 136, 137, 142, 147, 161, 162, 167, 224, 225, 227, 229, 250, 251, 259, 262
The Leader 14, 146, 152, 155, 156, 178
The Literary Gazette 13, 147
The Musical Gazette 13, 148

The Musical Times 13, 15, 22, 23, 24, 129, 138, 226, 227, 230, 233, 238, 239, 242, 243, 250, 254, 255, 263, 264, 269, 270, 274, 286, 287, 289, 290, 296, 300, 301, 302, 318, 328

The Musical World 8, 9, 13, 15, 18, 19, 20, 21, 22, 23, 25, 29, 46, 47, 48, 49, 55, 59, 60, 62, 63, 64, 65, 68, 69, 70, 72, 74, 84, 86, 87, 88, 89, 91, 92, 96, 97, 98, 99, 100, 101, 102, 104, 106, 107, 108, 109, 110, 111, 113, 114, 116, 117, 120, 124, 125, 127, 128, 129, 130, 131, 132, 133, 134, 137, 139, 140, 158, 161, 167, 168, 172, 173, 174, 178, 181, 182, 183, 184, 188, 191, 192, 194, 195, 196, 198, 199, 200, 201, 203, 204, 205, 206, 207, 211, 212, 213, 214, 215, 217, 218, 219, 220, 221, 222, 223, 224, 228, 230, 233, 234, 235, 236, 237, 238, 239, 240, 241, 242, 244, 248, 249, 250, 252, 253, 254, 261, 262, 266, 268, 269, 270, 273, 274, 285, 287, 288, 289, 290, 291, 292, 293, 296, 297, 327

The Pledge 42

The Saturday Review 13, 147, 154, 155, 162, 221, 222, 235, 305, 306, 319, 320

The Spectator 13, 57, 72, 73, 86, 120, 129, 130, 136, 150, 152, 157, 178, 189, 206, 287, 315, 319

The Tempest by Mendelssohn 59

The Times 12, 13, 15, 19, 22, 23, 25, 28, 33, 41, 42, 43, 44, 46, 48, 49, 50, 55, 59, 60, 61, 62, 63, 64, 71, 74, 83, 87, 92, 95, 96, 98, 100, 102, 103, 104, 105, 107, 108, 109, 113, 115, 117, 118, 123, 124, 125, 126, 134, 141, 146, 151, 152, 153, 154, 155, 160, 161, 164, 167, 169, 174, 175, 176, 185, 186, 188, 191, 198, 201, 203, 204, 205, 209, 210, 211, 212, 213, 214, 215, 221, 222, 228, 229, 234, 235, 238, 239, 244, 247, 248, 249, 250, 252, 254, 257, 258, 261, 262, 264, 266, 269, 274, 285, 288, 292, 294, 298, 299, 300, 303, 306, 307, 315, 328

Thomas, Ambroise 129, 238, 239, 242, 300

Thomas, Arthur Gorning 270

Thorndike, Herbert 302

Tietjens, Thérèse 171, 172, 173, 181, 182, 183, 184, 185, 188, 189, 191, 193, 194, 195, 198, 200, 215, 221, 228, 238, 247, 322

Trebelli-Bettini, Zelia 228, 322

Tristan und Isolde by Wagner 274, 275, 282, 320, 326

Un ballo in maschera by Verdi 11, 12, 26, 191, 197, 198, 199, 200, 201, 202, 205, 214, 220, 221, 224, 234, 235, 247, 257, 262, 322

Un giorno di regno by Verdi 316

Valda, Giulia 293

Valli, Ignazio 121

Van Gelder 96

van Zandt, Jennie (Madame Vanzini) 238

Varesi, Elena 247

Varesi, Felice 247

Vialetti 170, 174, 175, 177, 184, 322

Viallette 193

Vianesi, Augusto 242, 257

Viardot, Pauline Garcia 77, 132, 140, 322

Viscardello. See *Rigoletto*

Wagner, Richard 7, 12, 13, 18, 23, 25, 32, 111, 117, 118, 127, 128, 129, 130, 131, 132, 133, 134, 137, 138, 206, 207, 219, 224, 227, 233, 234, 236, 237, 239, 240, 241, 243, 244, 245, 247, 251, 252, 253, 254, 255, 257, 259, 260, 261, 262, 263, 264, 265, 266, 267, 268, 269, 270, 271, 273, 274, 275, 276, 277, 278, 279, 280, 281, 282, 284, 288, 289, 290, 291, 292, 293, 295, 298, 299, 302, 304, 305, 306, 307, 313, 316, 317, 319, 320, 325, 326

Waldmann, Maria 248, 249, 322

Ward, William 179, 181, 191

Weber, Carl Maria von 54, 104, 192, 242, 252

Weiser, Enrichetta 182
Werner, Zacharias 80
Werther by Massenet 307
Wood, George 241
Wylde, Henry 127

Zaffira 242
Zampa by Hérold 173
Zelger, M. 173, 201, 322
Zilli, Emma 304, 323
Zoja, Angiolina 77
Zucconi 140

This book need not end here...

At Open Book Publishers, we are changing the nature of the traditional academic book. The title you have just read will not be left on a library shelf, but will be accessed online by hundreds of readers each month across the globe. OBP publishes only the best academic work: each title passes through a rigorous peer-review process. We make all our books free to read online so that students, researchers and members of the public who can't afford a printed edition will have access to the same ideas.

This book and additional content is available at:
https://www.openbookpublishers.com/isbn/9781783742134

Customise

Personalise your copy of this book or design new books using OBP and third-party material. Take chapters or whole books from our published list and make a special edition, a new anthology or an illuminating coursepack. Each customised edition will be produced as a paperback and a downloadable PDF. Find out more at:
https://www.openbookpublishers.com/section/39/1

Donate

If you enjoyed this book, and feel that research like this should be available to all readers, regardless of their income, please think about donating to us. We do not operate for profit and all donations, as with all other revenue we generate, will be used to finance new Open Access publications.

https://www.openbookpublishers.com/section/13/1/support-us

You may also be interested in:

A Musicology of Performance: Theory and Method Based on Bach's Solos for Violin
Dorottya Fabian

https://www.openbookpublishers.com/product/346

Denis Diderot's 'Rameau's Nephew' A Multi-Media Edition
Edited by M. Hobson. Translated by K.E. Tunstall and C. Warman. Music researched and played by the Conservatoire National Supérieur de Musique de Paris under the direction of P. Duc

https://www.openbookpublishers.com/product/216

The Classic Short Story, 1870–1925 Theory of a Genre
Florence Goyet

https://www.openbookpublishers.com/product/199